PRIME MINISTER P.V. NARASIMHA RAO

The Scholar and The Statesman

PRIME MINISTER P.V. NARASIMHA RAO

The Scholar and The Statesman

Attar Chand

GIAN PUBLISHING HOUSE

NEW DELHI-110002

GIAN PUBLISHING HOUSE
5, Ansari Road, Daryaganj
New Delhi-110002

ISBN 81 - 212 - 0398 - 8

PRINTED IN INDIA

Published by Mrs. Gayatri Garg for Gian Publishing House, New Delhi 110002.

Laser Typesetting By Creative Typesetters, New Delhi

Printed At Goyal Offset Printers, Delhi

ACKNOWLEDGEMENTS

The writers are generally acknowledged masters in human intelligence. In India, may I request the Civil Liberty people who were very vocal for Kashmir and Punjab terrorists, take up the case of a writer (of Indian origin Britisher Salman Rushdie- the author of Satanic Verses) who is fighting for his life in this 20th Century for his 'sin' of writing a book?

We live in times when nobody can afford to wait for anybody. The pace of change is breathtaking in every field, in technology, in management, in R & D.. and unless a writer quick on the uptake he loses out. Like a Chief Executive, a writer, too must think fast and act fast and get his writings published and marketed whatever be the constraints. And of course the biggest constraint a Free- lance writer faces is that he cannot get finances from the public sector financial institutions. The question of any encouragement from the Government does not arise at all-thanks there is no need of a license for writing a book.

Sales turnover is the only indication of book business growth, as I see it. Other parametres like return on investment and profits flow automatically as long as one can ensure a consistent increase in turnover. Developing people, establishing stable management structure and a proper systems orientation are what I call the 'qualitative' indices of publishing business growth.

The present study could not have reached fruition without the encouragement of my wee-wishers, who suggested sundry improvements and provided nourishing guidance and a inspiration. I am much obliged to my fellow writers, journalists, academicians and professors whose writings I have consulted and taken notes, in parts or in full, in writing this book of global interest.

CONTENTS

List of Photographs

- P.V. Narasimha with President of India, R. Venkataraman, 21 June 1991.
- P.V. Narasimha Rao with the Press, June 18, 1991.
- P.V. Narasimha with his Family members and Indira Gandhi.
- P.V. Narasimha Rao Attending Congress Party Meeting, New Delhi
- P.V. Narasimha Rao with Rajiv Gandhi.
- L.K. Advani with Narasimha Rao
- Council of Ministers with R. Venkataraman
- Narasimha Rao, Chandra Shekhar and V.P. Singh.
- Narasimha Rao Swearing in as Prime Minister.
- Prime Minister Narasimha Rao.
- Courtesy: The Hindustan Times and Frontline.

ONE

PREFACE
FIFTY YEARS OF LOW PROFILE

The sober statesman from the South, Pamulaparti Venkata Narasimha Rao, has the distinction of being a scholar, and the statesman.

Rao, who will be 70 on June 28, 1991, faced the most daunting political task of his career in May when he became Congress president following Rajiv Gandhi's assassination which plunged the party and the country into a crisis.

The enormous goodwill of his partymen which catapulated him to the presidency of the largest and century-old party, speaks eloquently of Rao's loyalty to the part and its leadership.

The widely experienced administrator, affectionately called "PV", has handled several key portfolios Defaence, External affairs, Human Resources, Law, Health and education both at the Centre and in Andhra Pradesh, since he first became Minister in 1962. He has also been Chief Minister of his home state, Andhra Pradesh.

Born on June 28, 1921, P.V. Narasimha Rao comes from an agriculturist family in the Naxalite infested Karimangar district of Andhra Pradesh.

An intellectual by upbringing and a poet by temperament, he studied in three universities Osmania, Bombay and Nagpur, combining B.Sc with a law degree.

But his reputation as a polyglot overshadows his other talents and achievements. His linguistic repertoire includues proficiency in English, Hindi, Sanskrit, Telugu, Kannada, Marathi, Persian, Arabic, Spanish and French. Rao's multilinguism gained him recognition as one of India's most successful Foreign Ministers. Besides, his literary achievements include the Sahitya Akademi's frist prize for his translation of a monumental work of Viswanatha Satyanarayana, "Veyi Padaralu" (thousand hoods) into Hindi under the title of "Saharasa Phan."

He also translated into Telugu, a Marathi novel "Pan Lakshat Kon-Ghato" (but who takes notice), by the noted Marathi writer Hari Narayan Apte, which received much acclaim. For six years Rao was chairman of the Jnapith award selection committee.

Rao's political baptism took place during his student days when he actively participated in the protest against the Nizam Government's ban on the singing of "Vande Mataram" in his college in 1938. The agitation turned out to be a long drawn affair, interrupting his studies.

A Nationalist to the core, he gave up legal practice in the pre-Independence days when the State was subjected to repression by the British. He also took active part in the 1942 "Quit India for three years.

Rao got due recognition in politics after Independence. He was a member of the Andhra Pradesh Assembly for 20 years from 1957 and during the period served as a Minister for ten years and as a Chief Minister for three years.

He was first elected to the State Assembly in 1957 from Manthani constituency in Karimnagar district and since then had the privilege of getting returned to the Assembly several times from the same constituency.

He first became Minister in the Sanjiva Reddy Cabinet after the 1962 general elections and continued to be in office in the succeding Ministry of K. Brahmanada Reddy.

Although Rao held many key posts in the Union Cabinet, he was at his best when he was in-charge of the External Affairs Ministry both under Indira Gandhi and Rajiv Gandhi.

A serious experession that Rao bears on the face is rather deceptive, considering his penchant for humour often subtle and sometimes devastating that is reflected in his Parliament debates.

It was a tribute to his debating skill that when he made his first major speech in the Lok Sabha as External Affarirs Minister in 1980, the Opposition withdrew all their cut motions, paving the way for the unanimous passage of the demands for grants of his Ministry.

The area of leadership is no less researched. The charismatic theory held that leaders are born with certain personality traits. Early management psychologists modified this divine grace theory and suggested that leaders can also be trained to acquire the requisite qualities. Later studies attempted to correlate leadership behavious with effectiveness. The general run of the argument is that people oriented democratic leaders are likely to be more successful. However, no one has explained why, over a period of time, outstanding leaders fell from grace despite retaining the behavioural qualities that led them to glory. The mystery was explained by the contingency model of Flieder. The theory postualtes that leadership effectiveness is a function of the fit between leadership style and situational variable, leader follower relations and the power position of the leader. To be an effective leader, one must be able to diagnose the situation and adopt an appropriate style. Here lies the rub. A manager may painstakingly diagones the situation and evolve a solution but can a leopard change his sopts overnight? Another bit of conventional management wisdom from the human relations school suggests that an effective manager should not limit himself only to the official work role but go further and play the emotionally supporive role of the informal leader. You punish a subordiante in the morning for a wrong doing, only to apply the healing touch in the afternoon. While doing if you must neither feel remorseful nor confuse the subordinate about your motives. Power remains the driving force of all organisations depite its neglect by management pundit. It is the vital link connecting leadership to motivation. Power is the ability to get things done, the very essence of management. Absence of power creates anarchy. People may hate power but cannot live without it. The term is value-neutral and multidimensional. Managers control the behaviour of their subordinates since their own performance depends on the results produced by the subordinates. To that extent, leaders are also controlled by their subordinates. The power game has ominous ramifications as well. Every organisation has a few members who can hijack the entire system or bring it to a grinding halt merly by using their nuisance value. Betrand Russel in his classic treaties 'Power a new social analysis' suggested that Napoleon met his waterloo much earlier in Josephine who diverted French resources from defence to her personal comforts. Nearer home, corruption in the Indian system and power granted to the babudom' (bureaucracy) to meddle in the affairs of others. Experience shows that powers perpetuates itself. Recent efforts to liberalism have been stymied by a bunch of schemes who stand to lose in the process. Suffice it to say that power is the energy capitalisation of the institution. If used judiciously it multiplies the effectiveness of the leader and the organisation. But it is double eged wepons and its abuse will only lead to managerial impotency and organisational bankruptcy. Abdication of power is as bad as its misuse. Successful leaders have instinctively known the dynamics of power and skillfully used it in the pursuit of their missions. The basic problem in management remais one of acquiring and wielding power effectively without dysfunctional effects.[1]

Many a bureaucrat in New Delhi has worked with Narasimha Rao, since he has been the Minister for Home Affairs, Defence, External Affairs, Human Resources Development, Health and Family Welfare. They all think highly of him, of the pains he took in going through files and the clear way he set down his instructions. Jaipal Reddy however, questions Rao's achievements. "Show me one area where he has left his mark, he challenges. What then, accounts for the bureaucracy's affection for him? Reddy says, "The bureaucrats liked him because the was guided by them, and he vied with them only in the quality of English used in his notings. He did no rise above the most common failing of the Indian minister to prove that he knows better English than his bureaucrats." A CPI (M) leader makes a similar point when asked to react to the New Education Policy proposed by the Rajiv government, when Rao was Minister for Human Resources Development. At that time, Rao, was widely credited as being its principal author. The CPI (M) leader says "There was really very little new in the so-called New Education Policy except the elitist idea of navodaya schools. It was the work of an excellent draftsman who essentially stands for status quo; not the work of a visionary." Many veteran politicians say that they have always known that Rao lacks new ideas, but can implement them very well once the ideas are given to him. There was, however, no hint of this contradiction in the young Rao when he topped his school leaving examination at Osmania University in the erstwhile state of Hyderabad.[2]

The newest phenomenon in Indian politics is of course the "sympathy wave" though it is proving to be so elsuive. The low turnout on June 12, 1991 makes one wonder whether it is going to matter much any where. It is at its clearest in Tamil Nadu. But since the combined vote of the AIADMK alliance was set to drown the DMK before the assassination, the wave will not make much difference to the outcome. What will be interesting to see is whether it reverse the steady, though small increase in the DMK vote and steady and not so small decline in the AIADMK vote since the early 1980s. Therefore to see the real power, if any of the sympathy vote I would watch the results in Kerala. The sympathy wave there has not been confused by the apathy wave which has affected the vote elsewhere, but has to survive its encounter with the rocks of religious and caste indentities. The emergence of BJP, with its well dispalyed support among the higher Hindu castes has headened these identities again, stalling a recent trend created by the social politics of the Left and the spread of literacy.[3]

Considering the fact that Sonia Gandhi has flatly rejected the Congress Working Committee's choce of here as party president to succeed her slain husband Rajiv Gandhi and has refused to change her mind, the leaders are left with no alternative but to select a senior and non controversial person who has the added qualification of having kept himself aloof form the "coterie" which surrounded Rajiv Gandhi, as interim president. The presidential issue was finally settled by the AICC.[4]

Having committed the indiscretion of hastly electing Sonia Gandhi as party president even before Rajiv Gandhi's funeral had taken place, the working committee was now trying to retrieve the situation in the face of Sonia Gandhi's rebuff and thinks it can do so not earlier than May 29, after the ashes of late Rajiv Gandhi have been immersed at the sangam in Allahabad on May 28, 1991.

It will thus try to present itself as united party with committed leadership before thee electorate. The Congress resumed electioneering with a condolence meeting for Rajiv Gandhi at Ramlila Ground in Delhi on June 1, 1991.

It transpires that those who still insisit that Sonia Gandhi should change her mind and are undertered by her mind and are undeterred by her rejection have been making several suggestions in order not to give the interim president a free hand in running the party affairs. In this context the name of Arjun Singh was proposed for the post of vice-president of the party. But his opponents said this could no be and came forward with the idea that instead of one, the partys should have four representing four regions of the country and one each the Scheduled Castes and minorities. They felt that it was a crucial time for the party, which was in the midst of the election, and could not aford to project persons at the national level against whom allegations could be made by the opposition parties.

It is extremely unlikely that the suggestion for having a vice-president will take off the ground. Those who oppose the idea feel that it would present a picture of disunity and confusion at the national level. At any rate, the party has half a dozen general secretaries and thy would assist the interim president in the discharge of his duties as they did Rajiv Gandhi. Arjun Singh retraced his steps by writing a letter to P.V. Narasimha Rao in which he has stated that the thought of becoming Congress president had never entered his mind.

Another senior leader, Dinesh Singh, took the working committee members to task and asked them "to rectify the damage done by the undue haste" with which they had initially decided to requests Sonia Gandhi to become party president "when the mutiliated remains of her husband were still lying before her."

The so-called coterie however continue with its efforts to persuade Sonia Gandhi to accept the working committee's choice of her as party president. On being pestered repeatedly to change her mind and with seva dal volunteers shouting slogans inside No. 10 Janpath asking her to step in her late husbands shoes, the ordered that the doors be closed to such hangers on.

For the present Sonia Gandhi's house in out of bounds to the slogan mongers and their patrons. Most of those who have been pressurising Mrs Sonia Gandhi to accept the party presidentship belong to the Rajya. Those who were shocked by this drama pointed out that the "coterie" was motivated by considerations of retaining their hold on the levers of power rather than party interest.

The senior party leaders have by now reconciled to the choice of Narasimha Rao as interim president and feel that he represented the Nehru-Indira Rajiv tradition in political and economic thinking and is staunch Congressman whose loyalty has never been in doubt. In the present situation he is the least controversial person.

At any rate the longer the party gives the impression of being "headless" and presented a picture of strife, the greater would be the damage to its electoral prospects. They feel that the Congress-I would definitely gain from the "sympathy vote" and its logan of stability would sound more true after Rajiv Gandhi's assassination.

Initially, almost all the State Party chiefs and Chief Ministers had been persuaded to accept Sonia Gandhi's choice as party president though some of them had suggested that the PCC presidents and leaders of the Congress legislature parties too should be involved in the democratic process of selection of new party president.

Some leaders even suggested the name of Vice-President S.D Sharma who is also a past Congress president for the post of party president but Dr. Sharma showed no interest. He said in a statement that he had nothing to do with speculative press reports about his candidature for the Congress leadership.

Making it clear that he would not accept any political office under any circumstances he said particularly when elections are under way, constitutional functionaries must give an example of rectitude and perfect observance of constitutional and legal proprieties, especially concering the polls or the dignity of their office.

The party required a good deal more of resources because whatever was committed to the candidates had already been spent by them and they required money for another two weeks of campaigning. This was an issue which was discussed by the party leaders. The task had been entrusted mostly to the state party leaders.

Arjun Singh said in his letter to P.V. Narasimha Rao that the Congress party today has to discharge this duty with faith and determination to justify the trust of the millions and millions of the countrymen." A cruel fate has put us to test. Rajiv appointed us to the highest forum of the party. We are burdened with the unpleasant task of searching for his successor. For each one of us it is a heart-reading duty to perform."

"With whatever little knowledge and discretion I possess, I considered it my duty to propose the name of Sonia Gandhi to succeed

Rajiv as president of the Congress. The decision of the CWC to elect has president has the endoresement of every Congressman in the country. Her decision to decline the offer is totally in tune with the high sense of private and public propriety that the Nehru family has always maintained. Whatever be her final decision we must accept it respectfully."

"Our duty now lies in maintaining total unity in the party and make it a fighting instrument to ensure the democratic endorsement of the rich legacy that Rajiv has left to the nation. Throughout his political life he fought for the unity and integrity of the country and to preserve and protect the secular credentials of our polity. Only a totally united Congress party can carry forward the fight as he would like us to do."

"It is in this background that I see my duty to help strengthen the unity of the party. In spite of my making it abundantly clear some people are mentioning my name of as one of the contenders for the Congress presidentship. Kindly permit me to state categorically that I have never been and am not a claimant for the office of the Congress president. Since you are presiding over the meetings of the CWC, I thought it proper to communicate this to you. Let us all now resolve the issue at the earliest, so that our battle against the communal and casteist forces in the country is resumed with vigour and determination," Arjun Singh said.

Dinesh Singh is the second senior leader, after Vasant Sathe, to speak publicly on the leadership question. He said in a statement that "undue haste" in deciding to request Sonia Gandhi to take over the reigns of the party had damaged the reputation of the party.

Taking note of the fact that the opposition parties, particularly the BJP were taking advantage of the situation, he said, "Let the Congress return to its traditional ways of functioning and reaffirm its faith in its traditional policies of secularism, socialism and democracy," he said.

Dinesh Singh pointed out that in the past the process of selection was begun only after the period of mourning was over. Had this been followed, the criticism being made could have been avoided. Why this procedure was done away with is not clear. One week would not have made much difference. In any case it will be one week now before the decision is made. Having private meetings and its play in the media is giving an impression that the party is unable to choose even an acting president in a period of crisis. It also smacks of behind the scene manoeuvring which is damaging the image of the party.

"The Opposition parties, particularly the BJP, are taking advantage of the situation to say that only they can now provide a firm leadership and stable Government, when every senior leader of the Congress party is more capable of doing so.

"If Sonia Gandhi is not is a position to accept the responsibility at this stage. The seniro leader close to Rajivji is there. Acting presidentship will not place undue burden on his health. He needs no assistance to manage, the affairs of the party till an election by AICC can take place."

A meeting attended by former PCC presidents, president of the Indian Youth Congress,MPs and candidates of the Lok Sabha election expressed the hope that the Congress party has the tlent and the intrinsic strength to provide leadership at this critical juncture.

In a statement they said that "we feel that the Congress leadership, deprived on wise guidance of Rajiv Gandhi bears a speicial responsibility at this critical juncture. Our party's role has become all the more important in view of the hovoc caused by the Chandra Shekhar Government during its short tenure- a Government which set spies on a leader who enabled them to come to power, a Government which compromised the nation's dignity by altering our time tested foreign policy without consulting other political parites, a Government which encouraged the extremists and terrorists in Punjab and cleared the decks for the rule of anti-national forces in that State and last but not the least, a Government whose record in corruption is such that every honest and self-respecting Indian would hang his head in shame.

"The country has to be pulled back from this brink of disaster. We are confident that the enemies of Indian nationalism will be defeated. We had seen the prophets of doom predicting disaster for the Congress and for India's democratic system in 1964 and 1984 as well. As in the past, they will again be proved wrong."

The signatories include Birendra Singh, Tariq Anwar, Digvijay Singh, Ashok Gehlot, Ahmed Patel, Anand Sharma, Suresh Kalmadi, Jitendera Singh, Akbar Ahmed Dumpy, Aslam Sher Khan, Suresh Pachauri, K.V. Thangabalu and Bhubaneshwar Kalita.

The West Bengal Pradesh Congress-I Committee on May 26, 1991 unanimously urged the Congress Working Committee to immediately elect P.V. Narasimha Rao as the party see president Sidhartha Shankar Ray who had sent urgent telegrams to the four senior party leaders including N.D. Tiwari and P.V. Narasimha Rao, said that Sonia Gandhi would have been ideal to lead the party but as the was not willing to take up the responisbility her wishes should be respected.

Ray said that if she continued to refuse to accept the post, Rao, who was number two in organisation, should be immediately elected permanent president unanimously subject to confirmation by the AICC at a later date.

He said Rao should be authorised to lead the party in its remaining election campaign and "every other question will then be sorted out itself after the elections."

Now that the tumult and the shouting are over. It is useful to look upon the entire election experience of the last three months (April-June). We pride ourselves that we are the largest democracy in the world, and there are good reasons for being proud. By sheer magnitude, there is nothing compared to it anywhere else in the world-the Indian electroate this time, that is in 1991, is over 500 million; the total population of the US is about 300 million. A general election for the Lok Sabha every time brings home to the people of this far-flung country that with all their diversities, they belong to the same nation, that even the humblest peasant in the distant hamlet has the right to elect those out of whom will be chosen those who will be governing this land of ours. This awareness of the right and responsibility of choosing the ruler-the very essence of democracy-permeates them all. This explains the very large number of voter turn-out in the rural areas-larger than at the urban centres as a rule. Against this credit point of our parliamentary democracy-10 elections for the Lok Sabha and over 250 at the State levels in 44 years since Independence-we have to take into account the progressive erosion of the election process over the years. As this deterioration has now reached an alarming proportion, we can hardly afford to keep our eyes closed. The price of our turning a blind eye to all the degeneration that accompanies our electioneering nowadays would be the erosion of public confidence in the election system as it prevails in this country. The general election which has just concluded serves as a warning signal. It is an open secret that money power has come to play a very big role in our elections. It has grown from general election to general election until it has reached a menacing scale. It is admitted that the system of parliamentary election has become an expensive propostion all over the world. For us in India, its obscene intrusion is repugnant to the very image of democracy. Because, in this country, democracy is regarded as an affshoot of our freedom struggle, and the spirit of that struggle was symbolised by Mahatma Gandhi with his identification with the impoverished instead of with the affluent. It was the unwritten expectation in our early elections that those who served the nation with dedication would have a premium in the public eye at the time of the elections, and the flaunting of wealth and resources was at a discount. This basic ideology of the election system has been undermined more and more with every election. It is no doubt true that a modern election machinery of any large political party needs large-sacle funds, and the clolection of such funds from the rich and the super-rich is unavoidable.[5]

The technique of fund collection for political purpose has undergone considerable change over the years. In this respect, as in many others, the Congress as the party which has dominated the political stage for decades has set the standard. Before independence, the Congress as the party which has dominated the political stage for decades has set the standard. Before independence, the Congress depended on donations, both from the rich and the poor. Small donations came through mass collections while the larger ones came from those among the affluent who were loyal to the freedom struggle. After independence, the situation changed in a big way. As the ruling party, the Congress secured the shiphand over the business community, which was made to pay to the party coffers and secured, as quid pro quo, whatever concessions, permits and licences they could manage from the government. The entire business of raising funds by means, both open and devious, was handled by the organisation-bosses in the party, while the political leaders, by and large, did not get directly involved in it. As a mass party with a democratic appeal, the image of political leaders had to be preserved and could not be allowed to be sullied.

This neat division of labour within the leadership, however, broke down when the party split came in 1969. The organisation- bosses were all found on the side of the Syndicate, while Indira Gandhi's new Congress had to desperatly raise funds. Appeal for mass collection was not resorted to. Instead, approaches were made directly to the business establishments by the political leaders, including Indira herself, and funds were raised and kept by persons in her direct confidence without any reference to the AICC. Over the years, this system was perfected, and one used to hear about "levies" on business houses at the time of general elections. Individual Congress leaders at the State level managed to rope in their own respective patrons from among local business houses. Inevitably, an element of coercion came in during the Emergency and by the time the 1977 elections were held, the business houses chose their own favourites at many places. After Indira's return to power in 1980, a new element came into this business of party fund acquisition. There appeared the "cut- backs" and "kickbacks" on giant government purchases from abroad whether in Defence or other departments. Not for nothing did Indira make her memorable remark that corruption, after all is "a global phenomenon". It is in this category one has to place the alleged kickback from the German submarine deal and perhaps also the Bofors scandal. One could notice a more systematic arrangements of this department of party fund collection under Rajiv Gandhi. For obvious reasons, the full story of this aspect of party fund collection would not be known for years, if at all, because these have international ramifications as the very preliminary probe into the Bofors deal has amply borne out.[6]

Today, a new phenomenon in election politics-clearly shown in the 10th Lok Sabha general election-has been what may be termed as conspicuously activist intrusion of well-marked business houses trying to influence and pressurise political leaders, and through them the parties concerned. In other words, business lobbies are making frightening inroads into even our election politics. The enrichment of the big farmer in the last three decades-the fallout of the Green Revolution-has led to his mobilising muscle- men and gunmen to lord it over the village politics. Where political awareness among the peasant masses has not been organised, this menace has become acute. Out of this has come what's called 'booth capturing', the terrorising of the voter belonging to the underprivileged sections of society. If one goes slightly deep into the phenomenon of booth captureing and mass rigging, it is not difficult to trace their social origin. Since political leaders maintain their organic links with these village big shots, it is not difficult to identify the mafia of mastans who flourish particularly in the election seasons. In this latest general election the cancer has spread wide and deep. That accounts to large measure to the strange spectacle of "free and fair" elections being guaranteed by the posting of thousands upon thousands of armed security forces. This exercise at diagnosing the present malady would not be complete without a reference to the spectaculear decline in the integrity, probity and competence of the Election Commission, so blatantly symbolised by the conduct of the present incumbent as its head. The appointment of T.N. Seshan to the august office provoked controversy because he was known to be close to a particular political establishment, and it must be said to his credit that he has amply conformed that impression by his behaviour in the last two months. Though his almost non-stop pontificating one discern a touch of the megalomaniac, and he has left nobody in any doubt that he has not bothered to follow the wise principle that is the motto of judiciary that a judge has not only to be imprital but must be seen so by the public. Apart from this open bias in his conduct, Seshan's misdemeanour includes, among others, giving publicilty to certain allegations against of former speaker of Lok Sabha, allegations received by telephone calls-which has landed the Election Commission in serious conflict with Lok Sabha secretariat. Then there is his penchant for countermanding an entire election without himself following the rules the enjoins upon him to await reports of concerned polling officials, including the Central observers before passing sweeping judgements. Seshan has also been badly caught when telling the nation a patent untruth in a television discussion that the dates for the delayed polling of the second and third rounds were dictated to him by the Government, which has promplty come out with a denial. There are rumblings within the Election Commission itself against his conduct his conduct which needs to be looked into. It would be the job of the new Parliament to decide what action has to be taken to deal with Seshan's outstanding misconduct, and also to frame rules laying down code of conduct for the Election Commission so that our democracy is not further undermined by the Seshans of tommorow.[7]

The Congress on June 19, 1991 continued to grapple with the issue of electing the leader of its Parliamentary Party.

The main contenders for the post, P.V. Narasimha Rao and Sharad Pawar, could not come to an understanding among themselves although they discussed the issue at length. It appears that the consensus approach advocated by Rao's supporters is not acceptable to the Maharashtra Chief Minister.

The Narasimha Rao's camp gave the impression that an agreement had been reached between him and Pawar on Rao's uncontested election as the leader of the Congress Parliamentary Party (CPP) but the Maharashtra Chief Minister's supporters denied it.

Former Union Railway Minister Madhavrao Scindia was among the important party leaders who met Narasimha Rao and discussed the leadership issue with him. Scindia was very much in the fray and members of Parliament from different states were urging him to stand for CPP leadership.

A suggestion was reportedly made to Pawar that the leadership issue be decided by the Congress Working Committee (CWC) and the Central Parliamentary Board (CPB) and that the consensus arrived at should be acceptable to Pawar. But Pawar is understood to have maintained that though he was not averse to attending meetings of the party's top forums, he did not accept the proposition that the leadership issue could be decided by them. The choice of party leadership should be left to the Congress Parliamentary Party (CPP) in the true democratic tradition and its right should not be curtailed in any manner.

His supporters maintained that the Working Committee, as at present constituted, comprised mostly leaders who had lost in the recent Lok Sabha election and the Parlaimentary Borard members gave the impression that they were favouring a particular candidate.

Pawar's plea, which was supported by 40 members of Parliament yesterday when they demanded that the CPP should be left free to choose its leader, Members of Parliament, State legislatiors legislator and the AICC members. In a letter to the Congress president they urged him to told hold elections for the leader of the Congress Parliamentary Party "through the process of secret ballot". They strongly expressed themselves against the consensus approach which had damaged the Congress irretrivably. Signatories included Shyamlal Yadav, Yogendra Makwana, Shyam Nandan Mishra, Shyamdhar Mishra, N.C. Chaturvedi, Ram Vilas Pandey, Tulsidas Jadhav, M.R. Krishman, Jainul Basher, Y.C. Bhattacharya and Jaswant Mehta.

When Narasimha Rao and Sharad Pawar met in New Delhi, on June 1991, the two discussed the mode of electing the leader of the party in Parliament but could not reach a consensus. Later, answering questions at an impromptu Press confrernce at his Motilal Nehru Marg residence, Narasimha Rao said that both the secret ballot and the method of consensus were followed in electing the leader of the Congress party in Parliament in the past and said that either of them could be adopted even now.

Whatever the methodology, Pawar's supporters asserted that they stood by their demand for a "secret ballot" to elect the new leader in Parliament. "Nothing has changed", said Suresh Kalmadi, a Rajya Sabha member and a close associate of Pawar, pointing out that the fact was that the number of party MPs demanding a secret ballot had increased today.

Regarding reports that Pawar was no longer in the race for the leadership, Kalmadi said that a lot of "false and malicious rumours" were being spread involving the Maharashtra Chief Minister.

On the other hand, another Rajya Sabha member, Dr. Ratnakar Pandey, claimed that "90 per cent party members in Parliament want Narasimha Rao to be their leader. A consensus has already been reached."

A similar tone that "you just wait and watch the Congress will elect its leader in Parliament unanimously" was adopted by the party's treasurer, Sitaram Kesri, while talking to correspondents at Narasimha Rao's residence.

Talking to the Press, Narasimha Rao parried question on the demand of about 40 party MPs saying that the CPP should opt for democratic process for election of the leader. "I have no knowledge of the MPs statement containing the demand. But anybody can talk of secret ballot," he said. Asked about his meeting with Pawar, Narsimha Rao said: "Yes, we met today. We had met yestarday also. Pawar will come to meet me tomorrow also. It was a very good meeting. Whenever we meet, we keep two objectives in mind-how to strengthen the party and how to keep unity in the party."

Asked whether Pawar discussed with him the issue of "secret ballot" for electing the new leader in Parliament, Narasimha Rao said: "No".

Asked if he become the Prime Minister, would be make someone the Deputy Prime Minister, Narasimha Rao Said: "Whenever the Press meets me, I have a ground rule and so far everyone in the media has gone by it. The gound rule is that do not ask me a question which starts with an if."

However, a little later, Narasimha Rao told another correspondent that there would be no Deputy Prime Minister. "That speculation about the Deputy Prime Minister is wrong."

When a correspondent pointed out to Narasimha Rao that the Congress had taken great pains in bringing a legislation in Parliament to discourage defectors and whether in the present scenario the Congress would try to form the Government with the help of defections from the other parties, he said: "Our aim is to have a good rapport with all the parties."

"But if some party breaks up, how am I concerned? I am more concerned about my own party," Narasimha Rao said. Asked whether he visualised a break in some other party, the Congress president said: "I do not believe in fishing in the other parties" waters."

About the query whether the Congress would now welcome the old partyment, now outside, Narasimha Rao said: "A partyman can always walk out as the door is open. But if he wants to return to the party, then somebody has to open the door for him is the party's Working Committee".

Asked what was the view of a large number of newly elected MPs on the election of the leadership issue should be solved amicably and this should not lead to any wedge in the party.

"The Congress should not share the balme if some party splits on its own. I do not know if other parties will split or not but I can say with confidence that the Congress will not split," Narasimha Rao felt.

Meanwhile, Pawar, when asked to comment on his assessment of the situation, told correspondetns that "each and every Congress MP's opinion will be ascertained at the meeting of the Congress-I party in parliament as to who would lead it."

The All Inia Congress Committee-I's general secretaries in-charge of different States were busy in meeting new Lok Sabha MPs belonging to their respective areas in ascertaining their mood on the new leader in Parliament.

Pawar reportedly had two meetings with Narasimha Rao this evening and in between he conversed with the former Union Minister and an influential leader from Tamil Nadu, P. Chidambaram.

The secretary of the Congress party in Parliament in the last Lok Sabha, Era Anbarasu, at Narasimha Rao's residence told correspondents that he met the party president to tell him that all the 28 newly elected party MPs from Tamil Nadu were behind him.

Regarding the meeting of Narasimha Rao and Pawar, Anbarasu said: "An understanding has been reached between them but I do not know that details."

A leader belonging to the Narasimha Rao camp said that the party president wanted to make Sharad Pawar the Deputy Prime Minister but the State Chief Minister was still adamant on "secret ballot" for electing the leader in Parliament. "In fact, there would not have been any problem in making a nominee of Sharad Pawar the Chief Minister of Maharashtra and here at the Centre a ministerial portfolio of his liking would have been given to Pawar", he disclosed.

The tussle between the protagonists of a consensus and the standard bearers of election through a secret ballot had been going on since it became apparent that the party was destined to form a government.

Former Kerala Chief Minister K. Karunakaran, Madhya Pradesh strongman Arjun Singh who are in the Paralimentary Board, are said to be in favour of the consensual process. The name mentioned in this context is that of Narasimha Rao who has so far not admitted to being a candidate for the leadership position.

The younger member in the party led by Youth Congress Chief Ramesh Chennithala and NSUI president Manish Tiwari has have in a statement favoured the consensual approach. They said the new government must be of the correct blend of maturity, wisdom and "aggressive dynamism of the youth."

Kerala House continued to be the centre of hectic activity as new Lok Sabha members from various States called on Karunakaran one by one.

The AICC general secretaries, H.K.L. Bhagat and Balaram Jakhar, and former AICC general Secretary G.K. Moopanar were also present during the discussions.

The meetings were part of a wider discussion among senior leaders and new members of Parliament to evolve a consensus on the leadership issue.

Prof. K.V. Thomas, MP, said most of those who had met Sharad Pawar were also not for secret ballot to elect the leader. He expressed confidence that consensus would emerge tomorrow morning.

Meanwhile, Narasimha Rao, when asked if his party having failed to secure absolute majority, will seek support of other parties in Parliament, said "we will need support. We will have to work out the type of support needed by us."

The Congress President and the newly elected leader of the Congress Parliamentary Party (CPP P.V. Narasimha Rao, said in New Delhi, On June 21, 1991 that the election manifesto of his party as outlined by Rajiv Gandhi would be the agenda before the new Government. In an emotional reply to felicitations by a number of Congress leaders after the CPP election, Rao described the programmes and policies outlined in the Congress (I) menifesto as the national agenda and declared amidst thunderous applause that his party was committed to implement the manifesto to the hilt. Rao who spoke in English and Hindi alternatively said the only interpretation one could draw from the current election results was that the people had unmiytakable turned towards the Congress (I) after their sordid experience in the last 18 months. "The trend of the people is clear. With this trend we shall run the government and run it successfully", he said.

The Congress president likened the performance of his party in the recent election to that of a great cricketer who missed the century mark by a solitary run. Non one could say that the Congress (I) had not scored in the just concluded elections.

Rao said the emergence of Rajiv Gandhi on the national scene had solved the leadership probelm of the country for several years and not many realised the vacuum created by his sudden absence. The relationship between a leader and people was spiritual and not related to posts. It was this spirituality provided by Congress leaders like Mahatma Gandhi, Indira Gandhi and Rajiv Gandhi which was the capital and foundation of the Congress.

The newly elected leader began his speech on the note that he accepted the responsibility placed on his shoulders in all humility. With the unanimous support of the CPP (I) memebres, he enjoyed the support of millions of shoulders in the country. "As an individual I feel utterly humble before you but as a representative of a great party I feel like a colossus."

Rao said he preferred dialogue to speech in his style of functioning and would endeavour to have discussion at various levels within the party and through the Congress all over the country. He minced no words in suggesting that he would need every bit of support from every quarter to face the onerous tasks ahead. "You help me more than you have ever helped anyone. If you have helped Rajivji in X quantity, help me in 1000 X."

Referring to speeches of a number of members who had talked of the grave challenges in the absence of a leader of Rajiv's stature, Mr. Rao said he had no doubt that the Congress (I) was capable of solving each and every problem. Problem s and solutions were a continuing process and there could never be a probelmless situation.

"We don't have to be daunted by the daunting problems. This is the essence of the Indian National Congress," he observed. At another stage he said certain people had made politics a source of entertainment and spoke of the need for viewing the problems with all seriousness.

Rao recalled that seven years ago when he had proposed the name of Rajiv Gandhi as the leader of the CPP. He had never dreamt that it would be for the first and last time he would be proposing Rajiv's name for the job. Describing the assassination as merciless and cruel, he said it was a miracle that pople had recovered from it so soon. But in the case of the Congress the recovery was natural.

He said sometimes in history when great people departed, the task of fulfilling the larger goals fell on small people, and one had to cope with the changed reality. He had been associated with the job of drafting Congress manifestos for the last five elections, but the latest manifesto prepared under the leadership of Rajiv Gandhi was the most competent and was a meticulous programme of action. Rao said perhaps Rajiv Gandhi had a premonition that the task of carrying out the programmes outlined in the manifesto would fall on lesser shoulders and hence had made it so crysless than implement it totally and if the party failed, the blame would squarely rest on all Congress men and women. There can be no alibi, I am sure there will be no failures. The manifesto is the sum total of the tasks we have to address in the coming days and months." The newly elected leader said no country of India's diversity had so many achievements to its credit and the eyes of whole world were focused on events here. He depreciated the tendency among some people to look outside when the rest of the world looked towards India.

Narasimha Rao has the maturity to give proper guidance. Rao's selection as Prime Minister has been an ideal choice of Congressmen.

Instead of announcing his team in a piecemeal fashion as was done by some of his immediate predecessors, new Prime Minister, Narasimha Rao, has done well in constituting his ministry in one go, leaving little scope for speculation about further expansion in instalments. But a major drawback of the new Union Ministry is its unrepresentative character, particularly region-wise. The electoral debacle of the party in both Uttar Pradesh and Bihar has virtually foreclosed Rao's option of choosing from a large number of MPs from these two States. The most populous states of Uttar Pradesh and Bihar, which have played a major role in national affairs all these years, are poorly represented in the ministry. It is true that by including a few Rajya Sabha members in his team. Rao has tried to make up for the deficiency. But this strategy has not worked well. Similarly, the absence of Cabinet-level Ministers from States like Tamil Nadu and West Bengal is glaring. The most conspicuous omission, however, is that of some of Sharad Pawar's vocal supporters from Maharashtra despite the fact that the Congress has done extremely well in the State.

What is likely to cause discontent among partyment is the disporportionate weightage that has been given to the coterie. Some of the key members of the coterie have found berhts in the Cabinet. Mr. Rao could have easily managed the affairs of the country without their expertise and reputation. The most welcome inclusion in the Cabinet is that of the distinguished economist, Dr. Manmohan Singh. With him as Finance Minister, not only will India find it less difficult to secure, much required IMF loan the but well known for his pragmatic view and sound economic analysis, Dr. Manmohan Singh is likely to give the right direction to the economy at this critical juncture. Similarly, the inclusion of Arjun Singh shows he has tried to accommodate a leader who also had aspired for Prime Ministership, although it was Mr. Pawar who really put up some challenge. The inclusion of S.B. Chavan, Madhavrao Scindia and Madhavsinh Solanki is apparently aimed at using their considerable experience in the government. At the Minster of State level, the important inclusions are those of P. Chidambaram, Margaret Alva, Rajesh Pilot, M.M. Jacob and Eduardo Faleiro.[8]

Whatever the calibre of his colleagues, the Prime Minister's main handicap is that his party does not enjoy absolute majority in the Lok Sabha. Dependence upon outside help for his Government's survival is bound to cramp his style of leadership. Nevertheless an accommodating, non-controversial and tactful leader like him can be expected to secure the cooperation of not only his partyment but of others as well. However, good captancy lies not only in making the best use of his team but also in keeping party unity intact. This will require readiness to involve all senior leaders in the party in the decision-making and not letting a group take things in its own hands.

The Congress on June 22, 1991 described the composition of the Union Council of Ministers as a happy "blend of youth and matured and experienced" leaders.

The party spokesman, Pranab Mukherjee, said that the Ministry represented various sections of society. It has youngesters like Mamata Bannerjee, Youngest Cabinet Minister Ghulam Nabi Azad, and vet-tern like Sitaram Kesari, Vijai Bhaskara Reddy, apart from Prime Minister, P.V. Narasimha Rao.

The spokesman said that it was not always possible to give repre-sentations in the Council of Ministers as per the number of members returned to the Lok Sabha from a state. There were no such rules, he said in reply to a question.

Mukherjee said that lot of other factors like talent, sectoral and regional representations were taken into consideration. Apart from that the basic principle was that it was "the Prime Minister's Cabinet" and he had the prerogative to select it.

"It is his pack of cards, he can shuffle it the way he can," he commented.

Mukherjee described it as "rumours" that the Maharashtra Chief Minister, Sharad Pawar, was posing problems in the allocation of porfolios to the Central Ministers.

Describing that it was the "prerogative" of the Prime Minister to allocate porftolios, he said that one must "appreciate the delay."

About the National Front and Left Front's suggestion that the Lok Sabha Speaker, Rabi Ray, should continue as the Speaker, Mukherjee said that the normal practice has been that leader of the ruling party discussed with various party leaders. This time the same practice would continue.

Prof. N.G. Ranga, the oldest member of the Ninth Lok Sabha, who has been defeated in the just concluded elections asked the new members "to learn from the magnitude of failure of the last Parliament."

Prof. Ranga who was filling in the form for ex-member's pass, said the new members must support their parties in a "loyal and steady manner" so that parliamentary democracy was a success and "not a mockery".

Prof. Ranga, who held the credit of having the longest parliamentary tenure, said supporters of all the parties in the House should ensure that Parliament did not face "disastrous dissolution" before the end of its term as had happened to the Ninth Lok Sabha.

Ranga, the deputy leader of Congress in Parliament during the eighth and ninth Lok Sabha was defeated from Guntur Lok Sabha contituency of Andhra Pradesh by S.M. Lal Jan Basha of the Telugu Desam.

The nonagenarian Prof. Ranga visited Parliament House on June 19, 1991 and greeted the newly elected members.

He said that all the parties should function in a responsible manner and try to avoid the expenditure incurred on holding of elections.

"Finances of the Government have already gone awry and in parliamentary parlance the country has already been made bankrupt."

Suggestion that it is absolutely essential for the health of the nation that the three political goups, namely, JD/NF,CPI and CPM and Congress must jointly take on the responsibility of running the Central Government is likely to generate different and shrill reactions. The BJP for obvious reasons and because of its open anti-minority stand, a strident and rigid stand on Article 370 vis-a-vis Kashmir and its fundamentalist call to distort the universalism and tolerance of Hindu religion to the parochial shrill cry of Hindutva, obviously rules it out for sharing power at the Centre. The suggestion for the coalition politics at the Centre immediately provokes the question about the platform of or programme will be agreed to. But this controversy on ideological question is not so relevant, in the conditions prevailing in the country, as it was in 1953-54, when the overwhelming members of the Socialist Party led by Dr. Lohia repudiated the 14 point programme formulated by the Nehru-Jayprakash Narayan talks. Whether that decision was correct or not is immaterial now. The basic difference then and now is that at that time we had a functioning democratic State which was not in danger of collapsing in the absence of coalition. That situation no longer exists. The Indian state is on the edge of the precipice. The ground realities have to be taken seriously.[9]

The voting pattern in the assembly polls, when compared to that in the recently-held district council elections in the state, confirms as much. Though the LDF registered a 0.98 per cent rise in votes polled this time, the UDF had a 4.16 per cent growth when compared to the 1987 assembly election. This year, the LDF won 45.95 per cent votes and the UDF 48.52 per cent votes. While both the LDF and the UDF registered an increase this time, significantly, the BJP polled 3.67 lakh votes less in the 1991 assembly elections than it did in the district council polls, held barely six months ago. This section, in all probability, shifted to the Congress this time. Kerala also went to the polls after the assassination, and the fact that more women than men voted, indicates that the sympathy wave took its toll there. There are several other factors behind the LDF defeat in the state. Poll out comes in Christian dominated constituencies reveal that the community voted en masse for the Congress. The LDF's alliance with the Janata Dal too had an impact with the forward Nair caste, strongly reacting against the Mandal Commission, rejecting the alliance. And if, despite all these handicaps, the LDF still had a chance of doing well, (CPI (M) general secretary E.M.S. Namboodiripad's letter to Congress president P.V. Narasimha Rao well and truly queered the pitch for the Left. The letter, which read like an appeal for a repprochement between the Congress and the Left, propeled a large section of voters towards the Congress. "The voter would have thought that if the Left was going to align with the Congress after the elections, why not vote for the Congress straightway," a CPI leader reasoned. Up in the north, outside its bastions, the Left's performance was dismal. The Left, which hardly has any presence in the north, relied on its alliance with the Janata Dal to gather a few quick seats. Unfortunately, the Janata Dal's own lack of organisation or cadre in the rigion came up as an impediment for the Left. "And we underestimated the BJP's hold over the Hindus. It was our failure that we couldn't work at the grass root level and mobilise the masses against the BJP," a CPI (M) Member of Parliament admitted.[10]

The Nehru family's complete hold on the Congress, in a sense, started with Darbar's presidentship of the party and has continued since then, except for a brief period when Indira Gandhi was struggling to firm up her own power. With the routing of the Old Guard under S. Nijalingappa, the supremacy of the Nehru Gandhi family became a fait accompli. Since then the Congress as a party never did its own thinking. The thinking was done by Indira Gandhi and the coterie around her which kept changing with the party president's own imperious moods. Courtiers now appeared on the scene, men of straw who had nothing to their credit except a fawning desire to serve their mistress. In pre-independence day, membership of the Congress Working Committee was recogniation of an indivudual's national eminence. In post-Indira Gandhi days it became a reflection of a courtier's subservience. Once the Working Committee could boast of names that dazzled. But where once we had Mualana Abul Kalam Azad, today we only have he walked down Mohammad Ali Road, a Sitaram Kesari where once we had Babu Rajendra Prasad who was to become our first President and, a third rate lawyer called Janaradhan Poojari who can't get ten peopel to hear him (including himself and his body guard) were to address a meeting at Chowpathy. Men of straw they all are who strut on the national stage pretending to dispose of the fortunes of India's most distinguished national party. It is to sorry stage that we have come. But nothing is beyond repair. The domination of these insginificant courtiers has to be broken and the people have to come into their own; the

Bhagats, the Fotedars, the Bajpais and the Jhakars have to be summarily shown the door. Membership for the Congress will have to be thrown open as it once was during its four anna fees (24 Pasia) days. Those who love and honour the party will have to make a sincere effort to re-establish its glory and its relevance, It should not be up to Pranab Mukherjee (who has never won an election) or a Shiv Shankar, or an Arjun Singh (against whom there are several charges) to say who the Congress president should be. The decision should be left to the general membership of the All India Congress Committee to vote on and, perhaps the first thing that this body should do is to vote for the delection of the 'I (in Congress. Once and for all the Congress must be returned to the people. And never again should it be allowed to be the instrument of any one person, howsoever distinguished or noble. For a vibrant democracy to function, political parties must accept dissent. It is a cliche to say that the Congress was once an 'umbrella' party that harboured, even encourged dissent. For over two decades it was the Mahatma who was the arbiter of Congress destiny. But even he bowed down to the public will when, against his wishes, the party voted in Subhas Chandra Bose as the president for a second time. The Congress could shelter at one and the same time the conservative Vallabhbhai Patel, the socialist Jawaharlal Nehru and the revolutionary Subhas Chandra Bose. Vallabhhai could thunder at the AICC delegates and ask them to Please see that in the selection of delegates you eliminate all anti Gandhi elements' and be rebuked for saving that by Gandhi himself. That was party democracy. We have to revive the Congress and the *Chamchas* (sychophants) have to be booted out mercilessly. The people have to recapture the party from the predators who now hold it in thrall. With that achieved, the party and in consequence, the nation will be freed from the personality cult that for so long has prevented the growth of good leaders. It is time that the people finally come into their own. The time to free the congress from slavery is now.[11]

The minority Congress Government has apparently begun a search for a solid groups of Member of the Lok Sabha to lend it support for the Prime Minister, P.V. Narasimha Rao, has to prove his majority in the House within four weeks, as stipulated by the President R. Venkataraman, when administering oath of office to him.

To this end, the Congress has in all probability started talks with the CPI (M) leaders.

On behalf of the party, Buta Singh, former Union Home Minister, who has been reelected from Rajasthan, met West Bengal Chief Minister Jyoti Basu.

Buta Singh was accompanied by Harkishan Singh Surjeet, another CPI (M) politbureau member, when he met and talked with Jyoti Basu. Surject is believed to be close to some of the Congress leaders. He used to meet Rajiv Gandhi from time to time.

It is believed that the leaders discussed the question of CPI (M)'s cooperation with the new Government in the Lok Sabha. Buta Singh also presumably explored the possibility of whether or not the CPI (M) would lend the support of its 35 MPs in the House to the Congress in the event of the Congress (I) seeking a confidence vote in the House.

It is evident that the CPI (M) may not like to take such a step on its own, and would have to consult the other partners of the Left Front i.e. the CPI, Forward Bloc and Revolutionary Socialist Party for joint action.

The CPI (M) might like to lend its support to the minority Congress (I) to save it form collapsing in a non confidence vote. But this would probaly have to be a joint action with the CPI, FB and the RSP. The BJP has already decided to oppose a confidence motion in the Congress (I).

Meanwhile a two "day Central Committee meeting of the CPI (M), which commenced in the New Delhi on June 21, made an in-depth review of the election results.

The party's Politbureau member, Praskash Karath, said that the meeting had taken up discussion on drawing up a post-poll line of action. The party has not fared well this time except in West Bengal.

Prominent among those who attended the meeting include the CPI (M) general secretary, E.M.S. Namboodiripad, Basu, Surjeet, Nripen Chanravorty and E.K. Nayanar.

The CPI high command meanwhile has welcomed the formation of the new Congress (I) Government and said that the National Front-Left Front should determine its attitude to the Government by juding its policies andparaticies form issue to issue.

The CPI's National Council met here on June 20 and 21 adopted a resolution describing the emergence of the BJP as the second largest party in the Lok Sabha and the largest part in the U.P. Assembly as "a grave threat to the secular democratic fabric of our national unity and communal amity." The CPI said the BJP managed its success by "its divisive communal politics and exploitation of religion for narrow partisan political ends."

The National Council Resolution noted that the people were not interested in another midterm poll and "they expect this Government to tackle the burning problems and bring some relief to the masses."

"The NF-Left Front alliance, which fought the elections together, has to respond to this mood of the people in a positive and responsible manner", the CPI said.

The people wanted stability and unity of the country to be protected because political instability and the absence of a stable Government were prejudical to the vital interests of the common people, the party said.

The Left-National Front must rally all the secular and democratic forces, including those in the Congress, to combat and defeat the distruptive, communal and anti secular policies and actions of the BJP, to rouse the masses to protect our rich secular heritage and to defend the minorities, the CPI resolution said.

The party appealed to the Congress not to resort to any anti-democratic and unethical methods for securing majority.

The CPI appealed to all other Left formations to reorient their polities and join the Left main-stream, while maintaining the identify of the Left. We will have a properly functioning parliamentary coordination with the National Front. It said, the CPI as part of the Left Opposition, would coordinate its activites in and outside the Pralia-ment with other Left parties. What are the issue, however, on which the Communist today can join hands with the Congress without inhibition? Economic radicalism is one that can immediately be ruled out. Neither side can recreate the conditions of 1969 that made this a common ground. The days of 'garibi hatao' cannot return for the Congress. And, the Communists have yet to find their economic policy bearings in the post perestroika age of "liberalisation" when they can neither oppose nor support it. Also out of course, is "authoritarianism" as an anti Congress argument. It went with Indira Gandhi and it is only implausibly that the Communists have retained it in their polemics and the propaganda. With Rajiv Gandhi's assassination, it actually threatens of fall into disuse. The Communists also do not conceal the hope that "dynastic rule" will not longer be a hurdle to the dialogue mooted by the CPI-M general secretary.

The most promising of positive grounds for a Congress-Communist compact would seem to be provided by the prospect of "communalism" emerging as a potent force. Here is an issue where the ideological avowals and political interests of the two sides can be seen to concerge. It is majority "communalism" that has most consistently since Independence been perceived to provide such a gorund. The idea that communalism in the antithesis of Indian Communism, and not capitalism, is itself a legacy of the pre-independence Congress-Communist relationship and a testimony to the Nehruvian influence over the Left. What originally was a stance of opposition to all "divisive" forces and ideologies has by now been virtually reduced to an "anti-communalist" plant. The Communists have, for example, shed their pristine aversion to "Dravidian" politics, and now support movements for separate State of Uttarakhand and Jkarkhand. No such "historic compromise", however, is thinkable with the politics of "Hindutva". The need to isolate the political force of Hindu communalism, has, on the other hand, been the first argument communists could think of whenever they were going for an alliance or understanding with the Congress. The CPI did this during the Indira days and pressed their point to the extent of claiming that the Jana Sangh's participation in the Jayaprakash Narayan movement made it plainly "fascist". The then Dangeite party frequently twitted the CPI-M about its anti congressim putting it in communalist company. The CPI-M's response was never to assert that communalism or the Jana Sangh was not its main enemy, but only to claim that it was really more anti-communalist and anti-Jana Sangh than it rival.[12]

It was on the 'dual membership' issue, involving the Jana Sangh component of the undivided Janata party and the Sangh's links with the RSS that the CPI-M objectively helped dislodge the first alternative to Congress rule at the Centre. Such is the public's reading of the Marxist mind that, when Mr. H. S. Surjeet says his party will consider the subject of "realignment" after the elections, the CPI-M appears ready to do business with the post Rajiv Congress-I in order to keep the BJP at bay. It is not quite clear as yet whether another long-familiar argument for Congress- Communist cooperation will be invoked, but attempts are apparently being made in this direction. "Anti imperialism" did not cease to be shared paltform for them with the end of the colonial rule. Both the Communist parties have been among the staunchest supporters of the Nehruvian and Indiraite foreign policy, though the CPI-M may have had occasions to demur about the Soviet deviations from the straight and narrow path of proletarian internationalism in the Brezhnev period.[13]

The people have delivered their verdict, a mixed verdict, a somewhat confusing verdict, in fact a rather curious verdict. The Congress got a mandate almost and yet not quite. It missed the magical mark by a small number of seats. This is all the more remarkable because of its pathetically miserable showing in the two largest states of India, UP and Bihar, with some 139 seats among themselves. That it has still managed to get close to a majority is without parallel in the history of independent India. The first thing that strikes one is the absence of any uniform pattern. Not only has here been no national wave, there it no evidence of even common perceptions colouring the judgement of the people in the entire country. People in different states have had divergent perceptions and have voted accordingly. If in Madhya Pradesh and Rajasthan the people were powerfully influenced by the need for a strong, stable government at the Centre, further disillusioned by the lacklustre performance of their state governments, the people in Uttar Pradesh, Bihar and Gujarat apparently set no great store by stability. The sympathy factor after the brutal assassination of Rajiv Gandhi was certainly active in some states (Tamil Nadu most of all, but also in Maharashtra and Kerala and in a number of other states,) but it seems to have had very much less impact over the electorate in Gujarat or Uttar Pradesh, and perhaps none at all in Bihar. The resource of appeal in the name of religion and the Ram card has tilted the scales massively only in two states while the Mandal card has swayed voters only in the state of Bihar which in any case has allways been susceptible to the domination of caste, muscle and state power. Even the North-South divide stands broken this time. The Congress has done exceedingly well in states like Madhya Pradesh, Rajasthan and Haryana, but has been routed in Uttar Pradesh and Bihar, while it has put in a creditable performance in Western India and in Orissa in Eastern India. In has had a landslide victory in Tamil Nadu and stood its gound in Kerala and Karnataka for the Parliament elections in the South, but has suffered notable losses in Andhra. In many cases the disgust felt locally was reflected in the electoral behavious. This was evident in Assam and Haryana, both places where the Congress has benefited from the degeneration and stagnation that was associated with the previous regimes.[14]

If there is one glaring lesson for the Congress, it is that whereever Congressmen were able to unite and offered a determined fight, they did reasonably well and where they continued to engage in factional fighting or were otherwise in disarray, whether it was Uttar Pradesh or Gujarat or Andhra, they received a drubbing at the hands of the electorate. This is a way reflects both the strength and weakness of the Congress party and continues to determine its fate in different states. The Congress has also paid the price for supporting Mulayam Singh Yadav and the earlier act of allowing *Shilaniyas* to take place near the Babri Masjid. Clearly the Congress has lost its social base in UP and Bihar and would need to make a massive effort to recover even partially its support base there. The BJP has made a spectacular showing, increasing its tally in the Lok Sabha from 85 to around 115. Yet in the final analysis the windfall has come virtually from two states, UP and Gujarat, and it has registered only a nominal presence in South India. All said and done, the BJP's version of Hindutva stands rejected by a large majority of the country. Nonetheless, the BJP has certainly bagged the prize catch of UP, the largest state in the country, but this may also be the beginning of its troubles. If the performance of its administration there turns out to be as unimpressive as in Madhya Pradesh and Rajasthan and its handling of the Temple-Masjid issue proves too ham-handed, the consequences for it would be severly damaging. As far as the Janata Dal is concerned, its figures speak for themselves and confirm the earlier view of this writer that in India there is not enough space for two centrist parties, space that is currently occupied by the Congress. To provide a stable and durable government which would take hard decisions so sorely needed, the Congress would require the support of some other party or parties. In the present context it can turn only to the Left Group and/or the Janata Dal. The internal situation within the Janata Dal does not appear to be quite stable. Be that as it may, the political system must strive for a change in the basis and form of support that had hitherto been practiced. There is need for a more structured form of support and the Congress should think in terms of written agreements, as is done in many European countries. The dependence for such support should not lead the country from populism to more disastrous populism. The new Government would be well-advised to take all the tough and agonizing decisions required to put the economy on the rails and to rectify the deteriorating law and order situation in the first year itself, for no party would dare destabilise it during this period and, hopefully, by the second year the road back to some recovery would have started.[15]

The economic crisis must receive the highest priority and, therefore, the government must quickly formulate a package of measures which will carry credibility with the rest of the world. The tasks are daunting, but the country has suffered so much and so long that these are no longer vague.[16]

- Economy must be debureaucratised courageously.
- Respect for productive sections, forces and individuals must be incucated in the government. Parasites must be curbed; those who draw more from society than they contribute to it must be put in their proper place.
- The government must begin to trust the people: they must be presumed to be honest until proved otherwise.
- Deficit is to be reduced by curtailing unproductive expenditure, drastically phasing out subsidies, except where these are really needed in the interests of vulenerable and under-privileged sections and by ensuring that every paise of the

savings entrusted to the bureaucracy is productively and profitably invested.

- The government must withdraw from areas of economy where the task can be accomplished by individuals and voluntary associations of people.
- All practices, procedures and attitudes that delay decisions, protect inefficiency and restrict competition beneficial to society must be eliminated ruthlessly.
- All wages and non-wage incomes should be linked to productivity and needs of future growth.
- Above all, commitment to work ethic and productivity should be the core of economic philosophy.

Only in such a framework can the interests of the poor, unemployed and the deprived sections be protected.

ADMINISTRATION:[17]

- Restore respect for professionalism and integrity.
- Administration must be result-oriented.
- Rule of law must be restored.
- Simplify procedures, and end the regime of overlegislation.
- Build a durable and credible mechanism of interparty consultations.
- Give high priority to decentralisation of power, restructuring of Centre-state relations and introduction of grassroots democracy.

POLITICAL TASKS: [18]

- Postpone Punjab elections.
- Diffuse the Ayodhya issue and advise the state government to devise a consulative machinery to reconcile differences.
-

Take strict steps to protect life and property of all citizens without fear and favour.

P.V. Narasimha Rao, the Prime Minister, faces gigantic challenges. He is the tool of history to take India out of the gravest crisis facing the country after August, 1947. The whole nation wishes him good luck and success and he can count on the support and cooperation of all those who have the interests of the country at heart. It is a good augury that he is embarking on his momentous stewardship of the nation with enormous fund of goodwill.

Outgoing Commerce Minister Subramaniam Swamy announced with a fanfare that the country has turned the corner and produced a trade surplous in April of Rs. 135 crore. For the first time after several years, the imports were less than exports and this is attributable to the RBI import control measures against which Dr. Swamy had protested. Yet those curbs have helped him to show a trade surplous in April though he would take credit for the "vigorous export drive" of the Chandra Shekhar Government. If trade surplus is to come via import compression, it will be a short-lived satisfaction. Devaluation of the rupee has not been suggested by the IMF, according to its own statement, because in a floating regime of exchange rates, the rupee is being continually adjusted in relation to the basket of major currencies. The rupee depreciated by 12 per cent during 1990-91 but it could fall against the dollar sharply during 1991-92, until the Government is able to control inflation and put through an economic policy package. The normal monsoon and stable oil prices would provide a supportive environment for growth if the rate of inflation is brought down to well below 10 per cent in the current year. But any stiff dose of taxation involving commodities and revision of administered prices may thwart efforts to check the anti-inflation strategy. More than the budget, the Government would have to come up with reforms in the industrial sector and a beginning may be made with the policy changes announced by the National Front Government in May last but never implemented. These covered industrial approvals, support to small-scale sector and automatic clearance for 40 per cent foreign equity in designated areas. The IMF and the World Bank may, however, be expected to call for a more vigorous drive towards deregulation and privatisation. As the Government deals with the more immediate issues of fiscal and balance of payment deficits, which had brought the economy to the brink, the eight five-year Plan may remain a non-starter.[19]

Of late, the World Bank has been making a series of suggestions for the restructuring of Indian public sector corporation, including financial institutions. One need not have any objection to well-meaning advice from any quarter, more so if it comes from an agency that is a major source of financial assistance to this country. But this does not, mean that whatever the World Bank says is the last word in practical wisdom. We must weight its suggestions in the light of our politico-economic conditions and our perception of what is desirable and feasible. The main thrust of the Bank has been towards liberalisation of the economy and creation of a more competitive environment. But the pace of reforms has to match the new institutional framework and the requisite linkages we are able to build. It is against this backdropt that we must consider the latest World Bank suggestion to split the ONGC into three regional corporations, each as an autonomous entity. In so far as the diagnosis of the malady afficting the ONGC is concerned, no one can fault with the Bank's findigins that the commission has become an unwieldy body with too much centralisation impinging upon its efficiency. It is also true that its financial resources are declining, while the expenditure is rising. Clearly, the costs of amintaining essential communications and other services are enormous, even as the exploration programme is suffering for lack of funds. Recent report also revealed that the maintenance of oil wells has been neglected for long, necessitating closure of over 100 wells for urgent repairs. However, the remedy the world Bank has favoured has to be tempered with considerations of achieving maximum efficiency in the multifarious operations involved in the oil industry. There is, indeed, a case for splitting the ONGC. But rather than a geographical division and creation of regional corporations, it would be more appropriate to have a functional division. Thus, oil exploration, production, distribution and back-up services can each be handled by a separate corporation. Of course, these corporations may raise funds from the market, as the World Bank suggests.[20]

A functional split has the merit of ensuring that each corporation concentrates on its particular area of operation, while achieving the necessary coordination and economy in the deployment of its managerial, technical, material and financial resources. A geographical split, on the other hand, may mean increased overheads and sub-optimal utilisation of available resources. This model, in fact, can also be replicated to a great advantage in other major public sector industries like fertiliser and steel.

The Indian nation-state building process has entered a most critical phase. Though social science is not an astrology, the democratic and secular political system of the country is facing formidable challenges. This has been graphically illustrated by the course of events since 1989 and particularly during the recent mid-term poll to the Lok Sabha, through the rigging, booth-capturing, use of money and muscle power on an unprecedented scale and, above all, the fanning of communal and casteist passions.

Liberating, building, sustaining and safe-guarding the Republic and its objectives as ehshrined in the Constitution, of democracy, secularism, socialism and non-alignment, are the key tasks facing our nation today. Our liberation struggle under the leadership of Mahatma Gandhi was a unique event and heralded the beginnign of world-wide decolonisation. The building up of the Indian nation-state there after was a stupendous task. One-sixth of humanity, unified by the millennia-old concept of Indian civilisation and culture but divided in languages, ethnicities and religions had to be weilded together into a democratic, federal, secular, multilingual and multiethnic Republic. It was a task comparable to uniting the whole of Europe. To except that this task could be completed in four decades would amount to living in a make-believe world. It is necessacry and relevant to underline this aspect of the Indian reality because concerted attempts are being made, both within India and outside, to sap the confidence of the people in the democratic political system itself. This breeds cynicism. In fact, attempts are being made in India by certain political forces and personalities to erode confidence of the people in the political system and, above all, in the relevance of the secular and democratic political forces and parties. There is yet another dimension to it.[21]

The smooth assumption of power by the parliamentary representatives of the people elected to the Tenth Lok Sabha despite all the gunfire that claimed a former Prime Minister and a few other candidates for Central and State legislatures is proof, if any was needed, of the strength and resilience of the Indian democratic polity. The blood of two former prime ministers, a mother and a son, has nurtured this plant. The price of democracy is not only eternal vigilance but also sacrifice, even of life. Regrettably that price sometimes it too high because members of the intolerant frings who are afraid of the ballot occasionally go for the bullet. Yet the supremacy of the ballot over the bullet has been firmly established in India. It is difficult to pinpoint the involvement of foreign forces intent upon destablising even destroying the democratic system of India. The very nature of the intelligence operations of inimical powers makes it well nigh impossible to put the blame where it belongs. The sophisticated armoury of the terrorists and the ease with which they can challenge and subvert parts of the government of a country are unmistakable pointers to conspiracies hatched abroad. The bloodletting that has been going on in Punjab and Kashmir for quite some years now cannot by any stretch of imagination be described as home-inspired. True, some genuine grievances are there in very situation but they are resolvable by the use of argument counter-argument and ultimately the vote. Occasionally the use of the gun may also become understandable, though not justified, but presistent armed attacks on the state machinery, which is the guardian of the people's will, is an act of destabilisation, pure and naked. The empathy of forces like the LTTE with the erstwhile controllers of the state machinery in Tamil Nadu cannot be easily dismissed as figment of suspicion. What remains unidentified in such circumstances is not only the role of internal collaborators but also that of their foreign patrons and paymasters. But India can deal with them because the sacrifice of Rajiv Gandhior his mother is not of solitary nature. There are others too who can follow their example in blood. Hindustan shall never forget Maa Bete Ka Balidan (the sacrifice of the mother and son) and there are ever more sons and mothers who will not let the earlier sacrifices go in vain. The argument may sound rehtorical but it is a sound one. True, internally, rigging and booth capturing by money and muscle power have made a mockery of the polling process at several places, which is condemnable even in a solitary instance. No effort should be spared to combat this evil and if necessary, the constitution may also be amended to provide timely and swift remedies.[22]

The compuslory appointment of chief returning officers at state and district level from outside the state concerned may be one step towards ensuring an impartial poll. Senior police officers from outside states may also be compulsorily deployed as an additional step towards defeating the local goons. The Constitution may also amended to curtail the powers of caretaker ministers once an election is announced, there by preventing them from indulging in a last-minute being of favouritism and corruption. Simultaneously, giving more teeth to the Election Commission may also be debated to prevent it form being reducedd to a hapless spectator of rigging and both capturing. However putting things in perspective, even booth capturing is an exception to the general practice, though it hogs the headlines rather completely. Without any hint of complacency. It is worth remembering that by and large the general elections in India have achieved their objective. The people's will has always found its voice. The voters may look ill-equipped but they are quite uncanny in their judgement. The Indian voter in the rural country side may lack television, newspapers or even the reading skills but he has his ear firmly to the ground. His heart is in the right place and his memory not too fickle.[23]

Terrorism has psycho-pathological and political aspects. Psychopathology is reflected in the realisation of the seakness of the self. It is combined with the desire to exercise power over persons, events and processes. The normal indices of power in its coercive, productive and cooperative aspects are consensus- building in public policies. The psychology of the weak to become strong can issue forth in acts of solidarity of social groups that can be denoted as the social contract of the weak. In case this is not feasible, the psychology of spontaneity takes over. Spontaneity combined with a sense of individual heroism leades to violence which is senseless as also mystifying. The breaking up of the machines by the luddites in England was an example of spontaneity emerging from the fact of ignorance of social forces that cause a predominant reality on the fringe of which is desperate dissensus that is the source of such violence. Individual acts of violence, in themselves, suffer from the fact that they are against social consensus. Individual killings in zarist Russia made Lenin speak against that tactic. It is necessary to oppose terror since the psycho-pathological mind attempts to intimidate or subjegate through an act of violence. A psycho-pathological personality is characterised by emotional instability, impulsive and perverse, if not sadomasochist, behavious and one that has the abnormality of suffering from amoral and a social feelings. Individual killings in the arena of politics are much more complex than just individual crime. The killings of the Red Indians, the Jews, Patrice Lumumba, John F. Kennedy, Mahatma Gandhi and Mujibur Rahman, Ziaur Rahman, Ziaul Haq, Indira Gandhi are not acts of individual psycho-pathology. These killings had the prupose of obliterating a dominant political culture, and political personality. Terrorism is an attack on political consensus too. That terrorism is a politically organised and socially based phenomenon is made evident by history. From May 1793 to July 1794 France experienced the Reign of Terror. The Stalin phenomenon is marked by a reign of terror. The French and Gorbachevian rejection of this terror, which was marked by executions, is well-known and the latter is facing a different and ironical situation. Endemic violence in the USSR is not just ethnic. It is sponsored by political forces having paramilitary organisations and a fascistic history. Under siege have been the army barracks of the Red Army. Attack on soldiers and their families in the Soviet republics, particularly in the Baltic republics, is a quirk that bafflles both the Red Army and those who support the Baltics. The process of federation formation and Union treaty in the USSR is marked by both consensus and coercion. The German case of state terrorism is quite well known. This again raised its ugly head at the time of German unificiation. The accusations and counter accusations tht the US has levelled against the countries of Latin America and the Arab world reflect the malaise of transformation of individual terrorism into a systemic organism that besieges the consensus of a nation. The bombing of Libya to get at Gaddafi is no solution to the problem of terrorism in international relations or in the society itself.[24]

The terrorism generated by drug trafficking, alienation, poverty and desire for high levels of sensationalism cannot be ended by high-technology weapons that performed so well in the Gulf War. The latter means that arms bazar for the west has opened its womb as never before. Recurement patterns of terrorist acts show that a country is under a siege. That drugs and arms trade has its own logic cutting across regional security complexes involving extra- regional factors is proved by the endemic violence in Latin America, Pakistan, Afghanistan and Sri Lanka. In the countries of the third world, the nexus is nascent but the impact is astounding. If one goes by the cycle of individual assassinations. South Asia is rich in examples. The most greuesome is the assassination of former Prime Minister Rajiv Gandhi. Whether the arsenal of the contraption used in blowing up the leader of the party that called for stability was the one that the US army makes or not is besides the point. The fact of the matter is that terrorism in India does not have its roots in the system of arms-drugs syndrome, or indigenous arms industry development. It is much mercantilist in nature. The mushrooming of unlicensed arms production is a dangerous trend. It helps indirectly to erode the dominant consensus. Directly, it leads to physical liquidation. The sophisticated weapons that are being used in India-in Punjab, Jammu and Kashmir, Tamil-Nadu, the north- east-to put the country on the mat are the handiwork not of the homebrew. It is a heady foreign-made brew. In that specific sense, Rajiv Gandhi's murder is the result of foreign brew-the logic is mercantilist.[25]

The shadows of uncertainity lengthen and despondency deepens as the longest general election in recent memory comes to a close. But India must pull intself out of the gloom for there is no alternative. This is the only country we have and it simply party gets a working majrority in the Tenth Lok Sabha, it is not necessary that parliamentary democracy will withe to its death. And, it devolves upon the government to be in office to do whatever it can to restore the nation's receding faith in its own political class. The new government which, would have to deal with some of the biggest challenges facing India in recent decades. The priority items on the national agenda are as follows: First, political stability; second the economy; and, third, the battle against terrorism. The first task before the new government would be to dispel the impression that India has ceased to be a stable political entity. This impression is no longer confined to the prophets of doom in the West, but is increasingly gripping Indians. Progressively since V.P. Singh assumed office in December 1989, a sense of insecurity has grown, accentuated by the brazen practice of casteist and communal politics. A succession of unstable governments, petty intrigues and sinister conspiracies have combined to creat a fear of impending collapse-conditions in Delhi beign increasingly compared to those prevailing in the later Mughal years. It is essential that the next government dispels this impression. For that, it is an imperative that politicians abjure intrigues. That is a tall order, but if the leadership can hold firm, it will not be difficult to beat the conspirators back. Hard decisions have to be taken on the economic front too. Major policy correctives are necessary if India is to be palced firmly on a modern, technological, capitalist path of growth, cutting through the cobwebs of decades of "socialist" inefficiency. In their mindlessness, politicians scream from rooftops every time the IMF or other global financial institutions urge such corrective measures as drastic cuts in subsidies and greater liberalisation. The IMF would not have had to say this had we not been so hesitant to introduce sound economic sense into the system ourselves. Leaders of most political parties recognise the realities in private; in public they continue to spout the discredited, moribund jargon of a bygone age. We are truly doomed if this continues even after the next government takes office. The war against terrorism has to be pursued with the might and vagour that befits a state of India's size and importance. Among the first steps the new government may have to take is to dissolve the Pubjab assembly. The secessionist conspirators there need not be given a chance to form a government and thus legitimise their support base in the world's eyes. The Chandra Shekhar government's insane blunder in thrusting an election on Punjab has already boosted the secessionists morale immesnely. The next government must do everything it its power to smash their backbone. Similarly, a section of the Tamil refugees from northern Sri Lanka has abused India's hospitality by assassinating Rajiv Gandhi. It is essential to weed out the anti- India forces from among them. We cannot provide them shelter so that they may merrily countinue their conspiracies aginst India.[26]

Hopefully, a degree of consensus will be reached on all these issues. But, it is incumbent upon the Narasimha Rao government to pursue these policies with resolute determination. Those who oppose such policies are bound to stand exposed, for the Indian masses shall be grateful to any government which succeeds in snatching back order from the jaws of chaos.

The Congress faces the most difficult challenge of its post- independence history. In the first place, it has to throw up a colelctive leadership, cutting out infighting and the legacy of power grabbing. The second challenge for the Congress is to provide initiative for creating national consenus and cooperation on key issues, economic and political. A preconditions for this onerous task is to give up the urge for hegemony over power, since a bid for power monopolising will flop not being in tune with political realities as they have emerged from the Lok Sabha polls. The Congress should enlarge the forces involved in power sharing at the Centre. That certainly will pave the way for a new perspective in nation-building and bringing about a turn in national affairs so urgently needed.[27]

Meanwhile, noted lawyer and chairman Citizens Drive, New Delhi Lalit Bhasin said in New Delhi, on June 15, 1991 that his organisation had prepared an agenda for the new Government. The new government would need to review the foreign, internal and economic policies. His organisation had drawn up suggestions for these in the major spheres. Internationally, the government would need to review its role vis-a-vis the Non-Aligned Movement (NAM). With shifts in alliances between different countries it was necessary to consider the utility of NAM. Even the forthcoming NAM conference was known as the meet which will decide the destiny of NAM. Better relations with the country's neighbours could also allow for cut in defence expenditure which then could be utilised for priority spheres, he said. On the economic, front the roles of various agencies specially the public sector should be redefined. The public sector had proved to be highly inefficient and a drain on the economy. Stating that economic liberalisation should continue, he said any attempt at reducing the fiscal deficit would result in higher taxation.

The law and order situation in the country needed greater attention as also in the troubled states of Jammu and Kashmir, Punjab and Assam. Major problems could only be solved through a dialogue rather than a high repressive policy.

Referring to the reservation policy, Bhasin said that while reservation on bais of economic criteria was required there should be a time-bound reservation.

NOTES :

1. Inderjit Shrma. The Authority of Power. *The Business and Political Observer,* 19 June 1991.
2. Joydeep Gupta. P.V. Narasimha Rao. *The Sunday Observer*, 2 June 1991.
3. Pran Chopra. Old Loyalties Pitted Aginst New Politics. *The Sunday Observer,* 16 June 1991.
4. *The Hindustan Times*, 27 May 1991.
5. Nikhil Chakravarthy. Cancer of Money. *Patiot,* 16 June 1991.
6. *Ibid.*
7. *Ibid.*
8. *The Hindustan Times,* 22 June 1991.
9. Rajindar Sachar. By Sharing Power. *The Hindustan Times,* 19 June 1991.
10. Bishakna De Sankar. The left. *The Sunday Observer,* 23 June 1991. Se also India Decides Elections, 1952-1991. New Delhi; 1991.
11. M.V. Kamath. Congress Then and Now. Current, 8 June 1991.

12. J. Sri Raman. With Love From EMS. *The Hindustan Times,* 12 June 1991.
13. *Ibid.*
14. V.P. Dutt. In Search of Stability. *The Hindustan Times,* 23 June 1991.
15. *Ibid.*
16. R.K. Mishra. PV: The Tasks Ahead. *The Business and Political Observer,* 21 June 1991.
17. *Ibid.*
18. *Ibid.*
19. S. Sethuraman. Post-Election Tasks on Economic Front. *Patriot, 21 June 1991.*
20. *The Business and Political Observer,* 22 June 1991.
21. V.D. Chopra. Turbulent Days Ahead. *Patriot,* 17 June 1991.
22. Subhash Chopra. Democracy. *Natinal Herald*, 23 June 1991.
23. *Ibid.*
24. Rakesh Gupta. Political Violence in Society. *Patriot,* 19 June 1991.
25. *Ibid.*
26. *The Sunday Observer,* 16 June 1991.
27. O.P. Sabherwal. Implications of the Electoral Verdict. *National Herald,* 24 June 1991.

TWO

HUMILITY AND COMPASSION

Life is a vital, ever flowing stream perpetuating itself to eternity. Constant movement and perpetual change are the most outstanding characteristics of this life-force on this planet. It is the lot of man to share in the deeper aspirations of the universe around him and to share his own destiny as well as that of the universe, now by adjusting himself to the forces, now by putting the whole of his energy to mould the forces to his own ends and purposes. Human activities and thought always remain in the lap of evolution' and we find life marching towards perfection. Life is neither a bed of roses nor a path of thorns. It is self-realisation, self-determination and self-expression. A personal mishap does cover the entire sphere of human life.

A great deal has already been written, and a lot more is bound to be written in the coming days, of P.V. Narasimha Rao, the new Congress Prime Minister who took oath of office on June 21, 1991. Much of what has appeared in newspapers has dealt with his administrative and political careers. But there is a personal side to him which is not generally known, and this is largely because Rao has deliberately adopted a low profile all through his working life. I have known Rao for nearly two decades and have also had the good fortune of watching him perform as a Minister and a politician. But more importantly, I have had the opportunity of exchanging views with him on some occasions, and during these moments I have always found him come through as a human being with great understanding, humility and compassion. Rao has invariably been described as a self-effacing personality. Those who describe him so do it with a sense of charity because they know that he does not fit into the accepted framework of politician of the times. He prefers to keep himself, without intruding his presence on those who do not seek him out or on occasions where his will be the minority view. But any time, any leader or any colleague calls upon him seeking out his views, he can be depended on to offer his perceptions on men, matters and situations with out reservations. Narasimha Rao worked in senior capacities both under Indira Gandhi and later her son, Rajiv Gandhi. But there must have been very few occasions when he himself volunteered to approach them with his advice or even his perception of how a particular matter should be handled. But on all occasions whenever either Indira Gandhi or Rajiv Gandhi sent for him and asked him for his views, he would explain his point of view sincerely and candidly. Often, he would be aware that his point of view would not eventually be accepted. But this would not deter him from offering frank advice even if it is unpalatable on latter occasions. The description that would fit Rao most aptly would be: "Gentleman politician", alas, a breed which is slowly becoming extinct in India. He has all the attributes of a gentleman: he is gentle, inoffensive, courteous and civilised in his personal conduct. As a politician, he is skilled and experienced but given to enourmous restraint. As an administrator, he is a visionary, and inclined to think of the future rather than of the present. On the floor of Parliament, he can maintain his composure and cool in the face of extreme provocation. He has not been known to have list his temper even on a single occasion in either Houses of Parliament although the opposition has not spared him nor singled him out for mild treatment. The only occasion when he allowed himself to be provoked, as far as I remember, was during the question hour when he had to react sharply to a query on the spread of AIDS in India, and he advised the questioner to acquaint himself with the subject before coming into the House.[1]

A certain measure of ruthlessness is expected these days from a politician. Indira Gandhi was described in the early years of political life as a "goongi Gudiya"-a dumb doll by no less a leader than Ram Manohar Lohia. Those were the days when Indira Gandhi had not learnt that ruthlessness and political leadership go hand in hand. Once she had realised this, she could make a person squirm by only looking at him hard. One of the tragedies of Rajiv Gandhi was that he could not develop, during the five- year-tenure of the prime ministership, the level of ruthlessness which would have enabled him to match the combative tactics of the opposition. Had Rajiv Gandhi learnt to be more ruthless, he would perhaps not have made the statement in the Lok Sabha that neither he nor members of the his family had benefited by the payoffs in the Bofors deal. Rao is another of those politicians who do not know how to be ruthless. Indeed, he cannot even be politely offensive, or offensively polite. It is just not in his nature to be rude or crude. It is not in his temperament to be cause rancour in any one. He would rather stay silent or leave the scene of controversy than make his own contribution to the heat all round. This is hardly surprising in a man who was temperamentally more inclined to the pleaseures of reading and writing rather than to the rough and tumble of politics. "A good book is the life blood of a master mind", It is said. Yet, Rao had taken to politics like to water in the sixties. Had he been groomed for the political life by any other leader than the late Swami Ramanand Tirth, politics may have lost its appeal for him in course of time. Swami Tirth, who himself was a rare politician who combined the grind of politics with the elevating influence of spiritual approach, had picked up in the erstwhile Hyderabad State three youngsters of promise: Rao, Veerendra Patil and Shankarrao Chavan. It is as much a tribute to the qualities of discipline and earnestness of his chelas (disciples) as to his Swami Tirth's leadership qualities that each of them rose to become Chief Minister of their respective state. In the case of Rao, it was a fortuitous development that took him away from state politics and brought him into national politics. Had this not happened, he would not have been able to cope with the complexities of politics as they had developed in the late sixties, seventies and eighties. He would also not have become distinguished and respected enough to have been elavated to the topmost post in the party in the early nineties. For one thing, he was too mild-mannered to face the aggressive political tactics of the handful of powerful politicians who were beginning to dominate Andhra Pradesh politics. Secondly, local politics was turning to be caste-dominated, and Mr Rao being a Brahmin had no chance to challenge the up and coming leaders who were fully capable of exploiting the caste.[2]

Pamulaparti Venkata Narasimha Rao had his baptism of fire in the freedom struggle. Born in 1921 in Vangara village on 28 June Karimnagar district of Andhra Pradesh, he studied in Osmania and Nagpur universities obtaining B.Sc. and LLB degrees. He is also a recipient of *Sahitya Ratna* in Hindi.

The road to Narasimha Rao's Vangara village in Karimnagar district of Andhra Pradesh is, indeed, in eerie one. For as one proceeds on the 50-kilometre route along Hanamakonda in Warangal district, living beings begin to disappear and by the time one is in, what is described in hushed tones, as the 'dangerous interiors' spreading well over 20 kilometres, there is not a soul in singht. Though geographically, the Karimnagar district borders the Naxalite infested Adilabad district of the State, Naxalite's writ runs through the entire Warnagal Karimnagar-Adilabad belt. Karimnagar also touches Bastar in the neighbluring state of Madhya Pradesh. Politically, Krimnagar house Vangara, the native village of Narasimha Rao, Vangara is a remote village where the unspoken law is: No outsiders, no communication least it invites the fatal ire of the men who rule there". The Naxalities. Consequently, signals warning one to steer clear of anyone and everyone in Vangara and the reighbouring areas are flashed as one touches Warangal. They will, you are forewarned, kill you, or may be set the car a fire. In Vangara, suspicion pervades. Also there is an aura of intrigue. One is watched through half open doors. Somehow the message reaches those, it is supposed to, and they appear from nowhere armed with spears-and questions, in a semi- communicative language, relate to your identity and purpose. The journalistic credentials, once they are established, get response: icy faces thaw, spears are lowered and acceptability is almost immediate. And responsive. Perhaps you are one of them. Despite this closedcircuit existence, there is a political awareness among the 5,000 odd people living in Vangara. News travels and travels fast: They know that Narasimha Rao has been elected president of the Congress, following the assassination of Rajiv Gandhi. At a personal level they are happy because he (Rao) is yahan ka Rishtedar (country cousin). Politically they expect nothing from him because he is, according to them, not a doer. Rao had last visited Vangara in 1984, a little before being electorally rejected while contesting the Hanamakonda parliamentary constituency seat in the adjoining district of Warangal. They had voted him in, in 1977 and 1980, respectively. Rao later, represented the Ramtek parliamentary constituency in Maharashtra after which he never went back to Hanamakonda to contest. The relationship seemingly snapped and the electorate there forgot him, politically.[3]

Rao is not credited with having done much work for his constituency. Those who try to recall his "good work" have to go back 20 years when as Chief Minister of the state, Narasimha Rao had brought in the Urban Land Ceilling Act. Or even before that when as the State Education Minister he abolished the system of detention because of poor grades and introduced a common examination for the seventh class throughout the State. But for this the electorate has little to remember him for. Today, he remains for them merely the achcha aadmi (good man) with no "ruling power" or political clout. It is against this backdrop that his elevation to his present stature of president of the Congress-I did not even create a ripple either in his erstwhile constituency or in his native village. Response to the news was lukewarm. He is, somewhat, a forgotten figure. In fact, his elevation is being interpreted as being one which is "a safe bet" since he would most likely submit to the whim and fancy of those who wish to firmly hold the reigns of the party through him. The fact that Rao is not contesting the elections this time is cited as evidence of his "political oblivion". Rao has, by virtue of circumstances, rather than political desingn, always been a consensus condidate. Even in 1971, he was brought to power as Chief Minister because of the telangana agitation led by Dr. M. Chenna Reddy following which the then Chief Minister Brahmandnda Reddy had to quit because of the pressure from the high command in Delhi. The search was on for a "non-controversial pliable candidate" and Rao fit the requirement the best. History seems to have repeated itself now, two decades later, when once again Rao has been considered the apt choice as Congress president, since he fits in the slot of a noncontroversial person who would willingly step down as and when those who propped him would wish him to. His seniority, administrative experience and reputation of being a competent minister at the Centre, who handled important portfolios including that of External Affarirs and Home is, however, expected to stand him in good stead, during his tenure as Congress president.[4]

While Rao's elevation will certainly enhance the credibility factor, it is not likely to contribute substantially to the sympathy wave following Rajiv Gandhi's assassination. Though the Congress plans to initially whip up and later cash in on the sympathy wave electorally, the leaderlessness of the somewhat orphaned party has raised uncomfortable question in the minds of the electorate. They are confronted with the inevitable dilemma of "who after Rajiv Gandhi", thy being fully aware that Narasimha Rao's but a "stop-gap arrangement", till the elections. It is in this context more than any other that the electorate at least in this part of the south feels that had Sonia Gandhi agreed to lead the party she would have not only held it together but also been able to consolidate the sympathy vote as none other. The general feeling is that the party would have got a "bumper majority" as Sathyanarayanan chose to put it "had Sonia Gandhi been elected the party's leader. As against this neither the intelligentsia's view at her candidature would have eroded the sympathy nor dub her as a foreigner would have held good because the counter argument which is immediately furnished and which pales every other point into insignificance, is that considering the years Sonia Gandhi has spent in India, she is more Indian than a foreigner. In fact, this factor does not even seem to cross their minds as Nagabhushanam summed up; Sara bachpan to uska (Sonia's) Yahan bita, phoren ka raha kya link......kuchch nahin" (her childhood was spent in this country so what is foreign, what is the link....nothing). What seems to matter to a decisive chunk of the electorate here is that Sonia Gandhi is "Mrs of Rajiv Gandhi (wife of Rajiv Gandhi)", "But wohi jaanta aur kuchch nahin," said swamy (that is all that I know, nothing else). The fact that Narasimha Rao's candidature was reportedly backed by Sonia Gandhi was obviously helped matters which would in all likelihood result in his garnering support for the party in the forth-coming elections.[5]

Narasimha Rao topped his school leaving examination at Osmania University in the erstwhile state of Hyderabad. Despite his best performance, he was not allowed admission in a college in Hyderabad because he had taken part in an anti-Nizam procession. That led him to Nagpur University where he graduated in science. The brilliant academic record continued, Rao earning a gold medal while receiving his law degree from Bombay University. In academic circles sahitya Ratna Rao is known as a linguist, a man who known Telgu, Hindi,

Marathi, Sanskrit, Urdu, English and a smattering of Spanish and Chairman of the Jnanpith Award committee for many years, Rao is well known as the translator of Vishwanatha Satyanarayana's famous Telugu novel Veyi Padagalu into Hindi, and Hari Narayan Apte's Kon Gheto into Telugu. Both translations were published by the Sahitya Academy New Delhi.[6]

While practising as a lawyer, he participated in the Vandemataram movement in the erstwhile Hyderabad Staye under the leadership of Swami Ramananda Tirth. He was the general secretary of the then Hyderabad state Congress Committee. Later he became its vice president in 1956. The Congress in Hyderabad had to fight on the one hand the repressive rule of the Nizam and the Communists on the other. It was in this twin struggle, Rao learnt his political lession which found their echo later when he occupied political posts. During his tenure as the member of the Legislative Assembly, he held a variety of ministerial positions. He was Chief Minister of Andhra Pradesh from 1971-1973, succeeding Brahmaninda Reddy.

Unlike many of his contemporaries, Rao does not come from a family of politicians. He is, actually a lawyer by profession hailing from Vangara in Karimnagar district he was initiated into politics by Swami Ramanand Teertha, one of the leaders of the anti-Nizam movement. An MLA from Manthani in Warangal district since 1957, he became the minister of state for law and information in the sanjeeva Reddy government in Andhra Pradesh in 1962.[7]

Maintaining a low profile during the Emergency years (1957-1977), Rao was no favourite of Indira Gandhi at the time, it was dufing the period under the Janata Party rule that he proved his political capability, having been elected to the Lok Sabha for the first time in 1977 from Hanamkonda in Andhra Pradesh. As soon as he was reelected from Hanamkonda in 1980. Rao was rewarded by being made the foreign minister. During Indira Gandhi's most glorious days as an international leader, when India hosted the non-Aligned Movement summit and the commonwealth Heads of Government meeting it was Rao who was the trusted second-in command as foreign minister. A diplomat points out that it was Rao's intellectual stature that gave depth to foreign policy pronouncements during this period. And it was largely due to his hard work that the dying members of the NAM movement had been stoked. Rao in those days symbolised a split political personality. At one level, he played a highly successful role as a foreign minister; at the same time he was also the person who had been ignominiously defeated from his home state by a BJP candidate. There is a viewpoint which holds that Rao's defeat in Hanamkonda and his being assimilated into national level politics, was the outcome of his inability to play the rough-and- ready game of state politics.[8]

Indira Gandhi indeed, showed the trust she reposed in Rao by shifting him to the home ministery at a critical time, on July 19, 1984 less than a fortnight after Operation Bluestar. He was the home minister when she was assassinated, but so well known was his loyalty to her that apparently no Congressman even thought of charging him with negligence. After the success of Telgu Desam in Andhra Pradesh Rao probably knew he would have trouble retaining his Hanamkonda seat, so in 1984 he contested from Ramtek in Maharashtra as well. There was quite a bit of criticism about his "deserting" his home state, but his penchant for playing safe was reward when he made it to the Lok Sabha despite losing in Hanamkonda.[9]

Rajiv Gandhi made Rao his defence minister to start with but shifted him to the new umbrella minister of human resources development in September 1985. There was some talk about Rao having slipped from grace as he was no longer in one of the "big four" ministries, but that was quickly scotched when Rajiv gave him additional charge of health and family welfare in July 1986. In June 1988, he was made the foreign minister for a second term a post he held till the defeat of the Rajiv government. In 1989, unwilling to risk defeat in his home state, (which, incidentally, the Congress swept), Rao contested again from Ramtek. He was apparently helped along in his bid to retain the seat by Sharad Pawar, althought he has never been branded as anybody's man. His rise in the Congress hierarchy during the months the party was out of power has been ascribed by several Congressmen due to seniority rather than any other merit. But slowly, this plodder reached a position where he was the automatic choice for every senior party appointment including meembership of the Congress Working Committee. There is speculation that Congress president Rajiv Gandhi may have had some organisational post in mind for Rao after the coming elections, especially as Rao chose not to contest the bolls this time. Now that he has had great trust upon him, many Congressmen feel that after the elections the fact that he is not an MP will be used by his detractors to insist on the "one-man-one-post" principle.[10]

He shifted to Delhi as the AICC general secretary in 1975 and continued in that position till 1976. During this phase he played an important role in drafting the political economic and forgin policy resolutions for the AICC session at Kamagatur Nagar in Chandigarh. Rao believed that unless the Congress respected and honoured the hopes and aspirations of the masses would turn to extremism. In the 1977 general elections he was one of the few Congress stalwarts to with stand the Janata wave and enter the Lok Sabha from the Hanmakonda Lok Sabha constituency. In 1980 he became the Minister of External Affairs in Indira Gandhi's cabinet and later held the portfolios of Home, Defence, Human Resources Development in the governments of Indira Gandhi and Rajiv Gandhi.

Jaipal Reddy remembers those day well, since he was a close friend of PV's eldest son Rauga Rao, who is now a Congress MLA in Andhra Pradesh. As an Osmania University student Reddy often used to go to Rao's house. "I know he was quite free of corruption then, because I have seen the family suffer the pangs of genteel middle-class poverty As far as I know, he has been relatively clean throughout his career. Family planning enthusiasts who criticise Bihar chief minister Laloo Prasad Yadav for having nine children may also castigate Rao, since he has three sons and Five daughters. None except Ranga Rao' personal assistant in New Delhi makes it a point to say that he does not have any relative staying with him in the Capital. Two daughters are abroad. Reddy recalls Rao's wife satyamma as a "typical South Indian Brahmin house wife." she passed away in 1969.[11]

The Bungalow Number 9 in the Motilal Nehru Marg, New Delhi, which looked like any house in the row, suddenly came alive June 20, 1991 after it was decided that Narasimha Rao has been elected party leader. And thus, the decks were cleared for him to be sworn in Prime Minister of India on June 21. Rao is the first leader from the South head the government at the Centre. Anand Sharma, a known campaigners for Sharad Pawar, when asked to comment on the new development, said that the Congress was taking a unanimous decision on the issue of leadership. He hastened to add that there was no question of consensus. It was rather unanimity. He said that Pawar was never in the race immediately after that meeting, Rao went for the siesta as usual. A senior SGP officer come earlier to give instructions to their staff on security arrangements. 'Shamiana' (tent) was being erected in the lwans for the expected stream of visitors. The chairs were being unloaded form a van. The entry to the house was not restricted. The personal staff of Rao, some of whom are with him for years, were beaming with delight. When asked about the family of Rao, one of his staff members said that Rao, a widower, was living alone here while all of his three sons' were settled in Hyderabad. The eldest one Dr. P.V. Rango Rao, who is holding the Bachelor Degree in Journalism and doctorate besides other degrees is a member of the Andhra Pradesh assembly. The second one is a successful businessman. He is the managing director of the Sinclairs Television Pvt. Ltd, in his state, Andhra Pradesh. The youngest is an advocate.[12]

Rao is also the father of five daughters. The eldest daughter had three sons, the second one is the mother of two sons while the third one has three daughters. The fourth one is married to K.R. Nandan, an IPS officer who is the Additional Director, anti- corruption in Andhra Pradesh. She is the mother of twins, both daughters. The youngest has one son and one daughter. The ledest son of Rao who is an MLA is bachelor, the second one has three offsprings including two daughters while the youngest has one son. All the sons have reached New Delhi. A son-in-law who is in business with the businessman son of Rao is also in the Capital. He said that the other family members barring the families of two daughters who are settled in the United States of America, were expected to join Rao by June 21, 1991.

In the meantime, Chiranji Lala Sharma who has retained the Karnal Lok Sabha seat for the Congress for the fourth consecutive term came to meet Rao. He was followed by the Haryana contingent. They were asked to wait in a cozy room inside the main building. Within minutes, came the Punjab contingent, led by Beant Singh said that the Congress sticked to its decision to boycott the elections in Punjab and would like that the elections were deferred for the time being.

More Punjab Congressmen came. They were led by the hefty Vishwajeet Singh who hails form Punjab but represents Maharashtra in the Rajya Sabha as a Congress member. At 2.50 p.m. S.S. Ray and K. Karunakaran, the Congress leaders who had been asked by the Congress Parliamentary Board to ascertain the views of the party members of Parliament came in. "Nothing new" was the cryptic remark of Ray when news-persons asked him to comment on the new development. By this time, a group of students form Jawaharlal Nehru University, all hailing from Maharashtra trooped in to congratulate Rao.

Came Ghulam Nabi Azad, an AICC general secretary and Sita Ram Kesari, AICC Treasurer. At the same time, Romesh Bhandari who was humbled by the BJP nonimee from the South Delhi constituency. M.C. Bhandare and Vasant Sathe, another known detractor of Sharad Pawar also came to meet Rao, within minutes they were joined by V.N. Gadgil, another Congress stalwart who was humbled at the hustings in the Maharashtra despite a wave in the State in favour of the Congress. Mahesh Prasad, information Secretary to the Government of India also came to meet Rao. The horticulture department also came in the picture by this time. One of its van started inloading flowers pots in the Bungalow. The exotic floweres including the seasonal 'football lily' were put in pots at the entrance of the main house. The police also started searching all the shrubs and hedges. The time was 3.30 p.m. After five minutes another staff came under the cover of cleansing the bathrooms. Even bouquets, being brought by some businessmen were being screened by the security men. One Ali siddiqui who claimed to be the founder and organising secretary of the Aalami Urdu Conference and hailing form Hyderabad came in the picture by this time. He was busy in distributing three pages long bio-data of Rao. He pretended to be close with Rao. An aged person who is distantly related to Rao and has worked with him said that Rao was a quiet person and could not be carried away by flatterers, who were not in dearth in Delhi and started coming to his residence. He said that Rao was a religious man but not orthodox.

Meantime, Dr. Balram Jakhar came in after having a verbal dual with the security staff who tried to check his entry. With him emerged Rao form his room and dorve straight to the AICC office for the crucial meeting of Congressmen.

Many others came to meet Rao, but it seems that none of the visitors could meet the Prime Minister. However, another view was that Rao was busy in giving final touches to his Council of Ministers and preferred to meet only selected visitors.[13]

Narasimha Rao's stint as a chief minister was rather remarkable in view of the tradition of Reddy dominated politics in Andhra Pradesh. Althugh despite being a Brahmin, he made a commitment to introduce job reservation for backward classes, the move ultimately back-fired as it consolidated the ire of the landlords mainly Reddys of the state's prosperous, coastal region. Some analysts say this led to his defeat in 1984 in his home state in spite of Congress wave that was sweeping the country. His detractors say that, as Chief Minister, Rao spent more time in New Delhi than in Hyderabad. But in 1974, he was formally shifted to the Capital as a general secretary to the All-India Congress Committee (AICC).[14]

As Minister and Chief Minister of Andhra Pradesh, and subsequently as a member of the Union Cabinet, he has accumulated a wealth of knowledge and experience which would serve him as an asset in guiding the party in the critical times ahead. His advice will be eminently useful not only in organisational matters but also in handling administrative problems. It is well within his capacity to convert the present challenge into an opportunity. The delicate nature of his health may not allow him to undertake much physical exertion. But then he is capable of unleashing initiative in others and building an atmosphere in which a collective may function effectively. One can be sure that the loss of charismatic leadership will be well compensated by more vigorous operations of the collective. The rapidity with which the opinion in the vast and varied party has converged upon his and the all round welcome of his choice are assureance enough that the promise of stability and secularism which Rajiv Gandhi held out will be duly honoured by his suceessors.

Narasimha Rao, who is fluent in Urdu, gas given an assurance that his party would do everthing to promote the language.

This was stated in New Delhi on June 5, 1991 by Ali Siddiqui, the organising secretary of International Urdu Conference.

The organisation had arranged an international conference on Urdu in 1989 which was a attended by 250 delegates from all over the world, including Pakistan.

Welcoming Rao's election as the AICC president, Siddiqui pointed our that Rao was a great linguist. He was a master of several languages, including Urdu, Hindi and Sanskrit.

Siddqui recalled that way back in 1956 Rao had translated the speech of the then Prime Minister, Jawaharlal Nehru, who nominated him for the Congress ticket from Karimnagar parliamentary seat.

Siddqui, who contested the current Lok Sabha elections against Janata Dal leader, V.P. Singh from Fatepur constituency on the All India Urdu Morcha ticket, said Rao's election as Congress president had dealt a big blow to the BJP.

Rao will counter the communal propoganda of BJP because he can speak with authority on Hinduism in Hindi as well as in Sanskrit,"Siddqui added.

Siddiqui said Rao had assured him in a recent meeting that the Congress was committed to the welfare of minorities and also to the promotion of various languages including Urdu.

And finally, Prime Ministership a gift eight days before his birthday. At 70, Narasihma Rao is hardly expected to project the image of young India, something Rajiv Gandhi was able to do with his youthful image and zest for life. That vivid image of Rajiv Gandhi had over 40 Heads of State and dignitaries flocking at his funeral. But while the era is thing of the past, there is little reason to be depressed for Rao portrays courage, statemanship and experience just at the moment when the nation requires wise men to take over the reins. Rajiv Gandhi's assassination occurred at a time when the country was literally drifting economically and caught in the fierce Mandal-Mandir cross fire. The Congress, which was shattered by the dealth, was looking towards western Indira for leadership. Fifty-one-year old Sharad Pawar was expected to succeed Rajiv Gandhi and was probably the best equipped to do so.[15] But sometimes the best of friends some of whom displayed the most despicable traits of petty cunning, dirty tricks and resource management may be worse than foes.

Pawar's Delhi mission has failed but he has a long tenure ahead and will be best advised to wait it out for the "slog overs".

Just about the time when the Congress (I) looked like the national version of local Haryana Party, the senior men stepped in the seasoned Karunakaran from Kerala, the dignified and cool Arjun Singh from Madhya Pradesh, the elders like Vasant Sathe and N.K.P. Salve.

Consensus became an issue not because any of them had anything against Pawar, but only that dignity should be mainteined al all costs. That was achieved with Pawar's stunning announcement early in the morning. Sobriety has made a good beginning and the choice of Rao only enhances the impression that peace reigns finally.

The former External Affairs Minister and senior Congressman is not without minus points. He is old, he has always lived under the shadow of the Nehru-Indira Gandhi family. Absolute loyalty even at the cost of appearing ludicrous has been his forte. But the old man is not senile and even only two years ago, in his last assignment as country's External Affairs Minister, Rao is reported to have excelled himself. South Block endearingly referred to him as Mr Morose, probably a reaction to the seemingly bored expression on his face most of the time. Officials say that he was brilliant when attending to files and had the capacity to take decision. But, unfortunately, he would skip taking delegations abroad where major policy announcements would have to be made. "If he was required in washington he would probably end up in Nauru", said an official. Inspite of it, officials treated him with respect and still do. The era of towering personalities may be over but there is certainly place for men of stature.[16]

Rao often acknowledge how being a Brahmin has proved disadvantageous to him in the past, and how it would not help him in the future also. He gave poor health as the excuse for not contsting the 10th Lok Sabha elections but plaguing his innermost thoughts also would have been the difficulty of overcoming the disadvantage of his being a Brahmain and finding as suitable constituency. I once asked him why he was not projecting himself more forcefully in the Congress politics and the national scene and why he was continuing adopt a low profile when there was such an enormous good will for him in the country and party, thanks to his non-controversial personality. "You are asking me to change my style at this late age? How is that possible? I am content to serve my country and party in my own humble way!",he replied. As a minister, Rao fitted into any slot that was allotted to him. It is typical of the man that he tried to do his best and now sulk or skirk regardless of the protfolio.[17]

Narasimha Rao is a shy and reserved type of statesman but he is endowed with a fine sense of humour hardly found in a person. He also shuns publicity and avoids being photographed.

A tea to taller and a man of disciplined habits Narasimha Rao is an excellent tennis and badminton player. A computer addict he can speak with ease on literature and religious reflecting a fine blend of tradition and modernity a combination that India needs today.

Narasimha Rao, a twinkling star on the horizon of the East, has brought a message of hope, peace and prosperitty to the mankind.

NOTES :

1. Sridharan Viswam. A Philosopher Prime Minister. *Patriot.* 21 June 1991.
2. *Ibid.*
3. Kumkum Chadha. A visit to Vangara. *The Hindustan Times,* 9 June 1991.
4. *Ibid.*
5. *Ibid.*
6. Joydeep Gupta. P.V. Narasimha Rao. *The Sunday Observer,* 2 June 1991.
7. *Ibid.*
8. *Ibid.*
9. *Ibid.*
10. *Ibid.*
11. *Ibid.*
12. *The Hindustan Times, 21 June 1991.*
13. *Ibid.*
14. Jaydeep Gupta. *Op. Cit.*
15. *The Statesman,* 21 June 1991.
16. *Ibid.*
17. Sridharan Viswam. A Philosopher Prime Minister. *Patriot,* 21 June 1991.

THREE

THE SCHOLAR

A scholar by inclination there is little of an everyday, ordinary politician in the new Prime Minister P.V. Narsimha Rao characteristics which one associates with a politician these days: party intrigue, factional manipulation, electoral manoeuvre. He has all along in his long 50 years career as an active politician been far removed from, even above and beyond such manoeuvres. And yet he is not lacking in those political talents and skills which a leader in his role requires to possess. Though unlike Jawaharlal Nehru and Dr. Radhakrishnan, he often shows a remarkable resemblence to the two, especially in his intense passion for new ideas like Nehru and in his dedication to scholarly pursuits like the second President.

These are the qualities which earned him the respect not only of his partymen at large but also of many at home and abroad.

History was made on June 20, 1991 in the Central Hall of Parliament where for the first time a leader from south of the Vindhiyas who was chosen unanimously as the leader of the Congress Parliamentary Party to take over as India's ninth Prime Minister. That honour goes to 70-year old P.V. Narsimha Rao, a scholar and poet from Andhra Pradesh where he was Chief Minister years ago.

Rao's brief acceptance speech in which he showed his felicity in both English and Hindi won the hearts of his partymen, Mani Shankar Aiyer newly elected MP from Tamil Nadu, characterised the pseech as "the best in the Central Hall such the historic "Tryst with destiny" speech of Pandit Nehru in 1974.

For the first time too the CPP meeting was thrown open to the print media and the atmosphere in the high domed Central Hall was one of joy and jubilation.

Much before the meeting began at 4 pm newly elected members of the Lok Sabha and congratulated each other. There was much camaderie, banter and back-slapping as party colleagues from four corner of the country met after a gruelling election campaign and tension filled and staggered polling.

Not forgotten was the tragedy that had overtaken the party by the assassination of its leader, Rajiv Gandhi. Many mentioned it had said how they wished Rajiv had been alive to share and savour the suceess of the party.

A smiling colour portrait of the slain leader looked down the podium where Rao and other leaders were seated. Those who spoke said though Rajiv Gandhi was not alive they could feel his spirit pervading the meeting.

Arjun Singh, the party veteran from Madhya Pradesh proposed the name of Rao for the leadership of the CPP. Many, among whom were Shiv Shankar and N.K.P. Salve, seconded the proposal.

Each one who spoke referred to Rao as the best choice as he had enjoyed the confidence of both Indira Gandhi and Rajiv Gandhi.

Coice of Narasimha Rao to succeed late Rajiv Gandhi was no surprise. It did, of course, dampen the hopes of a whole hose of anti-Congress scribes and politicians who have come to believe that Congress baiting is the high water mark of intellectualism or political wisdom. For a week after the most tragic event of May 21, 1991 they poured on the party all manner of abuse and sarcasm. For them it was no period of national mourning. Their sense of decency and decorum did not preclude malicious raillery and snide flings even at the grief stricked lady at Janpath, New Delhi. At the end of it all Sonia Gandhi has emerged with dignity unimpaired and the Congress Party has demonstrated that it continues to possess, the wisdom and grace which had distinguished it form the flotsam and jetsam of Indian politics. If some people considered it totally dependent upon one personality or one family they had not understood the character of the party. In its century-long history it has survived the giant sized leaders like Lokmanya Tilak Mahatma Gandhi and Pandit Jawaharlal Nehru. It has also maintained its poise and stability when it has received unkind treatment from such stalwarts as Mohammad Ali Jinnah, Maulana Mohammad Ali, Subhash Chander Bose, Acharya Narendra Dev, Acharya Kriplani and Jayaprakash Narayan. Acknowledgement of this inherent inner strength of the party does not mean any partisan partiality. How many parties in the world have displayed the same capicity? The strongly knit Nazi Party did not survive Hitler and the Fascist Party of Italy went into oblivion after the departure of authoritative leadership. Nearer home can be recalled that fate of the Socialist Party, the Hindu Maha Sabha, the Swatantra Party, the Janata Party. All of them aspired to replace the Congress in the affections of people but have failed to find more than a mention among the footnotes to India's history. What of the current contenders, the Janata Dal and the Bharatiya Janata Party? The former has been no more than an ahdnoc contraption put together around V.P. Singh. It did not stay in one piece even for a year. And that too when dissensions meants loos of power. The magical skill in "managing contradictions", claimed by V.P. Singh, was nowhere in operation. The latter has been comparatively more stable. But that is because it is a lifeless marionette manipulated by an outside force, the Rashtriya Swayamsewak Sangh. It is well-known that the puppet master, in this case, does not allow the puppet to develop and grow to a point where it may have a will of its own. Its value lies only in providing democratic cover for the fascist style infiltration of the state machinery for internal sabotage and eventual coup. By installing Narasimha Rao in the helmsman's seat the Congress has proved that it has the human resource and the necessary wisdom to find the right man for the right moment. He has the siniority and experience to command respect throughout the organisation. His scholarship and quiet dignity is acknowledged even beyond the confines of the party, from the lowest to the highest, he is in a position to understand the problems of party building. And he is much more than a manipulated of the party machine, steeped as he is in the ideological lore of the Congress he will ensure the continuity of thought and approach hitherto associated with it.[1]

Even though Rao is for the time being only provisional president there is hardly any doubt that the choice of the Working Committee will be rectified by the AICC. There however, may be a demand that in the event of the party winning a majority he be drafted to head the Government but the reasons which kept him away from the electoral fray might prevail again. He has been telling friends that he has had enough of administration and would like to devote himself to party organisation. He is also a votary of encouraging the younger generation to take responsibilities. His knowledge of a large number of Indian languages will be of immense help in establishing personal communication through a charismatic personality has been cruelly snapped. At a time when the largest party was coming to terms with the grievous loss it had suffered some people chose to take political advantage of the traumatic situation. India's pride in this hoary cultural values and its inherently democratic temper received a jolt when an impression was sought to be created that there was no sympathy wave for the departed leader. The unwarranted assertions reflected neither the state of the nation (which did look upon the elimination of Rajiv Gandhi as a tragedy of tremendous magnitude) not the helpless of the Congress party. If anything it was a demonstration of the brankruptcy of politics slolely on the character assassination of Rajiv Gandhi. Accusations of dynasticism and authoritarianism had been indentified with Indira Gandhi and Rajiv Gandhi. Whoever differed from them was uncritically clothed in angelic robes. Devi Lal with his brood, V.P. Singh and Bansi Lal of Emergency fame, caste leaders like Ram Lakhan Yadav, demagogues and mafia leaders like NTR and Karunanidhi were all projected as costodians of the democratic conscience of the people. The election process even before the assassination of Rajiv Gandhi had disrobed them all but the tragic event in Tamil Nadu had brought out the sinister nature of the anti-Rajiv campaign with deeply moving poignancy. Fearing that the emotional backlash would sweep a side all the caly giants their drummer boys set about building dykes against it. The immediate response was to shift ciriticism from the person of Rajiv Gandhi to his party. It was sought to be shown as a bonless wonder, "leaderless", and "rudderless", trying like an orphaned child to find comfort in him of a mother firgure. Rather than appreciating the courteours grace and gratitude shown to the widow of the departed leader by offering her party presidentship they preferred to interpret the Congress Working Committee decision as bankruptcy of the party. Knowing full well that it was a unilateral gesture (in line of course with the best of the cultural ethos of India) without ascertaining the wish of Sonia Gandhi they lost on time in hurling indignities on her and the family. No way of condoling with a bereaved family though people like V.P. Singh did formally send condolence message.

The second part of the strategy was bold assertion that there is no sympathy wave in favour of Congress. The circumstances and the atmosphere in which the brutal murder took place inevitably led to the conclusion that Rajiv Gandhi was done to death not because there was personnel animus against him but because the politics which he represented was an anathema to powerful forces in the world. Indian people of the cloak and dagger activities of international agancies to miss the real significance of this dark deed.[2]

On a bright exhilarating day in Islamabad way back in 1981, one found P.V. Narasimha Rao engrossed in Urdu literature in a famed book shop. As the first Indian External Affairs Minister to visit Pakistan after the 1972 Simla Agreement, Rao had plenty of banqueting, diplomatic discourse and hard negotiations to attend to. But he still managed to break of from the tight official schedule to have a dip into the world of books. That was typical of the man; linguist, scholar, politician of the Gandhi-Nehfu mould, administrator of no mean calibre, above all a man of compassion who shunned rigidities. The man who after years of devotion and dedication to a cause has now taken his place in history as India's ninth Prime Minister. Narasimha Rao does not flaunt his attainments and has consequently been grossly underestimated. He has indeed been recognised as well read and well versed as a linguist. But in a political crowd in which the unlettered seem to predominate, these qualities do not take one far. If he could still climb the political leader to the top, it is because he is, in cricket terminology that PV occassionally deploys an "all-rounder." In 1982, as an accompaniment in the Pakistan trip with Foreign Minister Narasimha Rao, this writer noticed the break through he was able to register with earnestness and his people-to-people approach. It was a two-tier policy that Narasimha Rao adovacated in relation to Pakistan, one their being linkage between the Indian and Pakistan people, the other being State-level interaction. Narasimha Rao recognised the dualism in Indo-Pakistan ties. He set the pace himself if Islambad, for coming close to the people and this elicited instant warm response from Pakistan's intelligentsia and press stultified by the Zia regime's brutish stance to the printed word. It was the visionary and humanistic Narasimha Rao approach to Indo Pakistan relations that has in the last decade and a half brought about a gushing outflow of Indo-Pakistani cultural intercourse in music, poetry, and to an extent literature. One wishes this line of thought had been followed in greater depth from the point where Narasimha Rao left it. Watching in action Narasimha Rao's talent as a linguist during his two stints as Foreign Minister, one could well exclaim this is the stuff a foreign minister should be made of. With his grasp to eight language-French, Spanish, German, English, Persian, Urdu, Tamil and Hindi (not to speak of his mother tognue Telugue) PV could move among ministers of varied linguistic groups in international gatherings and could bring quick results, far beyond saving in terms of interpreters in better exchange of ideas.[3]

Because Narasimha Rao's first love has all along been no the literary side, he has evolved into a good writer, at home in many of the languages he knows. He was an ear for languages. His knoweldge of Urdu, Marathi and Hindi is as good as his own mother tongue, Telugu, and this enabled him to campaign in Ramtek constituency in Maharashtra as if he was a Maharashtrian and not an outsider. I have heard him speak in Parliament with equal efficiency and ease in all these languages. I accompained him on his visit to Pakistan when he was foreign minister years ago, and watched him talk to the Pakistanis in such chaste Urdu that they would all be surprised that a South Indian could speak the language without any accent. The honour of becoming the president of the Indian National Congress came to him without his seeking. Indira Gandhi and suggested his name for the Rashtrapati Bhawan, but she droppted the idea when leaders from Andhra Pradesh itself repressed reservations on the ground that three previous presidents, Radhakrishnan, Varahagiri Venkatagiri and Neelam Sanjiva Reddy belonged to the Telugu stock. It is true being a Prime Minister Rao will be thrown more and more into the intricacies and complexities of leading the country. But since he has a philosophical approach to life, he can be expected to say clear of controversies and give of his best to the nation.[4]

Although the new Prime Minister P.V. Narasimha Rao, cannot be said to have maintained a "personal rapport" which his predecessors, with the possible expredcessors, with the possible exception of V.P. Singh, had with the Nepalese leaders, old as well as new, his elevation to power has not failed to evoke considerable interest among a cross-section of the Nepalese intelligentsia.[5]

The former Prime Minister of Nepal, Kirtinidhi Bista, describes Rao as a "nice man, a man of understanding", under whose stewardship the relations between Nepal and India are likely to improve and the principle of "mutual benefit and cooperation" is expected to thirve to the satisfaction of both the countries.

Bista, who first met Rao when the latter was the chief minister of Andhra Pradesh, said: "He is a gentleman, with a receptive mind. Let us hope greater understanding will be displayed and genuine efforts made to help Nepal.

Asked to comment on Rao's assumption of office in India, the former Nepalese forign minister Mr Shailendra Kumar Upadhyaya recalling his numerous interactions with the "man of great wisdom" said, "I think he was quite responsive to Nepla's legitimate interests. I always found him very friendly and understanding. I am sure under his leadership, India will be able to solve its internal problems, and at the same time promote good will and understanding with its neighbours. I also hope that Indira, under Mr Rao, will play its effective role in strengthening the SAARC, making it a vilable political and economic framework for regional cooperation."

Analysts here recall Rao's "highly laudable" intiative concerning the formation of "Indo-Nepal joint commission as an umbrella to cover all aspects of bilateral matters between the two traditional neighbours. The commission however, did not make much headway owing to the 15 month long stalemate over trade and transit in the summer of 1989. A foreign office veteran opines that Rao's "aloofness and capacity to look at things in a detached manner" might produce positive trends in Indo-Nepal relations.

Another commentator, however, find Rao's aforesaid traits not so encouraging. According to him, he is likely to be influenced by the South Block bureacrats as far as external interactions are concerned.

The "coterie", he adds, will also begin to tilt the balance its way, not necessarity to the benefit of India as it stands today, not to the good of the neighbouring nationas who expect India to conduct differently in the changed regional and global context.

"P.V. Narsimha Rao is an astute politician, not a Machiavellian type" said Prof Lok Raj Baral. Rao he opines inherits the scholarly tradition of Nehru and Radhakrishnan. Mr Baral believes his (Rao's) intellect, experience and balanced views would be of great significance to Nepal. "He is not emotinally charged. Better still, he understands the realities of this regional". Even though Rao may lack the "personal sapport" with the new Nepalese leadership, his sustained role in India's foreign policy area will stand him in good stead when it comes to analysing and tackling the compelxities of Indo-Nepal relations, said Prof Baral, adding that Rao's understanding of the 1990 pro-democracy movement particularly its background is by no means, lesser than that of his predcessor the late Rajiv Gandhi.

Narasimha Rao may not have a Charismatic personality, but he has a very apt understanding of India's problems. He brings with him the grassroots experience in politics, having once been chief minister of Andhra Pradesh in the early seventies. He has never looked back since then, having adorned some of the key positions at the Centre. In this context, he represents a total continuity in some of the sensitive areas of national and international strategies. He had taken certain initiatives in the past which should provide positive signals for further strengthening of India's position in the comity of nation. In the eighties, it was the result of his efforts that the Indo-Pak joint Commission was set in motion. As External Affairs Minister, his record has been fairly good.

In fact, looking at the prevailing complexities of the economic situation proper appreciation of its global dimensions is a crucial factor in taking the country but of the mess. India has suffered in recent years because of the lack of right perspective of the changing economic realities all over the world. One can bank upon and his highly experienced cabinet team to apply correctives in India's economic framework in tune with global opportunities and realties. We simply cannot afford to work in isolation and fiddle with invisible options in the hope of putting the economy back on the rails. In today's trying conditions, India needs a large hearted leadership with a vision. One tragedy of the Indian polity has been that we have a large number of well-meaning but mediocre politicians specialising in short-term tactics and strategies instead of statesmen with the ability to see national and international problems in a broader perspective beyond immediate pulls and counterpulls.[6]

NOTES :

1. *National Herald,* 4 June 1991.
2. *Ibid.*
3. O.P. Sabharwal. Dialogue, Cousensus PV's Forte. *Patriot,* 22 June 1991.
4. Sridharan Viswan. A Philosopher Prime Minister. *Patriot* 21 June 1991.
5. *The Times of India,* 22 June 1991.
6. Hari Jaisingh. Man of the Moment. *The Business and Political Observer,* 22 June 1991.

FOUR

THE STATESMAN

Statesmanship is something which has to be painstakingly cultivated and acquired, provided one does not allow himself to be guided and misguided by a band of sycophants and time-servers. Politics has to be a matter of conviction. It has also to be related to the reality. It has, of course, to be mass based, but what really matters is the ability of the leadership to properly channelise their enthusiasm and resources in a positive direction for building an egalitarian society. Unfortunately, Indian politicians tend to surround themselves with a set of sycophants and so-called loyalists who build a human wall around them, isolating the leadership from the ground relities. We even fail to learn from Raja Vikramaditya who had Navratna (nine laureates) around him but only one court jester. Indian politics cannot see qualitative improvement, if it allowed to thrive on the pranks of court jesters. It has become absolutely necessary to keep some of the harsh facts in view since the country no longer enjoys the advantage of having charismatic leaders in our midst. Most of them represent sectarian intersts, with the result the country's problems get complicated. Though charismatic personalities do matter in changing the course of history, we need to appreciate that in our obsession with personalities we have run away from the tasks which spark the activity at the grassroots. In fact, the weberian phrase, charisma, has come to be abused. A number of leaders, both at the Centre and in the states, have benefited by it at the hustings. The process by which charisma is gauged and the effects of its electoral success have not always been helpful from the viewpoint of the development of democratic traditions or democratic institutions. If the charisma card is overplayed, it would erode democratic traditions and undermine the functioning of democratic institutions. To say this is not to underestimate the role played by some of the outstanding charismatic personalities since Independence.[1]

Fortunately for us, leaders like Jawaharlal Nehru, Indira Gandhi, MGR and Rajiv Gandhi had liberal outlook and solid grounding in democratic traditions. But, what needs to be properly understood and appreciated is that no charismatic characters are going to be able to master the sort of multi-dimensional problems the country is faced with. So, more than charismatic personalities, we need Lal Bahadur Shastris-leaders with common sense and rooted to the soil. Herein lies the opportunity for Rao and his experienced members of the council of ministers. Looking at the ground realities, there is no escape from collective leadership and consensus politics. As Prime Minister, Narasimha Rao has of course to set the pace for it. He has all the ingredients as a scholarly politician who is known for his sobriety, administrative and policy implementing experience and intellectual skills. His multilingual fluency including Telugu, English, Hidni, Urdu, Marathi and Spanish are well-known. So is his love for books. Though he will be subject to a lot of pressure from within the Congress and also without, his finesse will lie in keeping out of unsavoury controversies. This will mean tightrope walking in sensitive areas.[2]

After all the vicissitudes of a protracted general election has come a Prime Minister who is to run a Government that will rule through the most difficult phase of the nation's history since independence. When freedom come 44 years ago, the country had to bear the agony and the devastation of the partition blood bath and soon after, the shock of Gandhiji's assassination. The mosaic of princely states, large and small, were get to be integrated into the Indian Union bereft of resources but endowed with an indomitable will forged in the freedom struggle the nation not only survived but dared to go forward with an irrepressible determination. Today, four decades later, the nation is confronted with formidable problems which no other government had to tackle, all at the same time. And the question troubles everyone shall we generate the national will that can not only withstand all the torments that await in the coming days, but shall be able to take the country forward to better days beyond? For, it is not a question whether our people can bear all the burden that lies in store for them, but whether their will to over-power difficulties has remained in fact. The political uncertainties that have crept up in the last five years have sapped the vitality of the nation and a sense of helplessness prevails all over. The conventional parliamentary politics of the last two years provides a grotesque confirmation of this sorry state of things. In 1989 the Congress which had been rewarded with a record-breaking majority in the Lok Sabha, 415 out of 542, in 1984 was reduced to a minority, with only 197 out of 543 in 1989-an index of the declining public confidence in it. And so a new arrangement came up with the Congress out of power: the National Front led by the Janata Dal, with minority support in the Lok Sabha could get the support of the BJP on the one hand, and the left on the other, ensured for itself the necessary majority to run the Government with V.P. Singh as Prime Minister. Obviously this could not be a durable proposition, when in less than a year the BJP quit the coalition and forced V.P. Singh to resign.

Followed a more bizare arrangement: a breakaway janata Dal rump led by Chandra Shekhar formed the Government with the official support of the Congress-the classic example of the tail wagging the dog. When after a few weeks, Rajiv Gandhi withdrew support from Chandra

Shekhar's Government, the general elections were ordered and during the interim period the Chandra Shekhar Ministry continued, cynically breaking all norms expected to be followed by a caretaker outfit.[3]

It was in this sombre background of gathering despondency, the elections were held this time. The sullen mood of the electorate at the beginning was reflective of the all-pervading slump in the nation's morale; that was why political analysts stated at the outset that political parties were not sure of the mood of the voter. In a sense, the general election this time began as an inscrutable exercise for all condidates, and whatever the opinion poll makers predicted at the time was in most cases part of the partisan campaign in favour of different political parties-just as reputed newspapers turned virtually into organs of different parties, the first time this having happened so conspicuously in any general election in this country. Then came the shock of Rajiv's gruesome assassination. Along with the grief at the barbaric killing, there was widespread concern that the rampant violence that persisted in Kashmir, Punjab and in communal killings in different parts of the country, more than anytime since the partition days, could go so deep that it could brutally slay the leader of the largest political party in the country. It was this sudden realisaion born out of the shock of Rajiv Gandhi's murder that woke up large sections of our people. Apathy gave way to anxiety at the future of politics in this country, the voter be stirred himself and the congress party became activated at having lost its leader under fearsome circumstances. This was clearly perceptiable when the poll results finally came out. By all accounts, the Congress gained nearly 50 seats more as a result of this shock. It was thus more than what has come to be known as the "sympathy wave". It was also a measure of concern all round about the future of our politics.[4]

Within a day of the swearing in the P.V. Narasimha Rao Government is facing a serious problem. Unhappy over the Ministry formation, many newly elected Congress Lok Sabha member are refusing to take oath as Member of Parliament when the House meets soon. The number of such party members of Parliament said to be about 20 and they are mostly from Madhya Pradesh, Maharashtra, Rajasthan and Tamil Nadu. They are angry because they feel that "Rajiv Gandhi loyalists" have been ignored. In fact, some of them are said to have given an ultimatum to the Prime Minister to redress their grievance by giving berths in the Council of Ministers to those who have been winning the election for a number of terms and have remained faithful to the party as well as to the late Indira Gandhi and Rajiv Gandhi. This development in the party is also said to be responsible for the undue delay in the announcement of the portfolios. Instead of accommodating the loyal party soldiers." One party M.P. from Madhya Pradesh said, "the Prime Minister has made Ministers who have either been defector of have always been suspected in the past by the party high command as far as their loyalty is concerned." No doubt," he said, "many in the new Council of Ministers are those who were in the Rajiv Gandhi Cabinet too and we have nothing against them. But the faces of many new Ministers includes those whom the late Congress President had always suspected as their loyalty was always a question mark. But such people are suddenly back on centrestage behaving as if they are the party's bosses and interestingly a few of them have already started looking at themselves as the future party president and Prime Minister". There is strong resentment among many party M.Ps from Madhya Pradesh over the inclusion of Kamal Nath, who won from Chhindwara constituency, in the Council of Minister. He and another new Minister, Dalbir Singh, belong to the Arjun Singh camp. Then V.C. Shukla, who has been living the life of a defector for some years, has also been included in the Cabinet", said a party M.P. from Madhya Pradesh, adding that it was no justice if men belonging to only one camp were being made Ministers not only from Madhya Pradesh but from other States too. Similar complaints have been heard from party MPs belonging to Maharashtra and Rajasthan and some other parts of the country. The formation of the Narasimha Rao Ministry has caused resentment among the supporters of Maharashtra Chief Minister Sharad Pawar. They are unhappy over their exclusion. Senior party leader P.Shiv Shankar who like Narasimha Rao belongs to Andhra Pradesh has been ignored in the very first formation of the Cabinet. Shiv Shankar is the leader of the party in the Rajya Sabha. At the same time a section of the Congressmen are unhappy that some former senior Ministers have not been promoted this time. For instance, P. Chidambram, who was a Minister of State for Home Affairs in the Rajiv Gandhi Government and was also a member of the Political Affairs Committee then, deserved a promotion but has been appointed Minister of State again, although with independent charge, while Ghulam Nabi Azad, who was also earlier a Minister of state, has been elevated to Cabinet rank. The party people are saying that Chidambram has thus been equated with a newcomer like Kamal Nath and Ministers such as Mr. K. Ramamurthy. They hope that such injustices" would be corrected by the Prime Minister. The party MPs from Tamil Nadu are upset as no one from their State has been made a Cabinet Minister. Another Minister who feels down graded is Giridhar Gomango, who has been sworn in as the Minister of State. He is understood to have written to the Prime Minister that earlier he held the post of Minister of state for Communications with independent charge. But now instead of being promoted, he has been "demoted" to the status of the Minister of State only and the post was not befitting his standing in the party and the Lok Sabha. He was the president of the Orissa Pradesh Congress Committee and had won every Lok Sabha election. Besides this, fear was gripping some of the senior Ministers who took oath the other day and were waiting eagerly to know their protfolios. Some of them were apprehensive that if they are given unimportant portfolios, it will lower their image. It is said that the "coterie wants" Narasimha Rao to give insignificant portolios to those who can either be a threat to them or those who had put themselves in the race for either the Congress presidentship or the prime ministership. Meanwhile, party spokesman Pranab Mukharjee said there could not be any balnket rule to provide representation to a state in the Union Cabinet in proportion to the party members it sent to the Lok Sabha. Talking to correspondents, he said this was not possible as the Prime Minister had to consider many factors while forming his Cabinet including availability of persons and regional representations. Pointing out that it was the exclusive prerogative of the Prime Minister as far as the inclusion or exclusion in his Ministry was concerned, Mukherjee said that "it is the Prime Minister's Cabinet. It is his pack of cards which he can shuffle as he likes."

The party spokesman's statement came in the wake of reported unhappiness of the Maharashtra Chief Minister over the inadequate representation to the State, which has sent the largest number of the party MPs to the Lok Sabha, in the Union Cabinet. The State MPs have also expressed their feeling of being "let down".

Regarding the allotment of portfolios Mukherjee said the exercise might be delayed as it was for the first time in recent years that as many as 55 persons were sworn in as Ministers. Asked whether the announcement about the allocation was not being made as there was some hitch about the portfolio to be given to Mr. Pawar, Mr. Mukherjee said he did not think so. "Neither Pawar nor the Prime Minister had taken me into confidence (on the issue)," he remarked in a lighter vein. In his opinion the composition of the Union Council of Ministers was a "good one" as, among other things, it had a blend of young and matured persons.

Asked when the All-India Congress Committee would be sending observers to Maharashtra, he replied: "Let the post of the leader there be vacant first".

From Foreign Affairs, Narasimha Rao moved on to Home Affairs and later to defence and Human Resource Development the portfolio which under Rajiv Gandhi was a multi-purpose enlargement of the Edcation Ministry. In all these vital spheres of national life Narasimha

Rao produced ideas which helped take the country forward he was not just led by the bureaucracy. He deployed their considerable talent in the job at hand. The notable point is that Narasimha Rao has all these years been assigned the toughest jobs and it is in dealing with these sensitive tasks that he has left an imprint. From External Affairs-the portfolio that Rao held from 1980 to 1983-Indira Gandhi shifted him to Home at a crucial time. That was soon after Operation Bluestar when Punjab was torn between terrorist violence and thoughtless doings of the State machine. Narasimha Rao sought to apply the healing touch and did unleash measures which if pursued to their logic would have changed the course of events in Punjab by now. But his stint in Home was far too brief: Indira Gandhi's assassination cut short his term here, Rao's talent showed up in a bigger way in the Human Resource Development Ministry soon after. It is hardly known that Narasimha Rao has a passion for computers and mathematics. His university career that took him to law, despite his fascination for maths, left him regretful, but he still remained a computer buff. As HRD Minister, he personally keyed into his PC the entire new education policy elaborated during his own attachment to computers greatly appreciated. That Narasimha Rao took lessons in flying and attained a pilot's capability despite his age was another link between the two. With his studious mind, Rao may not have found his way into politics but for the fact that the freedom movement literally pushed him in this direction. In the Congress, he climbed up the ladder from the very grass roots, working at all levels of the Congress organisaiton. From 1957 to 1977, he was elected to the Andhra Pradesh Assembly. His tenure as Andhra Chief Minister (1971 to 1973) was a sort of grounding for him to develop his leadership talent as central minister subsequently. And it was Indira Gandhi who launched him into national politics, first as AICC-General secretary and thereafter as Union Minister. Narasimha Rao's brief period of stewardship of the congress after the assassination of Rajiv Gandhi reveals that he has great ability to respond to the biggest challenges that some his way. His leadership of the Congress election campaign during the weeks after May 22, 1991 is a reflection. At the same time these weeks also show that PV can discard his humanism and soft approach when dealing with die- hards and chronic situations.[5]

While being ushered in as Prime Minister of India there are some apprehensions being expressed that the low profile Narasimha Rao may be found wanting where tought political problems are involved, that his humanism may prove to be a handicap in critical situation. The fact of the matter is that it is the low profile Narasimha Rao who is the man needed to captain India's destinies at the moment. It is his ability for dialogue and consensus-making which is the need of hour dialogue within the Congress and outside-with parties whose support the Congress needs? That is what Narasimha Rao promised in his speech in the Central Hall of Parliament while assuming leadership fo the CPP-and his strength lies in that. If one considers Rao to be incapable of the bravodo and duplicity displayed by ministers during the last six months, so be it. The country can well do without these qualities.

The new Union Council of Ministers sworn-in on June 21, 1991 for the first time has a Prime Minister who does not belong to either House of Parliament. Dr. Manmohan Singh, eminent economist, is another Cabinet Minister who will have to get elected to either House within six months. When Sharad Pawar joined the team, he became the third one. He denied that the Baramati Lok Sabha constituency, which he had won in 1984 and which has been won with a large margin by his nephew this time, would be "vacated" for him. Pawar said he would prefer to get elected to the Lower House rather than seek a berth in the Rajya Sabha.

The new team has 12 Rajya Sabha member, five of them of Cabinet rank. The Rajya Sabha stalwarts sworn-in on June 21 are Shankaro Chavan, M.L. Fotedar, Sitaram Kesari, Gulam Nabi Azad and Madhasinh Solank. The ministers of state from the Upper House are Margaret Alva, H.R. Bhardwaj (both given independent charge), Balram Singh Yadav, M.M. Jacob, K.C. Lenka, Rudra Pratap singh and Rameshwar Thakur.

There are five women Ministers-Sheila Kaul, Alva two debutants, Mamta Banerjee and D.K. Tara Devi. Kamala Kumari is a Deputy Minister. The representation from Madhya Pradesh is perhaps the most impressive. Arjun Singh, Madhavro Sciundia, V.C. Shukla are all Cabinet Ministers, while Kamal Nath, a debutant, and H.R. Bhardwaj are Ministers of State.

From Andhra Pradesh, Kotla Vijaya Bhaskara Reddy is the Cabinet Minister, while junior Ministers include B.V. Rangiah Nadiu, Mallikarjun and Venkatswamy.

Besides Solanki, Gujarat has a long Union Minister in Mr. Uttambhai Patel. Delhi's sole representative is Jagdish Tytler. The Rajiv Gandhi Cabinet at one time had four Delhites. From Goa, Eduardo Faleiro returns to the Government, From Arunachal Pradesh, P.K. Thungon is also back.

Rajasthan, where the party has moved from zero in 1989 to 13, the line-up is Balram Jakhar, former speaker, Rajesh Pilot and a debutant, Dr. (Ms) Girija Vyas.

Besides Banerjee, West Bengal is represented by Ajit Panja, who was a Minister earlier. Orissa representatives are Giridhar Gamango, a young veteran, K.C. Lenka, who is a fresher. Karnataka, where the Congress performed impressively, has B. Shankaranand, S.D. Nayama Gowda, who defeated the former Chief Minister Ramakrishna Hegde, along with Alva and Tara Devi. From Kerala, there are four Ministers but none of Cabinet rank. S. Krishna Kumar and M.M. Jacob are old hands while the new ministers include Mr. Mullapalli Ramachandran and Prof. P.J. Kurien. Prof. Kurien was the chief whip of the party in the ninth Lok Sabha. Maharashtra, which has sent the largest contingent to the Lok Sabha with 37 MPs, has only two Ministers so far. Tamil Nadu, which brought impressive results for the party, has no representation at the cabinet level.

Prime Minister, P.V. Narasimha Rao, can see right throught people, an American newspaper quoted Sharada Prasad, Senior Information Adviser to the forme Prime Minister, Indira Gandhi, as saying. The thing about him is that he can see right through people. He's no push over, Prasad was quoted by the New York Times as saying. One would think he's a fuddy-duddy. But he's up on modern science and computers and math. He's one of the few in India who first had a personal computer. He'll put the focus on reconcillation. Some of the younger people in the party, you might call them pushy people, will heed his advice and counsel I hope. The paper quoted friends as saying that Rao is not merely an intellectual with an interest in politics, but a shrew, even calculating leader who could surprise the younger and restless Congress Party Politicians. Rao is very intelligent, extremely articulate, but in all fairness, he's considered quite indecisive, it quoted N. Ram an Indian newspaper (The Hindu) and magazine editor (Front line) as saying.

In fact, all politically, conscious Indians will agree that the taking over the rein of government by the Congress, under the leadership of P.V. Narasimha Rao on June 21, 1991 marks the beginning of a new phase in the evolution of parliamentary democracy in our country. What is new in the situation is that though technically speaking. It is a minority government; the Indian people and most of the political parties do not want another mid-term poll in the foreseeable future. This clearly reflects that the Indian nation is vitally intersted in the political stability of the country and no political party, including the Congress can ignore this sentiment of the people. This also partially explains why P.V. Narasimha Rao was unanimously elected as the leader of the Congress Parliamentary party. A close look at the new Council of Ministers constituted by P.V. Narasimha Rao shows that he, too, in keeping with the traditions of Jawaharlal Nehru, is following a policy of consensus. In the new Council of Ministers, he, of course, has given representation to all the States. He has also tried to bring about a synthesis among the Congressmen of the various age groups. Significantly, the induction of Dr. Monmohan Singh, a well known economist of inter-national repute clearly reflects that in running the administration of the country, Narasimha Rao will depend heavily on the outstanding intellectuals of the country who are not within the Congress hold. The politics of national consensus has begun to emerge, though within the framework of the traditions of one naional movement. There are quite a number of honest democrats in India who believe that a general election of the kind we recently faced will not help either in the evolution of democratic institutions or in stabilising the sense of nationahood among the people. The most agonising aspect of this election was that in the midst of the electioneering. Congress president Rajiv Gandhi was assassinated. This assissination clearly brought into sharp focus how the Indian political system has reached the brink of a precipice. Are they right? If they are, is there any alternative course for us? If they are not, can we dismiss some of the uglier and most dangerous aspects of our general election as inevitable in the process of the establishment of a democratic order in India? Never before since independence, communal and caste passions were raised to such a high pitch as they were in the recent elections. Communalisation and 'Mandalisation' of politics were the most outstanding characteristics of this election. In the process, the secular edifice of the country received a serious setback. These and other questions are, perhaps, not asked or answered vaguely and never precisely enough. However, they haunt all Indians aware of the many dark forces released during this election. Undoubtedly, these forces will leave a deep imprint on public life. Besides, these forces will also manipulate the irrational emotions of the people in the coming period and manage to emerge as key factors in the political drama of the country.[6]

An Indian general election based on adult franchise is a fantastic political exercise. Not only for the number of people involved in it, but in terms of the objectives sought, the methods adopted, and the ambitions of certain political forces. General elections in other countries are simple and definitive operations compared to ours, their purposes more compact and concrete and the quantity involved in them less numerous and less vague. In India, almost all the general elections and the general election of 1989 and 1991 in particular have been nothing more than attempts by different parties and groups in different parts of the country to push the Congress out of power. In this sense, the general elections have assumed certain unique characteristics. Let us not make any bones about it. Blind anti- Congressism has its own logic. Inevitably in such a sitution, throwing the Congress out of power becomes the central objective. As a result fo this, ancient tribal and caste contradictions, regional cultural contradictions, and modern social contradictions, all march together. The basic policies and the solutions of the problems recede into the background and blind anti-Congressism becomes the hall mark of electioneering. This is what really happened during the recent elections. This is only one aspect of the current situation in the country. There is no doubt that the era of one party domination in Indian political system has come to an end. This process began in 1967, entered a new phase in 1977, and another phase in 1989. This is a fact of life and cannot be denied, even if you assume that the Congress is not a movement but a well-knit political party. However, equally important is the fact that after every experiement of a non-Congress government at the Centre, it is the Congress which has always come back to power. How does one explain this phenomenon of the Indian political system? How is it that every experiment of a non-Congress government at the Centre whether in 1977, or in 1989, has proved to be brittle. There must be objective reasons for this. One reason is that despite its acts of omissions and commissions and notwithstanding its diversities and contradictions the Congress continues to be the only national force in the country.[7]

Rao now needs to address the realities thrown up by the electoral verdict. By denying majority to any party, the electorate has sent a clear message-that it wants the nation's affairs to be run by consensus, in other words by a coalition Government. Mr. Rao was concious of the reality, as the election results trickled and the prospects of a single-party majority receded. After the formation of the Government, he said then, they would have to decide on the form of cooperation with the other parties-whether it be an omnibus arrangement or based on issues. Mr. Rao, one can be sure, sticks to that position, but there is little evidence of a sense of urgency and others, in his camp, appear to dismiss the idea of allying with others and, thus, sharing power with them. A single-party dispensation, in the present context, has an element of in-built instability-and to ignore this and to create an illusion of stability could only create problems for the minority Governments-Indira Gandhi, who headed a minority set-up after the 1969 Congress split, dependent on the support of the communists and the DMK, was compelled to seek an early election. The National Front failed, though the then Prime Minister, V.P. Singh, believed that his was the safest Government (because of the compulsions of the BJP and the Left parties). What happened to the Chandra Shekhar Government is recent history. The danger in the present case is that the narrow Congress (I) deficit may full some of its sections into believing that they are secure. Any arrangement between the other two forces, the National Front-Left alliance and the BJP is ruled out as also a tie-up between the BJP and the Congress (I). They leaves only one possibility-the getting together of the Congress (I) and the National Front-Left alliance (as a whole or in part). That was what the signals exchanged between the leaders of the two sides were about. In the National Front camp, the issue was discussed thread bare and though opinions on the desirability of coalition differed, it was not ruled out. The public stand taken by the Front-that they would function as an Opposition party-made sense in the absence of an initiative. That, however, need not be taken as the last word. One can count on the sense of realism of Rao for a follow- up of his sensible approach, enuniciated at the vote-counting stage, while recognising the need for exploring all avenues of support and adopting a conciliatory line in response even to provocative questions, he disapproved the idea of augmenting the Congress (I) strength, through defections in other parties. It will not be easy to forge a coalition but, at some stage, the political parties will need to learn to work together. Yes, the difficulties are there-apart from other factors, the consequences of a Congress(I)-National Front coalition, with the Left support and apporval. Now, Rao conveyed a message of decisiveness bny finalising his team of 59 membners within hours of his appointment as Prime Minister. It produced a positive impact. This was in refreshing contrast with the past practice- even in situations where the Congress was comfortably placed (with four-fifths majority in 1985 election, for instance) -of appointing ministers in batches and instalements. the inductions- and exclusions-were almost a continuous process. What effect it had on the administration is well known by now.[8]

The team as such is a mixed fare. Arjun Singh, with his wide expericence in the Government and the party, S.B. Chavan and Madhavsinh Solank, both former Chief Ministers and Union Ministers, Mr. Madhav Rao Scindia and V.C. Shukla will be a source of strength. Mr. Rao will need to take not of the widespread public perception of the role and influence in the new set-up of the coterie, or the set of persons who had assumed the role of Rajiv Gandhi's confidants but were hated by a sizeable section in the party. The inclusion of two or three Ministers belonging to this category will only strengthen these perceptions. what was the difficulty in discarding a part of the baggage of the past? Rao chose not to confine his search for the Finance Minister to the Congress (I) Parliamentary Party, not particularly distinguished for the abundance of talent. He inducted an economist of repute, Dr. Manmohan Singh, who had the experience of dealing with international monetary agencies-which is what the daunting economic agenda will require in the near future. To get an indea of the type of direction he would give, one has to refer to his views, expressed in the recent past-when he did not have the slightest idea of taking up the onerous job of managing the economy, now in a shambles. He traced the origin of the present crisis to the early Eighties when the terms of loans from international sources hardened with the drying up of soft finance and the consequent recourse to commericial borrowing of which there was a big jump between 1987 and 1989. While the terms of borrowing changed, there were no structural adjustments in the sphere of economic management and in particular nothing was done to improve the productivity which remained static at the uneconomical level of the soft-loan era. Most of the changes, suggested by the world Bank, according to him, are needed to be carried out because of domestic reasons, and in particular there is the need to raise the capital-output ration and to improve the health of the economy. He, thus, made a case for harsh decisions in order to put it back on the rails. In his opinion, domestic controls which inhibit production need to be removed, exports pushed up and the budgetary deficit reduced. He did not accept the view that, in the present international economic environment, the scope for increasing exports is limited.[9]

Prime Minister P.V. Narasimha Rao struck the right note in his first address to the nation on June 22, 1991 by announcing his government's top priority to restoring the health of the economy. As an able administrator, he has realised what his first task was even before constituting a Council of Ministers. Fortunately his choice of a finance minister is impecable, and Dr. Manmohan Singh indicated in his first interaction with the media that he is in tune with the Prime Minister's economic thinking key to Rao's philosophy is an accelerated development pace promoted and sustained by an open-door policy to attract foreign investment, and preservation of the people's purchasing power by fighting inflation and strengthening the public distribution system. That he is not going to be weighed down by the constraints of dogma was clear in his assertion that India would continue the dialogue with the IMF and other multilateral financial institutions. Rao is right in pointing out that overcoming the economic crisis is a trans-party affair. If this approach does not ensure all-party support for his short-term economic policies, Rao's assurance of preserving India's economic policies, Rao's assurance of preserving India's economic independence should help the Left Front to shed its reservations about IMF loans. There is reason to apprehend that the Left Front may exaggerate the baneful consequences of IMF conditionalities. If it does, it will only be supporting the view that it is unable to get rid of its ideological blinkers even at a time when its Marxist fellow-travellers elesewhere in the world are leaving them miles behind on the road to libearalism. Rao deserves support from all parties for his agenda, for that alone will inspire confidence among governments and institutions whose help is crucial for India's economic recovery. If the Prime Minister did not sound rhetorical in his political assurances these nevertheless were sound in content. The promise to set up special courts to try communal offences and to raise a rapid action force to deal with communal riots will be widely welcomed by people who are seriously concerned at the vicious assertion of communal politics. In the same vein is a reiteration of the assurance according tostatutory status to the Minorities Commission. Rao has sought to avoid abrasive political jargon in presenting his agenda, for he possibly realises that he can secure cooperation for his minority government only through hard action and by not rubbing his adversaries on the wrong side.[10] Since most parties have expressed a disinclination to opt for an early mid-term poll, Rao has begun in an ideal condition. There need be no undue worry about political opposition offered just for the fun of it. This is a positive sign but, because it has come circumstantially, Rao's team will be unworthy of office if it were to fritter away the opportunity to prove its mettle.

NOTES

1. Hari Jai Singh. Man of the Moment. *The Business and Political Observer,* June 22 1991.
2. *Ibid.*
3. Nikhil chakravartty. Indian Politics. *Patriot,* 23 June 1991.
4. *Ibid.*
5. O.P. Sabherwal. Dialogue, Consensus PV's Store. *Patriot,* 22 June 1991.
6. V.D. Chopra. After P.V. Government, What Next? *Patriot,* 24 June 1991.
7. *Ibid.*
8. K.K. Katyal. Testing Time for PM's Skills. *The Hindu,* 24 June 1991.
9. *Ibid.*
10. *The Hindustan Times,* 25 June 1991.

FIVE

CONSENSUS MAN

The unanimous election of P.V. Narasimha Rao as the leader of the Congress Parliamentary Party is entirely in tune with the mood of the nation. No one, not even bitterest opponents of the Congress, would cavil at the choice or would have liked divisions within the ruling party. Consensus in the Congress lexicon has a meaning different from what the dictionary says. In the former it means bringing partymen around to supprt a particular candidate already chosen. Narasimha Rao, whould be India's first Congress Prime Minister not belonging to Uttar Pradesh, is an ideal consensus person. If he is not the most acceptable of all party leaders, he is certainly the least unacceptable of them all. As an embodiment of the old Congress culture untainted by the new, Rao is perhaps among the handful of senior Congress leaders who combine within them loyalty to the Nehru-Gandhi family with loyalty to the Congress ideals. As a Minister in the Congress Cabinets of Indira Gandhi and Rajiv Gandhi, Rao had been an outstanding success. There was no portfolio which he has not held with distinction and skill. He is perhaps among the few Congress leaders who will have no communication problems in most parts of India. Lacking charisma and a mass base, serious disadvantages for any ambitious politican, are the strength of Narasimha Rao. The Congress Party under him will have to depend on its performance and the manner in which it responds to the hopes and aspirations of the people. It remains to be seen whether Rao's clean image, competence and acceptability are adequate to keep the party and the government together. His skills as a politician and as a decision-maker are to be tested. Much depends on the kind of ministry he will have and on how he deals with faction leaders, family loyalists, state satraps, etc. As the head of a minority government, Rao will have to worry about ensurign the support of a centrist party like the Janata Dal or rely on the sympathetic attitude of the two Communist parties. The choice of Rao is the most ideal in sofar as rapport with non-Congress parties is concerned. He is not only highly respected by the leaders of all political parties but also can be trusted to carry them along with him in the making of crucial decisions. In a sense, the Opposition parties do not have much option other than supporting a minority Congress government, at least for some months to come. In such a circumstance, they would rather ofer to deal with a leader like Narasimha Rao than with personalities who are identified too closely with the Durbar politics of the Congress. The past months had been the most traumatic phase in independent India's history. Apart from the separatism related problems in Punjab, Jammu and Kashmir and parts of Assam inherited from the past, the country was subjected to the most dangerous kind of divisive politics based on religion and caste. The cult of the gun has entered the normal life of politicians in several states. Peace and stability have become national policy goals rather than administrative exercises. The socio-political situation in the country demands not only the cooperation from all the parties but also wisdom to agree on a set of minimum objectives where there would be no grounds for political confrontation. Also, such basic concepts as federalism, centre-state relations, secularism, etc, have to be redefined to remove the elements of friction that have entered the Indian society. Another stupendous problem, which will not have much disagreement among the parties is the tiding over of the internal and external economic crisis. Above all, the country must be allowed to lower the temperature and temper of the people. This is not the time to talk of either coalition politics or national government. Any government that goes by the name of the Government of India is the national government. Coalescing of minds is the need of the hour, not a coalition of parties. By temperament and image, Narasimha Rao is the most suitable person for the job. The country will be with him at this hour of crisis and expectations.[1]

The choice by consensus of the scholarly elder statesman, P.V. Narasimha Rao, as leader of the Congress Party in Parliament demonstrates the intrinsic strength and unity of the Indian National Congress and its ability to provide the much-needed stability to the country. Rao's election provided the answer to the anxious question "who after Rajiv", which was much tougher than the leadership issues that arose earlier after the deaths of Jawaharlal Nehru and Indira Gandhi. This was the first occasion after Independence when the party was bereft of the leadership of the Gandhi-Nehru family-a leadership sustained by sacrifices and people's affection. The party with, a 106-year-old tradition, which is in contrast with the brief life-spells of other centrist parties that had come up after Independence, is again at the helm of the Country's affairs. The election has by and large been smooth. The challenge in the initial stages by supporters of Sharad Pawar and the manner in which he pursued it only up to a point served to highlight the democratic credentials of the Congress Party. The demand by a section of members supporting Pawar for ascertaining the views of members instead of imposing a consensus choice was immediately agreed to by the party leadership and the process was initiated. It was recognised that Pawar and his supporters were entitled to their viewpoint on the need for a secret ballot but the majority of leaders preferred a consensus since at this crucial stage the party should not present an image of divising and infighting. Pawar has to be congratulated for the graceful manner in which he retracted and appealed to all membres of the party to support Narasimha Rao and thus arrive at a unanimous decision. Pawar explained that his endeavour was only for "affirmation of democratic principle in the functioning of the party". His sentiments on the need for a "united and democratic party", which could respond to the aspiration of the people for a strong and stable government reflects the view of every Congressmen for whom this was a day of rejocing at the continuance of the Congress tradition at the Centre coupled with respectful homage to the later leader Rajiv Gandhi. The wistful thought, expressed by the senior leader. Arjun Singh, who proposed the choice of Narasimha Rao for leadership, shared by all, was that but for cruel destiny the time and place would have belonged to Rajiv Gandhi. The dedicated resolve expressed by the leadership to follow in his footsteps should be reassuring not only to all sections of the party but to the people at large. Leadership change by democratic process, witnessed in other democracies like Britain and the United States, show that every leader has his individual style, not necessarily the same as those of his mentors. Rao's style can be expected to be mellow, mature and non-controversial. Though the Congress Party is short of a few seats for absolute majority in the new Lok Sabha.[2] Rao would not be under a handicap in pursuing the time-tested Congress policies of safeguarding national unity and promoting the economic and social welfare of the people, thanks to the positive attitude of the opposition parties in the hung parliament. He begins his term on a promising note.

Following Rajiv Gandhi's assassination and its failure to secure a majority in the Lok Sabha, the Congress was expected to strike a fine balance between two apparently incompatible but equally valid compulsions. Deprived of the awesome mystique of the Nehru- Gandhi family, the party was called upon, in the first place, to learn to function on a collective and transparent basis. The era when the "high command", a faint euphemism for the leader-could virtually dictate all decisions was well and truly a thing of the past. The decision-making process now had to involve the widest possible consultations among acknowledged leaders conducted in an open manner to ensure that extra-constitutional authority did not overwhelm it. Over the past two decades a handful of persons swearing loyality to the leader indeed wielded enormous power without commensurate accountability. In the absence of a dominating personality this was no longer possible. A Jawaharlal Nehru, an Indira Gandhi and a Rajiv Gandhi could and did hold the party together because each one of them effectively provided a rallying point to Congressmen nation-wide. No such rallying point existed at present. To be in a position to get its writ respected within the party, the "high command" now had to consist of individuals with proven administrative and political skills and a track record of public service who could be trusted to treat their colleagues enjoying popular supprt at the state and national levels with the deference due to them. The second compulsion relates to the precarious condition of the Congress. Since it had not been able to win a majority of its own in the Lok Sabha it was obvious that it would have to strain every nerve merely to survive in office. This was all the more imperative in viw of the colossal problems the new government will have to tackle. Nothing would have jeopardised its very survival more than factional infighting or a clash of personal ambitions. For this very reason it had to settle the contentious issue of the leadership of the Congress parliamentary party without delay and in a manner which precluded hostility and bitterness. Otherwise the party would have been hard put to seek and obtain-cooperation from the opposition parties to function effectively. This lesson had indeed been forcefully driven home by the two recent calamitous experiments of minority governments enjoying "outside support". The Congress leadership has managed, despite avoidable controversy, to reconcile these two compulsions. It redounds to the credit of Mr. Sharad Pawar that he took the lead to warn the country of the dangers inherent in deciding the leadership question on the basis of the kind of "consensus" that had prevailed in the past. The very fact that his supporters insisted on a secret ballot if the consensus process led to an impasse made it that much more difficult for coteries, caucuses or cabls to bamboozle the party. This insistence on presering democratic norms was naturally and quite legitimately interpreted as a sure signal that Mr. Pawar was a candidate for the prime ministership. Even his most acerbic critics could not deny that his candidature was indeed attractive: witness the Congress party's electoral gains in Maharashtra, the stability and progress the chief minister has provided to the state and his impeccable secular credentials. But then Pawar is too shrewd a politician not to have realised that in the larger interests of the party and in his own long-term interests, he cou very well afford to bide his time. Having successfully forced the "coterie" to go on the defensive, he is now better placed than before to enhance his reputation as a leader of national standing in the months ahead. His endorsement of Mr. Narasimha Rao's candidature paves the way for him to assume important national responsibilities.[3]

Rao's elevation to the leadership of the Congress parliamentary party has come about through a genuine-as opposed to an imposed-consensus. Given his vast experience of public life, his close association with successive Congress Prime Minister, his extensive familiarity with the strengths and weaknesses of the Congress organisation, not to mention his fine intellectual gifts, the party can trust him to steer it and the nation through these turbulent times. The allegations aired here and there that he was unduly influenced by extra-constitutional elements-be they sundry swamis or the so-called coterie-have been made before but they were revived as part of a malicious campaign to denigrate him with the avowed purpose of diminishing his chances in the race for the CPP leadership. His intensive and sustained interaction with Congress leaders deawn from all parts of the country to decide the CPP leadership issue should give the lie to the charge that he was a prisoner of the party's past habits. If anything, in the present circumstances, his ability and willingness to reach decisions through process of consultations should stand him in good stead as he seeks the cooperation of the opposition parties to meet the multiple challenges facing the country.

The spectacular success of the Congress in Maharashtra is expected to have wider ramifications on politics at the national level. The impressive Congress tally of 37 seats out of a total of 47 would not only give the State party the chance to play critical role in national affairs but also significantly boost Chief Minister Sharad Pawar's standing as a natinal leader. Juxtaposed against the Congress party's debacle in Bihar and UP, Maharashtra's emergence as the State which had returned the highest number of Congress MPs to the Lok Sabha along with the party's impressive showing the South could now be expected to bring about a shift in the Congress power structure away from the Hindi-speaking States towards the States south of the Vindhyas. In fact, it was precisely the prospect of Mr. Pawar's elevation to the national level that appeared to have, together with a sympathy wave, created a perceptible swing in favour of the Congress after Rajiv Gandhis assassination. Most importantly, post-Rajiv realities had compelled both the Chief Minister and his detractors in the state Congress party to realise that they had joint stakes in scoring a major win in the elections. A convincing win would vastly augment Mr. Pawar's leverage at the Centre by leaving the State for partymen with regional ambitions. Patch-up bids were therefore initiated to rectify the Congress's image of a house divided. For a party wrecked by constant dessensions and infightings, this had proved to be the crucial factor in boosting its electoral prospects. It helped marginalise the influence of both rebel candidates outside the pary as well as dissident leaders within. The defeat of influential rebels like Vikhe Patil, who contested as an Independent, and Banwari Lal Purohit, who had recently left the Congress to join the BJP, as also senior party leaders like V.N. Gadgil and Mr. Vasant Sathe, elucidate such a fact. In contrast to the Congress which had hastily set its house in order, rifts recently appeared in the

BJP-Shiv Sena alliance. The BJP's unease with the Shiv Sena supremo Bal Thackeray's rabble-rousing and demagogy of the worst kind, which included his infamous remarks on Nathuram Godse and Mahatma Gandhi, as revealed in an interview of A.B. Vajapayee to a Gujarati newspaper, clearly hinted that all was not well with the alliance. Besides, chinks had also appeared recently in the hitherto impenetrable ranks of the Shiv Sena. Differences within the organisation over the supremo's autocratic style of functioning had emerged into the open for the first time, especially in the Marathwada unit where several founding members had quit and joined the Congress Party. Not surprisingly, the BJP-Shiv Sena combine, their boastful claims notwithstanding, secured only nine seats as against the 14 they had won in 1989. The third contender in Maharashtra, the Janata Dal-led Progressive Democratic Front, was even worse, having been able to win only one seat as against its six last time.[4] Obviously, the absence of any effective organisation of the Janata Dal had prevented the party from converting the prevailing goodwill for it, especially in Maharashtra and the Vidharbha region, into electoral support.

It's like losing a general in the middle of the battle. We can't call off the battle nor can we wait too long to find a general who can take on to this battle. That is why I think what the party is doing today is the correct thing namely, electing a provisional president. The constitution provides for the election of a provisional president and for the AICC to ratify it, which every-one expects. I had said we must take, three decisive steps. The first, the CWC must elect a provisional President. The second, that shortly after June 16, the members of Parliament, both the elected members of the Lok Sabha and member of the Rajya Sabha should meet in the CPP to elect a leader and if we are the biggest party with a majority, that leader would become Prime Minister. The third step we should take is that the AICC should soon be called to elect a regular president. I think if the party is able to take these three steps without bitterness, without division, we would have overcome the crisis. The leadership is something which is thrown up in the crucible of struggle or a crucible of trial and tribulations. There are any number of examples in world history of a party providing a collective leadership, one of them being first among equals and then that first amongst the equals, by dint of his performance and emerging as an unquestioned leader. I believe that this can happen in India too. But in the foreseeable, future, at least for a year or two, I think we will be providing a collective leadership. And from that collective leadership it is possible that a leader may emerge taller than the others. I am not ready to give way to despair. I am confident that we will be able to resolve these questions of immediate leadership and long-term leadership quite satisfactorily. There are leaders without party and they think the Congress is a party without a leader. It is a very interesting combination but not likely. It is very much possible that some people who left the party may come back, but I doubt very much if the party would reach out to pluck a leader, so to say, from some other party and make him a leader of the Congress. That is not likely to happen. It all depends on how they conduct themselves.[5]

I think the CPP should elect its own leader and I think it will elect a leader shortly after June 16, I think today everybody should take his position as equal. As long as Rajiv Gandhi was there and he allowed anyone to act in any particular manner one must presume that he had given that person the authority to do so. But, now I think leadership mush be something which must be won by dint of performance and his acceptability to the people. It will be vital to keep the key positions in the hands of those who are elected by the people. This does not apply to Narasimha Rao. No one questions the electability of Narasimha Rao. He declined to contest election on health grounds and with the permission of Rajiv Gandhi. If he wishes to face an election I am sure he can face an election and he will be elected. I don't think what I have said implies to Narasimha Rao in anyway. He has always been elected to the Lok Sabha or he can always win an election, either in Ramtek or may other constituencies in Andhra Pradesh. We have many leaders and many whose credibility is very high. They may not have had national exposure but they can discharged their responsibility when given to them. Let's see how many of them perform well in this given particular time. I do not see any "goings" but many comings in once elections are over.....some sort of alignments may take place.[6]

Although in the past Congress had very strong leaders, the Mahatma himself guided the Congress, Jawaharlal Nehru was there but even then there was a collective leadership which at times was strong enough to resist even the tallest leaders. Take the case of the election of Subhash Babu. He was elected against the wishes of the Mahatma. Similarly, on several occasion Nehru's views did not prevail, even in small issues like the election to the UPCC. So the Congress was always a body of collective leadership. But, it broke down in 1969 after the split. Thereafter, it was a Congress party which had to be more or less run by an individual. And Indira Gandhi was fully conscious of it. She ran the organisation as if it was an organisation over which she had total control. Elections were more or less done away with, the working committee, the parliamentary board all along were nominated by her. The Chief Ministers were nominated, Congress legislature party chief PCC presidents, they were all nominated. This pattern was continued by Rajivji also. Now in the absence of a leader controlling the party doubts are being expressed as to whether the Congress party can function on its own. Whether the lack of a strong leader would result in the break-up of the party. Or that would weaken the party. I am one of those who do not believe that it is inevitable for the party to either break up or get weakened in the absence of one strong leader. Collective leadership could be just as effective. In fact, in the present times the general air of decentralisation all over the world and a collective leadership very much in practice, it shoudl not be very difficult for the party to adapt itself to collective funcioning. When the question of Congress presidentship came up, now, it was unfortunate that it was messed up in the working committee, initially. But sober opinions prevailed, to begin with, because the general elections are still in the process. The person who was number two to Rajivji and who is more or less the seniormost member and also non-controverial, is being made the Congress president-P.V. Narasimha Rao. And he should build up a collective leadership. He would be in to best position to do that because he is not dictatorial. If he can build up a collective leadership in running the party, it should equally be possible to build a collective leadership in running the government, when Congress comes in majority after the elections. There is plenty of material in the Congress. It is not that the Congress is less than any other party. If you were to compare, it would be clear that the Congress has more leadership material than any other party in the country. Its a question of bringing them together, giving them a feeling that now a collective leadership will function. I think had Rajiv lived after the elections he would have also attempted to introduce a measure of collectivisation and decentralisation because he was a modern man, he wanted to liberalise economy. You cannot liberalise economy without liberalising the political system. They go hand in hand. There is no difficulty in the Congress assuming and retaining its leadership role in the country. I think circumstances will bring the Congressmen together. To begin with, there may be attempts to acquire single leadership; all kind of loose talk is going on about individuals trying to assert themselves, to become leaders, in the mould of dictatorial leaders but I dont' think the party will accept it. It is also being loosely talked about that there will be a flow of money, outside influence etc. But, I don't think that by itself these will play a major role. The Congress party has a tradition of sacrifice, nationalism, of caring for the poor. All this talk of money etc. will not succeed. After the president is selected through the CWC under the constitution, it has to be endorsed within six months, by the AICC. In the present circumstances the process may be hastened.[7]

The Congress Party has undoubtedly been greatly shaken by the tragedy that has overcome not only the Party but the entire nationa. This is a period in which we are still shell-shocked. But the Party has a very historic tradition and at times of crisis it has always shown a great amount of resilience and inner strength. It has been a very very major blow to the Congress party. We have lost Rajiv Gandhi, a charismatic leader who had captured the imagination of the people at large. However, the last few days have shown that the Party has been able to gather its wits about it and after deliberation and consultations amongst Party member we have come to a consensus and decided on Narsimha Rao being our president. That in itself is demonstrative of the maturity and inner strength that exists in the Congress. There have been no splits, and despite of room forecasting all sorts of disasters about to overcome us, the Party has shown the resolve to meet even a crisis as major as this. Obviously, we have no leaders who can fully measure up to the personality of Rajiv Gandhi. But, a major emphasis should be laid on his manifesto and a public commitment made to implement it. This would help in maintaining our credibility with the masses. The Congress leadership will now have to pass into the hands of a representative collection of leaders who carry weight and credibility in their home states. I think if both these steps are taken, we can some what fill up the vacuum which we are experiencing. It is difficult to generate the sort of confidence that Rajiv generated in the masses, but certainly we can go some way towards filling the void, if we take such steps. There is a wealth of talent in the Congress Party. I do not think that there will be any clash between the middle-age politicians and the older generation of politicians. There can be a complete synthesis with each playing their own role. I think organisational elections should also be held. So long as we had a towering personality like Rajivji or Indiraji, may be, elections could be dispensed with, because everyone accepted their decision without demur or argument and also had confidence in their sagacity. That sort of person does not exist today, so if anyone now makes new appointements, it will be very difficult for him to carry the rest of the party along with him. That is why, organisational elections are absolutely necessary. In fact, the first phase is already over. The Congress is an organisation with years of history behind it and a specific ideology which has been dovetailed into the modern context by Rajivji. It is this ideology we represent and we have a responsible leadership which we can project. May be we do not have a charismatic "leader" but we can still claim to have a responsible "leadership". Nor does any other party have a towering personality. So not projecting a Prime Minister cannot be interpreted as a sign of weakness on our part. There are obviously two possibilities as far as choosing a leader of the Parliamentary Party after the elections is concerned. First, that we may arrive at a consensus like we did in the case of Narasimha Rao. Or second that we may have an election. If an election takes place, the victor should be wise enough to take along with him those who amy not have opposed him, for he would need the support of everyone to meet the national crisis. Conversely, the vanquished too must give their unstinted support to someone who gets elected democraticlly by a majority. This is the democratic way of functioning. If there is a consensus, well and good. But even if there is an election, I am sure good sense will prevail. We all have a major responsibility to shoulder to ensure that the party remains unified. We have to demonstrate unity in our resolve, so that we can measure up to the challenges that our nation faces. We must remain committed to Rajiv's memory and pledge to implement his agenda for the nation.[8] The Congress has earned the gratitude of an anxious nation by unanimously adopting Narasimha Rao as leader of its parliamentary party. This automatically makes him the next Prime Minister-the first from the south. This is a happy augury for the 106-year-old organisation which has been under tremendous strain following the tragic assassination of Rajiv Gandhi. At one stage, the party looked like losing its moorings but it has shown rare resilience and farsightedness in facing the most trying period of its chequered history. For, Rajiv Gandhi was not merely a party chief. He was a charismatic leader with an all-India following. The Congress had actually come to depend so heavily on the legacy of the Gandhi-Nehru family that it provided a sort of insurance against all calamities. Despite its faults, the party has shown a sense of purpose and direction. It did well to allow a free play to its various sections to interact in the leadership process. At one stage, a contest for the top slot looked imminent, but it must be said to the credit of Sharad Pawar that he bowed out gracefully showing statesmanship and political maturity.[9] The position of prime minister is not a bed of roses. It is probably the most difficult assignment in any democracy in any part of the world. In the first place, Rao will have to read cautiously since his party does not have an absolute majority on its own. It will have to bank on the support of other parties. This would mean a lot of adjustment accommodation. Even within the party there are bound to be some murmurings.

NOTES :

1. V.N. Narayanan. complete Consensus Man. *The Tribune,* 21 June 1991.
2. *National Herald,* 21 June, 1991.
3. *The Times of India,* 21 June 1991.
4.
5. P. Chiodambaran, The Spirit of Collectivism. *The Hindustan Times,* 9 June 1991.
6. *Ibid.*
7. Dinesh Singh. The Spirit of Collectivism, *The Hindustan Times,* 9 June 1991.
8. Madhavrao Sciendia. The spirit of Collectivism. *The Hindustan Times,* 9 June 1991.
9. *The Business and Political Observer,* 21 June 1991.

SIX

THE PEOPLE'S MANDATE: TRIUMPH AND DEBACLE

The Andhra Pradesh Chief Minister, N. Janardhana Reddy, said in New Delhi on June 20, 1991 that the Congress President, Narasimha Rao, could be elected to the Lok Sabha from his home state. Talking to newsmen soon after Rao emerged as the consernsus candidate for the leadership of Congress Parliamentary Party, Reddy said electing him from Andhra Pradesh would pose no problem. Reddy hosted a lunch in honour of Rao in Andhra Bhavan where a large number of top Congress leaders from the state were present. They included the former Chief Ministers, K. Brahmananda Reddy. Vijay Bhasker Reddy, and Chenna Reddy, leader of the Opposition in Rajya Sabha, P. Shiv Shankar, Prof. N.G. Ranga and R.K. Dhawan. Expressing happiness over the unanimous choice of Rao as the CPP leader, Reddy said the Congress Parliamentary Board, which met on decided that there should be a consensus.

Congress President, Narasimha Rao, has said that even if his party secured a comfortable majority in the current election to the Lok Sabha to from the new government at the Centre, it would seek the cooperation of other political parties in solving national issues.

"There are many national issues on which there is no party prediction and all parties should unite on issues on which there is no difference of opinion", Rao told a news conference in Bhubaneswar, on June 10, 1991. The Congress chief claimed that the party was on the winning trail and exuded confidence that it would certainly win a comfortable majority to from the next government. "From my election tours in Uttar Pradesh, Maharashtra, Andhra Pradesh, Rajasthan, Gujarat and Orissa I have seen a lot of determination on the part of the electorate to bring the Congress back to power for their love of Rajiv Gandhi, he said, adding the people want that the intention of those who assassinated Rajiv Gandhi should be defeated. Rao, however, refused to be drawn into any conversation on the likelihood of his becoming the Prime Minister if his party won an absolute majority in the elections. "As I have already said the party will choose its leader who will become Prime Minister", he told a questioner. "My first priority is to get my people elected to the Lok Sabha and I am not going to think of anything else before that But I must make it clear again that there is no problem at all on the leadership issue". When asked if there was any possibility of a person from outside being elected leader of the Congress Parliamentary Party, Rao said, "why should I rule out that possibility? How can I rule out that possibility? It is upto the party to decide". Rao said that he expected the party to retain its seats in the South and add more seats in the North to attain a comfortable majority. Asked as to what realignments would be possible if the Congress fell short of a majority leading to a hung Parliament, Mr. Rao said he was not thinking in those terms at all. "Besides, I don't answer questions begining with the word "if", he said. Replying to another question, Rao said that Sonia Gandhi was already considered to be a member of the Congress family and was "one among us" and the question of her party membership was a mere "technicality".

Explaining the party's stand on the letter of E.M.S. Namboodiripad, the CPI (M) leader, Rao said that "Namboodiripad had asked us to define our attitude towards his party and we in turn have asked them to define their stand towards us. That's all". "At the moment we are pitted against each other But I don't know what is the motive behind the letter. I don't speculate, it is your privilege," he told the reporters. He said that as long as Rajiv Gandhi was alive he was the party's sole campaigner, while the other leaders looked after coordination. But now all the leaders had been sharing the responsibility in the changed circumstances. "Should we call it group leadership" a reporter asked. "You call it whatever you like but I am putting forward before you the facts", Rao replied.

For the second time in less than two years the elections have thrown up a Lok Sabha where no single party enjoys a majority. This is going to be a handicap for the new House which is being called upon to tackle some of the most serious problem the nation is facing-Punjab, Kashmir the economic crisis and India's place in the world. As experience has shown a government not enjoying majority can neither survive for long nor tackle the tasks it is supposed to handle. Yet there is reason to remain hopeful about the future of the country. The elections have not been smooth. Rajiv Gandhi was assassinated, and many others lost their lives in senseless violence that marred the polls. There have been complaints about the malfunctioning of the electoral process. Yet the country has proved it can take care of itself notwithstanding an assassination and the spell of political uncertainty that was making many feel uneasy about the health of Indian democracy. Those who think Indian democracy cannot withstand shocks are being proved wrong. The Indian voter has often shown that he cannot be regarded as naive or a greenhorn who does not know what exactly to do in a challenging situation. There is in the present verdict a rejection of the kind of politics which tended to take the country backward in time. The electorate has rejected a clear attempt by certain parties to gain power at the Centre by the use of religion or a casteist platform. The Bharatiya Janata Party's was the most aggressive bid to come to power at the Centre, Mandir being its main card. "The voter has not thought highly of it. Despite the fact that the BJP has made a big gain by capturing Uttar Pradesh and improved its position in the Lok Sabha its leaders need to think why the voters, a majority of whom are Hindus, have not voted it to power at the Centre. They also need to seriously consider that their concept of Hindutva is not the kind of nationalism a majority of Indians want to believe in. The benefits of living in a composite culture are for our electors more convincing than the semantics of secularism, Communal vote-banks, pseudosecularism and minorityism. The Hindu, card as the BJP leaders would discover when they sit down to analyse their election results, is not immune from the Law of Dimnishing Returns. So also for the sectarian appeal the Janta Dal launched clearly whipping up casteist passions in the name of equity and social justice. Nowhere outside Bihar and Uttar Pradesh has the Janata Dal marked it presence. This is mainly because of the party's alienation from the urban middle class and the intelligentsia whose clout in Indian politics cannot be understimated. The party also suffered because of its inability to come out of the mess it had landed itself in over Mandal and its inability to see that social injustice and inequality in India required the breaking down of caste barriers and not raising them.[1]

Wisely, the voter has thrown the Samajwadi Janata Party (SJP) into the dustbin. It was an artificial contraption, a product of unprincipled politics, ambition and intrigue deployed to meet partisan needs rather than to serve even short-term interests of the country. None is going to shed a tear for it and its luminaries. The Congress has certainly improved upon its strength in the last Lok Sabha and has the chance of forming the government at the Centre. This can give it some satisfaction. But the party is faced with a serious situation. It has been wiped off from the nation's two largest States, Uttar Pradesh and Bihar, leaving the gound totally free for the BJP and the Janata Dal. How far this is because of the passions aroused by Mandir and Mandal or because of the failures of Congress's organisational shortcomings or its tactical mistakes is going to be the subject of a debate, but it will not be easy for it to capture these States back in the foreseeable future. Immediately the Congress has to elect a leader who can lead the government. With the chance of forming a government, the party can ensure its unity. On the ability of the party to elect its leader smoothly will depend the effectiveness of the government it is to form. The Congress also needs support from other parties to form a government. Who it seeks this support from-The Janata Dal or the Left-remains to be seen. The electorate has certainly shown an inclination for a government headed by the Congress in preference to other parties like the BJP and the Naional Front-Left combine. Yet it is a mandate that has been given a bit grudgingly, putting the party on a clear notice that it must set its house in order. The Congress-I leaders have to show that they can rebuild the party without the help of charismatic leadership. It is both a challenge and an opportunity. The Congress's rout in Uttar Pradesh is significant for the nation's politics. Except for Morarji Desai, who had a short tenure, all Prime Ministers have come from Uttar Pradesh. This has had a distorted impact on the country's politics. A Prime Minister from outside Uttar Pradesh can have a beneficial influence on the nation's federal polity.[2]

The May-June national poll of 1991 has new novel features held as it was in the most unusual circumstances and in the midst of, and profoundly influenced by, the assassination of Rajiv Gandhi. Its messages and warnings to the politicians who run our democracy for and on behalf of the people as well as opinion makers who influence political behaviour will be subjected to close security for weeks and months. One of the instant warnings the voters have issued, however, needs to be noted. The warning is to those who wreck political parties and alliances by defection and desertion. Not inspired by anything but just for power and self-advancement. Devi Lal who claimed to have brought the Janata Dal into being and made V.P. Singh prime minister in November 1989 was also the first to wreck the party and the subtle and delicate alliance system that was built as its scaffolding. His determined bid first to assume the office of deputy prime minister, and then to instal his son, Chautala as haryana's chief minister, led to the first grave internal crisis in the National Front.

Later, Devi Lal joined hands with Chandra Shekhar to break the Janta Dal and form a minority-minus government with supurious support from the Congress. In the last phase of his self-smeared political career, he even "campaigned" for the Congress and became a votary of that party. Now he has been cruelly and deservedly punished by the voters. It is not just his defeat in contests for both the Lok Sabha and the haryana state Assembly, it is the trouncing of his party that has been ruthlessly banished to the Haryana political wilderness. It is doubtful if Devi Lal will ever come back to political power. Without him, his sons are less than straw men, goons in political masks. Most of the Janata Dal members who deserted the party, joined Chandra Shekhar and wrecked the National Front regime have now been thrown into the wilderness by the electorate. Subodh Kant Sahay who in the maiden months of the NF regime had shown cheerful political promise, lost his security deposit in Bihar. Maneka Gandhi who was angry with V.P. Singh for not giving her a Cabinet position which, in any case, she did not deserve has also been punished. Chandra Shekhar's own party, Samajwadi Janata Dal, will have a token presence in the Lok Sabha, and the care taker prime minister himself will go down in the history of Indian politics with little more than a footnote. If newspaper reports are true, he has however, added a substantial amount of acres to his "ashram" at Gurgaon, which is not the people's reward for his widcat manner of running government.[3]

Look at Maulayam Singh Yadav. An ordinary man from the ranks of the lower peasantry, he made a very strong impact on UP politics in 1990. His stubborn stand against BJP and VHP on the temple- Masjid issue succeeded politically only because he had the full backing of the NF government in Delhi. This he denied later only to justify his defection to Chandra Shekhar. Maulayam Singh Yadav look another political plunge when he determined to govern Uttar Pradesh with the support of the Congress. The life-long opponent of the Congress now became a crooning apoogist for the party. What are the consequences of his double volte face? Not only is he and his party wiped out of UP legislature, the Congress itself has almost entirely lost the country's largest state which will be governed by BJP. The UP Congress was deadly against supporting Maulayam Singh Yadav but submitted to the command of Rajiv Gandhi. The voters have roundly punished politics of dire opportunism, an entirely lustful approach to politics. You will find the opposite in Bihar. Here, chief minister Laloo Prasad Yadav remained faithful to the JD and NF, and he has been amply rewarded by the voters of his state. Even BJP could not earn any significant political acre in Bihar, which is now the chief domain of Janata Dal. The voters have also punished mushroom politician lifted from the world of the celluloid. The electoral success of Dipika, who played Sita in the telefilm Ramayana, is offset by the trouncing of Rajesh Khanna in Delhi and Victor Bannerji in Calcutta. These two defeats will hopefully subdue political ambitions stirring up in the hollow bosoms of stars who seem to believe that Indian politics is now a natural extension of the Mobay movie.[4]

"Sahi Keh rahen hain" (saying right) ran the murmur as the crows nodded its approval at the new Congress president P.V. Narsimha Rao even as he waved his forefinger at the people at Shajahanpur, Uttar Pradesh and Pilibhit urging them to reflect. "Elections are no joke", he declared profoundly. And warned: "If the Congress is not returned, I guarantee that there will be another Lok Sabha election next year". Rao appeared to have shed his image of an old, ailing, marginalised politican and even seemed to be projecting himself as the permanent "leader" on his tour of central Uttar Pradesh. He made it a point to stress that he was an elder statesman rich in experience who had worked not only Rajiv and Indira but even Nehru. "Yes, we've lost our leader. But when the party comes back to power it will choose its new leader. The Congress can never be netraheen-without a leader. It has a traidition of renewing its leadership," he assured. Taking heart from the surpringly large and responsive crowd at Philibit an animated Narasimha Rao prepared his chaste Hindi with Sanskrit verses when referring to the masjid (mosque) and the Mandir (temple) that coexist alongside in Philibit, a symbol of the country's secular tradition which the BJP was irresponsibly trying to destroy. Openly battening onto the sympathy wave, Rao who spoke in the shadow of a huge cut-out of Raji Vandhi with his hand raised, said on a wistful note that when he sees these cutouts, "I also instinctively raise my hand and think for a moment that he's still with us". Unlike Shahjahanpur where the meeting had been packed basically with party wrokers, in Philibit the crowd appeared more varied, the tripples of applause more spontaneous. Rao was especially effective as he countered the BJP's bid to appropriate the Congress's stability platform following Rajiv Gandhi's murder. "This testifies to the BJP's conviction that Rajiv Gandhi would have delivered a stable government," Rao argued persuasively. Congressmen must have been ancnoyed by the response Rao got in Maneka Gnadhi's constituency, where the party's candidate, Manipal Singh Lodhi, seemed to the running third in the electoral race. But party workers here ramain disappointed that Sonia Gandhi has not yet reconsidered her decision. "Waiting for Sonia" was the theme in Shahjahanpur, too, where the rank and file party worker was convinced that Sonia of Priyanka would come to campaign for Baba Saheb (Jitendra Prasada). "He was very close to the family", Ashok Kumar Gupta, a social worker, said of Jitendra Prasada, who was Rajiv Gandhi's political secretary.[5] Sonia's name may not have been mentioned by the speakers at Shajahanpur meeting, but she looms large over Jitendra Prasada's post-Sriperumbudur election campaign. Liberally displayed all over the town were posters of the widow as she appeared on the day of the funeral dressed in black- bordered, white sari, head bowed, wearing dark glasses. Printed on the poster was "Sonia's message" - drawn from her statement declining the Congress presidentship, the only statement she has made since the assassination: "For the sake of the country for whom my husband and Indiraji sacrificed their lives, for its prosperity, unity and intergrity, strengthen the Congress." Although not many Muslims were to be sighted at Rao's meeting, Congress workers are certain that the constituency's 11 per cent Muslim vote is getting increasingly divided in their favour. There is, however, no firm evidence that this is happening across the board, especially in Shahjahanpur town. Laddan, a Muslim rick-shaw-puller at the rally site was, in fact, remarkably cynical about the sympathy wave: "These type of incidents happen because it is a former Prime Minister who has died, you see it as a tragedy and expect a sympathy wave. Why should it make any difference to us, when our sons die every day in riots?" A Muslim college lecturer felt that Rajiv's death had pur a damper on the election campaign as a whole. People were tired of election meetings. Sanjay Khan of Tipu Sultan fame and Ghulam Nabi Azad had come recently, and Madhav Rao Scindia and N.D. Tiwari were to follow. Narasimha Rao, according to him, was no draw. But then, as a local Congress leader pointed out, Rao's meeting was aimed also at boosting the morale of party activists dispirited by Rajiv's murder and worries about the future of the party. In that, it seemed to have succeeded. Only too aware of the sense of insecurity that had gripped party workers, Rao proceeded to assure them that under no circumstances would the Congress crumble. "This is not the time to be weighed down by sorrow or anxiety but to enter the field fighting," he declared. Barely a fortnight ago no Congress or JD meeting could take place without BJP supporters heckling the speakers and raising the Jai Shree Ram chant. But suddenly all that has stopped. And the Congress appears to have siezed the initiative. Narasimha Rao's meeting in Shahjahanpur may have lacked fireworks and was thinly attended, but party workers were heard to say in surprise, "He speaks well". Even if he didn't send party activists into delirium, at least he didn't disappoint. Battling the handicap of a South Indian leading the party into the poll, congressmen were reassured by "Narasingh" Rao's felicity with Hindi, if with no- thing else.[6] Narasimha Rao's visit to Hardoi and Lucknow did not evoke much enthusiasm, with the Congress presenting the spectacle of a depleted and dispirited force. At Hardoi, all activity ended 100 yards away from Gandhi Maidan, the venus of the meeting. There was little indication there largest political party was in town: Hardoi remained the sleepy and somnolent place it usually is.

Scheduled to arrive at 4.30 pm, Rao was running an hour late. A mere 3,000 people were present at the ground, which was ringed by heavily-armed Border Security Force (BSF) jawans, intelligence men and local policemen. People were being frisked by securitymen in plainclothes, while photographers and journalists had to get their cameras and tape-recorders checked. The general lack of enthusiasm and the strict security measures seemed to have dampened spirits. Even the local leaders, who usually make the most of such occasions and resort to all king of tactics to catch the leader's eye, were subdued.

In fact, none of them were allowed on the podium. Forced to sit behind the barricade, they came up one-by-one when their names were announced. The ubiquitous cheerleaders were also conspicuous by their absence. The audience, took, seemed in no mood to exercise its lung power. One of the speakers was actually embarrassed when he lustily raised a slogan to find the crowd absolutely mum. The sight and sound of Rao's helicopter infused some life into the otherwise listless auidence. The Party's candidates on the podium shouted slogans: "Rajiv Gandhi amar rahe", Indira Gandhi amar rahe", "Jab tak suraj chand rahega, Rajiv teranaam rahega", "Ma bete ka yeh balidan, yaad karega Hindustan." And, finally, came a full- throated response from the audience. But surprisingly, not a single "zindabad" was voiced from Rao and Tiwari, even as they drove to the dais from the adjacent make-shift helipad. Apparently, party workers and supporter's are still finding it difficult to accept the new leadership as an effective replacement for Rajiv Gandhi. Political observers regard this as an ill omen for the party. Partymen, too, displayed apprehension that the rally would be little match for that held by BJP stalwart Atal Behari Vijpayee at the same venue three days ago. Once on the podium, the aging and ailing Rao and Tiwari were offered water and electral. But, the drink failed to pep up the new Congress chief, as he found himself forsaken by most of the local leaders who immediately fawned on Tiwari. There were some spontaneous "N.D. Tiwari zindabads" from the crows, prompting local leaders to shout slogans hailing Rao lest the chief guest felt ignored.[7]

Tiwari was the first to speak. With his oratorial skills; he moved the hitherto distinterested crowd. The audience was, more than once, asked to raise its hands in a show of support for the Congress and it responded enthusiastically. Tiwari sought to convince the crows that by electing Rao the interim president, the Congress had displayed its inherent strength and unity. But he would go no further. His most complimentary epithet for Rao was "my elder brother" and, not once in Tiwari's speech did Rao graduate to "my leader". On his part, the south Indian Rao surprised all by speaking chaste Hindi. People heard him in rapt silence. Astute enough to realise that the state considers it its brithright to provide the country with a Prime Minister, Rao, who could be the PM in waiting flattered the state by saying that it alone was capable of seeing the Congress through. The partymen were pleased, but no enthused. The looks, the gestures and the aura of a dynasty seemed missing. So even when Rao left, there was a greater scramble to see the helicopter take off than to shake hands with him or raise slogans in his support. Perhaps, the Congress worker and the voter of U.P. who are both reared on the personalised politics of charismatic leaders like Indira Gandhi and Rajiv, are loath to accept and recognise leaders who were, lieutenants of the "great ones". The UP common man, it seems, is not prepared to accept anyone other than Sonia as Rajiv Gandhi's successor. It was no better in Lucknow. The very choice of Jhandewalan Park as the venue for the meeting was indicative that the party did not expect huge crowds. Though in the midst of Lucknow's busiest market, the park was half empty. Piqued at the way Tiwari was sidelined by the Congress Working Committee (CWC) in the selection of the party president, his supporters gave vent to their ire by shouting slogans: "Tiwari tum sangharash karo, hum tumhare saath hain" and "Desh ka nata kaisa ho, N.D. Tiwari jaisa ho". Started by the sudden outburst, Tiwari promptly reprimanded his followers. But the message had been conveyed nonetheless. Farrukhabad proved to be the saving grace. The meeting there evoked a better response and Rao was taken through town in an open-jeep.[8]

The 10th Lok Sabha election are, above all a single of the recovery of the Congress. The people's mandate this time is clear and unambiguous-the Congress should rule. It is this overriding result that is sought to be overlooked, by some quite consciously and with ulterior motives and by others who are trapped by stereotypes. The cry has gone up that we have a hung Parliament. E.M.S. Namboodiripad even nimbly theorises about it. He states that hung Parliaments are now going to be the rule and the norm. In fact, what has happened is that the BJP's bid to become the ruling party has ended in a failure. This cannot be concealed by the fact that it has made a big push forward in Up, performed well in Gujarat and picked up votes and some seats in Bihar, Gujarat, Andhra, Karnataka and Maharashtra. The BJP leadership tries to make out that from having two Lok Sabha seats in 1984 it now has one hundred or more. The advance is not to be denied. But it also cannot be forgotten that the advance was actually made in the 1989 elections. That was when the breakthrough was made thanks to the alliance between it and the National Front directly and indirectly with the CPI-M. CPI and their associates. The breakthrough which the BJP legions rushed was widened with the National Front in power. It was because of the opportunities provided to it in 1989-90 that it had the courage or, rather, foothardiness to proclaim its bid for power. The BJP has demonstrated tht it is a danger. It has shown that its path of advance is that of communal preaching rioting and killing. But it has also been demonistrated that power is still a distant dream of it Dilli Dur Ast (Delhi is still far)-that is the 1991 elections message to the BJP. There was another contender for power. That was the National Front of which the Janata Dal was the main constituent and which had the so called Left Front as its ally. How confidently and frequently did the leaders of this combine assert that they would win a majority. And how miserable has been the performance. Much more miserable has been the performance. Much more miserable would have been the outcome were it not for the outrageous handing of the law and order situation in Bihar by Laloo Prasad Yadav. He outdid the atroccious Chautala and will sooner rather than later, be politically punished in the same way. The Left Front parties in particular, and also all the patriotice and secular forces in the National Front combine should think over what has been the result of their reliance on casteism and Muslim communalism. Has it helped them or Right reaction? Has it damaged the Congress more or themselves? The Left parties an the Janata Dal have to wholly and sincerely abandon anti-Congressism. They have to wholly and sincerely abandon all hopes and designs of spliting the Congress. If they are to survive it will have to be together with the Congress in a broad patriotic front. The Samajwadi Janata Dal's leadership had hoped to have either on their own or no the basis of some kind of understanding a group that would be able to play a role of manipulation and manoeuvre that would bring it a number of gains. This hope has been dashed to the ground. Mr. Chandra Shekhar's more than dubious role in forcing an early election on the people has led to the political destruction of the party he still claims to lead.[9]

This brings us back to the outstanding characterstic of the elections-the mandate to the Congress to rule. There would have been no room for any doubts to be spread on this account and this party not suffered a devastating set back in Uttar Pradesh and Bihar. No doubt the peculiar cooperation and conflict between the communalists and the casteists in these two states hurt the social and mass base of the Congress. The immediate reason, however, for the debacle of the Congress in UP is the supprt it extended to the Mulayam Singh Yadav government which had to brutally handled the masses who had come to Ayodhya and which had fanned backward casteism. On top of it there was its won factionalism which reached ruinous proportions. In Bihar, factionalism and ambiguity about the phenomenon of backward caste fanaticism, played hovoc with the fortunes of the Congress. It stand did not win it fresh support while it eroded its traditional mass base. The Congress paid for not acting on the truth that all casteism is bad and dangerous, that the casteism of the backward castes has to be combatted quite as much as that of any other castes. In Gujarat the alliance with the Janata Dal (G) has proved to be quite as ruinous for the fortunes for the Congress as its own factionalism. Were it not for these blunders and weakness the Congress would have been for more effective in spreading its message of national unity and stability. Rajiv Gandhi's heroic campaigning and grievous death would, then, have brought it and the nation even greater dividends. Nevertheless, the fact remains that it is the Congress and its gallant leader, Rajiv Gandhi, which has inflicted a set back on the destabilisers. It has established a sufficient parliamentary presence to open up a realistic prospect of India, again, having a government that will govern. It has brought into being a situation where national recovery and advance would be fully posible. It is essential that the Congress should realise its own strength and its responsibility in full measure. It should demonstrate and that too, immediately its capacity to set up its structure of leadership. The Congress should certainly strive for consensus and agreement with all who are willing to strive together with it. There should, however, be no illusions on its part that even those parties and persons who may agree to ceasefire have, in fact, given up the war. It is not yet a farewell to arms on this part. The Congress while stretching out its hand to all should rely, above all, on itself.[10]

The saffron triumph in Uttar Pradesh and Gujarat is a significant pointer to the changing political complexion of the country. If UP is a mirror of the real India, then the installation of the Bharatiya Janata Party government in Lucknow should be a major concern for a Congress-led dispensation in Delhi. This fact in itself is bound to give jitters to the working equation between Delhi and Lucknow. At the core is not only the issue of the construction of mandir at Ayodhya-one of the central themes of the BJP poll-plank-but of establishing a non-confrontational relationship between the ideologically divergent camps. Not that opposing political parties have not ruled Delhi and Lucknow simultaneously in the past, but the circumstances in which the BJP has triumphed are quite unprecedented. That the BJP has on its own secured the highest number of seats both in the Lok Sabha and the state Assembly, unlike in the 1989 elections when the secured few seats even after seat adjustments with the Janata Dal, indicates the erosion of the centrist base in Uttar Pradesh. More than the Mandir-Mandal issue, however, it was the Mulayam factor that has affected the electoral fortuness of the Congress as badly as it has hurt the Samajwadi Janata Party (SJP). After having reduced his own government to a minority for the sake of calapulating Chandrashekhar to power at the Centre with the help of the Congress, and the way he handled the kar seva (free service) that led to what came to be known as the 'Ayodhya massacre', Mulayam Singh Yadav soon became the most hated politician in UP. Ths has vicariously affected the Congress which sustained Yadav's regime following the split in the Janata Dal. The blind support extended to Yadav by the Congress high command much to the chargrin of the state leaders virually killed the political initiative of the UP Congress. The party lost its credibility to the advantage of the BJP. The

Congress calculus wa sfraught with a number of imponderables. In Gujarat too, the high command put its state unit in an agonising position by forgoing an alliance with Chimmanbhai Patel whose is known to be an opportunist. Pate's JD(G) has hardly any platform except a vageu appeal to regional chauvinism which it could not push too far without making its partner squirm.[11]

Wrong alliance with wrong persons and for wrong purposes have cost the Congress dearly in UP and Gujarat. The Congress high command under the new leadership would do well to draw the appropriate lessons from the spectacular performance of the BJP in the two states. There cannot be shortcuts to power. Nor can power be built up without local back-up. The country's most violent and unendurably prolonged elections have once again failed to produce the eagerly sought-after decisive mandate for any single party or alliance. While the Congress has emerged as the single largest party, it will have to look for allies to form government with a requisite majority to govern. The question uppermost in every body's mind is will the country be, given the mixed electoral outcome, spared the ordeal of what followed the verdict of 1989 when a sharply 'hung' Parliament had brought polar opposites-the Left and the BJP-to join hands to support the National Front Government. Such an incongruous alliance had expectedly produced not only a severely hampered V.P. Singh ministry but also led to its early demise, giving way to an equally short-lived experiment of a minority Chandra Shekhar government which expended most of its energy in continuously haggling for Congress support which the latter had promised without joining the Ministry. The country paid a heavy price for the variegated poll verdict that it had produced. With a similar outcome again, is the country in for a similar traumatic experience is the apprehension being expressed in several quarters. The absnece of a clear mandate in favour of a single party seems to suggest that the days of one party dominance are over the time being and the country has opted, for whatever reasons, in favour of a coalition. Unfortunately, however, the country's turn towards pluralism in politics has come at a time when it can least afford it. Casteist and communal tensions are pulling the country apart even as a grim economic situation is worsening day by day. Separatist threats in the borders States continue to grow, encouraged actively by inimical powers across the borders. Taking advantage of the uncertainities prevailing at the Centre, Pakistan is already engaging in what amounts to a low intensity warfare in the North-West States of India. Indeed, seldom before has the need for a stable and strong government at the Centre been so acute. True, the admission by almost all political parties that an election-weary country cannot be put through another election certainly seemed to indicate that the pressures of the present political situation would dictate a hastened mood in leaders. But equally so the short life, not the full term of five years, accorded in a recent TV show by spokesmen of all major parties to the tenth Lok Sabha seemed to portend that the urgly game of power mongering is to unfold yet again. Obviously, party leaders do not appear to have learnt their lessons from the unfortunate experience of the ninth Lok Sabha when a weak Union Government was held hostage to the clashing-egos of politicians even as the problems of the country acquired crisis proportions. It is about time the leaders learnt to see the situation as what it is-an exceptionally difficult period.[12] Rather than returning to the people ever so frequently for a clearer mandate, or seeking to run governments with water-thin majorities, the party leaders should explore means by which a resonably stable and cohesive Government can function at the Centre.

The tenth Lok Sabha, which was constituted with the Election Commission on June 20, 1991 issuing an official notification, has came into being after passing through an unprecedented phase of trauma, violece, suspense and uncertainities. It has a few "firsts" to begin with. Chief Election Commissioner T.N. Seshan told newsmen that the notification listed the names of successful candidates frokm 502 constituencies, even though the polls have been held for the 511 out of the 537 seats. The results for the Guwahati, Banka, Salempur, Sasaram and Bikramganj constiuencies have yet to reach the Election Commission. Of these, the commission had put an embargo on the announcement of results in respect of Banka, Sasaram and Bikramganj (all in Bihar) pending an inquiry into irregualrities. But the embargo has since been lifted and the counting of votes was in progress. The inquiry was not yet complete in respect of two other constituencies, namely Munger and Begusarai (also in Bihar) and there would be no announcement of results till the inquiry is over. The Election Commission has already held as null and void the declaration of results in Aurangabad (Bihar) and Davangere (in Karnataka) and the counting of votes there would be done a fresh after the appointment of new returning officers as directed by the Election Commission. So, the names of nine constituencies have been kept away from the notification. It is also for the first time that the notification for constituting the newly elected Lok Sabha has been issued at a stage when the election process in all the States listed for the polls has not yet been completed. The elections to 13 Lok Sabha seats from Punjab are scheduled to be held on Saturday. Seshan later met President R. Venkataraman and presented to him a copy of the notification. The president had earlier directed that the new Lok Sabha should be constituted on or before June 20, 1991. The Election Commission had in fact to race against time today to complete the formalities for the notification a few of the States were slow in furnishing the required information about the election results as per the format laid down in the law and election rules. There were anxious moments for the senior officials in the commission working hard on finalising the formality and it was here that the much- trumpeted "superintendence and control" of the Election Commission on the election machinery in the States really failed. The final picture, as it emerged to day after the declaration of results showed that the Congress could muster only 224 seats, though it had fielded 493 candidates in all the States and Union Territories (except Punjab). It is for the first time that not one Congressman could get elected from UP (out of 85 seats)-The State which has in the past produced four Congress Prime Ministers. The second largest single party is the Bharatiya Janata Party, with a record strength of 119 members. For the BJP what is new is the election of a member from the Union Territory of Daman & Diu and two member from Assam. But in terms of a group in the Lok Sabha, the National Front-Left Front has a higher number of members, 127 to be precise. The NF-Left combine fought the elections jointly and have now decided to work as one group in Parliament. It comprised the Janata Dal, the CPI, CPI-M (at the national level), Telugu Dsam, Jharkhand Mukti Morcha, Forward Block, Revolutionary Socialist Party, among others, at the State or regional level. For that reason, the Congress will have to count on its allies, nemely AIADMK (11 seats) and the Muslim League (2 seats).

As separate entities, the CPI-M tally came to 35, CPI got 13 seats and the RSP and FB together got 7. The Janata Dal secured 53, the major share coming from Bihar (25 out of 49 seats). Polls for five seats in that State stand countermanded by the Election Commission.

NOTES:

1. *The Hindustan Times,* 18 June 1991.
2. *Ibid.*
3. Bhabani Sen Gupta. Defeat for wreckers and Defectors. *National Herald*, 21 June 1991.
4. Ibid.
5. *The Sunday Observer,* 9 June 1991.
6. *Ibid.*
7. *The Sunday Observer,* 9 June 1991.
8. *Ibid.*
9. Mohit Sen. What has happened? *National Herald,* 19 June 1991.
10. *Ibid.*
11. *The Business and Political Observer,* 19 June 1991.
12. *Patriot*, 20 June 1991.

SEVEN

THE SYMPATHY WAVE

The assassination of Rajiv Gandhi is the dominant issue of the last days of the election campaign. He is still its dominant presence as in life and so after death. This is not just a matter of a sympathy wave. It would be quite unnatural and a sign of total ingratitude if there was no sympathy wave. Rajiv Gandhi was rightly a greatly loved leader. Apart from the respect and affection for the party which he led he was also loved for himself. Millions were also heartbroken at the fact that a young man dignified in defeat had come so near to returing to the post to which the nation summoned him after his mother's murder and then blown to bits on the eve of his triumph. A young man who was interviewed just after the assassination was stating the bare truth when he said that crores of persons would queue up if somebody said that by his death Rajiv Gandhi could return to life. Let the wise heart of our people not be underestimated. The sympathy however is not for the person alone. His death is as much a message as his life and campaign were. He had been emphasising that the unity and integrity of India were under assault. He was stressing that it was the Congress alone which would be in a position to providea government to the country and that without a strong Central Government there was no possibility of the country surviving and progressing. Has this not been confirmed by his death? Is it for nothing that he was picked out for assassination? Why was his return to power feared so much? it would be ridiculous to imagine that millions upon millions are not reflecting on these themes, including those who may not have been earlier persuaded by the speeches and interviews of the slain leader. There should be no hesitation on the part of the Congress leadership to focus on this fact to the turmoil in the national mind. How can it help it if other parties did not have a leader life Rajiv Gandhi and now a martyr like him. The elections now more than ever than ever would be a contest between those who stood with him and stand by his perspective and programme for national recovery and advance. What is the height of hypocrisy, however, is the new claim to stability being made by the BJP in particular. It was the leadership of this party that had been most vociferously proclaiming that it was none other than Rajiv Gandhi who was the biggest force promoting destabilisation in the country. In fact their campaign was venomously directed personally against him. The Volte face, therefore, seems all the more nauseating. These leaders now state that the removal of Rajiv Gandhi has removed the one leader who could have promoted stability on behalf of the Congress. Now, of course they alone can provide it? This is their sympathy for the slain leader. The patent hypocrisy apart what has to be reiterated is that the BJP has today become the greatest divisive force in our country. P.V. Narsimha Rao has been rightly emphatic in pointing out that the BJP is not a rival to the Congress since it does not have the same perspective and values around which there could be both conflict and cooperation. It has another vision of India. Its vision is that of a fascist India.[1]

The point about the BJP, moreover, is that it is essentially negative. It can destroy, It cannot build. Using all the backwardness and distortions in our socioeconomic life, it has been able to build communal consciousness among millions of our people. It has been able to mount the most formidable challenge to our secular democracy since the partition of India. It has, however, done so by running down Islam or playing up the Muslim bogey. It has not been able to make of Hinduism the great unifying ideology that it is and to use it in the manner, e.g., of Mahatma Gandhi. That is, of course, because Gandhiji was a passionate believer in Hinduism while Advani and Vajpayee are equally passionate believers in communalism. It is this rousing of majority exclusiveness or antogonism by making a minority a meancing enemy that was and is the hallmark of the facist and Nazi movements. The logic of marking out a minority as a target of attack is that you keep doing this to one minority after another. For Hitler the Jews came first but not so far behind were the communists, then the social-democrats, then the liberals, the Christian church And so it went on an on till even the Nazis themselves did not know who was going to be the target next. This is the logic of totalitarianism. And the RSS-BJP are the representatives of totalitarianism and, by no means, of Hinduism. It was possible for Nazism to survive in and dominate Germany for almost two decades. It did so by savage repression and ferocious aggression. The BJP can and certainly will use repression if it gets a chance but aggression it certainly cannot manage. It can, however, be a satellite or strive to make India a satellite in the global designs of the political military and economic aggressors who, at the moment dominate the US administration. The satellite fascist regimes of spain, Hungry, Bulgaria, Romania, show that this has happened in the past-totalitarianism at home has gone together with subservience to the dominant aggressive totalitarian country abroad. Parallels are never exact and it is wrong to argue by analogy. This is true it is also true that history is all that there is for humanity to learn from. The BJP is aggressive against the minorities within the country but remarkably quiet and well-behaved when it comes to any discussion of any outrage perpetrated by the US imperialists. Whether it be Vietnam or Cuba or Iraq there has always been some excuse or the other which has kept it from condemning the US aggressors What about Pakistan? It is certainly a hate-object because of its Islamic theocratic character. The US aid to that country is certainly condemned by the BJP. But it starts from the wrong end i.e., its objection is to the character of Pakistan and not to the US which makes it possible for that country to become a menace to us. And it is definitely a part of the grand overall strategy of the US reaction to keep us embroiled in conflict with Pakistan so that we are not able to be the global power that in fact we are. The comparadore character of the BJP's communalism should not be missed. It is this compradore character that makes it so vicious an enemy of the Nehru-Indira Gandhi strategy. In fact, this is the character of the whole compradore intelligentsia. It requires malice of a particular vicious kind that make Khushwant Singh write in News Week (June 3) endores what Churchill had to say when the Independence of India Bill was being discussed in the House of Commons. He said "Power will go into the hands of rascals, regues and freebooters...These are men of straw of whom no trace will be found after a few years. They will fight among themselves, and India will be lost in political squabbles." Nehru, Indira Gandhi and Rajiv Gandhi are all found to be guilty and as responsible for Churchill proving right. The compradore Khushwant writes "Churchill's gloomy prophecy seems to be fulfilling itself. The current generation of Indian leaders have proved to be men of straw who spend their time squabbling with one another... Whether or not democracy will survive for very long is anybody's guess". We are going through a bad stretch. For this it is the mentors of Khushwant Singh and his ilk who bear the main burden of blame. Patriotic and secular political parties and leaders have made mistakes and have defects. These have now to be rectified so that the error of 'Churchill is again demonstrated.[2]

Both positive and negative elements are clearly discernible in the Indian polity. Positive signs may be feeble, but they do underline the basic soundness of the Indian nation and its ability to overcome any crisis situation. Nagative elements in the polity range from the general drift set in by politico- economic mismanagement to the constant threat posed to the country's unity and the democratic system by millitant and terrorist groups of different shades. The net result is that the polity is going through a trauma and transformation. The transformation is not confined to the Congress alone, though it directly affects the party's future course in the wake of Rajiv Gandhi's tragic assassination. The central issue here is not one of sympathy wave and the extent to which it would benefit the Congress. Some sympathy is inevitable in a situation in which the Congress has lost the tallest of its leaders. Rajiv Gandhi himself was a beneficiary of the sympathy wave following the assassination of Indira Gandhi by her own security guards. But the sympathy generated in the December 1984 election was specifically for Rajiv Gandhi as son of Indira and as President of the Congress. With Sonia Gandhi's refusal to get involved in politics, the sympathy factor this time will apparently not work in favour of a single leader but will either be for the organisation or for individuals who have had an excellent track record. The conduct of the Congress party so far has been reasonably good. The poll compulsions have at least publicly brought its leaders together in the hope of winning a mandate from the electorate. As things stand, the 105-year old Congress has no choice but to hold together and allow its senior leaders to settle for a genuine consensus on collective leadership through mutual adjustment and accommodation. The moot point is: can the Congress gather its strength and learn to work a perspective? A mandate would mean nothing in the absence of a new understanding of the complex task ahead. On the conduct of its leaders depends the future of the party as well as of the Indian polity traunatised by regional forces and terrorism. Terrorism, as some have learnt through experience, can never be appeased or compromised with. It has to be compromised with. It has to be confronted four-square. Most militant groups operating in Assam, Kashmir and Punjab have visible and not-so-obvious foreign links. And these links have been growing. The external manifestations of the terrorist 'fire' can still be controlled by turning off the fuel supply. But this will at best contain the symptoms and not the malaise. The ailment can be rooted out by reasserting the moral authority of the State. It is a pirty that the policies and postures pursued by the various central establishments during the past one decade or so have either been lopsided or misdirected. They have attempted to tackle the terrorist movements with the power of the gun, evading those issues that are responsible for their creation and sustenance. Small wonder that even well- intentioned reconciliatory moves have come to a naught. The threats from terrorist groups in Punjab are real. The need for introspection and heart-searching on why a section of the population known otherwise for its buoyancy of spirit is feeling sullen Perhaps, a twopronged strategy in this regard will help. In the first place, no mercy needs to be shown to terrorist groups which thrive on criminal acts. Secondly, a viable political initiative has to be constantly explored to help the process of reconciliation and readjustment between the central authority and the millitant groups. It is in this context that the importance of elections needs to be appreciated not only for Assam and Punjab but also for Jammu and Kashmir. To say this is not to deny that even if positive measures are taken, terrorism will takes long time to die out. Unfortunately, a political vacuum exists in Jammu & Kashmir. The leaders who reled the state failed both Delhi and the people they were supposed to serve. In fact, the Centre's handling of the Kashmir situation is a grim reminder of the failure of the leadership in correctly guiding the affairs of the state.[3]

The Kashmiri people have resented the fact that whereas the elections had, by and large, been fair in the rest of the country, they were made to suffer the manipulative politics of the Centre's favourite local leaders. At one stage, Dr. Farooq Abdullah was virtually a villain in the eyes of the Kashmiris, though he continued to enjoy the support of key persons in Delhi. Even the growth of Telugu Desam has had its sour note in terms of the hurt psyche of the local people, Mr N.T. Rama Rao came alive from the reel-life to become a real-life hero. He, of course, thrives on his dramatic postures. His recent fast was part of his desperate move to divert the Congress sympathy wave in his favour Whether he has succeeded in his designs or not will be known soon, It, however, must be said to his credit that he knows the fine art of political psychology. His action drew nationwide attention and to that extent NTR has succeeded in extracting some mileage out of his fast politics. Interestingly, the interaction of the regional parties like Telugu Desam, MDK, AIADMK and AGP with the national and peogressive and left parties have helped to evolve a new political culture both at the national and regional levels.[4]

The destabilisers are desperately trying to spread demoralisation. What has been their defeats they are trying to turn into a defeat for everybody. This is the meaning of the "hung" parliament propaganda. The lack of a clear majority for any single party in 1991 is sought to be equated with the ambiguous electoral verdict of 1989. In fact, there can be no equating of the two results. In 1989, the Congress, came down from a three-fouths majority in the Lok Sabha to less than two hudred seats. In 1991 the Congress-I has tormed back to being very close to an absolute majority with its allies. From being a defeated party it has come close to being a defeated party it has come close to being a totally victorious one. It is a reversal of fortunes. Unless the President completely violates all the norms and provisions the Constitution, the Congress should be reinstated as the ruling party of India even as this article appears in print. What the destabilisers were able to achieve in 1989 and what they went to all possible lengths to prevent in 1991 and what they went to all possible lengths to prevent in 1991 has been brushed aside. The Congress has pushed ahead on the basis of the programme and the personal appeal of the Late Rajiv Gandhi who represented the tradition and the tradition and the perspective of this truly remarkable party. When there is talk of the sympathy wave, there is often very little efforts made to analyse its content why was there such intense sympathy for Rajiv Gandhi? Is it not a fact that no effort was spared through the speeches and writings of his political opponents whether of any political party or of press and academic conglomerates to depict him as the archvillain of contemporary India? Despite all this the heart of India constricted with agony when this gallent and far-sighted leader was brutally killed. The spontaneous reaction of the people throughout the country was that the enemies of the nation had done the dastardly deed. The CIA in particular was singled out as the culprit. The sympathy was therefore not just personal. It was highly political. It is true that the sympathy wave alone does not explain the rolling foreward of the Congress. The difference between the May and June votes is a reality. But this difference is again a highly political one. The May vote was in most instances less than that of June because the assassination shocked the apathetic among Congressmen and Congress supporters to action. Complacency was replaced by alarm and anger. It let not to panic but purposeful action. In the midst of the fanfare about the Congress not having secured an absolute majority what is missed in many comments, mostly deliberately, is that the other two contenders for power-the BJP and the National Front-Left Front alliance-have lagged so much behind the Congress. yet both these contenders till the last moment were claiming that even after Raji Gandhi's murder it was they who would win and the Congress would be made irrelevant. The BJP in fact, was advised by its leaders to develop the killer instinct. These same persons stated that with Rajiv Gandhi gone the Congress could not now claim to represent the chance of the stability for the ntion. Those who had opposed the slain leader and ridiculed the plea, for stability now sought to usurp the plea itself. The National Front-Left Front alliance while opposing the BJP maintained till the very last that the Congress and its authoritarianism was the greater meanace and its return to Central Governmental power and to be prevented at all cost It is good that some of the statements of CPI-M and CPI leaders now advance a different thesis. These leaders including Jyoti Basu, no are willing to Judge the Congress-I government by its performance and, at any rate, they want such a government to be formed and remain in office at least for some years. In other words, anti-Congressism has been buried fathoms deep. The thesis of Namboodiripad that "hung" parliaments are now going to be the norm is both wroing and harmful. Wrong because it is based on a superficial comparison between that happened in 1989 and what has taken place this time. Harmful because it makes no distinction between the charactor of different kinds of coalitions. After all it is this harmful perception which enables the CPI-M to have no hesitation to go along with casteist, communal regionalist and secessionist parties of the

National Front. Namboodiripad has yet to shed his anti-Congressism or to repudiate the pledge he made in 1989 to demolish the influence on the masses of the ideology and programme of Mahatma Gandhi and Jawaharlal Nehru.[5]

The CPI-M said on June 16, 1991, that the early trends favouring the Congress-led United Democratic Front in Kerala could be ascribed to the sympathy factor following the assassination of Rajiv Gandhi and the accretion of BJP votes to the Congress. The CPI-M politburou member, Harikishan Singh Surjeet said since 1967 the party commanded a base of 37 per cent votes in the state and the difference in vote polled by both fronts was less than one lakh. "A swing of one to two per cent of the votes in the state can decide the fate of elections", he said. "The transfer of votes by the BJP to the Congress is a major factor in the Congress taking a lead according to early trends", he said, while commenting on the early trends that showed the Congress leading in 90 of the 140 assembly seats and the UDF leading in 17 of the 20 parliamentary constituencies. Commenting on the CPI-M performance in West Bengal, Mr. Surjeet said it was apparent that the Left Front had been able to break into the base of the Congress which was responsible for the Left Front's good performance according to early trends. Speaking on television, Govindacharya, the BJP general secretary, however, refuted Mr. Surjeet's charge of a tacit alliance between the BJP and the Congress in Kerala. He said no such alliance was possible because of his party's differences" Satya Prakash Malaviya said the country was going to have a hung parliament. Commenting on trends and results of the Lok Sabha elections available till now, Malaviya said. "It still appears that no party-will get majority and it will be a hung parliament". Is it true Narasimha Rao is going to Launch his election campaign from Tirupati temple in Andhra Pradesh tomorrow?

I have made it clear that I am going to UP tomorrow. Unless Tirupti when I go to Andhra Pradesh, that is not an area which had not been visited by the late Rajiv Gandhi. So there has been a demand that I should visit Andhra Pradesh. So I will start my visit from there and go to other places and come back to Delhi.[6]

Does Congress expect sympathy wave in the second phase of the election?

May I remind you what happened on May 21, 1991 is an event which is bound to have its effect on the minds of the people. Whether one likes it or not he people are devoted to Rajiv Gandhi and his sudden and the manner in which it occurred has shaken them. There is a sense of identification in the minds of the people with Rajiv Gandhi. In that situation, no one should be surprised if during voting they will do reflects this feeling.[7]

NOTES :

1. Mohit Sen. The New Stabilisers. *National Herald,* 7 June 1991.
2. *Ibid.*
3. Hari Jaisingh. A Polity under Siege. *The Business and political Observer*, 8 June 1991.
4. *Ibid.*
5. Mohit Sen. Prepare for Advance. *National Herald,* 21 June, 1991.
6. *National Herald,* 3 June 1991.
7. *Ibid.*

EIGHT

A WISE CHOICE -- THE PRIME MINISTER

Congress President P.V. Narasimha Rao, who was on June 20, 1991 unanimously chosen leader of the Congress Parliamentary party after Maharashtra Chief Minister Sharad Pawar withdrew from the race, was sworn in as the Prime Minister on June 21 at the Rashtrapati Bhavan.[1]

President R. Venkataraman invited Rao to form the Government afte their meeting on June 20 since no other party staked its claim to form the Government.

Rao has been given four weeks, from June 21 to prove his majority in the Lok Sabha since the Congress, which has won 224 Lok Sabha seats so far, falls short of an absolute majority in the House.

Rao discussed the current political and economic situation in the country with the President for about 50 minutes and was asked how soon would he like to be sworn in. He took a decision on the composition of his Ministry on June 21. The swearing-in has been fixed for 12.50 p.m. on June 21 in the Ashoka Hall of the Rashtrapati Bhavan.

The President handed a letter to Rao stating that as leader of the Congress, the largest party in the tenth Lok Sabha, he was appointing him as the Prime Minister. He invited Rao to form his Council of Ministers.

Rao's name for leadership of the Congress Parliamentary Party was proposed by Madhya Pradesh Congress president Arjun Singh and seconded by former Union Minister and leader of the Opposition in the Rajya Sabha, Shiv Shankar. Soon after, T. Chandrashekhar Reddy, secretary of the Congress Party in Parliament, sent a letter to the Rashtrapati Bhavan informing the President of Rao's unanimous election as leader.

Before going to the Rashtrapati Bhavan, Rao visited Rajghat, Shanitvan and Shaktistahal to pay homage to the departed national leaders and also called on Mrs. Sonia Gandhi at No. 10 Janpath.

The smooth election of Narasimha Rao, who is also the party president, after an over two-hour-long CPP meeting in the Parliament House's Central Hall was made possible by surprise withdrawal of Maharashtra Chief Minister Sharad Pawar from the race earlier in the morning.

Replying to the felicitation given to him on his election as the leader of the party in parliament, Narasimha Rao said the CPP by asking him to shoulder the responsibility would help to get the full supprt of millions of shoulders in the country.

Promising to implement the Congress's 1991 election manifesto in full without giving scope for any alibi, Rao said that "if we fail, the fault will be ours."

Felicitating Narasimha Rao soon after he was unanimously elected the CPP leader, Sharad Pawar, who attended the CPP meeting, described, him as a wise, mature and experienced leader, observing that "Narsimha Rao has been in public life longer than my age."

The irony was that the 70-year-old Narasimha Rao, who did not contest the Lok Sabha election this time on health grounds, become the Congress president and the CPP leader in less than one month of Rajiv Gandhi's assassination caused by a bomb blast near Madras on May 21, 1991 just a day after the end of the first phase of election in the country.

Though Narasimha Rao has handled several Key portfolios of Defence, External Affairs and Home at the Centre, he, at present, is not a member of the Rajya Sabha also. He would have to get elected to the Lok Sabha within six months.

Narasimha Rao's name at the CPP meeting for its leader was proposed by Arjun Singh, former Madhya Pradesh Chief Minister and, at present, the Pradesh Congress Committee meeting, which had then "unanimously elected" here without consulting her. But Sonia Gandhi had refused to accept the party presidentship the very next day. Later, the same CWC had unanimously elected Narasimha Rao as the Party president.

However today, P. Shiv Shankar, the leader of the party in the Rajya Sabha, seconded Mr. Narasimha Rao's name for the CPP leadership. The motion was also seconded by N.K.P. Salve, the party's deputy leader in the Rajya Sabha, B Shankaranand, former Union Minister, A.R. Antualy, former Maharashtra Chief Minister, Sheila Kaul the AICC general secretary and P.A. Sangma.

Narasimha Rao's election as the CPP leader rung the curtain down on the high political drama in the Capital after Sharad Pawar stated tht the leadership decision should not be foited on the party by the Congress Working Committee or the Central Parliamentary Board and suggested a secret ballot indirectly offering himself as a candidate.

This had sparked intense political lobbying in the party with supporters of Narasimha Rao demanding a unanimous election while Pawar's supporters arguing that this question should be settled through a democratic process, meaning a secret ballot.

Both Narasimha Rao and Pawar, in fact, met a couple of times during the last few days to discuss the party affairs, including the issue of leadership. Their and the other senior party leaders' aim was to solve the leadership crisis amicably.

Narasimha Rao had declared that it was up to the CPP whether its leader should be chosen by a consensus or through a contest. But Pawar's decision to opt out of the race came after he concluded his discussions with the party colleagues this morning, which reportedly gave him the impression that a contest for the CPP leadership through secret ballot might turn out to be an expensive deal with no fruitful results, and that it might also affect his political career in future.

Narasimha Rao arrived in the high-domed Central Hall of Parliament 10 minutes late, at 4.10 p.m., soon after AICC general secretary Ghulam Nabi Azad infored the party members belonging to both the Houses the purpose of the meeting.

Professor P.J. Kurien, Chief Whip of the party in the previous Lok Sabha, then proposed AICC treasurer Sitaram Kesri's name for presiding over the meeting.

The assembly then observed two minutes' silence in memory of Rajiv Gandhi, After this, Azad informed the members of the procedure adopted for knowing the mind of the majority. he said the Central Parliamentary Board in its late yesterday night meeting had authorised K. Karunakaran and Siddartha Shankar Ray to as certain the party MP's views about the method of electing the new CPP leader, whether by consensus or by secret ballot. Azad urged Karunakaran to tell the party MPs about their assessment of the mood in the Congress.

Karunakaran said that he and Ray, after meeting 90 per cent members of the Lok Sabha and the Rajya Sabha, had found that they were in favour of electing Narasimha Rao unanimously at a time when both the party and the country were faced with a serious situation. "There was not single dissenting voice," he informed.

Presiding the crucial meeting, Kesri Called T. Chandrashekhar Reddy, a secretary of the CPP, to make his opening remarks. Reddy said that the MPs were assembled there with mixed emotions and it should actually have been an occasion for the re-election of the late Rajiv Gandhi.

Reddy urged the partymen to re-dedicate themselves to the ideals of Rajiv Gandhi and assured them that the mandate of the people given to the party would not be betrayed.

Moving the motion proposing the name of Narasimha Rao, Arjun Singh said this was a time to "search out hearts and make sure neither vaulting ambitious nor a demand for self cloud our vision.

Extending whole-hearted support to the leadership of Rao, Singh said it should be theendeavour of all the partymen not to betray the legacy of Rajiv Gandhi. He urged the partymen to fight the nefarious designs of certain forces and stand by the ideals of the late Rajiv Gandhi.

Singh was confident that Rao would holdhigh the rich traditions of the party and inspire confidence among partymen.

Seconding was the motion, P. Shiv Shanker said the sacrifices of Mrs Indira Gandhi and Rajiv Gandhi shoudl not go in vain and urged partymen to the occasion to keep the party united.

The motion was also endarsed by N.K.P. Salve, B. Shankaranand, A.R. Antulay, Sheila Kaul and P.A. Sangma.

Salve said he was confident that Rao would "steer the country skilfully and safely out of the troubled waters."

The Congress had always emerged strong after every crisis and this time too the people would not be betrayed by the party, salve felt.

Sheila Kaul hoped that Rao would spare no efforts in keeping the party united and vibrant to face several challenges before it.

Antulay, former Maharashtra Chief Minister, hoped that the party would continue to maintain democratic traditions and uphold the rich traditions of the Congress under stewardship of Rao.

Shankaranand said that Rao was one of the few leaders who were actively associated with the party right at the grassroot level. He hoped that the anti poverty programme would be further stepped up to amielorate the lot of the downtrodden and weaker sections.

Aangma lauded the unanimous election of Rao as the CPP leader and hoped that the country would tide over the present difficult situation under his leadership.

Addressing the party MPs, soon after his election as the XPP leader, Narasimha Rao promised to implement the party's 1991 election manifesto "to felt hilt without giving scope for any alibi."

The manifesto given in the form of a national agenda by late Rajiv Gandhi would be implemented in all seriousness, Narasimha Rao said adding that "the challenges might be hard in the implementation but we have the will power to fructify them."

In his opinion, the manifesto for the 1991 elections was the most comprehensive and meticulously drawn one. The clarity of the manifesto was such that the last man and last village in the country could understand it.

"We cannot just do less than the full implementation of the manifesto. If we fail the fault will be ours and there would be no scope for any alibi." Narasimha Rao said, pointing out that this would be the sum total of the task before the party and "we will run the Government successfully."

Rao said the Congress was capable of solving each and every problem. However, the solution to one might result in another problem. "This is a continuous process and we would have to tackle them. If problems ceased to exist, life also ceases to exist," said the CPP leader, who felt that by asking him to shoulder the responsibility would help to get the full support of millions of shoulders in the country.

When Narasimha Rao arrived in the Central Hall for the CPP meeting, most of the party MPs and the other leaders present inside stood up, clapping to welcome him. But Sharad Pawar and some of is supporters around him kept on sitting.

During the entire CPP meeting, Pawar sometimes thumped his desk or joined the othes in clapping but on many occasions he just sat, listening carefully.

if anyone else after Narasimha Rao was the centre of attraction, it was Pawar. Before the beginning of the CPP meeting, the mediape sons surrounded him, asking questions, and the photographers and television cameramen "shooting" him.

After Narasimha Rao's election, Pawar, however, went over to the dais to personally congratulate him on his becoming the CPP leader.

During the meeting, the Press photographers and the party MPs bad a small tiff as the former were blocking their view in the dais. Many times the MPs shouted asking them to sit down.

At one stage, there was a brief scuffle between the watch and ward staff of Parliament and the photographers. Kesri loudly urged the photographers to clear the space in front of the dais. In this drama, two press photographers, in fact, began fighting among themselves, casuing an embarraseement to the Press corps.

After the meeting, Narasimha Rao accepted the bounquets and congratulations from the party MPs and then went out through a side door. Outside, at the main entrance of Parliament, some party workers, including MLAs from Madhya Pradesh, for quite some time kept on shouting "Rajiv Gandhi amar rahe". Similar shouts had also been heard in the CPP meeting, at which a garlanded colour portrait of Rajiv Gandhi was kept just behind the dais.

Till late June 20 night, Pawar and his supporters were adamant on secret ballot for the election of the party's leader in Parliament.

While a two-member All-India Congress Committee panel comprising Siddhartha Shankar Ray and K. Karunakaran had already began consullations with the party MPs in the morning in a bid to ascertain their views on the method of electing their views on the method of electing their new leader, Sharad Pawar in a Press statement declared that he had decided to support the candidature of Narasimha Rao.

Before issuing the statement about his opting our of the contest, Pawar met Narasimha Rao for five minutes and told correspondents soon after that "I have decided to extent constructive support to him."

"I am in favour of consensus on the election of the leader and I have decided to support Narasimha Rao", Pawar Said. The Chief Minister, during his meeting with Narasimha Rao, was accompained by senior Congress leaders, P. Shiv Shankar, N.K.P. Salve and Najma Heptulak.

Pawar in his statement had appealed to all the members of the CPP to support Narasimha Rao and thus arrive at a unanimous decision.

Later, Pawar's supporters said that the unity of the party was of paramount importance and, therefore, they were in favour of a consensus candidate.

In his statement, Pawar said: "I welcome the Congress-I president's acceptance of my demand for ascertaining the views of the members of the CPP in the decision of the leadership of the party."

The Prime Minister-designate, P.V. Narasimha Rao's swearing-in cermony has been fixed at 12.50 p.m. to avoid the inauspicious Rahu Kalam which lasts from 10 a.m. to noon, on June 21, 1991.

A Rashtrapati Bhavan communique issued after Rao had met the President stated: P.V. Narasimha Rao called on the President On June 20 everning. The President personally handed over a letter to P.V. Narsimha Rao which reads as follows: "As the leader of the Congress, the largest party in the Lok Sabha, I appoint you as the Prime Minsiter of India and invite you to form the council of ministers. I advise you to establish your majority in the Lok Sabha within four weeks."

What's Narasimha Rao's personal view? In the event of the congress scoring a clear majority would he like a relatively younger leader to take over as Prime Minister or would he prefer a more experienced person for the top job?

"It is for the Congress Paraliamentary party to decide. Let us see the contet; let us see who all are elected? Only after that can the part think about it. I'm sure they will come to the right conclusion."[2]

The Congress president P.V. Narasimha Rao, met Sonia Gandhi at her residence Janpath, New Delhi soon after the was elected leader of the Congress Parliamentary Party.

Before driving to Janpath. Rao visited Rajghat, Shakti Sthal and the samadhi of Rajiv Gandhi and paid homage to the national leaders.

Rao also visited the Congress headquarters at Akbar Road, New Delhi and the election control room there, before leaving for Rashtrapati Bhavan to meet the President, R. Venkatarman.

Many are apt to make the mistake of seeing the election of P.V. Narasimha Rao as the Congress Paliamentary Party's leader and therefore the next Prime Minister, as a compromise meant to keep the seat warm for somebody else. This would be misreading the event. The election of Rao promises "a wind of change" in India's political life. Despite his 70 years, he has been elected to represent the desire for change and reconciliation the nation, scared by the prevailing turbulence in our society, desires above all else. Stabilitity is too equated with perpetuation of an unpopular status quo. If a cohesive central leadership accelerates, without fracturing thebasic eocohesion of our people, overdue changes in our society and economy then a stable government will have served its purpose. If stable government retards reforms and aggravtes intra-party contentions and confrontation then there would be no real stability at the Centre. Bearing in mind this two-fold aim, the Congress party could not have had a better leader than Narasimha Rao at this juncture. The nation is tired of stridency in utterances of persons in authority, of artificially aggravated societal conflicts, of political adventurers forming caucuses not only in the congress but also in almost all parties. The Congress in its long years in office allowed its lower level organisation to shrink, leaving a vacuum to be filled by the political parveun. New groups have grown, led by persons with criminal prophesities. These fill the emptiness created by the denial of normal part activities by the Congress at district and grass-roots level. Narasimha Rao's appointment as the Congress leader may well mean that the decline of the organisation would be arrested, the Congress would rediscover its own party constitution and learn to act on its democratic precepts. Were this to come about in the party's affairs, this would be no mean gain because the eclipse of the Congress in many parts of the country has left a void which is currently being not by alternative parties but by local bulkies and the reactionary rich. To link Rao's appointment with the hope that this would arrest the Congress's further decline is not to state a non sequitur. Mr Rao is no scion of a great political family, though he has loyally served the leaders thrown up by the country's most illustrious political and the previous generations of self-sacrificing leaders. He remembers a great deal: he has in his persona the admirable trait of the previous generation of leaders-their self-restraint, capacity to submit themselves to the requirements of public weal, and unwavering faith in pan Indian nationalism. These common attributes helped to create a political leadership to be found in all parts, providing a political intelligentsia to be found in all parts, providing a political intelligentsia (or call it elite), without which post-independence stability and all round development could not have been achieved.[3] The physical demise of this leadership, which has not been supplanted by moder, patriotic, disciplined and younger leaders, is at their root of today's political crisis. Rao's elevation holds out the promise that the rootless whizz kids and adventures would either have to withdraw from the field or learn to climb the party leader by stages.

Narasimha Rao would be the first Prime Minister from a South Indian State. Uttar Pradesh, home of all but one Prime Minister, has voted itself our of the race. In any event, this absurdity of looking for the Prime Minister in UP alond had been carried to the point where the practice was being seen as dicrimination. Biju Patnaik, no stranger to the politics at the centre, outspokenly attacked this pernicious convention as extrapolating UP's problems in the affairs of the rest of the country. Rao's selection reverses this untenable convention. Prime Minister must be chosen on merit, though in real life a leader without a strong following in the party is most unlikely to fill this office. In this case, Narasimha Rao happens to have had support from partically all States, including those elected from the north eastern States on the Congress ticket. Rao will need a strong team. The internal situation is so grave that he might want to have a leader of Pawar's stature at the Home Ministry. Rao taken upon himself the arduous burden of running a government in a crisis ridden country of a time when his party has failed to secure an absolute majority. He has made a policy statement, opting for the Gandhi Nehru frame work of policy. His strong emphasis on this, and his non abrasive and conciliatory style should make it possible for him to secure a large measure of cooperation from non-BJP parties occupying the opposition benches. He has had good rapport with the Left wing parties, this should help him moderate the contentious issues which are bound to reappear in the tenth Lok Sabha. The country would wish him well.[4] Purely, in personal terms, it is not quite appropriate to compliment him on his elevation to this high office. He had not sought it. Circumstances have thrust it on him. His selection has been a wise choice.

In electing the senior party leader and experienced administrator, P.V. Narasimha Rao, as the leader of the parliamentary party, the congress has taken the first step towards a healthier political exisitence. Even if the insistence on a "consensum" rather than a contest might suggest a shying away from what should be normal democratic practice, the anxiety to avoid the overtones of a direct contest is understandable. First, the Congress is only now emerging from theprotective cocoon of the Nehru-Gandhi dynasty, a treansition that is particularly painful, forcing as it does the centry-old organisation to come to terms with the blunt fact that it will have to redefine its identity in the context of contemporary political realities. Second, given that the Congress has failed to get an absolute majority in this election, having been nearly decimated in the two key states of the Hindi heartlend, Uttar Pradesh and Bihar, it can ill afford to present the image of a house divided just as it is preparing to form a minority Goivernment. Thus the Maharashtra Chief Minister, Sharad Pawar, a powerful contender for the top post gave in with good grace, clearing the way for the consensus candidate, Narasimha Rao. We congratualte Rao in his well deserved selection. Having been a senior Minister in the Governments of Indira Gandhi and Rajiv Gandhi, and for the most part possessing a record of sober political counsel on the several critical issues, Mr. Rao is the best person to lead the party at this juncture. Which it might be held against him that he does not have a mass base to speak of, in this favour is the point that in contrast to the strong currents of opposition that the candidacies of various faction leaders are bound to evoke, Rao's choice will be reatively non- controversial, thus ensuring a good measure of stability for his leadership. Rao's election creates a record of sorts in the fact that he is the first Congress (I) parliamentary party leader from outside the State of Uttar Pradesh. This is certainly a healthy symobolic touch for the fedral character of the polity.[5]

Having been entrusted with the leadership of the post-dynasty Congress. Rao has aqu unique opportunity to restructure the organisation's democratic traditions and structure. The organisational elections which process was interrupted by the announcement of general elections must be taken up again. The other crucial aspect of the internal democracy which was so visibly absent in the era of Indira Gandhi and Rajiv Gandhi-iof involving a wider range of political counsel within the party on several key decisions-must be reactivated.

Narasimha Rao takes the centrestage at a particularly critical moment in this country's political life. The frustrating verdict of Election 91 has injected an element of instability into the present context, given that the minority Government of the Congress cannot embark on a very ambitious programme without the support of the Opposition. For the moment, the National Front- Left combine have said that they would prefer to sit in the Opposition and give support on certain issues. While one might understand the "political dilemma" that these parties face, as V.P. Singh put it the other day, it must be pointed out that the country is passing through a very critical period and the search for a "consensus" on issues relating to national security, national unity and law and order cannot be dismissed as a cliched political response. Too much is at stake for the country to be satisfied with the promise from the National Front and its Left allies that they will support the Government on certain issues. The National Front and the Left should consider very seriously the suggestion that they join the Congress in a coalition Government. True, it might mean surrendering their own political interests and putting the national interest firt. But the country needs a respite from the abrasive accents of the politicking of the last two years and the best healing touch would be for the Congress to sit down with the National Front and the Left to work on a point-by-point agreement on the agenda of the new Government. The implications of the challenge of the BJP are far too serious to ignore. The bruising events of the last two years which started with the unlocking of the gates of the main structure of the Babri Masjid-Ramajanmabhoomi complex and culminated in the Rath Yatra and its aftermath of a crescendo of communal violence have badly frightened the minorities. The first priority is to reaffirm the commitment to a secular polity, in tones that are loud and clear. Several hard decisions await the new Government-on Punjab, Kashmir and Assam. On the various secessionist threats. On the economy, where politically sensitive choices will have to be made such as having to go to be nimble in its response to what is fast becoming an alarming deterioration of the law and order situation. Rajiv Gandhi's assassination highlighted dramatically the vulnerability of this country and its leadership. The new Government will have to painstakingly grapple with each and every implication of this horrifying event in terms of reexamining certain policy courses and goals in the arena of national security.[6]

We urge Rao and the Congress to invite the National Front-Left combine to join a coalition Government which can bring the requisite confidence and support to the decisionmaking process at a crucial period. The last two years have demonstrated how the national interest was held hostage by partisan considerations. Issues as critical as Punjab have been politicised. If the Congress is serious about seizing this opportunity to present itself as a party that can govern, its first task should be to obtain a national consensus on the major issues involving national security, national integrity and the economy and to start implementing that collective resolve.

There can be no doubt about the genuineness of the consensus which led to P.V. Narasimha Rao's election as the leader of the Congress Parliamentary Party on June 20, 1991. Unlike on most earlier occasions, it was ascertained through a verfiable procedure and in an ambience of openness, which in turn perhaps owed much to the demand for an election raised by supporters of Sharad Pawar. While welcoming this development and hoping that it paves the way for the restoration of democracy in the internal affairs of the Congress, it is difficult not to recognise the fact that Narasimha Rao received the support of the majority of Congress MPs because he is considered to be amenable to external influences and therefore capable of being manipulated by the party bosses and the infamous "coterie". it remains to be seen whether he rises above his image. Meanwhile, it does not require clairvoyance to conclude that following the example set in Delhi, such Congress Chief Ministers as am may be elected in the near future in the states ruled by the party, will also tend to be pliable. The matter could have been dismissed as internal to the party and no outsider's business. But the point needs to be made in the extremely difficult circumstances in which India finds itself today. The economy is in a mess. The balance of payments situation has perhaps never been a critical. Violence continues unchecked in Punjab and Jammu and Kashmir. Harsh decisions will have to be taken to pull the country out of the mire. Some of these, like the lifting of subsidies on fertilisers and power for agriculture, will provoke sharp protests and perhaps violent demonstrations. To cope with such situations, Rao will not only have to be firm but, given the minority, status of his government, able to carry a section of the opposition with him. For this and for the sake of his own credibility as well as of good government, he should try to distance himself as far as possible from the "coterie" and its malodorous members.[7]

After spending over a year and a half on the opposition benches, the Congress is all set to return to power at the centre. That its leaders are somewhat excited at the prospect of the party forming the government again is understandable. But they all need to remember that with power comes a great deal of responisibility. The electorate has shown a tilt for the Congress with the hope that it will be able to provide a stable government. Living up to the people's expectation would call for unity in the party as well as its capacity to select a leader who can take the entire party with him and provide an effective government to tackle such serious issues as the economic crisis, Punjab and Kashmir. The

Congress Parliamentary Party need not worry about the fact that there are several aspirants for Prime Ministership. The main question is whether the CPP can choose one of them as its leader without ruffled feelings. There are only two ways to choose a leader: by a consesnus or by an election. There are plus and minus points in both approaches. Selecting a leader by consensus will be the best course provided it does not amount to the imposition on the party of someone who in effect is a nominee of a small group. A consensus needs to be evolved by widest possible consultations and whosoever is selected in this way should reflect the wishes of most sections of the party. If such a consensus cannot be evolved then the Congress Parliamentary Party should not shy away from electing a leader by a secret vote. Choosig a leader by a secret vote is democratic and whoseover wins should be given cooperation by all leaders of the party including the losers. Also, elections of the leader by a secret ballot need not be regarded as an attempt to disrupt party unity. The Congress after all chose Indira Gandhi its leader by a secret ballot and political parties in other democratic countries do it quite often. What matters is the willingness to accept the outcome of the exercise. The Congress has also to start thinking about how best it should goven the country. The party does not enjoy a clear majority in the new Lok Sabha and unless it can muster the support of another group or a party it will find it difficult to provide a government that can pull the country out of the mess it is caught in Congressmen have perhaps to give up their traditional resistance to sharing power with others. If the Congress party feels it cannot form a viable government on its own it should not hesitate in inviting either the Janata Dal or the Left parties to join a coalition led by the Congress. At the same time neither of the two parties should resist such approaches when made. Some of the pre-election rhetoric has to be forgotten by all in national interest. The overriding factor that should matter is that the new government must last its full term without any worry about its survival. The country afford to have elections every alternate year.[8]

Most political parties centred on one person generally faced difficulties in sorting out the succession question. The Congress Party could have got caught in this problem after Rajiv Gandhi's assassination, but it has succeeded in resolving the leadership issue without much trouble. Credit for this should go to P.V. Narasimha Rao who has been chosen as the leader of the Congress Parliamentary Party, and Sharad Pawar, his main challenger who preferred party unity and stability to his keenness to be Prime Minister. The Congress Party does not enjoy majority in the Lok Sabha and a split over the issue would have made the task of forming the government difficult. Rao will now be able to form a government, hopefully stable with the support of other groups. On Rao's shoulders lies tremendous responsibility. He is taking over as Prime Minister at a time when the country is caught in a serious economic crisis and when Punjab and Kashmir questions require urgent attention. He is a sober man and has a fund of experience of heading such key ministers as Home. Defence and External Affairs. He, however, enjoys the reputation of one whoo would analyse the pors and cons of a problem well, but would leave the decision to others. He has to provide a decisive leadership to his government making it clear that he is going to reflect the wishes of his party and the Council of Ministers and not of a coteire of men who like to exercise power from behind the scenes. A hung Parliament as well as the serious problems facing the nation would require sustained efforts by Rao to take others in the party along. He will also have to ensure that there are regular and meaningful consulations with other political parties so that a national consensus can be evolved on the economic crisis, Punjab and Kashmir. Successive governments have failed in evolving such a consensus on key issue during the last few years and this has proved costly for the nation. The first move in this direction has to come from the new Prime Minister.[9] Rao also needs a team of competent ministers to help him. His Cabinet should have the best talent available in the party, representative of all sections. But it will be important that competence more than loyalty is used as a criterion for finding ministers. Much will also depend on his willingness to restore the forgotten, but essential, principles of parliamentary form of government where major decisions are collectively taken by the Cabinet.

It was typical of the Congress that it gave the impression that of being in the throes of a grave crisis over the leadership issue before the choice finally fell on someone who, on hindsight, was the obvious persons from the beginning. The reason for the feverish activity, however, which preceded Thursday's meeting of the parliamentary board was the entirely legitimate ambition of diffirent senios leaders to win the coveted prize. There is nothing wrong with such an expression of a healthy democratic temper, although in the Congress it seems to arouse the visions of a split. It is also possible that the intensity of the campaign was the result of the party's new-found freedom of action. Having abdicate their responsibility in playing a role in the question of determining the party's leadership and policies to one family all these years, the Congress politicians may have found the less constrained atmosphere after Rajiv Gandhi's death almost like a heady tonic. The fact that there were quite a few contenders for the top post in spite of Mr. Narasimha Rao's earlier selection as the party president also indicated that the Congress (I) has still retained, men of both talent and the necessary drive despite the manner of its functioning from the early seventies. That Sharad Pawar should have been one of them is hardly surpirsing. In a way, he represents the archetypal Congressmen. Sharad and seemingly competnet, with a chequered background who is known to enjoy the support of a section of businessmen. The party's fine showing in his home State was clearly a point in his favour unlike N.D. Tiwari's case. But it was probably Pawar's peripatetic past which spoilt his chances, for if there is one factor which had assumed crucial imortance in Congress politics since Indira Gandhi's time, it was the concept of unfinching loyality, the willingness to stand by the party's leadership through thick and thin. There is little doubt that Mr. Narasimha Rao demonstrated this ability in full measure, even if it seemingly placed him in the ranks of those subservient yes- men who surrounded their leaders like shadows. And it is exactly this test which Pawar failed, not only because he had once left the party and could return to it only after Indira Gandhi's death, but also because he always gave the impression that he could do so again. It goes without saying that while Pawar's elevation might have seemed on the surface to be the victory of a pragmatic man in tune with the volatile times, it would nevertheless have introduced an element of instability into the political atmosphere. But the unsimiling man from Andhra Pradesh is totally different and, although he lacks the Maharashtra Chief Minister's political base, his tenure in unlikely to be marked by any wild flutuations in matters of policy and attitudes. It is perhaps this realization which made the partychoose him, for the prime need of the hour is the induction of a sense of stability based on the Congress's close ties with jittery allies and determined approach to the various critical problems in both the domestic and foreign field.[10]

The scholar-statesman. Pamulaparti Venkata Narasimha Rao could not have asked for a greater challenge than leading the Congress Party and also holding Premiership at this crucial juncture. His suave and sophisticated exterior hides a tough inner personality that was shaped by strong political, economic social convictions in an eventful political career spanning five decades. He always sought and handled with tremendous skills and finesse tasks that many would prefer to avoid. He brings to his new assignment as Prime Minister a wealth of experience as a lignuist, journalist, scholar, lawyer and a successfull administrator. He distiugished himself in every field of interest, be it literature or diplomacy. Rao, popularly known to his friends and admirers as "PV" shot into fame with his land reform measures as the Chief Ministers of his native Andhra Pradesh. Unmindful of the repurcussions and threat to his own self and career, he went about formulating a realistic land reform policy which made the masses extremly happy and the landlords angry. He was warned by many that his land reeforms would cost him his job. But Rao was determined to implement the land reforms with the support of Indira Gandhi who was then the Prime Minister. As the revolutionary measures were implemented he saw to it that in the Assembly elections in 1972 nearly 75 per cent of the Congress tickets were given to candidates from the Scheduled Castes, the Scheduled Tribes and the backward classes. The two measures won for the party an unprecedented number of 220 seats in an Assembly of 270. This electoral success was the beginning of his political troubles. Landlords and vested interests who saw in him a relentless reformer decided to strike before he went ahead and implemented the land reforms fully and then undertook the urban land ceiling he had on his hand. The agitation against the land reforms took the shape of the separate Andhra agitation which turned violent eventually forcing Rao to tender his resignation. That marked the end of a 20-year stint in the legislative Assembly where the represented the Manthan Assembly counstituency.[11]

What are Narasimha Rao's chances of becoming leader of the Congress Parliamentary Party in case the Congress is voted to power?

I have answered this question times without number. We are at a stage when a new Congress President has been elected. I am starting my campaign tomorrow. I will not come back to Delhi till the campaign is over, except for a few hours now and then. This is the stage. Why do we have to jump the gun and start asking questions as to what is going to happen after a fortnight or after a few weeks? I would appeal to you not to do this because, number one, you are not going to get a categorical answer from me or from anybody in the Congress. The Congress Parliamentary Party is going to be formed after the election. It is that body which has the right, the power and the privilege to elect its leader. How do I know as to whom is it going to elect as its leader? My request to you is not to raise the question. It is a question which does not arise at this stage.[12]

Prime Minister, Narasimha Rao, attended his office in South Block for about 90 minutes on June 21, 1991.

Rao had discussions with officials of the Prime Minister's Office, including the Principla Secretary, S.K. Mishra, and the Special Secretary, Surinder Singh.

He broadly discussed with them the agenda for the next few days and asked them to work out priorities and the tasks for the Government.

The Samajwadi Janata Party (SJP) today welcomed the unanimous election of. Narasimha Rao as the leader of the Congress Parliamentary Party and expressed the hope that he would be able to provide a stable Government.

Reacting to Rao's elections at the CPP-I leader, SJP a spokesman S.P. Malaviya said: "I wish Rao very well in the days to come. I hope he will be in a position to provide a stable Government, which may also let the Lok Sabha complete its full five year term.

Asked about the SJP's approach to the new Government, Malaviya said: "We will support it one issues". Malaviya emphatically ruled out the possibility of the SJP's merger with the Congress. "On the contrary, we will go all out to build our party, from the panchayat level onwards," he said.

Jathedar Rachhpal Singh, president of the Akali Dal (Master Tara Singh), today congratulated P.V. Narasimha Rao who has emerged as the unanimous choice for the leadership of the Congress (I) Parliamentary Party.

Addressing a press conference in New Delhi, on June 20, 1991 he said Narasimha Rao was the right choice as he had acquitted himself well in all the assignments given to him by Indira Gandhi or Rajiv Gandhi.

The first priority for the new Government, he said should be to solve the Punjab and Jammu and Kashmir problems. Along with this, the new Government should make every effort to expose the conspiracy behind the assassination of Rajiv Gandhi at the earliest. With this end in view, it should ask the CBI to become more active and also set up a committe comprising three Supreme Court judges to look into the wider aspects of the conspiracy. This apart, the Government should set up a board comprising representatives of all political parties to independently investigate the case.

The Congress could have easily got a majority had there been no dissidence in the party. During the campaigning for the current elections, he had been to Pune and to his surprise found that after the assassination of Rajiv Gandhi some of the local MLAs and the corporators openly opposed the official candidate. In Delhi, the situation was no different and it was his firm belief that had there been no dissidence in the party it would have won at least three more seats in the capital. In view of all this, he sai, the party president should appoint a committee to identify all those Congressmen who had worked against the official candidates. he stressed that strict action should be taken against all these leaders and workers so that discipline is restored in the Congress (I).

The Jatehedar appealed to the Government to provide complete security cover to Sonia Gandhi, Rahul Gandhi and Priyanka Gandhi.

He said this was important because in Delhi "We are safe thanks to God and not the security". He said often persons like him who had been given security cover were provided escort cars which frequently broke down. For this, however, the police alone were not to be blamed.

President R. Venkataraman's decision requiring P.V. Narasimha Rao to test his strength in the new Lok Sabha was a surpirse. This course, it appears is considered necessary. Venkataraman laid similar conditions on two earlier occasions. In December 1989, V.P. Singh, leader of the National Front, was asked to seek a vote of confidence in 30 days and later in November 1990. Chandra Shekhar, was given 11 days. Both of them fulfilled that requirement. In 1989, the President was given a letter mentioning the decision of the BJP and the Left parties to extend "unconditional support" to the National Front. And last year, the Rashtrapati Bhavan communique spoke of the President's prima facle satisfaction "that Chandra Shekhar's group, with the support of other parties could provide a viable government." It listed the names of the parties. This time, there is no such reference perhaps because the Congress (I) is not that heavily out-numbered as the ruling parties were on the two previous occasions. The non-Congress (I) parties have now talked of constructive cooperation but there is no formal commitment.[13]

NOTES :

1. *The Hindustan Times,* 21 June 1991.
2. P.V. Narasimha Rao Talks to Vinod Sharma. *The Hindustan Times*, 9 June 1991.
3. *Patriot,* 21 June 1991.
4. *Patriot,* 21 June 1991.
5. *The Hindu,* 21 June 1991.
6. *Ibid.*
7. *Indian Express,* 22 June 1991.
8. *The Hindustan Times,* 19 June 1991.
9. *The Hindustan Times,* 21 June 1991.
10. *The Statesman,* 21 June 1991.
11. National Heraldn, 30 May 1991.
12. Narasimha Rao in an Interview. *National Herald,* 3 June 1991.
13. *The Hindu,* 21 June 1991.

NINE

CABINET REALISM - THE TRUST TO GOVERN

In less than 24 hours of his appointment as Prime Minister P.V. Narasimha Rao produced a 54-member three-tier Council of Minister which was sworn in by the President, R. Venkatarman, on June 21, 1991 Sharad Pawar, Maharashtra Chief Minister, who, at one stage, planned to contest against Rao for the leadership of Congress Parliamentary party, too, will be inducted into the Cabinet. Three Ministers of State and one Deputy Minister could not be present for the oath-taking ceremony, including them, the new team's strength will go up to 59. The break-up of the three tiers is as follow: apart from the Prime Minister, 14 Ministers of the Cabinet rank, 33 Ministers of State, including 14 with independent charge, and six Deputy Ministers. The first category includes party seniors like Arjun Singh, S.B. chavan, Balram Jakar, V.C. Shukla, Vijaybhaskara Reddi and Madhavsinh Solanki.[1]

The most interesting was the inclusion of Dr. Manmohan Singh, a distinguished economist of international repute for the key portfolio of Finance. Dr. Singh had served under various administrations and till recently was the Economic Adviser to the Prime Minister. New to the world of politics, he will have to be inducted in Parliament in the Rajya Sabha, most probably. A right man for the right job. The portfolios of the new ministers will be announced tomorrow but the Prime Minister told Dr. Singh of his new charge.

In the new pattern of collective leadership in the post-Rajiv era, Rao will be depending on the counsel of senior colleagues, like Arjun Singh, pawar and S.B. Chavan. Notable among the Ministers of state with independent charge are Margaret Alva, H.R. Bhardwaj, Kamal Nath, P. Chidambaram, K. Ramamurthy, Ajit Panja and Santosh Mohan Deb. The other Ministers of State include, M.M. Jacob, Rangarajan Kumaramanaglam, S. Krishna Kumar, M. Arunachalarm, Eduardo Faleiro. Among the six Deputy Ministers are Salman Khursheed and Madam Girija Vyas.

Five of the full-fledged Ministers had served as Ministers of State in the Cabinets of Indira Gandhi and Rajiv Gandhi. They are Madhavrao Scindia, reputed for his competent handling of the Ministry of Railways, Sheila Kaul (Indira Gandhi's aunt), Sitaram Kesari, Jaffar Shareif and Ghulam Nabi Azad, Balram Jakhar was formerly the Lok Sabha Speaker, Arjun Singh was the Governor of Punjab at a crucial time of the Rajiv Longowal accord. He then moved to the Centre as

Minister and later had the distinction of functioning as the Congress (I) vice-president under Rajiv Gandhi's stewardship.

The state-wise representation is unenven, Andhra Pradesh has the largest number eight with the Prime Minister and Reddy as Cabinet Ministers, Madhya Pradesh has three Cabinet rank Ministers, Arjun Singh, V.C. Shukla and Scindia, and Dalbir Singh, Tamil Nadu is not represented at the senior level, though there are four Ministers of State Childambaram, Kumaramanglam, Ramamurthi and Arunachalam. Rajasthan as one senior Minister two Ministers of state and one Deputy Minister, Gujarat, one senior Minister, Orissa and West Bengal two Ministers of State each.

The mighty Uttar Pradesh which in the past provided the Prime Ministers for the Congress Governments and accounted for a big contingent in the Central Cabinets, is pathetically represented only by Sheila Kaul at the senior level, apart from the juniors at the lower tier. For Bihar's representation, Sitaram Kesri, A Rajya Sabha member, came handy to the Prime Minister. M.L. Fotedar and Ghulam Nabi Azad hail from Jammu and Kashmir but were elected to the Rajya Sabha from other states. V.C. Shukla was External Affairs Minister in the Chandra Sekhar Cabinet not long ago.

It was an ambience of bonhomie and goodnatured jibes at the swearing-in ceremony on June 21, 1991. Lighter moments peppered the ceremonial occasion, livening up the atmosphere.

Adversaries were seen hugging and shaking hands, Madhav Rao Scindia and V.C. Shukla, who do not see eye to eyem for one. For supporters of the politicans, few who could man age an entiry into the hall, it was a struggle to get to shake hands with their heroes.

Scribes, guests and MPs-elect, were all bursting with curiosity over the size, shape and composition of the Council of Ministers. The list was a closely guarded secret. For some, it was a pleasant surprise. From among the audience, they walked up to great President R. Venkataraman, thanked Prime Minister P.V. Narasimha Rao and took the oath, all in a daze.

The surprise element would be gauged from the fact that Ms. Mamta Banerjee was absent when her name was first announced. She came to know only through the TV and reached the Rashtrapati Bhavan some 15 minutes later and was sworn in.

Dalbir Singh and Chinta Mohan too were not present when their names were called our rushed in later three persons Rudra Pratap Singh, Rameshwar Thakur and Ms. Tara Devi would not be sworn in Ministers of State.

When another was announced, the Minister to be walked up and began to take the oath. Just than another amn stood up, leading people to think that perhaps the wrong one was at the mike. But a quick check proved that everything was oky.

The whole gathering burst into laughter with even the President joining in, when a UNI reporter got up when the name of Shanta Ram Potdude was announced, people even began clapping fort this "peoples minister", when he made his position clear. He was only trying to move to the back of the hall to talk to some one.

For Mr. Girija Vyas, it was no laughing matter. She had come to Ashoka Hall to be sworn in. But the security staff, unable to identify her, asked her to wait near the entrence. Then one of the securitymen went up to the spefial enclosure and checked the "veracity" of her claim and only then escorted her in.

Fro P.V. Rangaiah Naidu, who found it difficult to get a pass to witness the swearing in cermony, it was a sommon from the Andhra Pradesh Chief Minister, Janardhana Reddy, which saved the day. But for that, he would have been sitting at Andhra Bhavan and watching the ceremony over TV. Despite the fact that a valid pass in his name was sanctioned. The junior staff of the Rashtrapati Bhavan's invitation section played truant. Luckily for him, summons of his Chief Minister enabled him to arrive at the Ashoka Hall in time to be sworn in.

Guests began arrving an hour and a half before the "muhurtam." The first to arrive, other than the officials responsible for the whole show, were the visual media packed into a raised enclosure. And then the long wait, jostling for position.

Then followed the guests. The former Prime Minister, V.P. Singh, was guided to a seat by an escort. But soon he was asked to take the next one. The confusion lasted for a couple of minutes more, while his wife. Sita Devi, kept standing till the matter was sorted out. After the arrival of Prime Minister, Chandra Shekhar and the Prime Minister-designate, Narasimha Rao, the bettery of photographers and video cameramen demanded a group picture.

Some of the ministers took the oath in English and some in Hindi. The Prime Minister, the first person from South of the Vindhyas to occupy the post, took the oath in fluent Hindi.

With the 54-member three-tier Ministry headed by Narasimha Rao, India has, after months of polotical and economical uncertainty, finally got a full Union Government. This in itself is a matter of great Solace to a by a now election weary people. Not only has the election of the Congress party leader, belying the worst fears of most people, been amooth, but the announcement of the Ministry has revealed that the party suffers from no dearth of experience and talent. More than half the members of the 54- member Ministry have been Ministers before. The inclusion of some who were said to be members of the much reviled "coterie" in the Government probably was inevitable, given that they were the Rajiv loyalists and shedding them, assuming that the new Prime Minister was inclined to exclude them, would have sent a wrong signal to the power centres in the Congress party. Narasimha Rao, after all, received unstinted backing of the "loyalists". However, it is well that the new Ministry is as complete as it can be. This should reinvigorate a letharigic administration after months of being in political limbo. Expectedly, the new Ministry reflects the tried and tested style of Congress Politics where loyalty combined with pragmatic political manoeuvring the criteria for the selection of Ministers-The news about the inclusion of Sharad Pawar later Mr Pawar has confirmed this after his graceful withdrawal from the leadership contest, indicates that he does not see his future confied to Maharashtra alone. Prime Minister Narasimha Rao too has said that Pawar would join the Ministry-His inclusion would give strength to the Union Ministry. Factors like community, region and caste have invariably influenced Ministry-formation, this time being no exception. In fact, a tilt away from the Hindi-speaking States implicit in the significant representation from the Southern States in the Council of Ministers marks an important departure from the past. The fact that nearly a third of the members of the Council of Ministers belong to the South reflects as much the shift of Congress strength from the North to the South as the party's desire to consolidate such again. Maharashtra, which has the distinction of returining the largest number of MPs to the Lok Sabha, has not had an adequate presence in the Ministry. By contrast, Andhra Pradesh has more than its due. The endeavour has been to have all states represented, even though the poll verdict inevitably is reflected in the Ministry. If Bihar and Gujarat have few Central Ministers, it is because there are not enough Coingress MPs from these States. The North-East has obtained sufficient representation. Despite that UP sent only four Congress MPs, three have been included in the Ministry. Madhya Pradesh, the only Hindi speaking state where the Congress has done well, has secured a rather large presence in the Union Ministry. Ghulam Nabi Azad and M.L. Fotedar, new Cabinet Ministers are members of the Rajya Sabha; neither has been sent there by Jammu and Kashmir. Overall, the formation of the new Council of Ministers breaks new ground.[2] Narasimha Rao, intending to consolidate, would not have wanted to rock the party's power structure.

The new Council of Ministers, sworn in along with Prime Minister, Narasimha Rao by the President has many experienced hands and some promising new comers to steer the country out of the current difficulties and give it an efficient administration. At the selective Cabinet level, Rao has included senior Congress office bearers like Balrak Jakhar, Ghulam Nabi Azad and Sitaram Kesri. The only non-political personality inducted into the Cabinet is Dr. Manmohan Singh, the eminent economist whose vast experience in handling domestic as well as international economic issues will serve the country well at a critical time. All the other Cabinet ministers have rich experience in the party and governmental wings. The team is strong at the Ministers of State level with representation being given to various states and sections. In refreshing contrast to the recent phenomena of piecemeal cobbling of the ministerial team and administration of oath on an mass scale, Rao was able to present a proper three- tier Cabinet at the very furst opportunity. Each of the Ministers took the oath separately as it should be. The task before the new government is challenging. Apart from combating violence and iterorism is states like Punjab and Kashmir, the social tensions arising from the exploitation of the Mandal and Mandir issues in the past months have to be diffused. Almost the first deciwion of the new Prime Minister was to recommend postponement of the Punjab and Kashmir, the social tensions arising from the exploitation of the Mandal and Mandir issues in the past months have to be diffused. Almost the first deciwion of the new Prime Minister was to recommend postponement of the Punjab polls. If the sane counsel of the Congress in this respect had prevailed earlier, at least some of the incidents like terrorist killing of candidates contesting the polls would have been avoided. On the economic plane, both short term and long-term tasks have to be attended to with a sunse of urgency, reversing the drift of the last 18 months. A foreign exchange crisis has to be staved off. Resort an IMF loan for the purpose would involve the formulation of a set of measures to satisfy the requirements of the international banker on whom we have a legitimate claim in situations like the present. Some of the measures like containment of fiscal deficits and easing of economic regulations would be undertaken by us even other wise. The pruning of subsidies to contain the deficit would involve some hard decisions. The reforms will touch the Public Sector. The planning process, which has been derailed, has to be revived. The Eighth Plan, which notionally is in its second year, will have to be properly formulated. The delayed presentation of the budget would provide the government with an opportunity to indicate the direction of the new economic policies. Mr. Narasimha Rao would no doubt be devoting attention to revamping of the administration, remedying the ills brought about by political interferece in postings and transfers.[3] The style of the new Prime Minister, who does not believe in one upmanship, would suit the requirements of the new political situation. His penchant for arriving at decisions through discussion and consesus would be advantageous in working with an Opposition on whom the government would have rely for parliamentary passage of government business.

At long last India has a government which can be trusted to govern. Many hoes can and will bepicked in the composition of the concil of ministers that P.V. Narasimha Rao announced on Friday. But, clearly, the very swiftness with which he has been able to present has team should gradually dispel the uncertainty which has prevailed in the country since well before the collapse of the V.P. Singh government in November 1990. It should also send out a powerful signal that the new Prime Minister, who has so far enjoyed the reputation of being mild, means business. The inclusion in the cabinet of tried and tested administrators, many of whom boast of a mass base of their own in their home states, should instill confidence in the nation that the Centre is now in surer hands. The four tied council of ministers conveys the impression of a broadly representative and compact team. Most of the regions of the contry have found representation, albeit unevenly. Due weight has been given to social groups, particulary to delits, tribals and the miniorities. Women have not been neglected. The mic of experienced hands and greenhours does not lend itself to controversy. Above all, this is not a top heavy team. The Prime Minister has ensured that his senior colleagues will be assisted by younger elements so that the former can attend to matters related to policy and strategic issues. It can be argued with good reason that the cabinet should have been more proportionately balanced; States like Kerala and Tamil Nadu, which gave the Congress massive civtories a spectacular triumph, is underrepresented. On the other hand west Bengal has no cabinet-level minister at all. The non-inclusion of senior leaders who were associated with Sharad Pawar's candidature must also raise eyebrows for it conveys the unfortunate impression of bias. All this, however, should not detract attention from the compulsions under which Rao had to put his government together. Lacking a base of his own, he had to ensure that he would not have to look constantly over his shoulder to preempt pressures that might be brought to bear on him. By finding berths for those who, drawing on their proximity to the late Rajiv Gandhi, might be tempted tothrow their weight about he has in fact guaranteed the stability of his government.[4] This stable character is sound to be strengthened once he inducts Pawar into the Cabinet. For the moment, however, Rao should be complimented for making the Congress government appear to be a reasonably homogeneous team which is willing under his firm yet conciliatory leadership to attend to the grave problems of the nation without the slightest delay. One excellent pointer to this is the decision to defer the poll in Punjab until September.

New Prime Minister, P.V. Narasimha Rao, has gone about the task of Ministry making in a quick and business like manner. With a 58 member Ministry sworn in immediate past, the new Government is in a position to tackle the challenges facing the nation without delay. In a sense, therefore, the quick completion is to be welcomed after the virtual absence of a credibel and serious administration during the last two years, and more particulary during the Chandra Shekhar interregnum. If in the goverall impression the image of the Cabinet is not particular bright or spectacular, one cannot overlook the limitations that the Character and composition of the Congress (I) parliamentary party impose on its leader in choosing the team, indeed, the Minister does not look very different from the kind of government Rajiv Gandhi would have formed except perhaps for Madhavsinh Solanki who was regarded as an unfriendly critic and the Cabinet Minister-designate. Sharad Pawar, who was seen by Rajiv Gandhi as being diriven by an ambitious to play an active role in national politics rather than remain confined to Maharashtra. Their induction symbolises a mild assertion of a collectiv eleadership in the party, and a move away from the prejudices and inbitions of the past. At the level of the Cabinet Ministers, Narasimha Rao has opted for continuity and all but one are established political figures. A surprise but welcome choice is Dr. Manmohan Singh who with his experience of economic management and wide acceptability is ideally suited to handle the current economic crisis, in particular the loan negotiations with the international Monetary Fund. If in the Ministry as a whole there are 28 first time Ministers, except for a handful, all of them are well known political functionaries who could have been expected to be part of a government. In term of regional representation, Narasimha Rao's Ministry appears morebalanced than V.P. Singh's or Mr. Chandra Shekhar's. The absence of political heavy weights from Uttar Pradesh and Bihar is explaned by the party's rout in the two key states. But otherwise, Rao has been able to draw upon the Congress parlia-mentary party's wide base in both the Lok Sabha and the Rajya Sabha.[5]

The Ministry is its overall composition reflects desire to unify and carry along all elections within the Congress(I) in the post Rajiv Gandhi context. Arjun Singh, the former party vice president and experienced administrator who was also the archietct of the party's impressive performance in the Madhya Pradesh gets the number tow slot. There are established adminstrators which are S.B. Chavan and

Viyahbhaskara Reddy, those like Madhavro Scindia and P. Chidambaram whose performance as Ministers in the Rajiv Gandhi administration was appreciated, high profile party activits and effective parliamentarians such as Kamalnath, Jagdish Tytler and Rangrajan Kumaramangalam, organisation men like Balram Singh Yadav, Ashok Gahlot and K. Ramaurthy and nominees of regional bosses. the coterie and sundry family loyalists are also well represented. The virtual completion of Ministry making at this stage, however, does raise some fears over the minority character of the new Government. The Congress (I) and its allies are 15 short of an absolute majority and some stability would be imparted to the government only if they are able to come to a firm arrangement with the Janata Dal and the Left. The Janata Dal and the parties of the Left have so far declared that they would prefer not to join in a coalition, but that could well be a part of their posturing so as not to seem too keen to rush into a power sharing arrangement. The Congress(I) itself has not made any serious effort to bring them into the government nor does it seem to have tied up any other arrangement for support. The 58-member Ministry offers little scope for expansion and induction of a substantial number of Ministers from other groups should coalition materialise. It remains to be seen if. Narasimha Rao was wise in closing the door a to a coalition government so firmly at this stage.[6]

With the installation of Narasimha Rao as Prime Minister, a new chapter begins in Indian politics. The circumstances under which he has taken the reins of power in Delhi have been both difficult and complex. But Rao has shown his political acumen and pragmatism in choosing his council of ministers. He has thus opened his new inning in right earnest, and with a sense of direction. The fact that he has promptly constituted a three-tier ministry shows his decisiveness which is the crying need of the hour amidst the general state of drift this nation has been witnessing for quite some time. Ministry-making is a tough job even in a normal situation. But Rao has apparently been prompted the larger considerations of cohesive functioning and the need to take the party along on a new course of adjustment and accommodation of varied interest groups. The new cabinet is undoubtedly comprehensive with a number of stalwarts occupying key positions. This in itself should provide positive signals in the polity and generate confidence about the unity of purpose and action among Congressmen as well as in the country as a whole. confidence building has to be a priority item in the prevailing situation in the country which does not have the advantage of the charismatic personality of Rajiv Gandhi.[7]

There are as many as five chief ministers whose experience in the states can be of immense value at a time when the country is faced with knotty problems in Punjab, Assam and Kashmir. There are, of course, some larger issues of centre-state relations which will also have to be tackled tactfully and firmly. The fact that some of the younger ministers like Kamal Nath, P. Chidambaram, Ashok Gahlot, Rajesh PIlot and Margaret Alva have been given independent charge of some of the key portfolios should provide dynamism to the functioning of the government. The inclusion of Dr. Manmohan Singh enriches the cabinet's expertise on national and international economic issues and should generate confidence amongh all those who want the country's woes to be takkled with professional skills, speed and determination.[8]

However, the real challenge for Narasimha Rao lies in knitting the heavyweight members of his cabinet into a purposeful and cohesive team, working together and not pulling in different directions.

The constitution of the P.V. Narasimha Rao Minister shows that the coterie has emerged victorious with almost 50 per cent of the Cabinet Ministers owing their allegiance to it. They include Makhan Lal Fotedar, Sitaram Kesri, Balram Jakhar, Shila Kaul and Ghulam Nabi Azad.[9]

Even among the Ministers of state, there are a number of them who maintain close links with the coteire. They are H.R. Bharadwaj, Santosh Mohan Dev, K.C. Lenka, Balram Singh Yadav, Rudra Pratap Singh and Rameshwar Thakur.

Then there are Ministers who have not only been close to the coterie but belonged to the late Sanjay Gandhi bridgate brigade as well. they are Jagdish Tytler, Ashok Gehlot and Kalpanath Rai.

In fact, a number of Ministers in the MOS category appears to have been chosen by the gang which, controls Number 10 Janpath, residence of Sonia Gandhi. The Ministers falling under this category include Margaret Alva, P. chidambaran, Mamata Banerjee, Eduardo Faleiro, Girdhar Gamango and P.J. Kurien.

According to some party insiders, the new Prime Minister, while choosing his team, has gone totally by the advice of the coterie rather than the Ministers' capability. There are few good parliamentarians in the new team. Most of the prominent coterie leaders, it may be noted, are in the Rajya Sabha. They are Makhan Lal Fotedar, Sitaram Kesri, R.K. Dhawan, and Capt. Satish Shrma.

Narsimha Rao has called the first meeting of the Union Cabinet on June 22, 1991 to take stock of the economic and political situation in the country with special reference to Punjab and Kashmir. A high-level meeting will also be held to discuss the critical economic situation and

Dr. Manmohan Singh has been asked to set about the task of applying the necessary correctives to put the economy back on the rails. Rao attended office on June 21 briefly and held discussions with Principal secretary S.K. Mishra and the special secretary Surendra Singh. The change of Government has expectedly fanned speculation about a likely reshuffle of bureaucrats, but there is little chance that the new Prime Minister will replace bureaucrats for the fun of it. He has a clear idea of the tasks he has set before himself and would like the top bureaucrats help accelerate the process of accomplishing them. There is little doubt theat that certain bureaucrats, who had endeared themselves too much to politicians and were doing their bidding in disregard of administrative norms, shall be replaced. Certain Ministers in the recent past have tried to politicise the bureaucracy and use it for furtherance of their political aims. Such bureaucrats are unlikely to find favour with the new Government. But, by and large, the bureaucracy has welcomed the change and hopes that the new Government will define its goals and assign tasks to officials, Mr. Rao has clearly hinted that efficient, hardworking and upright bureaucrats shall receive his appreciation.[10]

But certain changes are inevitable and the minor reshuffle that takes place will be governed solely by the consideration of putting the right officials in charge of the right departments. It is, therefore, not unlikely that changes will be made soon at the level of the Cabinet Secretary, the Principal Secretary, the Finance Secretary, Information and Broadcasting Secretary and Industry Secretary. The possibility of a couple of bureaucrats being moved from the states is not ruled out. The speed with which new Prime Minister Narasimha Rao finalised his Council of Ministers and the delay in allocating portfolios have let pressures build up among sections of the Congress for larger representations to regions and groups in the party. Some Members of Parliament feel that their talents have not been recognised while others argue that their seniority has not been taken into consideration while classifying them as Ministers of State (Independent charge) and ordinary Ministers of State. The disgruntled elements feel that due notice should be taken of their resentment, but it is unlikely that Rao will undo things in 24 hours, thought his mind is not closed on correcting any commissions. Prime Minister Narasimha Rao will endeavour to carry all sections of the party with him and he is temperamentally unsuited to "coterie" politics. He may seek to correct the impression some partyment have of his being guided by the "coterie" in all his actions. With too many aspirants for too few posts, it is not easy for him to satsify every Congress Member of Parliament. Narasimha Rao is said to be working on reorganisation of the Ministers to make for greater coordination and efficiency in the Government's functioning. A certain regrouping or portfolios is thus on the cards.[11]

Government's first task is formulation of the Central budget for 1991-92, which is already delayed by four months. The Budget will reflect how serious the Government is in addressing itself to the enormous tasks facing it. The Congress Party and, therefore, Rao, who had a hand in drafting its election manifesto, is committed to do certain things in the at least first 100 days in office. Another set of commitments requires to be fulfilled in a year's time. The 100-day programmes include reintroduction and passing of the Constitution Amendment Bills on Panchayati Raj, reserving for women 30 per cent seats or positions in all statutory bodies and committees, including panchyats and nagarpalikas and arresties and, in particular, roll back prices to levels obtaining in July 1990 in the case of diesel, kerosene, salt, edible oils, cycles and two wheelers, electric bulbs, cotton sarees and dhotis, stoves, including smokeless chulhas, new- sprit, postcards, inland letters and envelopes. The party is committed to maintain a stable tax regime for five years in respect of direct taxes, maintain stable tax rates through the fiscal year in respect of customs and exide excise duty duties and exempt profits from taxation, if they are reinvested in low and middle income group housing, highways, roads and bridges, non-x conventional energy generation, school buildings and drinking water supply. It has promised to increase interest rates for small savings, establish a composite rapid action force to quell communal riots, introduce and pass a Bill to maintain the status quo as on August 15, 1947 in respect of all places of worship and to foreclose any new controversy and to establish a Backward Classes Development corporation. Having returned to power after a 19-month gap, the Rao Government realises that the programme is an ambitious one and not outside the realm of controversy, particularly when it comes to amending the constitution or tackling the issue relating to palces of worship.[12]

In an appeal to the Congress president, Prof. Kishore Gandhi, secretary, Centre for National Integrity and Development, said in New Delhi, On June 20, 1991 that the post-elections scenario is unfolding both a challenging and promising agenda for the Congress leadership for taking the country forward to bring to fruition the dream of Jawaharlal Nehru, Indira Gandhi and Rajiv Gandhi.

The two non-Congress Governments have brought India to crucial crossroads during the last 18 months and the sensitive people are looking before and after as to how to arrest the forces of secessionism and terrorism that are threatening the unity and integrity of the country. The country needs a functionally viable Government comprising outstanding statesmen and men of high intellectual calibre and administrative capability. The intellectual climate of opinion revolves around the fact that the Congress should explore the possibility of inductiing Dr. Karan Singh, Sidhartha Shankar Ray and Dr. Manmohan Singh in the Cabinet, Such an effort would give a new outlook to the Cabinet and produce extremely meaningful results", he added.

NOTES :

1. *The Hindu,* 22 June 1991.
2. *Patriot,* 22 June 1991.
3. *National Herald,* 22 June 1991.
4. *The Times of India,* 22 June 1991.
5. *The Hindu,* 22 June 1991.
6. *Ibid.*
7. *The Business and Political Observer*, 22 June 1991.
8. Ibid.
9. *The Indian Express,* 22 June 1991.
10. *The Hindustan Times,* 22 June 1991.
11. *Ibid.*
12. *Ibid.*

TEN

HIS HONESTY AND COMMITMENTS

Warm felicitations came in from political party leaders and organisations on P.V. Narasimha Rao becoming the Prime Minister.

BJP president Dr. Murli Manohar Joshi wished him well. Goa governor Bhanu Prakash Singh said "Mr. Rao's leadership would gear up the nation to effectively meet the challenges confronting it."

Janata Dal president S.R. Bommai wished all success to the Prime Minister who he said "can be depended upon to do full justice to the difficult tasks before the government."

Bommai said being a veteran freedom fighter, erudite scholar, administrator and a sober intellectual, Narasimha Rao can be depended on for doing justice to the handling of complicated problems like the law and order situation and the deteriorating economic crisis.

Tamil Nadu Governor Bhishma Narain Singh extended his hearty congratulations and best wishes.

Himachal Pradesh Governor Virendra Verma assured him of full supprt. Panthers Party President Bhim Singh, who called on Rao, extended him full cooperation in resolving the Jammu and Kashmir problem.

Former Assam Chief Minister Prafulla Kumar Mahanta congratulated the new Prime Minister and assured him that the AGP would extend all help and cooperation to the newly formed union ministry. He said the AGP would not tolerate any divisive forces which might affect the integration of the country.

Former Tamil Nadu Chief minister janaki Ramachjandran also greeted Mr. Narasimha Rao an his assuming office as the prime minister.

Manipur Pradesh Congress Committee and Congress legislature party also congratulated Rao on his becoming the Prime Minister.

Pondicherry Lt. Governor Harswarup Singh said "Your vast experience would help the country overcome the challenges." The All India Newspaper Editors Conference welcomed the election of P.V. Narasimha Rao.

President of the Bengal Chamber of Commerce and Industry Dr. Abhijit Sen expressed the confidence that the new government would take bold economic policy initiatives to pull the country from the present difficult situation to make it a "modern and vibrant" economy.

President of the Merchants Chamber of Commerce C.K. Somany said, "with his profound erudition, long experience, enormous sacrifice and unflinching dedication, Rao will succeed in providing a dynamic leadership to the nation."

D.K. Roy, president of the Bengal National Chamber of Commerce, said the major objective of the new Government should be to curb inflation, tackle the foreign exchange crisis and finalise the 8th five year plan without further delay.

Meanwhile BJP leader L.K. Advani, described the size of the ministry "outsized the proportion of minority government."

The All-India Shaheed-E-Azam Rajiv Gandhi Workers. Command Force on June 20, 1991 welcomed the unanimous election of P.V. Narasimha Rao as the leader of the Congress Parliamentary Party.

In a statement its chairman, Anwarul hassan expressed hope that with Rao's elevation the party would be able to provide a stable Government at the Centre.

Describing Rao as the talented and efficient leader, Mr. Hassan said that he in his meeting with the new leader urged him to tame "talented men in the cabinet."

Wishing Rao well in the days to come Mr. Hassan also expressed the hope that "Rao will be in position to provide a stable government which will let the Lok Sabha complete its full five year term."

Hassan said that he told Rao about the post-election scenario which was "unfolding both a chellenging and promising agenda for the Congress leadership for taking the country forward in order to bring to fruition the dream of Jawaharlal Nehru, Indira Gandhi and Rajiv Gandhi."

He said that the two non-Congress Governments have brought to "cross-roads in the last 18 months". And therefore the sensitive people were looking up to the Congress to "arrest the forces of secession and terrorism that are threatening the unity and integrity of the country.

Meanwhile, Standing Conference of Public Enterprises (SCOPE) in a statement welcomed the election of P.V. Narsimha Rao as the leader of the Congress Parliamentary Party and the Prime Minister of India.

Extending his felicitation to Rao and his council of ministers, Moosa Rajza, Chairman (SCOPE), said that with Rao as the Prime Minister, the stage has now been set for a stable and active government to take charge. He hoped that with his rich and varied experience as a statesman, the country would make all round progress and development.

He said that the Congress Party in its manifesto has already recognised the crucial role that the public sector has played in the growth of economy, industry and employment.

The All India Congress Committee (Kisan Congress) Vice-Chairman, Romesh Sharma, expressed his jubiliation over Rao's unanimous election to captain the nation during the hour of crisis.

He said Rao would fulfil the gap left by Rajiv Gandhi and take India into the realms of unity, integrity and prosperity.

The Hindustan Andolan and the Lok Swaraj Andolan welcomed the verdict of the people and hoped that the Congress Party, which has won the largest number of seats, would be able to form a stable Government on a permanent basis to enable it to effectively tackle the serious political, economic and social problems facing the country.

The Andolan expressed its happiness that the new Prime Minister, P.V. Narasimha Rao, was a person noted for his intellectual" attainments and honesty.

Delhi Pradesh Congress Committee president, Prem Singh congratulated P.V. Narasimha Rao, on his being elected unanimously the leader of the Congress party in parliament and also his becoming the Prime Minister.

He, a statement expressed his fervent hope that under the able leadership of Narasimha Rao, the cvherished dreams of Rajiv Gandhi for a new strong India would be realised. Also the nation would lead towards the path of all round development prosperity and its pestige in the comity of nations would be restored.

Prem Singh said that the unanimous decision of the Congress Parliamentary party has once again proved that the Congress was the only party which is a savious of democracy in the country and is totally united.

He, on behalf of the DPCC assured the new leader of the party. fullest cooperation of the entire Delhi Congress.

The Bombay Stock market welcomed the government of PV Narasimha Rao with cautious optimism.

The market seemed set to return to a bull phase after a long spell of uncertainity due to the Gulf war, political instability and the foreign exchange crunch.

Stocks opened substantially higher today and the BSE sensitive index opened 35.10 points higher at 1371.85 and the BSE national index 11.71 points higher at 666.17.

However, the news of Pranab Mukherjee, not being inducted, was one of the resons for stocks to react sharp by mid-session. This saw the sensitive index declining to the day's low of 1353.32 points and the national index to 662.41 points. But, they regained and the sensitive closed at the current year high of 1361.72 points, showing a net gain of 24.97 points, while the national closed with a gain of 9 points at 663.46.

On the kerb, late evening, Reliance Industries was quoted Rs. 151/152, Tata Steel Rs. 192/193, ACC Rs. 2,600/2.610 and Great Eastern Shipping had buyers Rs. 57/58.

Induction of the former RBI governor Dr. Monmohan Singh has raised hopes that he would be given the finance protfolio.

The market is looking forward to the fiscal budget, expected to be announced July-end and successful negotiation of the IMF loan to tide over the foreign exchange crisis. However, although current trading sentiment in the stock markets has improved slightly, profit-booking at higher levels continued.

Institutional investors are expected to take a decision whether to make substantial investments or continue supporting the market at lower levels, which they have been doing past couple of months. Their decision is expected to be taken within a fortnight, when institutional funds are expected to start getting indications on the impending budget, early July.

Although profit-taking was seen in a few scrips, many stocks posted good gains. Shipping shares were in the limelight.

PHD Chamber of Commerce and Industry (PHDCCI) president S.S. Kanwar has welcomed P.V. Narsimha Rao as the new prime minister, and hoped that with his varied experience, the government would pursue pragmatic economic policies to put the economy back on rails.

Kanwar has advocated bold and innovative decisions, a dynamic liberalisation policy, abolition of the MRTP Act, sale of equity shares of profit making public sector under-takings to the public, and an aggressive role for the private sector.

He also appealed to all the parliamentarians, irrespective of their party affiliation, to accord the highest priority to bail out the economy from its present crisis.

The PHDCCI Chief lauded the emphasis on higher productivity by all regional and national parties in their manifestores.

While felicitating P.V. Narasimha Rao on his becoming the Prime Minister of India, heading the new council of Ministers, L.K. Modi, president, North Indian Chamber of Commerce and Industry, said: "The rich and varied experience of Rao would give the country a strong leadership, a stable Government and a new policy thurst."

Modi said that Rao combines himself with matured pragmatism and wisdom which have helped him to forget a vision about the future.

Modi felt that the new Government should give the importance to economic policies and would-create a conducive atmosphere for furtherance of industrial growth, trade and exports. The nation has to forge ahead in many sectors and has the potencial to become an international player in many commodities and services, he said.

He extended the support of the business community to the new Government in its efforts towards striving a new dynamic, liberant and futuristic India.

Dhruv M. Sawhney, president, CEI, on behalf of the 2,6000 member companies, drawn from all sectors of Indian industry, small, medium and large, private and public sector, has extended to Narasimha Rao felicitations and best wishes on his assumption of the august office of the Prime Minister of India.

The CEI suggested that a massive, united effort was required to put India on its normal development and growth path and, in particular, the combined efforts of Government and industry, under the leadership of the Prime Minister, could be crucial to achieving this objective. The CEI has pledged to the Prime Minister its fullest support.

A meeting of the office bearers of the INTUC under the presidentship of G. Ramanujam also congratulated Rao on his election as the leader of the Congress (I) parliamentary party and welcomed his formation of the Government.

Dr. B.K. Modi, chairman and president of Modi Group of Industries, in his message said that the industry had a great hope in the Congress (I) and looked forward to the thrust it had received under the care of Rajiv Gandhi and also hoped that the party's manifesto with regard to liberalization, disinvestments and deregulation would be implemented whole-heartedly.

Chief Minister of Mizoram, Lalthanhawalah, today offered his felicitations to P.V. Narasimha Rao on his assumption of office as Prime Minister.

In a message, the Chief Minister expressed hope that "with his intellectual acumen, vast administrative experience and deep commitment to the service of the country, Rao would be of the country. Rao would be able to give the type of service, which the nation badly needs."

In Hyderabad, the Andhra Pradesh BJP chief M. Venkiah Naidu, said the state unit was "happy" that Rao had becomes Prime Minister since this was the first time that a person from the south and particularly from the state had held the high office.

Naidu said his party hopes that the state would benefit with Rao taking over his new post.

He has, however, critical of the Cabinet formation, stating that it was "oversized, considering the fact that it was a minority Government. Also, nearly every third Congress (I) member of the Lok Sabha from the state is a Minister now," he said.

Himachal Pradesh Minister, Shanta Kumar, congratulated Rao on his assumption of office.

In a telegram to Rao, Shanta Kumar hoped that under his able leadership, the country would forge ahead on the path of progress and prosperity and solve the problems facing the country.

He assured Rao of his full cooperation to the Centre in the matter of development of the State and the country's unity and integrity.

The National confederation of Banke Employees representing over 3000,000 bank employees in the country has also greeted Rao.

In a statement in Hyderabad, P. Lakshminaraiah, general secretary of the Confederation, said it was of the first belief that under Rao's mature leadership, the country would be able to overcome the crisis in several spheres.

The Tokyo-based Organization for Industrial, Spiritual, and Cultural Advancement (OISCA-International) has expressed the hope that Narasimha Rao will be able to achieve the programmes set out by the late Rajiv Gandhi.

In a message conveyed through the OISCA-Indira president, D.N. Sinha, the OISCA-International president, Dr. Yoshiko Nakano, also welcomed Narasimha Rao's unanimous election.

In a message from Guwahati last night, the former Assam Chief Minister and Asom Gana Parishad (AGP) leader, Prafulla Kumar Mahanta, said the AGP would not tolerate the disintegration of the country and would extend all cooperation for the country's progress and prosperity. The AGP had never bowed to divisive forces, he added.

The Nutun Asom Gana Parishad working president and former Home Minister, Bhrigu Kumar Phukan, in a message, also congratulated Mr. Rao, saying that under his leadership peace would be restored in the country.

The Orissa CLP(I) leader, Basanta Kumar Biswal, and the PCC (I) general secretary, Sitakanta Mahapatra, also welcomed Rao's appointment.

Soviet President Mikhail Gorbachov on June 22, 1991 congratulate P.V. Narasimha Rao on his taking over a Prime Minister and said he was well known to Soviets as prominent Indian politician, statesman and a sincere friend of their country.

In a telegram to Rao, the Soviet leader said, "We highly appreciate close friendly ties with India."

Gorbachev also congratulated Rao on his 70th birthday and said he was well known to the soviets as a "loyal associate of Indira Gandhi and Rajiv Gandhi" as well.

Gorbachev said, "our cooperation in international affairs, based on noble principles of the Soviet-Indian Treaty of Peace, Friendship and Coopertion and Delhi Declaration, continues to be an invariable constant in the efforts of the world community, aimed at buinlding a nuclear-free and non-violent world."

Pakistan Prime Minister, Nawaz Sharif, and the Bangladesh Prime Minister, Khaleda Zia, are among the leaders who have greeted P.V. Narasimha Rao on his assumption of office as Prime Minister on June 21, 1991.

In his message, Nawaz Sharif said his "friendly meeting" with Rao in New Delhi, at the time of Rajiv Gandhi's funeral, had "encouraged me to believe that, through close contacts and sincere exchange of views, we can enhance mutual goodwill, confidence and trust between our countries."

The government and people of Pakistan "are also convinced that a peaceful settlement of the outstanding issues would foster normal, good neighbourly relations and pave the way for the expansion of cooperation between our countries to the mutual advantage of both."

Sharif also expressed the hope that India would make further strides in its development effort under Rao's "sagacious leadership."

In her greetings, Khaleda Zia of Bangladesh assured Rao of her country's "best cooperation" to "work together...(with) the friendly people of India."

Nothing that Rao's assumption of office coincided, more or less, with her own coming to power in Bangladesh, Mrs Zia said: "This provides us with an excellent opportunity to work together for further strengthening the existing close and friendly relations between our two countries."

Other world leaders and several heads of state also sent messages of P.V. Narasimha Rao on June 21, 1991, felicitating him on his assuming the office of Prime Minister.

The Bhutan King, Jigme Singyee Wangchuk, expressed confidence that under P.V. Narasimha Rao's "wise, selfless and far-sighted leadership," India would forge ahead towards-peace, progress and stability and continue to play a vital role in the international arena.

The King said he looked forward to working closely with Rao to further strengthen and consolidate the deep and abiding ties between Bhutan and India.

Prime Minister of Nepal, Girija Prasad Koirala in a message, sought Rao's support towards the "very important task of consolidating parliamentary democracy after the completion of the general elections."

He also expressed confidence that the "traditional relations" between the two countries would be further strengthened to the mutual benefit of the people of Nepal and India.

The Indian business community in London has accorded a cautious and measured welcome to P.V. Narasimha Rao's choice as India's new Prime Minister.

The businessmen seem less interested in the choice of the leader than in a stable Government though many of them had a distinct preference for Sharad Pawar as Prime Minister or at least some important position at the Centre.

"It is not a question of preference. We want a reasonably clean, stable Government, and we hope with Rao we get one," industrialist Sawraj Paul told India Abroad News Services.

He said the choice of Rao was "under the circumstances a good solution". He said Rao was a sober man who could work to putting the party and the people together." "The status of Indians is going down, and if this is't done, it will go down further," Paul cautioned.

The people of India, he said, "deserve a better Government than they have had for the past few years." The voter, according to Paul, had shown that he was not satisfied with any party.

"It is a signal to all parties to put their act together. It is the voter who has won," the industrialist said.

Some businessmen said privately they would have liked to see Sharad Pawar as, Prime Minister, "But perhaps the best way would be for both to work together as a team," a businessman said.

Others said they were glad there had been a consensus, but that they would have been happier with a consensus on Mr. Pawar.

Many, however, welcomed the appointment of Rao. Piara Singh Khabra of the Indian Workers Association seeking Labour candidature for the Southall seat, said he had met Rao when he came to Britain with Rajiv Gandhi. He said, "Rao is an intelligent man and I shall support his nomination in the present circumstances."

The Non-resident Indians in the United Kingdom have expressed hope that the appointment of P.V. Narasimha Rao as Prime Minister would bring in political stability in the country, facilitating larger foreign investment.

S.P. Hindjua said a large entrepreneurial and managerial reserve, economic potential and smooth leadership transition exhibiting political stability of the country will enhance the confidence of foreign investors and the NRIs.

The general secretary of the India League, S.N. Gaurisaria, described Mr. Narasimha Rao as a distinguished scholar and an able administrator of vast experience and hoped that he would provide the country the much needed strong and stable Government.

Meanwhile, the British media has taken special notice of the induction of Dr. Manmohan Singh into the Union Cabinet.

The Daily Telegraph quoted Dr. Singh, having said "we have to take control of inflation. We have to modernize and take India into the 21st century as a modern, unified nation."

The Guardian hailed Dr. Singh's appointment as "the most imaginative."

"The cambridge-educated Dr. Singh will be in the vortex of the economic storm breaking over India, involving a $ 70 billion debt, a balance of payment crisis, rising inflation and strong pressure from international lending agencies, such as the IMF, for austerity and drastic reform," the Guardian commented.

In Kuala Lumpur, the Prime Minister of Malaysia, Dr. Mahathir Mohamad, felicitated Narasimha Rao on his appointment and expressed the hope that the existing close and cordial relations between the two countries would be strengthened further under his leadership.

The State department spokesman, Richard Boucher, on June 21, 1991 said that the U.S. was looking forward to working with the new government under P.V. Narasimha Rao.

U.S. Officials and international organizations in Washington are awaiting an indication of the Prime Minister, Narasimha Rao's policies,.

Immediate U.S. interpretation of the decision of the Congress parliamentary party to choose Narasimha Rao as its leader and hence the new Prime Minister of India was that the country has chosen a veteran who may be depended upon not to rock the boat and build a consensus among the disperate members of the newly- elected Parliament.

As seen here, India is greately in need of coping with the difficult foreign exchange situation, which needs resort to the International Monetary Fund and a firm hand in dealing with terrorism in Punjab and Kashmir.

India also needs, for the medium and long term, dynamic, new, private enterprise-oriented economic policies which will lift India's growth rate and thus automatically ease social tensions which are partly due to unemployment and lack of opportunities for educated youth.

Whatever Rao says will give clues to the direction the world's larged lemocracy is taking.

Meanwhile, the Indian National Congress of America (INCA) has congratulated Mr. Rao and called on people to fully support him at this crucial juncture.

The Chairman of INCA Kamal Dandona, said "each one of us owes Narasimha Rao the utmost trust, faith and confidence."

"After 18 months of turmoil and the worst decline in India's econom) since Independence, the people of India have realised that only the Congress (I) can satisfy the diverse needs of India", he said.

He urged all political parties and people to move forward with the conviction that whatever the differing philosophies, India comes first.

The New York Times has, meanwhile, pointed out that the paramount task before the new Prime Minister will be to keep the country intact.

In an editiorial entitled "Why India's Unity Matters", the paper said if chaos triumphs in India, the tremors won't be contained. "Indian disunion would be a clamity for human rights. It would fragment markets and acclerate a regional arms race fed by new rivalries."

"Growth has slackened, inflation is climbing and just servicing foreign debts consumes 30% of export earnings. Opening up an over-regulated economy could help. So can a reduction in an ever rising arms budget.

"But the paramount task will be to keep India intact. New Delhi has oscillated from appeasement to repression but to no avail as communal and separatist insurgencies whirl out of control."

The Times said unless the Congress Party musters support from other centrists, India's secular tradition is at risk.

Enfeebled by its long dependence on a family dynasty, the Congress party has no obvious leadership choice. Its dilemma is sharpened by the turbulent rise of a Hindu nationalist party which is placed second in the voting, it said.

The Times said history suggests a terrible cost if India dissolves. Tens of millions were uprooted and hundreds of thousands killed when Britain agreed in 1947 to the creation of Pakistan as a separate Muslim state. Partition bolstered the claims of other disgruntled minorities.

If Sikh separatists prevail in Punjab and if Tamils gain indepndence, the clamour would spread. Disunion means certain upheaval and probable communal massacres, it said peril has helped sustain India's secular democracy in the past.

"A violent election, interrupted by the assassination of Rajiv Gandhi, has left it without a majority or a visible leader. Hindus, Muslims and Sikhs are mired in quarrels, regions clamour for self-rule, and everyone complains about corruption, the economy had an ossified bureaucracy.

ELEVEN

DEMOCRACY AND NATIONALISM

Our democratic system is surely under strain and people are disillusioned with the sort of vote-bank politics that has been practised in recent years. The world's largest and most vibrant democracy requires quality control. Indeed, the crumbling of democratic institutions can be halted if we seek qualitiative change. The crisis engulfing us is beyond personalities and groups. They have to be handled firmly and unitedly. It needs to be appreciated that the populist politics of mandir and Mandal cannot take us very far. We have the wherewithal to cure the sickness afflicting the policy if we move beyond personalities and think of our common interests in a rejuvenated India. The task facing the Narasimha Rao government is tough. But since people do not expect miracles from him, he has a fairly good chance to find pragmatic answers to the country's manifold problems. Nevertheless, one should bear in mind that the 1991 verdict is a watershed in Indian electoral politics. Not in terms of number of seats secured by one party or the other though that is significant it itself but in the larger context of future trends in the polity, especially when it no longer enjoys the protective cover the Nehru-Gandhi charisma.[1]

We must develop a new surge of impulse and strive to build a homogenous national psyche to struggle our of the against divisive forces which threaten do mismantle the very foundation of Indian nationalism. Wait I have seen in this election is simply unbelievable. I could have never imagined that the Indian society which is known for its adherence to refined values of religion and spiritualism, full of love, tolerance and non- violence should have so recklessly thrown to winds all norms, basic human decencies. Democracies have thrived only in civilised societies, they have never been sustained in societies lacking in tolerance and maturity. So as a Congressman I have to, with renewed vigour, fight back to the last drop of my blook. It is true that for the Congress party, its leader has always been a strong pivotal point in keeping us bound but milions of people in a political party are not bound to each other merely because of a leader. A political party its not religious our a spiritual group comprising men following the will of the spiritual leader. Right from the days of Mrs Gandhi and earlier in its history of 106 years this party has comprised of in whom certain basic values of public life, certain basic values of nationalism have been common. "Whatever the magnitude of our grief and however irreparable our loss in the assassination of Rajivji, it will be the gravest disrespect to his supreme sacrifice if we do not take up the crusade for the values he cherished. There is a lot of disinformation and misinformation about the functioning of the Congress Party and I would like to clarify these misunderstandings. I've already spelt out the basic postulates and ideas that bind us as Congressmen. To us democracy is an article of our faith, the very basis of our party's existence the very way of our life. No question had ever arisen about its democratic functioning in the pre-independence India. After Panditji Nehru took up the reins, party elections were held. Mrs Gandhi suceeded in the same atmosphere. There has never been any restriction an expressing dissent. In 1969, a most unfortunate situation developed when reactionary politcians at the state level were our to thwart the progressive policies of Indira Gandhi. The very peopel who Indira Gandhi supported in the state politics revolted. Had they succeeded the party would have lost its very basis and foundation for its existence. It could never have played a role which it was duty bound to pay in the service of the people. It is true Indira Gandhi was forced to be wary of politicians at the state level who'd derive strength for he and go against party interests to aggrandise their own self-interest. She indeed worked in a system which she had to depend on a few trusted people to manage the affairs of the party-Indira Gandhi with her experience, training and background and perfect political judgement could work in a system which was more centralised. Rajiv suceeded in the same system. But he realised that the system which worked so successfully under Indira Gandhi was not so successful under him. The failure at the hustings in 1989 compelled him to consider evolving a new system. Rajivji vigorously worked to revive inner party democracy by organising election right from the block level and work insistently for the same. We must, as soon as possible revert to total inner party democracy but in the meanwhile I hope all the Congress will make a totally dedicated and determined bid to liquidate the highly dangerous communal forces which are seeking legitimacy in this election.[2]

For much of the time India had a multi-party democracy, but a single party reality. This did not matter too mush so long as the single party itself was 'many parties in one' and each part of it was a reflection of and responsive to one or another major segment to society. But when the one party became the voice of one person and an are for the power play of a clique, the absence of other cridible parties meant that other voic either fell silent or, lacking recognisable forums, reduced themselves and the polity to a babel. The elections in 1989, and even more the present elections have changed all that perhaps for good. Some changes for the better have also taken place recently within each of the democratic and secular alternatives. The Indian Left, learning from what has been happeing in Europe (though actually it was itself the pioneer in some of these fields) has quietly given up much of its ideological dogmatism, while remaining more wisely selection in doing so than either of the two Soviet models, Mikhail Gorbachev and Yeltsin. The Janata Dal, one hopes, has learnt that even a good platform needs a good organisation to back it. Otherwise, it cannot mobilise its constituency. And it need not become more exclusive than in necessary for political clarity; otherwise, it has no way of compensating itself if it loses some of its constituency to a predator. The Congress one hopes, has learnt from its experience in Maharashtra (and the opposite experience in U.P.) that dynamic and authentic leaders in various States and regions are an asset for the party and only and insecure, incompetent or autocratic Central leadership need consider them, to be a threat to its own pre-eminence. The recent tussle for leadership in the Congress may be seen by some to have been an ugly squabble. But it is also a sing that life is returing to the limbs in the Congress. Otherwise, the party might never have got as close to a contest as it did. Nor would the final outcome, Sharad Pawar's acceptance of P.V. Narasimha Rao as the victor, have resulted so much form his assessment of the party's support for the two candidates. The outcome would have been decided through whispered messages carried by half visible operators. If these are signs of depersonalisation and decentralisation of power within the Congress, the Government formed by it might also catch the winds of change just as the reverse happened when the malady spread from the party to the Government. But certain apprehensions persist. How deep is the change in the Congress? And which is the real Congress? The one which really wanted and nearly asked Mrs. Sonia Gandhi to become next prime minister united declined outsightly? Or the one which said there was nothing wrong with a contest for the leadership? A second worry arises form the fact that in the wake of the election results, neither the Congress nor the alliance made a straightforward affort to ensure that the new Government would have a convincing majority in Parliament which should have been quickly attempted by both when the country is struggling to regain credibility in the world of international finance. The effort by each side was to keep the other side guessing in order to squeeze the best bargain out of it. Which each watched through the corner of its eye the Congress tally in the elections returns. The third worry relates to the BJP side of the fence. What filled its electoral sails was partly the winds of public support. But it was also in part the hot breath of the inflammatory campaign of the VHP. How is the BJP going to dismount this tiger[3]

The democracy which we achieved in India after a long interval and by moving on the path of non-violence taught by Mahatma Gandhi, the father of nation has now become centre of Rajiv Gandhi in a massive bomb blast at Sriperumbudur near Madras clearly indicates that it is not murder of Rajiv Gandhi but murder of democracy. Rajiv Gandhi was an outstanding personality of his time and did remarkable things for bringing peace and prosperity not only in our country but abroad also during his short regime. He always made efforts to maintain unity and integrity of the country. He said, "We have to be read to make sacrifice for the sake of India, to strengthen India, and take her for war." He played valuable role in acheving independence and security for the member countries when he was the Chairman of the Non-aligned Movement. His vist to China pledged and marked the commencement of new phase for the development of our bilateral relationship. On December 29, 1988, he attended the 4th SAARC sumit at Islamabad and said that cooperation in South Asia must be formed by this larger vision. He appealed to the members to act with a remarks speed. In India he had also gone through many changes. He took a major step towards the full equality of women in developing their potential for the benefit of humanity. He realised the participation of industrial labour and rural workers in building of modern India. He made an effort to settle Punjab problem on July 24, 1985, in a meeting with Longawal. In all, Rajiv Gandhi stood for democracy, secularism, nationalism, self-relience, stability and partriotism. His assassination was not just to murder him, it was to destroy all that he stood and fought for. He was a great believer in democracy and in the people of India. It is the enmies of our democracy who were out to destroy Rajiv and the democratic foundations of our policy.[4]

India today is the world's largest democracy. The future of democracy in the world as a whole, and particularly, in the developing countries, depends on how Indian democracy fares. When we talk of safegurading the Indian Republic we are referring to the second largest nation-state the largest democracy of the world, comprising one-sixth of humanity. Of the four largest nation-states in the world China, India, the Soviety Union and the United States India and the US are democracies while the Soviet Union is passing through an agonising process of democratisation. China is not a federal state, and neither China nor the US is a multilingual state. Hence, it is no exaggeration to say that uniting thenations of the global into one world will largely depend on the success of the nation-building process in India as also progress towards integration in the European Economic Community of the deocratisation of the Soviet Union. It is against this backdrop that all developments relating to the future of the democratic political-system in India need to be objectively assessed. In this sense, the fate of the democratic political system in India has an international significance. The harsh reality of the Indian polity today is that in the post-

Nehru period, the integrating forces have been weakening and forces of disintegration have been on the ascendancy, though this process developed in a zig-zig manner.[5] What some of the Indian scholars, social scientists and jouralists have failed to grasp is that thetype of turbulence and violence which India has been witnessing in the recent years in the process of nation-state building is not unusual.

No democracy can be run without a strong and disciplined party system. Parties represent the people who are sovereieign but who cannot directly run government perhaps the most damaging weakness of the Indian polity now is its party system, which is undemocratic in the sense that most of the parties do not conduct proper organisational elections and the premier party, the Congress, as had no election since 1972. The Anti-Defection Law was rushed through Parliament in the '80s when the Congress-I suddenly feared the loos of Maharashtra. Its loopholes must now be blocked and its general political purpose made much stronger. Chndra Shekhar violated even the fundamental idea of the anti- defenction law when he took into his Cabinet MPs who had been disqualified by the speaker for acting against the letter and spirit of the law. Couriously there was no storm of portest from the mass media, while the Congress-I in its eagerness to keep the Shekhar ministry, in office as long as it suited its own interests looked on with closed eyes. In beefing up the anti-defection law, members who defect in violation of the laws strict requirements must be immediately dismissed from Parliament. We must also introduce the system of recall, giving the voters the right to recall an MP who has disappointed them bitterly. Defection itself must be made more difficult. One of the most striking aspects of the voters verdict is that most parties have suffered in the states they govern. West Bengal alone has been defended, most convincingly by the Left Front that has reasserted its two third majority in the state legislature had begged most of the Lok Sabha seats. Sharad Pawar has given a tremendous performance in Maharashtra where he has kept both the BJP and Shiv Sena at bay, and has thus emerged as the strongest Congress leader in the country. The pattern also extends to Bihar where Laloo Prasad Yadav has defended the JD fortess. In the rest of the country, the ruling parties have lost ground. BJP's poor performance in Madhya Pradesh and Rajasthan show that voters are more concerned with good government than with religious politics with roti rather than Ram. In Gujarat, Chimanbhai Patel another arch-defector, could not get for his contrived party a single seat in the Lok Sabha. The LDF lost Kerala not because of the "sympathy" vote but for failing to respond adequately to people's needs and demands. In Andhra Pradesh, the performance of the Congress-I has helped TDP to stage a remarkable comeback. Devi Lal lost haryana for the maythem style of politics. In Karnataka, the Congress-I was able to give a good performance but lost quite a number of seats of BJP. In Uttar Pradesh, the impressive electoral success of BJP is larded with irony BJP can no longer make the Ram Temple a political issue. If it determines to build the temple, it is free to do so but if the ries to demolish or remove the mosque, then it will not only betary ananti-Muslim bias but also invite the wrath of the whole country. Tensions will arise between BJP and VHP. The quality of BJP political leadership in the state in doubtful. The BJP leadership will be well advised to send one of its national leaders to head the government in the country's largest, most populous and politically most explosive state.[6]

I do not belong to the pessimist group which feels alarmed at the rise of regional gorces. The rise of regionalism mainly underlines the failure of the national parties, including the Congress to adequately respond to the local hopes and aspirations. Though we have overcome the initial shock and have to accept most of the regional parties as part of the political reality we are yet to fully appreciate new regional equations and postures.

We need to acknowledge that loyal and regional roots do not make a political outfit anti-national. The showing of a regional flag only underlines glaring gaps between local hopes and national perspectives. A happy amalgamation can definitely be evolved from these divergent possitions. I will go step further in asserting that the Indian nation will find its real roots when regional leaders come forward to stake the leadership claim at the national levels. Indeed, for a multi-ethic polity to achieve stable political integration, it ought to be responsive to the aspirations of ethnic groups, including their craving for a real rather than a symbolic share in political power at the levels. This alone can ensure a sense of belonging and stake in the mainstream national politics. The Congress has done its bit. Even other national parties have begun to view things in a large per spective on alliances which might ultimately help to evlove a two party system. Viewed in this context, the BJP's tragedy so far has been that it has mainly confined itself to the Hindi belt. In the present election, it has widened its political base by putting up candidates all over India. This is a healthy development for the party, though the BJP has a long way to go before it finds itself acceptable in different parts of the country.

Perhaps its rise would be faster if it forges alliances with local and regional parties as it has done with the Shiv Sena in Maharashtra. For theoretical purpose, imagine the BJP's tie up with Telgu Desam. This could be a formidable combination in Andhra Pradesh. The point I take to emphasise is that it is obsolutely necessary for Delhi-centric national parties to find their genuine levels of understanding and adjustment for the vitality of India's democratic polity. The unity and integrity of the country is, of course, not negotiable. Looking at the gravity of problems facing the nation, it is absolutely necessary that all patriotic forces, irrespective of party label, or ideology, be firmly committed to upholding national honour and dignity. In the final analysis, what is needed is not the mere survival of the Congress as the dominant party or the creation of a viable alternative of it, but to correct the distortions that have crept in the polity.[7]

NOTES :

1. Hari Jaisingh. Man of the Moment. *The Business and Political Observer,* 22 June 1991.
2. N.K.P. Salve The Spirit of Collectivism. *The Hindustan Times,* 9 June 1991.
3. Pran Chopra. New Hopes and Aspirations. *The Hindu,* 22 June 1991.
4. P.K. Jaiswal. Murder of Democracy. *National Herald,* 22 June 1991.
5. V.D. Chopra. Turbulent Days Ahead. *Patriot,* 17 June 1991.
6. Bhabani Sen Gupta Defeat for Wreckers and Defectors. *National Herald,* 21 June 1991.
7. Hari Jai Singh. A Polity Under Siege. *The Business and Political Observer*, 8 June 1991.

TWELVE

COMMUNALISM, CASTE POLITICS AND SECULARISM

In an interview, Narasimha Rao has spoken about communal darkness engulfing the country after the assissination of Rajiv Gandhi and the BJP has been accusing the Congress for being responsible for this communal darkness. What is his comment? Congress has never been responsible for any communalism in this country. By its very nature by its 106-years old history, service, by its activities and by its programmes it has been anti-communal to the core. This has to be understood very clearly. I emphasise this with all power at my command.[1]

Narasimha Rao on June 8, 1991 has urged the people to defeat communal, casteist and divisive forces, which were out to disturb harmony in the country in the name of religion and caste. "There is no other alternative for the people but to vote for the Congress, which alone can ensure stability", he said. Addressing a meeting of party workers at Sheoni airport on June 7, Rao, without naming any political party, said during the last 18 months the country had been brought to a sorry pass.

He asked partymen to sink their differences and work unitedly. "Where is the parliamentary party?" asked Rao, in reply to a query as to why the Congress did not name its parliamentary party leader. When a newsman asked if Sharad Pawar would be the leader, the Maharashtra Chief Minister, who was present at the press meet quipped "Are you fed up of me?" However, Rao said he could not name a particular person for the post. He also clarified that he was the full-fledged Congress President and there was nothing provisional about his appointment, Rao said the party's policies were clear and would be implemented with continuity. Rao said the people, particularly in the North, have "realised their mistake" by voting for oppositon parties which could not provide a stable Government and the country had to go for the mid-term polls involving a stupendous amount of Rs. 2,000 crore, Rao ridiuculed the Bharatiya Janata Party's claim to provide a stable government stating that it had a following "only in three states of country and had no following in the rest of the country. He said that while the BJP wanted to divide the country on religious, grounds, the National Front led by V.P. Singh, was "dividing the country through the Mandal Commission implementation. Narasimha Rao said in his recent interview that Ayodhya problem could have been solved a long time back if some bad elements had not mismanaged it. I would like you not to misquote me even to me.[2]

Congress President (Narasimha Rao). There is no question of misquoting. In the Times of India interview this morning, you had said it.

I am going to repeat what I told Dilip Padgaonkar of Times of India. My point is this is not an intractable question. I am convinced, hundered per cent, that a solution was attempted. What really scuttled that attempt was the syndrome of certain political parties politicising it for electoral purposes. Number one, the Shilanyas itself should have been a white flag, a flag for peace. The temple was not going to be constructed. But the Shilanyas was to be performed. This was a kind of formula which would have put off the other steps beyond the election. The idea was that it should not become an election issue. Others had other ideas. They precisely wanted to make it an election issue. They would not have it solved it in any other manner. They wanted to garner votes in the election. I have absolutely no doubts about their motivations and it is crystal clear to anyone who goes into the sequence of events as they happened. So, I am quite certain that if this syndrome, politicisation syndrome, is done away with, the solution would not be very far in coming.[3]

Religion has heaped the beliefs, values and attitudes of people in India over the centuries, and to a great extent, this is true even now. Religion as conceived and religion as practised through rituals and dogmatic interpretations shows its historical transition over the year from spirituality to subservience to socio-economic-political vested interests. The communal problem, as it is understood now in India, is one of meeting the claims of the minorities and offering them sufficient protection from majority action. Minorities in India are not racial or national minorities as for instance, they are in Europe; they are religious minorities. Racially, India beign a patch-work and a curious misture, no racial questions have arisen or can arise in India in future. Religion transcends these racial differences, which fade into one another and are often hard to distinguish. Religious barriers are obviously not permanent, as conversions can and do take place, and a person changing his religion does not thereby lose his racial background or, his cultural and linguistic inheritance. It is aginst this background that the goings-on among the various political parties in the newly elected Lok Sabha will have to be watched. There is hardly any doubt that the Bharatiya Janata Party and certain casteist forces in other political formations will be key actors in the drama. There are obviously two options before the Indian nation. One option is that a national government should be formed at the Centre, including the Bharatiya Janata Party on the plea that this alone will bring about political stability in the country. From all indications, it appears that President R. Venkataraman is the main architect of this concept. Whatever may be the subjective and objective reasons which have impelled the President of India to evolve this concept, any move in this direction will reverse the wheels of history and the entire process of the modern nation-state building in India would become lopsided. In fact, it will not incorrect to say that the idea of the socalled national government will give a new stimulus to the move of transforming India from a secular demoratic state into a theocratic state. This will have its chain reaction within the country and give a new boost to revivalist and fundamentalist force in the entire world, and the developing world in particular.[4]

The other option is that all the secular forces in the country unite and provide a stable government. The initiative for this has to come from Congress, the oldest party in the country, and which from all indications will be the largest party. Only a united Congress can take this initiative boldly. The new Congress leadership should spell out a time bound programme for democratisation of the country, on the one hand, and for radical changes in the economic structure of the country within the existing frame-work on the other hand. The Indian Left, the CPI-M and the CPI should come out of their narrow shells and see for themselves that building socialism in India is not on the immediate agenda. The capitalist world itself is passing through a period of transformation. A new structure of the world capitalist economy as well as that of the world community at large is beign formed. As far as stages of economic, social, cultural developments are concerned, the world is not longer divided into two conflicting parts. In future, it may become even more multifarious, polycentric, and at the same time, more systematic. There is every possibility that the non-socialist part of the world may become an intermediate zone between the socialist and capitalist countries. Historically speaking, the objective reality in the given context demands that all secular and demoratic forces should unite to give a lead to the country. But will they do it?[5]

The legendary peasant leader of Avadh in the 1920. Baba Ramchandra had converted Siyaram (Ram and Sita) into political slogan, Peasant activists used this as the form of greeting to distinguish themselves from the Zamindars and Taluqdars. Indeed, the mass use of Siyaram became a form of preasant nationalist protest in colonial U.P. Seventry years later, Ram again provided the nucleus of protest in UP as Jai Shree Ram became the rallying electoral cry of the BJP. But it would be a gross mistake to assume that the BJP's spectacular electoral showing in the just- concluded election was founded entirely on a religious hysteria built around the call to restore Ram to his alleged birth place. Without Ram and Mulayam Singh Yadav's Ravanesque attempt to combat it, the BJP may not have succeeded in sweeping UP, but the party's victory is owed to factors that go well beyond the temporary exuberonce of spirit that generated in the Ram lehar wave. Finally, the BJP has succeeded in positioning itself as an all India party, providing a ready-made national alternative to the Congress. The stunning expansion of its influence is not reflected in the number of seats it has picked up. It is a vagary of the electoral system that it has secured only for seats in Karanataka after polling 29 per cent of the vote; or more strikingly, not getting even one assembly seat in West Bengal after obtaining an astonishing nine per cent of the votes. Through its new found presence in Assam (interestingly, in the Bengali-dominated Barak Valley), Karanataka and Andhra Pradesh, the BJP has finally succeeded in overcoming it biggest handicap-- that it is a party of north Indian Banias alone. Even its claim to being the pre-eminent party of the Hindi belt was questioned, because the fulcrum of the Hindi heartland, the Aryavart, had always eluded its grasp. The BJP was hitherto confined to the heartland's fringes-Himachal Pradesh, Madhya Pradesh and Rajasthan. But now, it is the party of government in Aryavart Uttar Pradesh. The symbolic importance of this success cannot be understimated, despite its mediocre performance in Rajasthan, poor showing in MP and rout in Bihar. Conversely, it has posed a serious problem for the Congress. For the first time in the history of independent India, a party rules Delhi with just five MPs (four, excluding Rajiv Gandhi), from the Gangetic belt. In fact, it is the Congress's claim to being an all-India party which may now be challenged on account of its catastrophic performance in UP and Bihar for a third time in a raw (1989 Lok Sabha, 1990 assembly and 1991 Lok Sabha). Indeed the BJP's real success has been its seizure of the most important component of the Congress vote. Upper castes almost throughout India have evidently voted for the BJP in substantial numbers. Although numerically, they may not be a decisive factor, they continue to be the opinion making segment of India, especially in the semi- urban and rural areas of the country. With the Muslims crossing over to the Janata Dal and the Harijans divided, the desertion of the upper castes-Particularly Brahmins-has cost the Congress dear. The significance of the Brahmin breakaway, too, should not be understimated. Ever since its inception, Brahmins have been dedicatedly loyal to the Congress. As the only all-India caste their stake in India's unity not only has historical roots, but is also crucial to their retaining a position of pre-eminence. The uneasy feeling that the congress is no longer the party which can aggressively protect Indian unity appears to have caused their drift towards the BJP.[6]

Parliamentary democracy has survived the multiple challenges posed by the advocates of one section of society by another also the sinister attempt to disrupt it by the gruesome assassination of its foremost leader. The bomb that tore apart the handsome body of Rajiv Gandhi was a serious attempt to tear apart the system built on the values generated during the struggle for national indepedence. That it was so has been proved by the contemplation in certain circles about stopping the election process and setting up a national government which should launch on formualting a new Constitution. All credit to the wisdom and restraint of the Indian people who neither showed signs of despair and acquiescence to the sinister suggestions nor rose in anger which would have cleared the way to an unprecedented anti-constitution coup. The survival, however, is no cause for complacence. The challenge of distruption has been averted but not eliminated. For the first time in the history of free India the electorate has been approached to support an alternative concept of nationalism That the party advocating it has failed to get a majority in Parliament and form a Government should be no comfort. The country has to think hard how and why the Hindutya protagonists picked up courage to be bold and brash. There has to be honest heart serching any acrimoney-free discussion on who has gone wrong how and where? In would be a clossal tragedy if those who are wedded to the concept of democratic secular, nationalism end up exchanging polemics. That would only pave the way for the success of the challengers. The country is going to face apart from the ideological challenge a serious problem of communal violence. In the course of half-a-decade long confrontation over the Ayodhya dispute the religious sentiments have been roused to a fever pitch. Even the smallest excuse will be punced upon to give vent to volatile emotions. And there is enough of destructive weaponery spread all over the country, especially North India, which can come handy for the marauders and arsonists. Communal violencve has been all through the instrument of communal polarisation. The riots in the late twenties had prepared the ground for lunching the Rashtriya Swayamsewak Sangh. It has won its spurs in the Hindu-Muslim riots that rocked Nagpur in 1927. The partition riots provided it the opportunity to win nation wide recognition as a consequence of which it felt bold enough to launch on political carrer with the formation of the Bharatiya Janata Sangh. Its political prospects brightened up in the backdrop of the spate of riots which stared as a backlash of riots in the then East Pakistan and in the wake of the anti-cow slaughter agitation. It is not only during the run up to elections that communalists resort to violence. Whenever in an election they play a prominent role the elections are followed by violence, no matter whether they win or lose.

This time the RSS cadres are going to feel specially frustrated because the Bharatiya Janata Party had roused high, though false, hopes that they were going to win a majority. If they have been thwarted they are now being told, it is because of the Muslim vote. This situation requires extraordinary vigilance not only by the custodians of law and order but also by leaders of public opinion, more particularly by the political parties. Peace and harmony between the communities can be safeguarded only if the secular parties resist the temptation to indulge in one-up- manship. Special care will have to be taken of the anti-social elements in all the communities. Unfortuantely they have acquired prominent position in the political life. Whatever party these elements may work for during the elections in a communal situation they are taken over by the communalists. The other challenge that the BJP can and perhaps will, pose is of a stricly secular character. It is well known that the economic situation is grave. The treasury was not empty when the Janata Dal had taken over but it certainty is touching the bottom today, whoever takes over the reins of Government after this election will have to administer a rather stiff does of taxation. This plus the conditionalities of the IMF (which seem unaviodable) will cause deep holes in the pockets. The BJP will use its being in opposition to its advantage and try to mount an anti-taxation and anti-price rise movement. For it would be an opportunity to launch a major offensive aginst the economic and foreign policies of the Nehru frame-work of that the signs are already available in the unbridled diatribes of the BJP ideologues and its intellectual supporters. Nehru-baiting and Congress-baiting have been a fashion of late particularly after the enthronement of Lohiaism under the aegis of Janata Dal. The non-Congress parties have been indulging in an unseemly competition in denigrating Nehru and trying to push up lesser luminaries to his level. The rush for putting up the protraits of Ram Manohar Lohia and Dr. Shyama Prasad Mookerjee in the Central Hall of parliament is only a symbolic expression of that tendency.

Post-election scenario will be a testing time for the wisdom and sagacity of all the parties. All of them have had fairly extensive experience of association with the RSS sponsored political outfit. It smuggles itself into mainstream with a winsome smile and kicks the leader at the first available opportunity. Despite this the temptation to do down Congress has repeatedly landed them in close proximity to the BJP. That has been the genesis of the view that Congress is more dangerous than the BJP that Congress is the fountainhead of communalism. It is with such skewed perspective that the Left leaders of Trade Unions included the Bharatiya Mazdoor Sangh for joint action in support of the demands of the working class. The same mindset in responsible for the seemingly innocent theory that communal problem cannot be effectively tackled without involving the BJP. More recently, the promoters of national government idea also wanted it to be included in such a set up. This is not to argue that non-Congress non-BJP parties should merge their identities into the Congress. It is however a plea for changing the style of democratic competition. Genuine differences of opinion on approach to peoples problems are bound to be there but the debate should not be allowed to transgress democratic proprieties and degenerate into mudslinging and character assassination. Fascism thrives when people are despaired of democratic process. Both the ruling party and opposition have the responsibility to save people from sinking into cynicism. Party structures should be revived with each unit developing capacity to deal with problems as its own level. The BJP-VHP campaigns have been able to influence people mainly because the grassroots level organs of parties became weak through disuse.[8]

What has been happening in India, in the name of politics and government making is the mere extension of the inner conflicts and contradictions of the Hindu community. The community has been at war with itself for centuries and the added political colour of the siege within ever since Independence (and perhaps before) has made things worse. Formerly, the war had been at socio- economic levels. After Independence, ever since the majority community was called upon to take over political power, the socio-economic strife that had dodged the Hindu society for centuries, has permeated the political scenario as well. What we witness today is not a turmoil or national churning caused by political ideologies of contradictory natures, but the perenial was with the Hindu society itself. It is for this reason that we have political parties and factions which do not have much differences among themselves. Take for instance, the present three groups which are in the forefront of the political race- V.P. Singh's contraption, BJP's platform or the Congress. The three parties do not differ from each other in any drastic manner. True, they might currently be using some slogans of extreme variations, like the Mandal, Mandir, Stability etc. But we know that they do not mean much by these slogans, and that all the three groups are not going to do much about what they have promised. V.P. Singh would not, perhaps, be able to go in for Mandal whole-heartedly. BJP too will not be able to build the temple so easily as it promises to do and, in fact is may not be able to achieve the goal at all, if it formed government, since any forced construction would endanger the unity of the nation, which is so dear to that party! And we know that unless the ruling party is well organised and stable it cannot give us a stable government. Hence we do not take that slogan seriously from the Congressmen. Apart from these passing populist slogans, these political parties are not very different from each other. There are more commonalities among them than conflicting views and stands. And yet, they have been quarrelling and competing among themselves and vying to form the government. This has caused a lot of political fluidity and socio-economic retardation. These conflicts and quarrels are, as we said, backlashes or rather carry-overs from the conflicts within the Hindu society. All the three major political groups are, in fact, trying to establish their supremacy, over the bulk of the Hindu society. in order to gain political power. Each group does it in its own way. The conflicts and siege within the Hindu fold have been caused mainly by casteism. A look at the way each party has put up candidates for the Lok Sabha polls would elucidate the point. More than political ideology, it is the caste equations in the constituency that have been the deciding factor for the selection of candidates in most places, even in the case of parties which claim to be secular and comopolitan. Even the pre- election quarrels, lawlessness and violence have been mostly casteist wares. Hence if we want to build a truly democratic India, with economic progress as its main aim, the first step should be to free the Hindu society from its internal siege and conflicts. This is possible only if we build up a casteless society. Are we ready for that?[9]

Probably the most heartening aspect of the election results is the unequivocal rejection of the divisive Mandal manifesto by the people. This has exposed the limits of casteist politics and, hopefully, will serve as a standing lesson to all leaders who seek to appeal to the basest instincts of the masses. Unfortunately, appealing to caste sentiment is a low-cost operation and, consequently, holds out a devilish attraction for politicians. From Ram Manohar Lohia to Charan Singh, V.P. Singh to Laloo Prasad Yadav, casteism has been the short-cut to political fame. Again and again, the people have given them the drubbing they deserve, but the pursuit of petty gain made politicians repeatedly succumb to its fatal charm. Much is being made of Laloo prasad Yadav's success in Bihar. True, he appears to have mismeriseed a section of the electorate into believing that a caste was will lead to their emancipation. But hypnotists before him, such as Karpoori Thakur, came a cropper by practising the politics of backwardism and it is a matter of time before the hallowness of the Mandal plank becomes plain to Bihar's electorate. Mercifully, however, the rest of the country has unhesitantingly rebuffed the messiahs of Mandalism. The Janata Dal's rout even in states such as Karantaka has shown it up for what it truly is-a Gope (Yadav) Dal, in the tradition of the erstwhile Lok Dal. But even the Lok Dal was not a single-caste party. Its leader was Charan Singh, a Jat and his endeavour was to create an allien OBC alliance. This time Jats, disenchanted with allegiance to the BJP. Indeed, history will record V.P. Singh as the BJP's principal ally. It was he who gave the party the necessary legitimacy; it was he who enabled it to emerge from the fringes of north Indian politics to become a contender for power in New Delhi. Despite the lip-service he countinues to pay to secularism, he is the BJP's real friend. It was also his casteist politics that created a nationwide revulsion against the Janata Dal, there by eliminating its chances as a possible challenger to the Congress hegemony over the middle ground politics. Even in 1980, Charan Singh's Janata (S) had won 40 seats in the Lok Sabha, 33 of them from UP alone. Compared to Charan Singh's performance, V.P. Singh's achievement is hardly impressive. Without Laloo Prasad Yadav's temporary success in Bihar, the Janata Dal would have sunk without trace. If the party has any serious interest in surviving as a viable political entity, it needs to revise its strategy drastically. It is clear that Mandal will get the party thus far and no further. The self- limiting nature of pure backward politics was in fact, evident to many Janata Dal leaders such as Biju Patnaik, Ajit Singh and R.K. Hegde, but the impression that V.P. Singh is the sole vote- catcher, presented their views from being given the importance they deserved. It is still not too late for the party to make the necessary correction. If that means Laloo Prasad Yadav walking out, it does not really matter, for Biju Patnaik and Hedge do not gain from his presence anyway. But even more important is that the contemptuous rejection of Mandal should alert other political parties against falling prey to the temptations of casteist politics.[10]

Reservations for the socially educationally and economically deprived sections is one thing. Mandal, which seeks to unleash a civil war, quite another. In this moment of the triumph of social unity, praise needs to be showered on the brave students through out India who gnenerated the emotional environment leading to the rout of Mandalism.

The victory achieved by the Janata Dal and its partners in Bihar is nothing short of spectacular. With 39 seats out of 44, the results of which were declared so far, already in their kitty, they have proved how effective the Mandal card is in a caste- conscious State like Bihar. It is as much the victory of the Janata Dal as it is of Chief Minister Laloo

Prasad Yadav, who is the architect of the winning combination. The worst to be hit by the Mandal fury is the Congress-I whose disaster is exemplified by the humiliating defeat Dr. Jagnnath Mishra suffered in Madhubani. Obviously, neither the sympathy factor nor Hindutva had any effect on the voters of Bihar as has been highlighted by the failure of the BJP even to retain the nine seats it had in the ninth Lok Sabha. Nevertheless, allegations of electoral malpractices have nobbed some sheen of the Janata Dal's victory which would not have been possible but for the caste consolidation under the Mandal banner. There is not a single constituency in Bihar where the backwards of Muslims or tribals do not constitute the majority. Besides, the State has for long been one of the strongholds of the Communist Party of India. Thus, a combination of all these forces is bound to be invincible in any electoral context. The Congress which drew an blank lost both on Mandal and Mandir issue with its backward caste supporters goimg the Janata Dal way and a section of the upper castes shifting its loyalty ot the BJP. The ambiguous stand of the party on the Mandal question and the clandestine support some of its leaders extended to the violent anti-Mandal agitation cost the party dearly. And to confound its problems, the Muslims, who dreifted away from the party following the Bhagalpur riots, are yet to return to the party fold. Even the BJP, which has won only five sets so far, could not escape the Mandal tornado which swept the State, particularly North Bihar. It could notch up a few seats only in the tribal-dominated South Bihar where the Mandal card had a relatively muted appeal. However, even there the pride of place was taken by the Jharkhand Mukti Morcha, a Janata Dal partner which own all the six seats it contested. The Mandir issue did not at all influence the voters despite the fact that it was in Bihar that L.K. Advani's rathyatra was forcibly stopped. The BJP can, however, take solace from the fact that it could push the Congress to the third position in many constituencies.[11] Because of the near-polarisation witnessed in most constituencies, third forces like the IPF which had won a seat in the 1989 election could not make any impact. If the Janata Dal has benefited from the alliance, so have all its partners.

The Mandal lobby within the Janata Dal finally had its way in the political affairs committee meetings earlier this week and got it to decide against extending even issue-based supprt to the Congress government at the Centre. Even as Janata Dal leaders like Ajit Singh, Biju Patnaik and Ram Krishna Hedge were arguing for support to the congress government, if not a coalition, Mandalites led by the Bihar Chief Minister Laloo Prasad Yadav and socialists like George Fernandes succeeded in convincing the leadership that it would be the best for the party to sit in the opposition. The decision, which now has been ratified by the coordination committee of the National Front and the Left Front, is reported to have been guided by the consideration that there was no reason for these parties to suddenly abandon their anti-Congress plank at a time when its vigorous propagation in states like Bihar had paid dividends. But the factor that appears to have been determinant for the decision is that the Congress had not even appealed for help largely because its assessment is that the NF-LF cannot dare pull down the government in near future. "The Congress has not even asked for help when it is their responsibility to run the government. Why should we offer ourselves on our own?" asked Laloo Prasad Yadav. All the constituents of the NF-LF are aware that it would be disastrous to pull down the new government in near future and thus the assertion that the two fronts would adopt "a positive approach". In concrete terms, as a senior JD leader put it, it means that "we will perform all the tasks of the opposition and expose the ruling party on all the issues possible, though we will not vote against the government. The chances are that on most issues, we will abstain after registering our disagreement". A section in the JD also felt that they had to face reverses in all but two states because of the absence of party organisation in most parts of the country which resulted in the party's inability to "spread the message of secularism and social justice." This section would want the entier JD attention to be focused during the next few months on revamping the organisational structure at least in states like Madhya Pradesh, Rajasthan, Orissa, Maharashtra and Karanataka where "natural sympathy" for the JD is said to be existing. Advocates of this point of view also argue that the JD did manage to get a good percentage of votes in many parts, despite a lacklustre campaign and the BJP's offensive. This section of the party also appears to be happy with the selection of P.V. Narasimha Rao as the leader of the Congress Parliamentary Party as "it has made our task easier". The fact that Rao is a Brahmin is likely to give credence to the National Front's allegation that Congress leadership continues to be a monopoly of the upper castes. "Had Sharad Pawar become the Prime Minister, things would have been different. First, he just might have accepted the implementation of the Mandal report. Also, his shrewdness and drive might have caused problems for us", commented a senior JD leader. In this context, an opinion also seems to be gaining ground that the party president S.R. Bommai should be replaced by someone like Sharad Yadav who is more clearly identified with the Party's public image. However, it is too early to predict how strong the opinion may become during the next few months. The party feels that the Congress government with its uncomfortable numericals strength in the Lok Sabha would not be able to bring about "much significant change" in the state of affairs wther on the economic or the political fronts. Besides, "if the BJP government in Uttar Pradesh is unable to deliver what it promised in terms of a clean and efficient as well as on the Ayodhya temple issue, the Janata Dal would certainly gain," the party leader feel.[12]

Even as the new Congress government at the Centre looks to the National Front and the Left Front for sheer survival, the contradictions between them on social and political issues, most notably the Mandal report, appear to be far too many for any smooth workable arrangement to evolve. The indications are that haggling will be a regular affair and that only the growing strength of the Bharatiya Janata Party (BJP) will prevent it from pulling down the government. A premature toppling of the government would further empower the BJP in its endeavour of coming to power at the centre. The Janata Dal has made it clear that the new ruling party cannot expect any blanket support from it. The extension of its qualitative supprt to the Congress would depend on the latter's response to its commitment to social justice and secularism. The election saw the Janata Dal's base having practically shrunk-in terms of seats-to Bihar and Uttar Pradesh and the party's assessment is that these are the areas where its plea of implementing the Mandal Commission report and protecting the minorities, has paid rich dividends. The Janata Dal's assessment is that if it has to extend its base, it must be able to contain the BJP and that the only way to do it is split the Hindu votes while further consolidating the support of the minorities. The Bihar Chief Minister, Laloo Prasad Yadav, had been very successful while adopting this approach. It resulted in a sweep of the Lok Sabha seats in the state for the party. Unless the Congress takes a sympathetic stand on the implementation of the Mandal Commission report it will have to feel cagey about support from the Janata Dal, the biggest constituent of NF. However, the Congress leaders argue that their party cannot take a "very unequivocal" position on the Mandal Commission issue because this will result in all the "anti-Mandal votes" going to the BJP. The other assurance that the Janata Dal wants from the union government as stated by Laloo Prasad Yadav is that it would not alow construction of the temple at the disputed site in Ayodhya, in case the BJP government in Uttar Pradesh decides to go ahead with it. But this the Congress may find difficult to concede at the outset. The assessment of the Congress is that its support to Mulayam Singh Yadav contributed to its poor performance in UP. And now, can a party which finds its vote bank seriously eaten up by the Janata Dal on the one hand, and the BJP on the other, afford to take such a blanket position in the absence of any moves from the BJP? Among the parties constitutiong the Left Front, it is the CPM, more than the CPI, which has strident differecnces with the the Congress. The latter has a past record of supporting the Congress on vital issues in the '70s and, by virtue of never having headed a state government, the CPI's perception of the Congress as a threat to federalism is much less.[13]

Such is not the case with the CPM. West Bengal chief minister, Jyoti Basu, has already gone on record saying that the Left would remain in the opposition and that giving issue-based support to the minority Congress government would imply that the BJP would becoem the main opposition party. At the same time, he said the kind of support to be extended would have to be discussed. His initial statement implies that if such a support is given to the government, the LF government in West Bengal may become vulnerable to Congress pressure. Also, his views possibly stem from the fact that it is an imperative for the CPM to let the government function and instead concentrate on reversing its electoral setbacks. The Left Democratic Front in Kerala came in for a drubbin, while by opting out of the Tripura polls, the CPM had made it much easier for the TUJS. Now, having been effecitively contained mainly to west Bengal, CPM's strategy would perhaps see how far it can use the lever of its support to the Congress to reassert itself in these two states. The Left Front has repeatedly stated that before any arrangement for cooperation is worked out, the idea would be thoroughly discussed by the Front Constituents. However, the recent controversy over their participation in the Punjab polls puts a question mark on their claim of unity. While initially both parties had decided to boycott the polls, the CPI later reversed its decision. In the face of open criticism from the CPM on this count, the CPI came up with the justification that the former had ignored its request for a joint review of the boycott decision, forcing it to go ahead alone.[14]

If Uttar Pradesh has seen Hindu consolidation, Bihar is witnessing a sharpening of caste division. Isn't this equally dangerous.

Well, the implementation of the Mandal Commission's recommendations have not quite been along the right lines. It is not a question of just providing some jobs. In any case, the jobs are not there. What is needed is a sustained effort to improve the lot of the backward, to bring them up. Perpetuation of the caste divisions and the resultant tension is not the answer.[15]

A casteless India is an almost impossible dream. Not merely because casteism has become an inalienable part of the Indian life after centuries of paratice, made firm with a religious sanction for it, but also due to the economic divisons effected by the system over all these years. It is impossible to eradicate caste and create an egalitarian society based on equalities of all sorts, including that of birth, because everything in this country is done in such a way that prepetuation of the old vice is ensured. It is ironical, because everybody, even the most orthodox section of the Hindu society, is aware of the evils of the caste-based socio-economic and political system. Every now and then we hear ardent pleas for the abolition of the archaic order, and yet every thing is decided in this country only after taking into account the caste factor. Mahatma Gandhi (and now the newly elected Prime Minister, Narasimha Rao) too, had perhaps understood this national double-speak and that is why he did not make any vehement plea for eradicating the system He was mostly intersted in eliminating the harsh others was marked by this zeal. All the latter day Mahatmas, too, followed the same line. Efforts by various political groups that wanted to win over the bulk Hindu vote were aimed at keeping the Hindu fold undivided at the political level, although at the socio-economic level, it had always been fragmented into two broad groups: the upper class castes, on the one side, and the lower castes, on the other. Reservations were intorduced for the economically bottom line castes mainly with a view to keep them within the Hindu fold by providing to them some compensation for the centuries-long deprivations, so that politically they would fall in line with the bulk-group of Hindi society which wielded political power. It is hardly surprising, therefore, that every political party, first considers the caste equations in every area before putting up the candidate for either a municipal election or parliamentary poll. One party, the BJP, which had very little use of this practice in the past, too, has fallen in line with others these days. The stigma of being an upper caste outfit it sought to be erased by giving tickets to Harijans, Adivasies, and other predominant castes in different areas. This is a double-edged weapon. For it ensures better prospects in winning political power and, at the same time, tries to bring about social unity among the warring factions of the Hindu Societ. The catalyst of this change, however, was VP Singh with his Mandal mantra that had aimed at dividing the Hindu society further on caste basis. That unnerved all parties, including the BJP and the Congress, each of which was busy enticing the bulk support of the Hindu society, in order to gain political power. Both the parties, the BJP and the Congress, have never advocated total abolition of the caste system, not on religious grounds, but it was an easy way to manipulate the much-needed bulk support, with Mandal trying to create a new casteist equation, the BJP and the Congress were trying to counter it with their own populist slogans. The one which countered the Mandal menace would win the political power. The Congress suddenly tried to suppress the socio-economic issues raised by the 'revolt' within the Hindu fold by appealing to nationalistic fervour and stability of government. The BJP took shortcut. It sought to sidetrack the problem of socio-economic origin, that threatened to divide the Hindu vote bank, by finding a religio-spiritual slogan that would transcend the casteist equations, and which is expected to keep the Hindus united. And so, if the BJP manages to win political power, by rallying all the mutually warring Hindu factions under the banner of the Mandir, it would prove that Ram is still more popular than 'roti'. But the question remains: how long will this common spiritual fervour keep the socio-economic problems under the carpet? Unfortunately, there seems to be no end to the dark tunnel in which the nation has been trapped during the past two decades.[16]

The Congress president, P.V. Narasimha Rao, has given a new slogan to the party: "Stability with secularism". In his statement after accepting the decision of the Congress Working Committe elect him president of the party, Rao said in New Delhi, on May 29, 1991 the fundamental fact in India was that "there can be no stability without secularism". What India needed the most was a strong and stable government that could protect the unity of the present and nourish the vision of the future. Only the Congress could play this role. "No other party is in any position to do so, least of all the BJP, tainted as it is by communalism", Rao observed. "The BJP only means the institutionalisation of communal strife and hatred. As for the National Front, it simply does not have even the minimum number of credible candidates to make any sensible claim: it was an opprotunistic conglomeration that accepted casteism as its creed for political ends. It cannot deliver the goods. It has already begun to crumble under the pressue of events", Rao said. Paying tributes to Rajiv Gandhi, Rao said the leader of the nation was tragically assassinated "just as he had reached the threshold of victory in the current election". The tragedy had thrown India and its democracy into a profound crisis. For the Congress, it was an hour both of the deepest gloom and the greatest challenge. "As so often during its 106-year existence, history has thrust upon the party of Mahatma Gandhi, Jawaharlal Nehru, Indira Gandhi and Rajiv Gandhi the responsibility keeping India and Indians together", Rao said. The ideological and institutional strength of the Congress could lift the nation from the giref of the deepest tragedy to meet the greatest of challenges, he said. "Rao the Congress feels proud of the example set by Sonia Gandhi and the personal courage she has shown in this tragedy as well as her deep commitment to the future of her Congress party and her India," the Congress president said, adding: "We are grateful to Sonia Gandhi and the personal courage she has shown in this tragedy as well as her deep commitment to the future of her Congress party and her India," the congress president said, adding: "We are grateful to Sonia". On Rajiv Gandhi's assassination, Rao said: "We will one day find out who assassinated Rajiv Gandhi-but we already know why he died!. He laid down his life for India's unity and for the future of her youth and the poorest of the poor; for the oppressed minorities, the down-trodden and the outcasts. Like his mother, he gave every drop of his blood to his mother-land. "We will not allow Rajiv Gandhi's dreams to die with him". Assuring all that he would do his best in his new assignment, Rao said: "Let us get on with the job together. I am sure this is what the people want, what the thousands upon thousands of congress workers want".

Eminent intellectuals attending a meeting called by the Krishna Menon Society to discuss the theme "India: the prospect after three assassinations have stressed the need for liberal, secular and progressive political formations to come together on a single platform to tackle the "national crisis" arising out of Rajiv Gandhi's asrassination. They have said that the Indian National Congress, the secular centrist parties and the Left bear a special responsibility in this context. "For they have to come together to resist the assualt on secularism and parliamentary democracy in our midst at the same time as they might any attempt to impose a hegemonic world order on under developed politics of Asia, Africa and Latin America." Moreover, the common front of all liberal and progressive forces in India is necessary to bring together the people in a "grand alliance" pledged to building a new and equitable society in our midst.

The statement issued by Prof. Ravinder Kumar, Director, Nehru Memorial Museum and Library on behalf of the intellectuals said: "As the people of India recover from the shock of the assassination of Rajiv Gandhi, it is appropriate to dwell on the course of happenings which led to this tragic event. It is equally appropriate to look to the future and fashion a world view best designed to create in our midst a sane society in which outr citizens can live with dignity." Recalling that the people of India were drawn into a struggle fro national liberation under the aegis of Mahatma Gandhi and Jawaharlal Nehru with very specific objectives in view, the statements said that both these stalwarts civilisation into a modern state under whose umbrella citizens pursuing different religions could interest freely with each other. Those associated with the freedom struggle had brought for freedom fully aware of plight of the exploited people elsewhere and they were determined to made common cause with such people. However, the endeavour of the people of India for a new and better life seriously alarmed those who looked upon her resurgence as a secular, democratic and industrial polity with the most profound misgivings. "Small wonder then that the first victim of reaction was Mahatma Gandhi whose assassination in 1948 was an attempt to shatter the dream of a society in which citizens who pursued different religions lived together in amity", the statement said. The statement added that over the last decade the attempt of anti-national forces to create divisions within our society.

It is a critical juncture in India's history. The cult of violence, the cult of religious fanaticism and fundamentalism has to be curbed. Somebody has to steer, with firmness and resolve, this country out of the mess that we have landed ourselves in. We will have to exert and assert ourselves if we are to develop as a progressive and what is more a civilised nation. Luminaries like Vasant Sathe, Nikhil Chakravarty and others have suggested a National Government. I would favour such an arrangement. But can we over-come the problem of bloated-egos and self-advancement? We are yet petty and small men and women when it comes to putting the interest of the country before our own. We should think seriously of switching over to a presidential form of government within a time-frame beginning with a new constituent Assembly to deal with a changed environment and changed times. There should, in fact, be a national referendum on this matter at the earliest so that our federal structure, our centre-state relationship and above all are unity is not threatened. It is pointless to start a debate on whether all like-minded politicians, former Congressmen, etc. should join the Congress. The imperatives are for "Nationalist and Secular Forces" to transcend their narrow political differences and make a concerted effort to bring economic and political stability to the country. Let each one of us stand where we do and first rescue and then strengthen the political system which has been ruthlessly subverted, corrupted and criminalised by power brokers, middlemen, manipulators and commission agents to borrow Rajiv Gandhi's phrase.[17]

The future will see an acute struggle between the forces representing secular, democratic and progressive politics and the fascist onslaught of the BJP-VHP-RSS-Bajrang Dal combine. Only Narasimha Rao in the present seenario can lead the challenge to the anti-secular reactionary forces. Congress rule enriched secularism and raised its defences whatever social order that preserves the country's economic and political sovereignty. The Janata Dal has all but sold us down the drain and the BJP for all its talk of Ramrajya, will do it even sooner. In the given situation, only a government formed by the Congress party can safeguard our economic and political independence, specially because it will not be in a position to take arbitrary decisions but will be guided by its time-tested policies.

NOTES

1. *National Herald,* 3 June 1991.
2. *National Herald,* 3 June 1991.
3. *Ibid.*
4. V.D. Chopra. Turbulent Days Ahead. *Patriot,* 17 June 1991.
5. *Ibid.*
6. Chandan Mitra. For the BJP It was a Famous Victory. *The Sunday Observer*, 23 June 1991.
7. D.R. Goyal. Post Election Challenges *National Herald,* 15 June 1991.
8. *Ibid.*
9. K.V. Chacko. Paradox of Caste Politics *Patriot,* 5 June 1991.
10. *The Sunday Observer,* 23 June 1991.
11. *The Hindustan Times,* 21 June 1991.
12. Uday Shankar. Mandalities Prevail in JD. *The Sunday Mail,* 23 June 1991.
13. Uday Shankar and V.V.P. Sharma. Stand on Mandal Crucial for Survival. *The Sunday Mail,* 23 June 1991.
14. *Ibid.*
15. Jyoti Basu on secularism. *The Sunday Mail,* 23 June 1991.
16. K.V. Chacko, Paradox of Caste Politics. *Patriot,* 5 June 1991.
17. Vijai Singh Mankottia. A Summer of Shame. *The Hindustan Times,* 16 June 1991

THIRTEEN

THE HINDU-MUSLIM DIVIDE

The ascendancy of P.V. Narasimha Rao to the coveted position of Prime Minister represents both contiunity in terms of the Nehru-Gandhi legacy in the Congress; change for not being part of the charisma of the Nehru-Gandhi family which in itself is a significant pointer to the future thrust of Indian politics. PV, as the new Prime Minister is popularly known to his friends, belongs to the traditional school of politics. Yet, he is forward-looking and liberal in outlook. He comes with a very rich experience as an administrator, having been closely associated with governmental functioning right from the days of Indira Gandhi. This in itself speaks volumes of his capacity to survive against all odds. Rao was actually all set to call it a day in politics and move to Hyderabad with his trunk-loads of books when the series of events following the tragic assassination of Rajiv Gandhi changed the political course for him and forced a transition at a most delicate moment in the Congress fortunes. As a person indisposed towards politics of confrontation, there could not have been better choice than PV for the prime ministership. This trait assumes considerable significance in the context of the emergence of different power centres within the Congress as well as the fractured society ravaged by politics of casteism and communalism.[1]

The changed political scenario after the assassination of Rajiv Gandhi has completely baffled the Muslim leadership which was already jolted by the behaviour of minority voters in the first round of polling on May 20. Muslim voters had largely defied Muslim leaders' and Jama Masjid Shahi Imam Abdullah Bukhari's call to vote for the Janata Dal. Now after the death of Rajiv Gandhi, as the campaigning for the second and third phases of elections begins, there is a perceptible change in their attitude towards the Congress. Reports from various States on the pattern of voting by the minority reveal that despite the call, unlike in the 1989 elections, a substantial section of Muslims had also voted for the Congress and the Samajwadi Janata Party (SJP) this time. In 1989, Muslim voters had voted for the Janata Dal and its allies. There is nothing like sympathy wave in favour of the Congress after its leader's death. Muslim leaders say, but his secular stand and utterance against the Bharatiya Janata Party (BJP) on the eve of the elections certainly influenced their minds. This happened despite Muslim leaders' appeal against the BJP and the Congress, holding the latter responsible for allowing the lock at the Ayodhya shrine to be opened and shilanyas to take place near it. The Congress was no less communal, they had said. The deep fear of the Muslim leadership now is that a decisive split in the minority vote between the Janata Dal, the Congress and the SJP, particularly in Uttar Pradesh and Bihar, would only benefit the BJP. At the same time, they are not in a position to change the trend. A greater number of Muslim voters would vote for the congress following Rajiv Gandhi's death, they admit. In Uttar Pradesh and Bihar, majority of the minority votes would still go to the Janata Dal, but a good number of them would now also go to the Congress. In Madhya Pradesh, a larger section of this vote-bank was turning to the Congress while in only seven to eight constituencies where the Janata Dal's position was strong, Muslims adhered to the party. However, a crack in the vote-bank in these constituencies is already apparent.[2]

In Gujarat, the minority vote was already divided between the Janata Dal on the one hand and the Congress and Mr. Chimabbhai Patelo's Janata Dal (Gujarat), mainly because Patel as Chief Minister had been able to successfully control recent communal riots in the State. In Rajasthan, similarly, the vote is divided between the Congress and the Janata Dal against the BJP. A final agreement between the Assam minority front and the Janata Dal had not materialised before the elections and so the vote in that state is divded too. In Kerala, a fresh rapprochement between the Congress and the Indian Union Muslim League (IUML) has helped the former. And in other parts of south a mixed feeling among Muslim voters prevails. Obviously reiteration of the same appeal by the Indian leadership is unlikely to help now. Consultations between leaders of the Quami Mushawarat Committee, the Qaumi Morcha, the Muslim Majlis and the Majlis-e-Ittehadul Masalmeen have not been able to resolve their dilemma. Interestingly, Muslim leaders now do not even criticise the Congress and in case of a hung Parliament they would not bother if the Congress and the Left, the Congress and the Janata Dal or the Congress, the Janata Dal and the Left came together to keep the BJP out. They lack courage to make a revised appeal to vote either for the Janata Dal or the Congress, against the BJP, falling in line with the voting pattern. Such an appeal, they fear, will lead to division of votes in favour of the Congress. Split in the Janata Dal had also divided Muslim leaders and they were finding themselve put in a dilemma. They had tried to resolve the issue by adopting a mid- way approach that the minority should vote for V.P. Singh (the Janata Dal), in Mulayam Singh Yadav (the SJP) in the Assembly elections. The fresh dilemma they find too difficult to resolve. They may not be able to make any fresh appeal to the minority before the second and third phases of polling. The only consolation they find is that the changed circumstances are likely to bring adverse forces together. One must face the reality as it comes. Would not minority votes still matter if they go enbloc to a party? Yes, they would, they can, Muslim leaders agree. But they are helpless.[3]

Keeping with the practice, the Muslim voting pattern varied from area to area. The "tactical" voting expected to favour any candidate capable of defeating the BJP was resorted to but not everywhere. Thus, some Muslim-dominated contituencies were lost to the BJP. While in the Capital, UP, Bihar, West Bengal and parts of the Andhra Pradesh the National Front and Left Front combine got a bulk of the Muslim votes, the Congress cornered the Muslim votes in the south, Madhya Pradesh, Rajasthan, Gujarat, Assam, Haryana and most parts of Maharashtra. The Samajwadi Janata Party (SJP), which was expected to get substantial Muslim support because of the firm stand taken by the chief minister of UP, Mr. Mulayam Singh Yadav, on the Ayodhya issue could not do so barring some contituencies in UP and Haryana.[4]

The JD had endeared itself says to the Muslim to such an extent that they voted for its candidates even though they looked unlikely to win. In the prestigious New Delhi constituency, the BJP stalwart, L.K. Advani, would have been humbled by the Congress candidate, Rajesh Khanna, had the JD candidate, Ms Manju Mohan, not secured most of the votes in the Muslim-dominated areas like Nizamuddin. Mohan got a total fo 20,439 votes while the margin of Mr. Advani's victor was only 1,526 votes. Similarly, the JD candidate for the Chandni Chowk Constituency, Kishore Lal, polled a majority of votes in the Muslim-dominated metropolitan segments comprising Matia Mahal, Ballimaran, Qasabpura, and Ajmeri Gate while the victory margin of the BJP candidate here was only 2,774 votes. In the East Delhi constituency, the Janata Dal's Ramvir Singh Bidhuri scored 1,58,712 votes while the victory margin of the BJP candidate B.L. Sharma, was a little over 60,000. In all these constituencies, the Congress suffered from a strong JD presence. Scenario repeated itself in UP. A similar split in Muslim votes in some of the UP constituencies where Muslims constitute 25 per cent to 47 per cent votes helped the BJP win. In Rampur, the BJP's Rajendra Sharma, won as the Muslim votes (47 per cent of the electorate) were shared by Congress, the JD, and the SJP. All these parties fielded muslims. In the Domariaganj constituency, where Muslims constitute about 35 per cent votes, the former Congress minister Mohsina Kidwai lost to the BJP's Ram Pal Singh as the National Front candidate, Ms Seema Mustafa, also polled a sizeable number of votes. Yet another constituency where the BJP won because of the split in the Muslim votes in Balrampur. The SJP's Maulana Muzaffar Hussain Kachhachawai, who is also the convenor of the Babri Masjid Action Committee, came second while the JD candidate, Fazlul Bari was third.

However, in Bihar the Muslim votes escaped divisions and the JD remained the major beneficiary. For instance, the convenor of the Babri Masjid Movement Action Committee, Syed Shahbuddin won the Kishanganj parliamentary constituency by a margin of over 80,000 votes although there was another strong Muslim candidate, M.J. Akbar of the Congress. In the Bettiah constituency the JD candidate, Faiyazul Azam won the seat by securing 2,83,073 votes while the Congress contender, Mr. Sagir Ahmad, came third with only 29,454 votes. The charisma of V.P. Singh reached the far off constituency in Lakshdweep where Muslims constitute about 94 per cent of the population. The JD candidate Dr. Mohammad Koya lost to the Congress candidate, P.M. Sayeed, by only 281 votes. In Kerala, the Muslims by and large voted for the United Democratic Front, particularly the Indian Union Muslim League and the Congress. The biggest gainer was, however the IUML which won a record number of 19 assembly seats, besides the two traditional Lok Sabha seats.

In Assam, where Muslims constitute about 26 per cent of the total population, the Muslims rejected the United Muslim Front this time and it could manage only a few assembly seats. In the last assembly elections, it had won above 30 seats. In the last assembly elections, it had won above 30 seats. This time the Muslims voted for the Congress in large number as it is evident from its tally: 6 Lok Sabha seats out of the 12 whose results were declared till this evening, and 65 assembly seats out of the 121 results declared. There are a total of 126 seats in the assembly.

However, in West Bengal, the Muslims by a large voted for the Left Front as it is evident from the fact that out of the five Muslim MPs from the state, four belong to the Left Front. In constituencies where both the Congress and the Left Front fielded Muslim candidates, the Left Front contenders came out tops. For instance, Zainal Abedeen of the CPM won the Jangipore constituency as against Mr. Mannan Hussain of the Congress. Similarly in Katwa, the CPM candidate, Saifudding Chaudhary won the election by defeating the Congress contestant, Nural Islam by a margin of over 1.5 lakh.

The electorate is indecisive about which way to go. It is in view of this that the Bharatiya Janata Party gains political relevance in the States of Andhra Pradesh and Karanataka. The ground support to the BJP which is comparatively limited here as against in the North does not come from the fact that it is propagating the Ram Mandir, it comes from the "chance and change theory" where in the electorate in the Hindu-dominated areas in Karnataka and some parts of Andhra Pradesh feels that the Bharatiya Janata Party should be given a chance and a change would be for the better. Venugopal, for instance, feels that the leadership of the BJP is sober, educated and mature and is unlikely to have a leadership tussle which the Congress may get embroiled in: "after all in BJP the fight for the Prime Ministership will be at the most between L.K. Advani and Atal Behari Vajpayee. In Congress, once it comes to power, there will be a virtual battle with innumerable self-styled leaders." Even for the lukewarm supporters of the Congress comprising sections of the urban electorate, the sympathy factor of the post- assassination period is being overtaken by the concern for the future. The Muslim electorate, however, seems to have consolidated itself in favour of the Congress in many parts of these two States, both for emotional and practical reasons. Emotional, because they feel that the Congress is perhaps the only party which is secular and consequently the only one which is capable of providing security to the Muslims. Here the Janata Dal and the Bharatiya Janata Party are both seen as divisive parties which through their respective strategy of pampering the Muslims and Hindus separately are creating an irreparable divide between the two communities. The Congress, most feel, does not talk in terms of the Hindus and Muslims but propagates secularism-a secularism which to the Muslims now means security. The practical, strategic reason for the Muslims to vote for the Congress in this part is that is likely to defeat the BJP. This also would overtake whatever personal sentiment V.P. Singh has been able to generate among the Muslim electorate, who more than his stand on the Babri Masjid, recognise that fact that it was he who announced the Prophet's birthday as a national holiday. As things stand the Congres's vote bank would seemingly stem from its traditional electorate, the sympathy wave, its secular image and its capacity to pose a serious challenge to the BJP.[5]

The array is starkest in Uttar Pradesh and Bihar, both as regards the loyalties of religion and caste with for off Kerala presenting a variation in which the higher caste Hindu sentiment is rising against the diverse tides of Christian, Muslim, and lower Hindu caste Ezhava identities. Neighbouring Tamil Nadu is a lake in which you can measure the sympathy wave because it contradicts the myth of the north-south, Aryan-Dravidian, Brahmin non-Brahmin, dark-fair divides; this wave measure a Dravid, non-Brahmin, southers, dark-skinned sympathy for the fair scion of an Aryan and Brahmin family of the far north. The Muslim factor is most worth looking at in the Chandni Chowk constituency in Delhi; in the Agra, Kanpur, Faizabad, Muzaffarnagar, Badaun, Azamgarh, and Shahjahanpur constituencies in Uttar Pradesh; and Madhubani and Begusarai in Bihar. These constituencies, except Kanpur, Muzaffarnagar, and Badaun, are also interesting in the context of caste, along with Allahabad in UP, and Arrah, Buxxar, and Muzaffarpur in Bihar. The largest single chunk of voters in Chandni Chowk are traders, the most dedicated among the supporters of BJP, and the very next block are the antithesis, the Muslims, who in this constituency have not only the general inclination of the Muslims this time towards the Janata Dal but also the fatwa of the Imam to reinforce it. Pitted against these specific loyalties is the more diffused but the older general loyalty towards the Congress among these two communities, as well as among the third strongest, the Scheduled Castes. The result will show how far the Muslims have shifted their loyalty to the Dal as a reaction against the deeper saffron of the traders this time, of how far they have stayed with the Congress as a better way of stopping BJP. The Congress used to win Shahjahanpur on the strength of a triangle of support: Brahmin-Muslim-Harijan, a spread which supported its claim to be a "national" party, while the Jats and the backward castes, though once with the Congress, were taken away from the late 1960s onwards by a predecessor of the Janata Dal, the Lok Dal. Now BJP is drawing off the Brahmin cream while the Janata Dal is trying to retain the Lok Dal legacy, and at the same time is also trying to take away the Muslim vote. What might blur educations from the results, however, is that the Muslim support for Janata Dal in this region is being confused by wrong selection of Janata Dal candidates in the wastern UP region. The Muslim factor has further dimensions in Kanpur, where riots have deeply segregated Hindu and Muslim localities. Last time this worked in favour of the CPI(M) candidate, Subhashini Ali, because to the Muslim she added her own labour and lower caste votes. But now there is a growing affinity between the Muslims and Hanijans as a backlash against the emotion-charged consolidation. of the higher Hindu castes behind BJP. And there is a candidate here now of the BSP, which claims to be the Harijans' own party. Subhasini Ali's spirit may therefore face a bigger challenge this time.[6]

A tougher test of this new Muslim orientation lies in Badaun, where the Muslim vote is said to be a decisive factor and the choice lies between a rich Muslim candidate of an influential family, the Sherwanis, fielded by the Congress; a pillar of the new backward caste politics, Sharad Yadav fielded by the Janata Dal; and a Swami Chinmayanand (not of the Geeta Pravachan fame) fielded by BJP, who is more famous for his social work than for his politics and has little paint of communalism. Which will be the way for Muslim politics here? The old way (the Congress), the new way (Janata Dal), or the neutral way (the swami)? A similar dilemma faces the Muslims in Faizabad, in choosing between a good man and the new social justice platform of

Janata Dal. Their problem is that the good man here is the Congress candidate, and he is losing the upper caste votes on account of the hard-sell Ram politics of BJP. This is making the Muslims wonder whether to stop BJP first with the "good man" shield or to take the road of "new politics" into the future. As you go eastwards the road becoms smoother for the new politics, except for another fasinating fork at the very end. In Azamgarh, Chandrajit Yadav of the Janata Dal is a secular sociaslist, a Mandal enthusiast to boot, and has the backing of the largest block, the Yadavs, and the next largest, to the Muslims. There are no inner contradictions to worry the Muslims here. In Madhubani, in north Bihar, the upper castes are divided between the Congress and BJP (a common factor almost throughout the Gangetic belt) and by reaction and conviction the Muslims and the backwards are with the NF-LF candidate though he has to share the Harijans with the Congress.

The building up of the Indian nation-state comprising one-sixth of humanity divided in languages, ethnicities and religions was certainly a stupendous task. To expect that this task could be completed in four decades would amount to living in a make- believe world. It is necessary and relevant to underline this aspect of the Indian reality because attempts are being made, both within India and outside, to sap the confidence of the people in the democratic political system itself.

The Government will set up speical courts to try communal offences and a composite rapid action force to quell communal riots. Prime Minister, P.V. Narasimha Rao, said in New Delhi, on June 22, 1991, in his first national telecast after assuming office that Minorities Commission would be provided statutory status to enhance its effectiveness. "We are committed to protect the constitutional and legal rights and the legitimate interest of the religious linguistic and ethnic minorities", he said.

NOTES :

1. Hari Jai Singh. Man of the Moment. *The Business and Political Observer,* 22 June 1991.
2. Abhay Sinha. Changed Scenario Baffles Muslim Leaders. *Patriot,* 2 June 1991.
3. *Ibid.*
4. *The Times of India,* 21 June 1991.
5. Kumkum Chadha. A Visit of Vanagara. *The Hindustan Times,* 9 June 1991.
6. Pran Chopra. Old Loyalties Pitted Against New Politics. *The Sunday Observer*, 16 June 1991.
7. *Ibid.*

FOURTEEN

NEHRUVIAN MODEL OF DEVELOPMENT

New Prime Minister Narasimha Rao, in his first nation-wide broadcast on June 22, 1991 spoke at length on the economic crisis plaguing the country saying there were no soft options before the nation as the people had to be prepared for sacrifices to preserve their economic independence. He said his government welcomed direct foreign investment and offered to remove all "obstacles that come in the way of allocating foreign investment on a sizeable scale. He promised to strengthen the public- distribution system and announced that the delayed Central budget would be presented within a month. He said the dialogue with the International Monetary Fund would be continued to tide over the precarious balance of payments situation. He promised remunerative prices for farm produce and assured that the interests of the poor would be protected and the momentum of growth maintained in the process of adjustment. He said India would maintain its unblemished record in meeting its international obligations and streessed the need for fiscal dicipline. Narasimha Rao said formation of his "broad-based Council of Ministers was only the beginning in the beginning of a programme to reach out to the people in every nook and corner of the country. "My team understands the heabeat of the people", he said. The Governments vision was to create employment eradicate poverty and reduce inequality. Mahatma Gandhi said that it was his ambition to wipe every tear from every eye. That is vision which will inspire the work of my Government".

The Prime Minister painted a grim picture of the economy and said there were no economy and said there were no "soft options" but expressed confidence that the crisis would be overcome. He said the dialogue with multilateral institutions, particularly with IMF, would be continued to tide over the precarious balance of payments situation. Devoting the major part of his ten minute address to the economic crises besetting the country, the new Prime Minister said "there is no time to lose. The Government and the country cannot keep living beyond their means year after year." He said there were no soft options left and underlined the need "to tighten our belts and be prepared to make necessary sacrifices to preserve our economic independence, which is an integral part of our vision for a strong nation". Narasimha Rao assured the people that Congress Government attached the highest priotiry to restoration of the health of the economy.

Prime Minister P.V. Narasimha Rao's real acumen will be known the way he handles the organisatinal problems and tackle the multi-dimensional crisis facing the country. The economy is in a mess. The national offers are empty. The foreign exchange crunch boggles the mind. India's international credit rating is the lowest over.

The Union Cabinet at its first meeting presided over by the Prime Minister P.V. Narasimha Rao on June 22, 1991, observed a one minute silence as a mark of respect to the former Prime Minister Rajiv Gandhi, before opening its formal proceedings. The Prime Minister discussed with senior officials the immediate measures requiring to tide over the difficult economic situation.

An official spokesman said the broad options before the Government were analysed by the Prime Minister at his an over two-hour meeting with the officials. Dr. Manmohan Singh was also present. While reviewing the economic situation, the problems that had to be immediately attended to and the broad options before the government were taken up. The Prime Minister had on June 21, said tackling the economic situation would be one of the top priorities of the new government. The nation was faced with a depleted foreign exchange reserve mounting fiscal deficits and inflationary spiral. It also has to take a sift decision on the question of IMF loan and possible frame a budget in the shortest possible time.

The party that has ruled India for 40 of the 44 years of Independence has promised to rein in prices, create jobs on a massive scale, aoolish poverty, deprivation and unemployment and usher in dynamic growth magically, while reducing the tax burden and giving the mixed economic sector its head. Although most of us are no more economists that our former prime minister, about one thing I am clear" Rajivnomics or the programmatic options pur forward by the other 'mainstream' parties, will not do the things promised during the 1991-election manifesto.

Dr. Manmohan Singh, is of the firm view that there should be a national consensus on urgent economic issues facing the country and the next two years should be made use of to restore the health of the economy through a package of hard measures.

Talking to newsmen after his swearing-in as the Cabinet Minister on June 21, 1991, Dr. Singh said that India is passing through critical times and from day one, the new Government would have to tackle the burgeoning fiscal deficit which had been at the root of the present serious economic crisis. He underlined that fiscal system is linked to the balance of payments crisis and unless the deficit is curbed, confidence in the economic health of the country will not be restored.[1] Dr. Singh has already discussed the economic situation with Prime Minister P.V. Narasimha Rao and he has been given a clear indication by the Prime Minister that the Gaovernment will back his measures to put the economy back to rails. The former Deputy Chairman of the Planning Commission as also RBI Governor, talked to a number of senior officials in the Government and exchanged ideas on the nature of the problems. Dr. Singh pointed out that he would take a fresh look at the existing economic policies and discussions would be held in ritht earnest with the Internaional Monetary Fund (IMF) on structural reforms in the economy. He emphasised that the world economy is increasingly becoming interdependent and India will certainly have a place in it on its own terms. Dr. Singh said that the package of economic reforms including deregulation would not be implemented at the cost of social justice to the weaker sections of the population. He was emphatic that in the next two years, austerity would have to be practised all round and the better off sections would have to shoulder a greater burden to ensure growth with equity. Dr. Singh gave a clear indication that the next two years would be the period of consolidation of the Indian economy which would give a breathing space to the Government to enter the world economy with strength and confidence. New Finance Minister opined that the country is now prepared for hard decisions and the Government must take the people into confidence about the dimension of the crisis and the sacrifices the people would have to make. He exuded confidence that the reforms would be brought about without adding to inflatioanry pressures. Further, there will be no cut back in the social sectors including education, health, drinking water and other essential rural programmes. Dr. Singh while favouring the need to disinvest holdings in some public sector undertakings, did not support privatisation as a panacea. Meanwhile, sources in the Rao Government said that the Finance Ministry will tackle the problem of the present foreign exchange crisis by pursuing vigorous export promotion, effective import substitution, establishing an appropriate exchange rate mechanism and increasing productivity and effeciency in the economy. Consistent with the objectives of economic growth, the new Government will pursue debt management policies so as to avoid India falling into a debt trap. Special attention will be paid to avoiding disbursement delays in externally assisted projects and for the efficient utilisation of borrowed funds. Public and Private sector banks will be allowed to raise off shore funds and the Rao Government will also permit the establishment of new mutual funds, particularly pension funds in the private sector.

Those who prefer the readoption of the Nehru model of development today-that is what professor Ravinder Kumar and his fellow signatories underline-implicity recognise this. They also recognise that the role of the State has to expand, not contract; that the market has to be married to a rational system of commands. Whatever the net content of such a marriage, it cannot accommodate the kind of liberalisation regime that has been associated with a higher rate of growth but an ostensibly skewing process of distribution. That exactly, is the dilemma. Liberalisation has accelerated the pace of expansion of the size of that section of the population, which is lebelled for convenience as the 'middle class'. It has also raised the level of consumerist aspiration. It is this middle class which provides the market for capital spoilt by the habit of super-profit. And it is a larger section of this middle class which occupies strategic positions at differect levels of the state apparatus,. Many members of this class are waiting for a bonanza in the new budget, particularly inspired by the BJP's promise of raising the exemption limit of personal income tax to Rs. 40,000/- and by the assurance from both BJP and Congress that the interest rate on 'small savings' would be increased. Will it be possible to persuade them to accept austerity for the sake of redistribution? There is no known Nehruvian recipe for such a combination of conflicts and complementaries as operates in India's political economy to day. The collaborative reconcilition of confliciting interests that marked the Nehru era of Indian history, cannot be re-established in the situation that prevails in India today. At the level of economic theory, a reasonably high savings ration as the precondition for economic growth has to be of a lower priority at least for a few years to come. Of course, if, and only if, a visible redistribution is seen as a conpulsion for a democratic system. At the level of correlation of social groups, an expanding middle class has come to be coterminus with a faster concertration of income and wealth, and a high savings- ration. In simpler political terms, poverty and rising inequality provide additional inputs to those who present Ram Rajya and national unity, as interchangeable concepts; or moral purity and order (as opposed to corruption, anarchy or violence) as inviolable commitants of Hinutva as the world-view[2]

That kind of Hindutva is one source of challenge to the democratic potentiality of the Indian society today. Its votaries can keep changing their slogan depending on the demands of relevance and credibility. On the other side of spectrum too, there will be no dearth of political formations advocating radical changes, including, if need be, changes that would drastically affect the existing beneficiaries of economic policy and the political power structure. What happens to 'centrist' politics under such opposing pulls and pressures? Perhaps, the advocates of the Nehru model are flexible enough to accommodate social justice in a more concrete and effective manner. Perhaps, there is a realisation now, at least among the sincere liberals, that for parlimentary democracy to survive, and for the communalist to be countered in time, there is no soft option of the kind that was available until the early 70s.

And that the expanding chorus in favour of the 'free' market system is proving to be challenge to parliamentary democracy. It is not for nothing that the ideologues as asking the Congress to revert to the Nehruvian path, with modifications where necessary. It is not easy for the historically most important political party of the country to change its earstwhile persuasion. At the same time, it is not easy to survive as a major party without a conscious commitment to convince the people that it is serious about improving their lot. Right now, the Left is not a major challenge to the Congress or any other formation which retains a tolerable framework of class reconciliation. The threat comes from the communalist right, particularly because theocracy can only divide the society and the market. The rulling party will have to clinch some of these basic issues before it presents the regular budget. How the issues are cliched will greatly influence the turn of events during the next two to three years, and thereby the direction which the political process will acquire, Another midterm poll, will depend, not so much on the number of seats won in this election, as much as on the extent of credibility the new government can earn for itselt. But this time the creadibility in the eyes of the poor will count much more than that in the eyes of others. For, whatever one may try, the poor are in the majority, and most of them are fast changing from mere numbers into discerning human beings.[3]

Few people in India, including perhaps many in the major political parties, realise how much threat or fragile economy poses to the sovereignty of the nation. Over the last four years or so, the economy or more precisely the finances of the country have been badly managed. First the facts about the three crucial aspects of our finances, viz. 1. fiscal and revenue deficits, 2. foreign exchange reserves and 3. the foreign debt. According to the Government's own estimate given by Finance Minister Yashwant Singh in his budget speech on March 4, 1991, the fiscal deficit, i.e. the gap between the Government's revenue and its total expenditure is somewhere around 8-5 per cent of a Gross Domestic Product of about Rs 5,00,000 crore. The actual figure may turn out to be a little higher. The revenue deficit in the interim budget, presented by the Finance Minister to the Lok Sabha in March 1991, is estimated at about Rs. 10,770 crore. The Indian record until the 1970's was quite different. Even in 1980-81 the first year after Mrs. Indira Gandhi's return to power, the revenue deficit of the Government of India was just Rs 1,715 crore. By 1985-86, it grew to Rs 5,586 crore and reached a staggering figure of Rs 12,436 crore in 1989-90 when the

Rajiv Gandhi Government was voted out of power. The Government of India was responsible for over 2 per cent dissaving a year. The foreign exchange story is somewhat similar. Around 1979-80 India's foreign exchange reserves were approximately US $7 billion, more than enough to give India a good cover for its prevailing level of imports. By 1989, the country's foreign exchange reserves fell to $4 billion a low level considering the import needs of the economy. What is worse is that the external deficit on current account grew from $ 3.4 billion in 1980-81 to $ 9 billion by 1989-90.

As is well-known the foreign exchange reserves today are good for supporting only a few days import requirements and the Reserve Bank has virtually to pursue a hand to mouth policy.[4] The calamitous position of foreign exchange reserves is further compounded by the state of India's foreign debt. In 1980, India's foreign debt was just $ 18 billion. In 1991 the World Bank estimates our foreign debt at $ 72 billion or overs Rs 1,40,000 crore. A four-fold increase in less than a decade much of it due to reckless high cost commercial borrowings. And this does not include the liabilities on account of NRI deposits. This level of debt and its servicing costs has clearly put the country in what is called the debt trap. The debt service which was estimated at 8 per cent of export earnings in 1980-81 is now estimated at almost 30 per cent-far above what is regarded as a safe level. The Indian credit rating has already fallen so low, former Prime Minister Rajiv Gandhi's assassination compounding it further, that the Central Government in of whichever party, will be in no position to withstand heavy international pressures. Unfortunately for India, the Soviet Union which had come to its rescue so often in the past, itself is seeking a $ 100 billion assistance from G-7, the club fo the world's seven rich and most industrialised nations. India, therefore, will have to fall back upon the IMF and the World Bank which again will mean the G-7. A good question is, why did India which had a sound-record of managing its finances come to this pass? It is quite apparent that the Congress Government at the Centre, especially after 1986, decided on a gamble of high growth with large domestic borrowing plus budget deficits and also large international borrowings at high commercial rates. There is little doubt that the higher performance of the Indian economy was fuelled a great deal by these twin deficits-both domestic and foreign. The gamble may have paid, if the Indian export performance had been good enough and the productivity of the high cost domestic and foreign borrowings was satisfactory. Unfortunately, the political system did not seem to have bothered about the systematic 'export prevention' which our governmental system has been practising for a long time, nor did it bother about the low productivity of use of borrowed funds whether domestic or international. The Indian financial mandarins, who in the past had been prudent and perhaps even over-cautious, either did not do their homework or were overruled by their political masters. Even if they were overruled, they certainly owed it to themselves and to the country to alert the nation about the disastrous path on which we were going.[5] They did nothing of that sort and in fact scoffed at public criticism as unduly pessimistic and negative. It is true that the forex crunch is not new and the situation has been critical since the Gulf conflict exploded in August last. As petroleum prices aboroad rose, the increase in the petroleum import bill depleted our reserves. By January 1991, the reserves had crashed to about Rs. 1,800 crore, or less than the amount needed to finance two weeks of imports. Had the IMF not stepped in with a $ 1.8 billion loan under the first tranche and the contingency oil facility, India would have defaulted on the repayment of its foreign loans. Mercifully the crisis was averted and forex reserves went up to Rs 4,600 crore by end-January.

All this is old hat. But it is necessary to look back to understand why foreign exchange reserves have fallen by about Rs 2,000 crore between end-January and end-May 1991. The drop in reserves in the Petroleum import bill, the shortfall in exports and the resultant rise in the trade deficit. Thus, in 1990-91, India's trade deficit soared to Rs 10,644 crore, showing an increase of Rs. 2,914 crore over 1989-90. However, this was adequately covered by the Rs. 3,200 crore loan from the IMF in January. In the subsequent period, for two reasons, the fall in reserves cannot be attributed to the trade deficit. First, our oil import bill must have come down as the end of the Gulf was brought about a fall in world prices of crude oil. Second, while exports may not be doing as well as they should, the fact remains that the severe import squeeze unleashed by the RBI has resulted in a noticeable contraction in imports. Therefore, alongwith the drop in oil imports, the non-oil trade deficit should have recorded a decrease in April and May this year. Already in the previous year 1990-91, the non-oil trade deficit had fallen sharply to Rs. 876 crore from Rs. 2236 crore in 1989-90. Indeed, it is not unlikely that the non-oil trade balance in the first two months of the current year may negligible, if not possitive. Reasons for the drop in reserves obviously lie elsewhere. What deserves a closer look is the fact that on May 30, the day SBI sold the confiscated gold in Zurich, Standards and Poor, the US agency, lowered India's debt rating to the speculative grade or the last investment grade BB-plus from BBB-minus. This was the second time in a year that standards and Poor had downdgraded India's credit rating and its latest move implied that investment in the country had become a risky proposition. Earlier, the other US agency, Moody's and the Japanese Bond Research Institute had already placed

India in the last investment grade. The latest downgrading by Standards and Poor also means that India will now be unable to tap the short and medium-term funds market in the US. This is the crux of the problem. Ever since the Gulf crisis, India's credit rating has been consitently falling and foreign banks have become increasingly wary of lending to India. Consequently capital flows that financed the deficit on the current account have all but dried up. Even non-resident Indians have become uneasy about parking their funds in India.[6]

Reports are that the net increase in FCNR deposits during 1990-91 was about Rs.230 crore, or less than 10 per cent of the increase of Rs.3,000 crore that took place in 1989-90. This is despite the fall in interest rates abroad and the high interest rates offered to NRI's by the Government of India. Similar fall has occurred in direct foreign investment. After reaching a high of Rs. 317 crore in 1989, DFI flows to India crashed to Rs. 123 crore in 1990. It cannot be ignored that foreign lending and investment has stopped flowing in simultaneously from all sources. The hard fact is that foreign lenders have lost their confidence in India's ability to manage its economy. It is no coincidence that the Standards and Poor's move to lower India's credit rating came in the wake of Rajiv Gandhi's assassination, which signalled a period of political uncertainty. Foreign lenders have taken a dim view of the Indian economy over the last two years as unstable coalitions at the Centre, have failed to implement critical economic policy decisions; the new industrial policy for instance. Political instability dealt a major blow to financial stability when the minority government headed by Chandra Shekhar failed to present the annual budget in January 1991 and postpones it by four months to end-June. Foreign lenders did not fail to observe that the postponement of the budget would delay measures to contain the budget deficit which in 1990-91 had soared to Rs 12,500 crore, 80 per cent ahead of the budget estimate of Rs 7,20 crore. Yet another postponement of the budget after Rajiv's assassination came as the last straw. For this implies that, if the usual buegetary procedures are followed, the new budget will be in place only by end-August. New tax proposals, therefore, will be able to raise additional resources only for half the fiscal year. Meanwhile, import curbs and slowdown in industrial production will retard the growth in indirect tax collections through customs and central excise. The budgetary gap, therefore, will assume alarming proportions unless of course, the government takes strong and determined measures to reduce the fiscal deficit. Till that happens India will continue to remain an untouchable as far as foreign lenders are concerned. Critics of trade liberalisation may feel confident that import curbs imposed by the RBI is just the right kind of medicine that needs to be administered to tackle the current malaise. But not the foreign banks and investors or even the NRIs. Piecemeal tinkering of the kind of the RBI has been indulging in will not only fail to arrest the slide in foreign reserves but will also fail to enthuse foreign lenders. They view the problem not as a crisis triggered by excessive imports, but as a crisis of confidence.[7]

It was lack of direction in economic policies after 1989 and failure the present foreign exchange crisis necessitating the sale of gold to meet international commitments, the Congress spokesman, Pranab Mukherjee said, in New Delhi on June 8, 1991[8]. Mukherjee, a former Union Finance Minister, pointed out that unlike the successive Congress governments which were able to mobilise internal and external resources to meet the needs of growth and development, the National Front Government which came to power in 1989 sent out wrong signals with comments like "empty coffers" and "debt trap". It was a short-sighted politics. The foreign exchange situation was not confortable for the country for most of the time, but the high growth rates of economy and the clear agenda for development of the Congress governments ensured that the needed resources "rolled on". This "roll on" process stopped because of panicky signals given cut by the National Front government. The Eight Plan was not finanlised and there was no clear direction in the Government's polices. Mukherjee spoke of the Congress Party's plan to manage the cirsis. which was spelt out in its manifesto. He made a distinction between "non-Government economy" and "Government economy", and said the it was the crisis in the Government economy that had to be checked quickly. Mukherjee noted that during 1985-91, the country's industrial output grew up nearly 60 per cent, exports increased by 200 per cent and capital issues went up by nearly 200 per cent. The macro factors such as infrastructure, agriculture trade and finance were managed effectively by the Government. The non-Government economy remained bullish even today as reflected in the latest growth rate of 8 per cent. "But the Government management of the economy has faltered. Hence we have a foreign exchange crunch, a credit squeeze and near paralysis on the infrastructure front. The slippage in the performance of sectors like coal, oil, carriage of railway freight and electricity generation might be around 10 per cent. He said that unless the crisis of the Government economy was checked swiftly, its repercussions would be felt in the Government sector and the achievements of the past five years would be wiped out. "The decline of public confidence will be hard to restore". Mukherjee who was addressing a press conference arranged specially for economic journalists at Jawahar Bhawan," spelt out the Congress Party's economic programme. He spoke of the role of government in the changed economic situation and of the importance of the poverty alleviation programme. Unlike his hard hitting briefings on political matters, Mukherjee spoke with sympathy about the problems facing the government in the economic field, displaying his mastery of the subject. There was a change of style in the way he patiently answered irritating questions, showing that he had mellowed over the years since his innings in the Finance Ministry. Mukherjee said that the Congress, under Rajiv Gandhi's leadership had grasped the dimensions of the developing crisis in government-economy. "It is clear to us that the Indian economy has changed dramatically especially in the relationsship between the government and non-government sectors. "out manifesto outlines a plan wherby the Government takes upon itself the task of managing the macro factors, while creating conditions for the sustained growth of the non Government economy." Mukherjee said the Congress realised that the Government could to play a "far more creative role" in the redistribution of wealth. The Government's welfare-related activities had to be enhanced. Mukherjee said that there should be no reluctance about adopting standard remedies like restoration of fiscal balance in the budgetary system by reducing wasteful expenditure, rationalisation of non-developmental expenditure, expanding the recvenue base and restricting defict financing. Asked whether the Congress would desist from going in for an IMF loan to meet the present situation if voted to power, Mukherjee said they would consider all options. If necessary they wouold seek an IMF loan and not "shy away" from it. The broad policy of the Congress to tackle the problem was "by pursuing vigorous export promotion, effective import subsitution, establishing an appropriate exchange rate mechanism and increasing productivity and efficieny in the economy". Asked about the reported observation of an economist, Dr. Jay Dubashi, that the World Bank was asking for a 22 per cent devaluation of the rupee against the dollar as the price for an aid package, Mukherjee said that with a proper economic agenda and absence of a sense of crisis, more favourable terms could be obtained from the bankers. One of the reasons for the current crisis was that there was a drying of short term external credit due to the panicky signals sent out by the Government. Mukherjee thought that if the Naional Front Government had worked on securing an IMF loan as soon as it came to power in November 1989 the conditionalities would not have been that stiff because of the many pluses of the economy. On Poverty alleviation, Mukherjee said the Congress Party's focus was not only to just lift the people above the povertyline, but to redefine the poverty line itself. By world standards Indian poverty is abysmal. The poor in India are not poor merely in the financial sense of the word. In addition they lack access to basic services such as public health and education. Mukherjee added; "Just because someone crosses the income-based povrety line does not mean the Government's job is done. The focus must be to improve the environment in which people live. Not just in terms of trees and parks, but in very real terms of hygiene and electricity, fuel and drinking water, literacy, and immunization." These were the tasks which the Congress had set for itself in the 1990's, he said. A note on "issues before the nation" circulated at the press conference also reiterated the "firm resolve" of the Congress to use the full power of the state to arrest the rise in prices. It said:" In particular the Congress is determined to roll back prices to the levels obtaining in July 1990 in the case of diesel, kerosene, salt, edible oils, cycles and two wheelers, electric bulbs, cotton sarees and dhotis of 40 counts or below, stoves including smokeless "chulhas", newsprint and postcards, inland letters and envelopes".[9]

Corrective action should have come by 1988-89. But apparently the Rajiv Gandhi Government hoped that some miracle would take place which did not. In 1989, perhaps, the Rajiv Gandhi Government thought that the corrective actions would be taken after it got a fresh mandate which also did not happen. The National Front Government under V.P. Singh obviously did not settle down to sort out the economic issues. In fact the National Front's Finance Minister Madhu Dandavate's budget of 1990-91 assessed a large foreign exchange deficit of Rs. 10,000 crore. It hoped for some relief through NRI deposits, commecial borrowings, etc. which by their very nature are highly volatile and suceptiable to all kinds of vagaries. The National Front Government compunded the financial ills of the country by loan waivers which is estimated to cost Rs 10,000 crore and increase in agricultural support prices-obviously a sop to its peasant consituency. The Gulf War of 1991 made the Indian situation even worse. The additional cost of oil imports, decline in remittances, and slow rise in exports compared to the import needs have all made the Indian economic situation grim. It is quite likely that the industrial production for 1991-92 will get affected. The overall economic growth rate will undoubtedly drop. And if the monsoons are not normal in the coming months, the domestic economic situation will become almost unmanageable. Thus India which was once a symbol of sound and prudent financial management, now faces loss of its financial credibility and an extremely difficult if not grim economic situation. It will need a lot of political grit and hard work to sort out the mess.[10]

The most important contribution of technological change in Indian agriculture since the mid-sixties was the dynamism and progressivity it imparted to agriculture by making farmers increasingly science and technology conscious. Of late, even small and marginal farmers in backward regions have been participating in this process of technological change. Attainment of self-suffiency in foodgrains is the most important outcome of this change. From the social and political angle, consilidation of the large farm sector through the development of capitalist relations has been a glaring feature. To this extent, there has been a weakening of traditional semifeudal relations in Indian agriculture.

There is increasing regional specialisation in production and a national market has been developed for outputs as well as inputs, including labour. The rural labour market in India is highly segmented and imperfect and yet, the green revolution has led to the emergence of a national market for agricultural labour on a scale never witnessed before. This market operates basically through contractors and other middlemen, and also thrives on the information and experience gained by first-generation migrants. In bringing about the gree revolution, the greatest price has perhaps been paid by migrant labour. They are subjected to severe exploitation by middlemen and the employers. High wage-levels in the areas of green revolution provided the incentive for migrant labour. The influx of migrant labour helped farmers contain further rise in wages while local labour found it increasingly attractive to get into non-farm rural occupations for which opportunitites had opened up in the green revolution regions. Working conditions for migrant labour have been miserable. Apart from the exploitation by middlemen and employers, their bargaining power is quite low. This explains why the relative share of wages in output has gone down steeply in areas undergoing technological change. Productivity and profits have risen at a much faster rate than real wages. Despite severe hardships for migrant labour and their exploitation, social tensions are not acute and, by and large there is an out appearance of peaceful transformation in green revolution areas.[11] Apart from the availability of unorganised and dependent migrant labour, this apparent harmony, is also explained by the prevailing land- tennure systems. The initial tenurial conditions in green revolution areas were generally favourable as they were characterised by the raytwari system of tenure and no by the zamjindari or other semi-feudal systems.

So even before the green revolution, tensions between local labour and large farmers were not as serve in these regions as in areas like Bihar, Thanjavur and Telengana where land tenures were outmobed. Further, despite hardships and exploitation, incomes of migrant labour are higher than what they would have been able to earn without migration. It is interesting to observe that despite the existence of such a large reservoir of labour, the rate of mechanisation was higher in the process of green revolution. This is because migrant labour lacks certain skills required locally and mechanisation of certain operations like ploughing and irrigation turn out to be cheaper even with the availability of migrant labour. This is another reason for the sharp decline in the share of labour in output green revolution areas. However, these events should not be interpreted as unbridled development of capitalism as a consequence of the green revolution. Instead, what we have been witnessing is the constrained development of capitalism in Indian agriculture. It has been constrained by two factors, viz the legal ceiling on land-holdings and the co-existence of small and marginal farmers on account of non-availability of alternative opportunities for employment. The real contribution of ceilings on landholdings in Indira lies not so much in the redistribution of land to the landless as in arresting the unrestrained development of capitalism through the accumulation of land.[12]

This partly explains why large farmers have not been able to drive away the small and marginal farmers from the profession. Another important reason for the persistence of the tiny sector is that agriculture is labour-intensive and economies of scale are not important.

It is true that, of late, the sale of land by the marginal farmers has increased and that they are joining the ranks of the landless. But this cannot be attributed solely to the development of capitalist relations in agriculture. In a significant measures, the observed 'proletarianisation' is attributable to the successive sub-division of holding on account of population growth, displacement of certain traditional household industries and the availability of more attractive alternative employment opportunities for some of these farmers. The small farmers capacity to survive and to use technology successfully is reflected in social relations in rural areas. The conflict of interests one witnesses on account of the green revolution, is not so much between the small and the large farmer, it is really between the large or capitalist farmers and the landless labourers, including particularly migrant labour. The contradiction between different classes of farmers arises mainly from the initial inequalities in the distribution of land and in the access to inputs. It is true that in the initial phase of green revolution, small farmers lagged behind the large farmers in the adoption of new technology. But more recent evidence indicates that, in course of time, small farmers access to inputs has improved and they have been able to catch up with big farmers in the use of modern inputs. Although the transformation appears, by and large, peaceful, though painful, in the green revolution areas, it has caused tremours in the backward areas, particularly those characterised by semi-feudal relations. In the process of migration, labour has become more skillful, enterprising and has considerably improved its Staying on account of the Rise in its income this has enhanced its capacity to right against in injustices. Paradoxically, their growing militancy is to be seen not in the 'alien' green revolution pockets, but in the familiar' surroundings of their areas of origin against landlords, money lenders and contractors. The rural unrest in central Bihar plains, in the Telengana region and certain tribal belts reflects the growing consciousness and staying power of the poor who are prepared to hit back. Their incomes and staying power have increased not only through earnings from internal migration but also from migration overseas, including the Gulf areas. Besides, there has been a significant expansion of poverty alleviation programmes such as IRDP, and Jawahar Rozgar Yojana, which have also imporved the incomes and the barganing power of the poor. The latest figures from the Planning Commission indicate a significant decline in the proportion of people below the poverty line.[13]

The proportion of migrant labour is quite high for certain backward areas. As a result of the rise in staying power and supply price of labour, real wages have started rising in such areas during the eighties. The wage disparity between the developed and less developed areas has started declining. The male-female disparity in wage rates is also coming down. On the whole, therefore, the development of capitalist relations following the green revolution in the developed areas of the country has led to an improvement in incomes and in the bargaining power of the poorest of the poor in less developed regions, even in the absense of formal organisation of labour. Tensions are becoming acute because the rise in agricultural productivity in the less developed areas is not as significant as in the areas which were the first to experience the green revolution. The latter also had the advantage of higher relative prices of output. There are certain other features of the green revolution which have directly benefited the poor. These arise from the fact that agriculture is highly labour-intensive, is a highly competitive industry and supplies essential commodities like foodgrains, Despite machanisation, agriculture is still more labour-intensive than many industrial activities and, what is more, it provides employment to the economically weakest sections of the population. The highly competitive nature of agriculture means that no single group of farmers can influence the quanitty of output produced or the amount of inputs deployed. Because of this competition and also because there is an early limit to the demand for essetial commodities like foodgrains, the green revolution has brought about a decline in the relative prices of foodgrains such as wheat and rice. This is how benefits from the rise in productivity on account of green revolution have been passed on to consumers. The poorer sections who spend a large proportion of their budget on foodgrins have benefited relatively more than the well-to-do from the decline in relative prices.[14]

Captains of industry are of the opinion that the new Government should address itself to the task of bailing the country out of the economic crisis which has cast an ominous shadow on the future. Speaking to the Statesman [15] some noted industralists highlighted issues that need immediate attention.

The Delhi-based industrialist, Raunaq Singh, said liberalisation and delicensing were the key measures to put the economy back on rails. He explained that they would result in unhindered production giving the manufacturer scope to export the products, consequently bringing in the much-needed foreign exchange. Singh recall that the brief bid by Rajiv Gandhi's regime to reduce redtapism attracted many foreign investors. He hoped that the Government would encourage privatization and reduce subsidiaries to sectors like fertilizers, eventually stop the practice altogether. Mr. Singh observed that there was no alternative to IMF loan under the present circumsatance. However, he added that it did not help any country to be debt. ridden.

Another leading industrialist, K.K. Modi, suggested that the Government should endeavour to ensure that the country would not be held to ransom by demonstrations, strikes and bandhs. The phase of trumoil through which the country was passing last year had brought work in the industry to a virtual halt. He felt that production ought to be export-oriented since only the inflow of foreign exchange would ease the BOP (balance of payments) crisis. Dweling on the measures that can be implemented, Modi said exports should be excise free. He observed that it was high time that the protective cover given to the Indian market (goods) was removed. The quality would improve and the costs would come down if the market was subject to international competition. He stressed that the foreign investment till 40% should be free from bureaucratic hurdles. Modi said that efforts should be made to ensure that the rupee-rouble controversy did not become the cause of loosign an old customer especially at a time when it was difficult to make in roads into any new market. According to the Dalmia group chief Sanjay Dalmia, free entrepreneurship had saved the bacon of many a failing economy. He felt that the IMF loan was only a short- term solution, and would serve a limited prupose. He opined that steps shouls be taken by the new regime to stimulate production which was essential for any economy to flourish. With reference to the Budget (which the Government would present soon),

Dalmia suggested that there was no need to increase taxes instead rationalization of rates would help to collect the desired revenue. He observed that "pledging" of bullion in European markets and struck a blow to the "Indian psyche". The actual damage to its image in the international market was less.

R.V. Kanoria of the Kanoria Chemicals observed that the new Government's priority was to clear the country's debts. Wrothless expenditure and carrying on with unviable public sector units had taken its toll on the economy. He said that subsidies to fertilizers had failed to benefit the common man who still found prices spiralling. Kanoria stressed the need to liberalize the issue of licenses to permit the setting up of more units. He felt that imports could be linker to expoerts, ensuring that foreign exchange was not wasted. R.C. Bhargav of Maruti Udhyog Limited (MUL) shared his counterpart's opinion that privatization of loss making public sector companies could prevent them from being closed down. To deal with the difficult economic situation we will undoubtedly need a stable and cohesive government with substantial majority to work out drastic structural reforms in the Indian economy. The government's expenditures will have to be pruned, the public sector effectively disciplines, productivity of financial resources raised all around, and urgent steps to improve our exports even if that means alowing foreign investments freely, although in the short run very little is likely to come. Fortunately, India has an extrememanagerial class and first rate entrepreneurs whose potential remains stymied by poor macro policies of the politicians and even worse by micro procedures which our middle and lower level bureaucracy has tied them in. Neither our politicians nor our bureaucrats seem to be able to remove the chains on our economy and people. The coming few months and the regular budget which needs to be presented to the Parliament will put the country to tough seats. India will inevitably have to turn to the IMF and the World Bank for help, Perhaps, for large help. Given to present international geopolitical and economic power structure, India may find that the poor shape of its economy may cost it a lot in terms of its sovereignty. It is, therefore, extremely vital that all major political parties work together to prevent any significant infringement of our sovereignty, lest we find our independence on many fronts gets compromised.[16]

NOTES:

1. *The Hindustan Times,* 22 June 1991.
2. Kumaresh Chakravarty. A Paradigm Lost. *The Business and Political Observer,* 13 June 1991.
3. *Ibid.*
4. V.A. Pai Panandikar, the Economic Crisis, *The Hindustan Times,* 6 June 1991.
5. *Ibid.*
6. Vivek Bharati. India's Liquidity Crunch. *The Business and Political Observer*, 6 June 1991.
7. *Ibid.*
8. *National Herald,* 9 June 1991.
9. *Ibid.*
10. V.A. Pai Panandikar. The Eonomic Crisis. *The Hindustan Times,* 6 June 1991.
11. C.H. Hanumantha Rao. It's Easier to Fight on Full Stomachs. *The Business and Political Observer,* 22 June 1991.
12. *Ibid.*
13. *Ibid.*
14. *Ibid.*
15. *The Statesman,* 23 June 1991.
16. V.A. Pai Panandikar. The Economic Crisis, *The Hindustan Times,* 6 June 1991.

FIFTEEN

STATES POLITICS

In his maiden speech on June22, 1991, Narasimha Rao said, that his Government would tackle "with determination and single- minded-ness" the problems in the three border states of Kashmir, Assam and Punjab. "While genuine grievances will be redressed, terrorism and other fissiparous tendencies will be dealt with firmly," he said.

The new Prime Minister Narasimha Rao has to endeavour to improve Centre-States relations, greater federalism and fiscal, autonomy so that the people in this country of diversity can determine their fate. On this score too the new government can bring peace to the troubled states.

The definitive verdicts in the elections to several state assemblies contrasts sharply with the temperance of the Lok Sabha results which articulate a desire for consensual politics at the centre to meet pressing political and economic challenges. In the states, the vote for change has been overwhelming in its intensity, and pugnacious in its impact. The people have opted for strong state governments which can resolve problems of law and order, and of regional development. Detailed results are awaited, but certain trends are evident, and they hold warnings for the new governments as for others. Voters have summarily rejected discredited or non performing ruling parties. In Haryana the aspirations of the Chauthala clan have meet a fitting end. Also rejected is the regionalism of Bansi Lal. The Congress, however seems not to have learnt any lessons from the fall of its adversaries. There are ominous signs already of schisms in the party. In Tamil Nadu too, the unprecedented vote for the AIADMK is a damnation of the Karunandhi regime. The DMK's rejection was complete long before the elections. Jayalalitha faces pressing issues of public distribution system, jobs and housing, apart from the law and order crisis born of the presence of LTTE cadres among Tamil refugees. For the Congress the problem will come in how well they combine being her allies while also being watchdogs of public interest. In Assam, incomplete results again show disillusionment with the AGP which dissipated a passionate public mandate in internecine welfare and insatiable greed. The results of West Bengal and Kerala are object lessons both for the Congress and the left parties. In Bengal, the performance of Mr. Jyoti Basu's government and his own national stature contrasted sharply with a Congress party suffering from a death wish. The state party chief had not touch with ground reality. His colleagues were too busy fighting him, and each other. In the end, they all sank. In Kerala, the Congress recovered rapidly from misunderstanding with of its front partners.

Even otherwise through the last four years, it had kept itself alive with popular campaigns against the lack lustre Nayanar ministry.[1] The most summary verdict has been in UP. Maulayam Singh Yadav's handling of the Ayodhya issue fatally contaminated the Congress, his one time ally, as it did the parent Janata Dal. The Congress also paid the price of infighting, clouded vision, and above all, a failure of leadership. The wise people of UP have now told the BJP to mop up the law and order mess it created. The BJP's real test comes now.

The immediate task is to do something sensible about Punjab, Jammu and Kashmir and Assam. Polling is scheduled in Punjab and Assam and the Congress is ranged against the idea of going through with Punjab elections at this point. This is a divisive and dangerous vacillation because apart from sending the wrong signal to the people of Punjab it raises the possibility of playing arbitratilly with democratic, constitutional institutions. Holding these elections in the face of the threat of separatism, secessionism and armed extremism will mean taking some risks. But what the Congress seems dead set against is the path of cooperation among all national parties and regional forces which are opposed to the pro-Khalistan extremists. One hopes that the late Rajiv's message about Punjab not being ready for democratic elections within India will not turn out to be a self-fulfilling prophecy, where part of the problem is an anti- federalist party at the centre. This brings me to yet another task before a new government in Delhi. It is learning to live with Opposition experiments democratically and sportingly, developing a new culture of dealing with adversaries after people have had their say at the polls, being intelligent about Centre- State relations and respecting cooperative federalism in a way that does not belong to the mainstream political culture here. If the newly installed government makes a sound start on this front, there is bound to be a noticeable improvement on the front of national unity and political democracy within a year. Then perhaps, Indian democracy could turn the corner. We should wish ourselves luck.[2]

It certainly was not like 1984 But the sympathy vote coming to the Congress in the wake of Rajiv Gandhi's assassination was not insignificant either. Though it is a hypothetical assertion, psephological trends show that Rajiv in his death gifted the Congress at least 30 seats-possibly the eventual difference between the party's ability, now, to form a government with outside support and it having to form a government only in coalition with other parties. Had the sympathy factor not worked, the Congress tally may have been around 180-185. In such a situation, the support of the Left alone, which has 55 seats in the Tenth Lok Sabha, would not have sufficed. It would have required the support of the Janata Dal (JD), Telugu Desam or others-naturally for a high political price. It is perhaps not an exaggeration to say that Rajiv's martyrdom has given his party a better chance of providing a functional government. On the face of it, the most dramatic manifestation of the sympathy factor came from Andhra Pradesh. In the first round of polling in the state, which was on May 20-that is, pre-assassination-the Congress won only three of the 15 seats. In the next round, on June 15, it bagged 21 of the 25 seats, making clear that the voters sympathy had shifted to the Congress following Rajiv's death. But this is only part of the story, for behind the number of seats won lies a more accurate index of the shift in votes which is demonstrated by the change in percentage votes. And by that yardstick, the sympathy factor was relatively muted in Andhra. In the first round of polling in the state, the swing away from the Congress was seven per cent. In the second round, the swing away was two per cent, indicating a sympathy factor gain of five per cent. Surprisingly, in Uttar Pradesh, where the Congress performance was dismal in terms of seats, the sympathy factor was much more pronounced. In the first round of polling, on May 20, 1991 the swing away from the Congress was a whopping 14.6 per cent, which came down to a swing away from the aprty of 4.7 per cent in the June 15 polling-connoting a gain of 10 per cent for the party. It is another matter that the Congress base vote was so narrow this time round that even a 10 per cent increase in votes caused by Rajiv's death did not help the party to win seats. In Rajasthan, the sympathy vote was even higher. The Congress vote in the state, which was going up in any case, showed a one per cent increase in the first round of polling. The went up to 14 per cent in the second round, indicating a sympathy factor of 13 per cent votes. It is possible that the factor was exaggerated in Rajasthan because the constituencies that went to the polls in the second round-mainly the tribal seats in south- western part of the state-are traditional Congress seats. Likewise, in Madhya Pradesh where the party was poised to do well, the sympathy factor caused a surge in the Congress vote. In the first round, there was a four per cent swing in favour of Congress, which went up to 10 per cent in the second round. But once again, the second round polling was in areas where the Congress has been traditionally strong, which possibly gives such a pronounced sympathy factor swing. Though the electorate's emotional response to the assassination was most visible in Tamil Nadu, the swing in the party's favour was only two per cent. This is because the Congress-AIADMK combine had swept the polls last time too, and the present performance, although a further improvement, could only be so much as to show a relatively small swing. All in all, the sympathy factor appears to have helped the Congress in winning a larger number of seats in areas where it was already strong.[3]

Andhra Pradesh, Prime Minister P.V. Narasimha Rao's home state, has been given the maximum representation in his Council of Ministers. Of the 58 ministers, eight are from that State, two Rao himself and Vijaya Bhaskar Reddy of the cabinet rank, four Ministers of State including M. Mallikarjun and Chinta Mohan, and two deputy ministers.

Uttar Pradesh which returned only five Congress candidates including the late Rajiv Gandhi to the Lok Sabha, has got six ministers. Sheila Kaul is a Cabinet minister while Kalp Nath Rai, Balram Singh Yadav and Rudra Pratap Singh, are the Ministers of State and Salman Khurshid and Ramlal Rahi deputy ministers. Khurshid, who won the Farukhabad seat is the son of Karnataka Governor Khurshid Alam Khan. Maharashtra, where the party fared very well securing 37 of 47 seats has got only two minsters, S.B. Chavan, Cabinet rank and Shantaram Produkhe, Minister of State. None of the known supporters of Chief Minister Sharad Pawar, who withdrew in favour of Rao from the contest for the leadership of the Congress parliamentary party, finds a berth in the ministry. Madhya Pradesh gets as many as three Cabinet rank ministers, the highest for any State-Arjun Singh Madavrao Scindia and V.C. Shukla, who rejoined Congress just before the elections. It also has two ministers of State Kamal Nath and Dalbir Singh. Tamilnadu which returned as many as 28 congress members to the Lok Sabha has no representation at the Cabinet level. However, four of them have been made Ministers of State-P. Chidambaram, M. Arunachalam, P. Kumaramangalam and K. Ramamurthi. Another State where the Congress poll performance was very good. kerala also goes without representation at the cabinet level. It has four Ministers of State Mullapalli Ramachandran, M.M. Jacob, P.J. Kurien and S. Krishnakumar. Yet another Congress bastion. Karnataka, has five ministers. B. Sankaranand and C.K. Jaffer Sharief are the Cabinet ministers, Ms Margaret Alva and MS Tara Devi will be ministers of State and S.D. Nayama Gowda, who trounced Janata Dal leader R.K. Hedge in Bhagalkot, Will be a Deputy Minister. Bihar, where the party drew a blank at the poll, will be represented by two of its Rajya Sabha members Sitaram Kesari, who will be a Cabinet minister and Rameshwar Thakur, who has been made a Minister of State. M.L. Fotedar and Ghulam Nabi Azad, who hail from Jammu and Kashmir, but represented Uttar Pradesh and Maharashtra respectively in the Rajya Sabha, have been made Cabinet Ministers. The representation for other states is as follows: Rajasthan four-one cabinet Balram Jakhar, two ministers of State and one Deputy Minister. Gujarat one, Madhav Singh Solank (Cabinet rank). Orissa and West Bengal two Ministers of State each, and Tripura, Assam, Meghalaya, Delhi, Goa. Arunachal Pradesh, and Pondicherry-one Minister of State each, Assam has one Deputy Minister also. Well-known economist Dr. Man mohan Singh, who as a technocrat has been included into the Cabinet comes from Punjab.

The Congress impressive performance in Assam, surpassing even its own expectations, can be attributed to a considerable extent to the 'sympathy' factor which played to large a part else where in the country. Sriperumbudur must have had a special resonance in Assam. Not only was it the first State after the assassination of Rajiv Gandhi to go to the polls on June 6 and 8, but the State Congress had itself suffered badly at the hands of terrorists before and during President's rule. The verdict from an election which was peaceful and saw a large turn-out should therefore be read as a decisive vote against the politics of violence and secessionism and for the resolution of ethnic and autonomy claims by democratic means. The AGP and break-away Nutun Asom Gana Parishad must blame no one but themselves for their disastrous fall from 63 Assembly seats in 1985 to just over a quarter of that number in 1991. A less than mediocre record in office, unfulfilled promises on the immigrant question, capped by factional wars and allegations of corruption against party leaders explain the losses sustained in their former strongholds in the Brahamputra Valley. In the end the two AGPs could not count even on the All-Assam Students Union to compaign for them; the sympathy generated by their Government's dismissal from office last November could not work any magic. The inability to reach out to tribal people and linguistic and religious minorities in order to extend to AGP's original but limited base, and the recent dangerous firtation with the outlawed ULFA, have contributed to the overall failure. The price for the AGP's narrowly chauvinistic platform is that it has been reduced to a size indistinguishable from other small regional outfits.[4] The victories of the Autonomous State Demand Committee and the All- Bodo Students Union-Bodo People's Action Committee will strengthen demands for autonomous status. The BJP's path-breaking inroads into the communally sensitive Barak Valley is another pointer to the kind of tasks that will fall to the new Congress Government under the leadership of Narasimha Rao. And the ULFA, which has been as good as its word and avoided interfering with the elections, must be dealt with firmly and skifully. It is a tough set of challenges that the Congress ministry will be inheriting. The Prime Minister-designate, P.V. Narasimha Rao, said in New Delhi on June 20, 1991 that he was yet to decide whether his cabinet colleagues would also be sworn in alongwith him at Rashtrapati Bhavan on June 21. In a brief that with newsmen after his meeting with the President R. Venkataraman, Rao parried questions on whether his government was going to recommend to the Election Commission deferment of the Punjab elections, scheduled to be held on June 22. He said he could not answer any question about elections in Punjab "without being sworn in as Prime Minister or without the government being constituted." However, the Congress stand on Punjab is well known. The party has decided to boycott the elections in the troubled state. It has repeatedly demanded that the assembly and Lok Sabha elections there be postponed as the situation in the state was not conducive to holding a free and fair poll. Regarding the chief election commissioner's decision to postpone the Punjab elections, Prime Minister Narasimha Rao, said on June 21, 1991 he welcomed it. The Congress had been seeking a cancellation of the Punjab elections as the situation in that state was not conducive to the holding of a free and fair poll, he said. "The elections have been postponed and let us watch the situation now," Rao said.

Communal violence and caste-riots played a decisive role in the battle of ballots in the states. The electorate's behaviour in places which witnessed voilence on caste and communal lines was guided by intense polarisation on religious and sectarian lines. Even the traditional bastion of the Congress crumbled in the face of consolidation of the electorate on religious and caste basis. For instance, in Allahabad, which comprises three Lok Sabha seats, the Janata Dal won all seats. The place, considered to be the Congress stronghold because of the long association of the Nehru family with it, had witnessed anti-Mandal protests on a large scale. The Congress ambiguous stand on the reservation issue cost the party dearly and it could not win any of the 14 assembly seats in the district. On the other hand, the saffron effect too could not match the pro-reservation wave and the BJP could bag only three seats from the urban areas. The rural areas rejected the Ram wave altogether and gave their mandate in favour of the JD which won 9 assembly seats. At the same time, the electorate's behaviour in Varansai, a district bordering Allahabad, is a study in contrast. Considered to be a stronghold of the communists and socialists, the three parliament seats, Mirzapur Bhadohi, Varanasi and Chandauli, were won by the BJP, Political observers here feel that had it not been for communal riots just two days before the polling on May 20, 1991 the results would have been different. So intense was the Hindu consolidation in the district that even the backward-dominated Lok Sabha seat, Chandauli, was won by a not-so-known BJP candidate, Mr. Anand Ratan Maurya, by defeating the JD's state unit president, Mr. Kailash

Singh Yadav. Similarly, in Varanasi, the ex-DGP, Mr, S.C. Dixit, won against his formidable rival, Mr. Ram Kishore of the CPM. Of the 14 assembly seats in the district, the BJP won 10 seat. Paradoxically enough, the two neighbouring districts, Allahabad and Varanasi, which are equally important religious places, the election results were completely at variance. While in Varanasi, Hindutva torch bearers ruled the roast, in Allahabad, Mandal protagonists influenced voters. The Congress faced decimation in both the places. A trend-analysis of the election results in the other east UP parliamentary and assembly feelings on voters. In Gahazipur which borders Varanasi, of the two parliamentary seats, one was won by the CPI and another by the JD. In all, the National Front bagged all the parliamentary seats. The trend was confirmed in the assembly seats too. Of the seven assembly seats, two were won by the BJP and the rest won by the National Front alliance. The simple reason for this strange voting, as explained by the political pundits, is that the caste factor dominated the scene in the district. The district had witnessed two caste clashes in members of the Harijan community were persecuted by the caste Hindus. The situation led to consolidation of voters on caste lines against the dominant upper caste Hindus.

The persution by the Muiyam Singh regime in eastern UP areas where L.K. Advani's rath yatra was scheduled to pass through helped Hindu consolidation on a large scale and enabled the BJP to a smooth victory in most of the places. Since in none of these places caste-conflict was evident, the Mandal factor did not work against Hindu consolidation. Though economically backward and predominatly inhabited by backwards and Harijans, the two Lok Sabha seats, Gonda and Balrampur, went to the BJP. Of the 10 assembly seats in the district, the BJP won nine and all with good margins. The effect of the Ram wave in this sleepy district could be judged from the fact that the BJP candidate from Gonda, Mr. Brij Bhushan Singh, an SJP leader involved in several cases, won simply because he joined the BJP just before the announcement of elections.

Similarly, the BJP had a clean sweep in Gorakhpur and Basti where it won all Lok Sabha seats and claimed most of the assembly seats. In Deoria, the trend was, however, different. Of the three Lok Sabha seats, Padrauna, Deoria and Salempur, the BJP won only in Padrauna while the JD, leader, Mohan Singh, won in Deoria and Harikewal Prasad of the JD won in Salempur. The assembly results of this district which borders Bihar were, however, astonishingly different. Of the 13 assembly seats, the BJP won 10 seats. The trend suggested that voters behaviour in electing, MP's and MLAs was not the same. Apart from the east UP district, the major gain for the BJP has come from the districts ravaged by frequent riots. The BJP won the Kanpur Nagar and Dehat Lok Sabha seats. Three successive riots in Kanpur had already polarised the electorate on communal lines. This was evident in the assembly results too as six out of the seven seats in Kanpur Nagar were won by the BJP. Interstingly, Kannauj Lok Sabha seat adjacent to Kanpur was lost by the BJP despite the presence of the high profile BJP candidate. T.N. Chaturvedi. Similarly, in Aligarh, where repeated riots have shattered the district's economy, the BJP won two Lok Sabha seats, Hathras and Aligarh. Of the 10 Assembly seats, the BJP won six. In Budaun where communal riots took place last year, the JD fire-brand, Mr Sharad Yadav, lost to the erudite Swami Chinmayananda. Though the district has large assembly seats, the BJP got three. The JD also won three seats while two were shared by the Congress and the SJP.

What appears to have come as a major surprise for political observers is the results from Budaun district where the BSP had dominated the scene in the last election. This time, of the seven assembly seats, the BJP won all the seats. The BJP candidate won the Budaun Lok Sabha seat too. The apparent reason for this winning spree of the BJP is Hindu consolidation in the district which witnessed one of the most serious communal riots that shook the state in recent times.

The fact that communal violence played a crucial role in the elections could be judged from the fact that the BJP candidate. N.P. Singhal, retired DGP, lost to his JD rival. The Samabhal Lok Sabha seat of the district was also won by the JD. Though the district is communally sensitive, there had been no riots since 1980. The stable law and order situation, of this sensitive district did not alow Hindu consolidation the BJP suffered a major setback in losing both the Lok Sabha seats.

Maulayam Singh Yadav who received Congress Party's support is down but not out. He will now devote his time and energy on building up his party's base from block to the State-level and is confident of occupying the centre stage in the State politics. He opined that the Bharatiya Janata Party has temporarily succeeded "in misguiding the innocent voters on the issue of the Ram temple". He said "it is now for the BJP to build the Ram temple at the disputed site since this was their (BJP's) main election plank". Asked how the BJP could build the temple at the disputed site in view of the status quo order issued by the three-member special bench of the High Court, Yadav replied that "every leader of the BJP had been assuring voters that if voted to power, the construction of the temple will begin within a month. It is for them to fulfill their assurance." When quizzed further whether the BJP had come to stay. Yadav said, "No party can stay in power for long by inciting religious feelings of the people and igniting communal passions, and the people will soon realise that they had been cheated". He refused to entertain further questions on this subject. To another question, Yadav replied that he would now concentrate his time and energy on building the party organisation in the entire State-from block to the state-level- and hold conference with party workers. "This is my struggle based on principles which aims at maintaining communal harmony. This may be a long-drawn out struggle but our principles will ultimately emerge triumphant", he added. Ask how he viewed the victory of the BJP in UP, he replied it was a victory of negative politices and votes. They (BJP) misguided innocent people in the name of religion and Ram temple which would now boomerang on them. "No Government formed on communal frenzy can last its term in any society", he asserted.

When asked what would his party do if the construction of the Ram temple was bogged down in legalities, the Chief Minister said the temple was BJP's main election plank and "let them construct it at the site they had been demanding for years." "We too were in favour of the Ram temple, but at a different site so that the Babri mosque is not demolished", he pointed out. Yadav said he accepted the people's verdict but refused to discuss the reasons that led to the debacle of his party in the elections. Since his own election has been countrermanded, Mr. Yadav ceases to be a legislator. But he is fully prepared to contest the elections as and when the Election Commission holds it. He has no idea whether the countermanded elections (one for the Lok Sabha and five for Assembly from his home district of Etawah) will be held in November or December.

It is no secret that Yadav is unhappy with Prime Minister Chandra Shekhar over his utterances against the Mandal Commission which drove away the backward (OBCs) voters into the Janata Dal camp. He is also maintaining a distance from Deputy Prime Minister Devi Lal whose various acts of "omission and commission" made the SJP a laughing stock.

Winning for the fourth consecutive term is no simple achievement. It only proves that, despite drastic changes in issues and electoral calculations, the Left citadel in west Bengal remains intact. The CPWM-led Left Front's victory was expected, going by the pre-electoral trends visible in this State. Not even the fervent optimists in the Congress had expected this Left bastion to collapse. West Bengal witnessed a high 70 per cent voter turn- out in the first round of polls before Rajiv Gandhi's assassination. Hence, the sympathy factor had not played any role there, unlike Kerala, where the CPM-led Left Front has been defeated by the Congress. High participation of voters is itself an in dication of the importance attached to elections by West Bengal voters, unlike the electorates in most States where voter turn-out has been under 53 per cent, signifying voter disillusionment arising from the inglorious end of the 1989 Lok Sabha. While the exact constiutaency-wise break-up in terms of percentage of votes cast, and the different factors influencing voters behavious visa-a-vis the final outcome is yet unclear, the Left has once again been able to way rural Bengal and vast sections of urban voters in its favour. However, the deeper truth in West Bengal lies in the dissatisfactin of the common people with industrial stagnation, lock-outs, electricity shortage, unemplyment and vast trerrains of poverty, in spite of land reforms. If the Congress, with its stable 40 per cent support base, had wished to utilise this discontent and turn it into votes in ints favour, it miserably failed, and for obvious reasons. And hoc WBPCC president Siddhartha Shankar Ray has won the Chowrangee seat but he was unable to organise the factions of the party into one chohesive unit. Fourteen years of Left Front rule has not been a golden era; but given the situation, the voters have decisively opted for the Left. The Left Front has secured an absolute majority in the Assembly and secured 29 Lok Sabha seats, with the CPM alone winning 182 Assembly and 22 Lok Sabha seats. The Congress has won 42 Assembly seats (it won 40 in 1987) and five seats in the Lok Sabha (it won four in 1989). Clearly, the party has singularly failed to learn from its past bungling, nor are its petty faction leaders likely to unlearn a great deal which has brought the WBPCC to its present sorry pass. The WBPCC remains the happy hunting ground of Calcutta-based faction leaders, with little or no contacts with the rural hinterland. The BJP has drawn a blank in spite of contesting 42 Lok Sabha seats and 290 Assembly seats. West Bengal has been consistently secular. Communal rabble-rousers have failed therein recent years. BJP candidate Victor Bannerjee's defeat from South West Calcutta should be a reminder that even star power cannot sell of it is not the politics the Bengal electorate currently prefers. However, the BJP has secured the third position in some border districts.[5] This should concern both the Left and the Congress, and especially the latter, because it is their traditional support base which has cracked under the BJP pressure. The GNIF has won three seats in the hills, with its subdued call for a separate State-an issue, which would certainly add to the worries of the new Left Front Government.

The 501 members of the newly constituted tenth Lok Sabha have been judged primarily on the basis of their commitment to the respective positions they or their parties had taken in 1989. As the details of the results indicate it is clear that the voters have swept the broom to clear out those who deviated directly or indirectly from the anti-Congress mandate of November, 1989. Instead, those who stood by their party's ideology and leadership and followed a consistent and honest political line have been voted the Congress out of power in 1989 in the hope that the opposition would stick together and would not repeat its 1979 blunder of paving the way for the return of the Congress party again. According to political analysts, the voter has been particularly harsh to the Bharatiya Janata Party by exploding its myth of emerging as the real and the only national alternative of the Congress. By giving it 119 seats of the 480 it contested, the voter has summarily rejected the claim of its leadership that the election was "between the BJP and the others". It is clear that the people have not pardoned the BJP for deviating from the strident anti-Congress political ideology and resorting to purely religious issues. The party has been confined mainly to Uttar Pradesh, Madhya Pradesh, Rajasthan, Himachal Pradesh, Delhi and a few pockets of Karnataka. Compared to its opponents-particularly the non-Congress parties-the BJP had enormous resources at its disposal, including a fleet of aircraft and vehicles and an overflowing cornucopia of funds. But down the line, its political arrogance an confrontationist approach drew the voters away from it. People have shaken the party even in its traditional strong holds. It has undoubtedly managed to improve its tally from 86 to 119 and to almost double its share of votes in the country by spreading its net from Arunachal Pradesh to Kanyakumari. But it was delivered a crushing blow even in its citadels like Madhya Pradesh, Rajasthan and Himachal Pradesh. In the Capital, L.K. Advani, its prime ministerial candidate, barely scraped though by a slender margin of 1,500 votes against a political lightweight, Rajesh Khanna. In Haryana, the party could win only two Assembly seats aginst 18 it has in the dissolved House and most of its Lok Sabha candidates secured third of fourth positions. The Congress, too, has gained only in those States where its local leadership maintained its independent character. But as far as the party is concerned, the gain of 36 seats is not merely a bounty coming from a disunited opposition and the assassination of its leader. Even then the decline of 3.5 per cent in its votes is far less than the steep fall of 9 per cent between the 1984 and the 1989 elections. It is obvious that the nation is having second thought about the Congress. There is clear evidence that the party picked up few extra seats in Andhra Pradesh, Madhya Pradesh and few other States after Rajiv's tragic death. But even if Rajiv were alive, the beneficiaries of Congress losses would have been those who stood by the 1989 mandate and not those who betrayed it.[6]

The new government be required in the short-term to initiate measures for the restoration of normalcy in Jammu and Kashmir and bring the state back into the national mainstream. Here again, it will be unable to take any initiative unilaterally and will have to depend on a national consensus, which it itself will have to bring about. Thus, apart from hard decisions which await the government in the economic and budgetary fields, equally hard decisions await it on the political front. The communalisation and criminalisation of politics has already jeopardised the law and order situation. Failure to act with firmness and determination on the domestic front will add to the deterioration of the situation. However, the most important question that has a direct bearing on the shape of things to come relates to the Congress itself. The fact that for the first time in the party's history it will not offer a Prime Minister to the country from Uttar Pradesh is not important as the other related fact that for the first time the Congress parliamentary party will have no member from Bihar, and less than five members from Uttar Pradesh. Considering that these two States from the main base of political power in India, the absence of representation from them is bound to create tensions of a new kind for the party, and lead to subterranean rivalries and jealousies and conflicts between the defeated members from these two States and the victorious members from other States. A situation in which members from the two States sending the largest number of members to Parliament have no say in the decision-making processes has not been faced by the party till now. Such a situtaiton can be dealt with, and the tensions arising from it controlled, only by a strong leader. There is no denying that the country is crying out for a stable government which will address itself to the manifold tasks of governance from day one. But no party riven by factions, and motivated only by considerations of power and pelf, and given to the soft life, can deliver stability in the long run. The absence of a comfortable majority makes the tasks of governance that much more difficult in a country which even in the best of terms is not easy to govern. The absence of a strong leader who can hold the party together can be neutralised to some extent if there is a new style of functioning, and collective wisdom is given preference over coterie manipulation. But if the Congress fails to draw appropriate lessons from the plight it find itself in, its rule will most probably come to and end within months rather than years. It can survive that fate only if its elected members approach their task with a greater sense of responsibility and responsiveness, and tailor their conduct to the new political realities which contains seeds of discontent and disenchantment which can turn explosive in no time. The Congress needs to galvanise its leaders not only to "manage" the party but also to "manage" the people when elections come next if it intends to become the mainstream political party in India all over again.[7]

The study on Centre-state fiscal transfers by Dr. Rajah Chellia and Govind Rao of the National Institute of Public Finance Policy (NIPFP) has brought out some glaring distortions in the existing system of transfers through the planning and finance commissions. Its main formulations pointing towards wasteful duplication of funds, inadequate criteria to assess backwardness, excessive weightage to population and the need to enhance the states share in taxes merit a serious consideration. Centre-state fiscal relations, which have evoked a fierece controversy in the past, are bound to come to the fore once again with the new configuration of political parties in power in the states. Although the Congress seems set to return to power at the Centre and has regained hold over Haryana, Kerala and Tamil Nadu, almost half-a-dozen states are still under non-Congress rule. More pertinently, after the departure of Rajiv Gandhi the last vestige of supreme authority in the party, even the Congress-ruled states are bound to assert their regional interests more openly. It will, therefore, be appropriate to arrive at a broad consensus on the norms governing fiscal transfers. The NIPFP study has rightly underlined the need for taking into account the disadvantages of certain states arising from the shortfall in their revenue raising capacity. This factor has inhibited the states ability to provide adequate funds for public services. The wasteful duplication of funds is attributed to the compartmentalised functioning of the planning and finance commissions and the artificial distinction inassessing the plan and non-loan needs of the states. It is well known that non-plan expenditure does not always imply non-development expenditure. More often than not, such expenditure relates either to the maintenance of engoing projects or those projects which do not form part of the plan but have a vital bearing on the socio-economic development of the states. It is, therefore, essential to take an intergrated view of the states development needs. Equally important is a review of the resource raising instruments available to the states so that they become more self-reliant and do not have to look towards the Centre for financing every little project. In the German federal system, major resource raising powers are vested with the constituent landers which, in turn, contribute to the central kitty in accordance with certain specified criteria.[8] There is no reason why we should not bring about necessary modifications in our federal financial structure to ensure more fiscal autonomy for the States. This will sure enable them to develop faster in a spirit of healthy competitions.

Indeed, Narasimha Rao will be judged by his ability to lead and perform in the crucial areas of Punjab, Assam and Kashmir and of the economy. He has so far shown a dignified and sober response to the traumatic cirsis that the Congress was faced with. He has handled Sharad Pawar firmly but tactfully. His council of ministers is broad-based, having a number of stalwarts. Their experience should help to take the country forward. However, more than tactful skills, he has to generate confidence even abroad.[9] He has to take the initiative in speeding up the process of normalisation and political renaissance in the turbulent states.

NOTES :

1. *The Business and Political Observer,* 20 June 1991.
2. *N. Ram. What nent? Current* 1 June 1991.
3. Arindam Sen Gupta. The Sympathy Wave. *The Sunday Observer,* 23 June 1991.
4. *Indian Express,* 21 June 1991.
5. *Patriot,* 19 June 1991.
6. Prabhu Chawla, 1991 Lok Sabha Elections. *Indian Express,* 23 June 1991.
7. S. Viswam. Managing the Mandate. *The Hindustan Times,* 23 June 1991.
8. *The Business and Political Observer,* 19 June 1991.
9. Hari Jaisingh. Man of the Moment. *The Business and Political Observer,* 22 June 1991.

SIXTEEN

TERRORISM AND SECURITY

Prime Minister P.V. Narasimha Rao in his first nation-wide address on June 22, 1991 asked the people to prepare for sacrifices and tighten their belts to restore the health of the economy and promised "decisive" action to solve problems. He also declared that his Government would deal with terrorism and the communal situation with determination and single-mindedness to safeguard the unity and integrity of the country.

India has come to a pass where terrorism has struck roots in the mercantilist on goings. It is a new development. That India suffered communal violence, linguistic agitation and communist insurgency in 1947 is well known. Communists changed tactic and gradually those beyond redemption reduced themselves into sects of Naxals. The Communist insurgency was a reflection of the acts of violance of those who suffered from absolute deprivation. Linguistic reorganisation evinced, apart from cultural aspirations of the people, the desires of those who were suffering not from a sense of absolute deprivation. They suffered from a sense of relative deprivation, i.e. those sections of the society who had propertity but who wanted a larger share in the cake. That this has assumed meancing proportions, say in Punjab, Jammu and Kashmir and the north-east must be read in the context of anti-India psycho-pathology of its neighbours. The communal violence that was witnessed in 1947 has grown by leaps and bound after an initial lull and needs to be reckoned with. Communal riots began as sporadic events in industrial and middle class towns for a few days. Today, in the late 1980s, the situation is that towns are under section 144 for months and yet communal carnage flares up. Historians and empiricists have attributed the growth of the phenomenon to the middle classes and petty traders. Some had identified it with the underworld and their shady deals with political parties. In 1990 when the Toyota-Kamal march took place, blood flowed in the streets and lanes of Indian cities and mobilisation of people took place in the Hindi heartland in the nake of Ram and Social inequity. Both wanted to change the political agenda of India. Seen in that context, the slogan of Congress stability could not be regarded as status quoist or revisionist. It was denoting self-preservation of a nation that began on the path of democratic peaceful experiment with social change. The use of violence against this way has made nobody wiser or stronger. Those for communalism and for social equity are still struggling to get a mass base. The greatest tribute that these forces are paying to Rajiv Gandhi is their adoption of the slogan of stability. No body, today after his assassination, is talking of coalition politics. Is this an indication of things to come at the hustings? Perhaps. The political class in India needs to think hard about terrorism. They need to rise above personal greed. Liberalisation of the economy is on the agenda. So, it appears is the privatisation of the public sector. If arms industry is completely privatised and if India develops an arms bazar owing to the breakdown of the dominant political consensus, it is the political class in India that will be responsible. And the people who allow this cannot blame their gods but themselves. Seen in the larger context, political terrorism is a phenomenon which has begun to raise its ugly head in a large number of countries. That in a difficult period of transition from a highly centralised political system and 'command economy' to democratisation, decentralisation and market economy, terroristic violence, and ethnic conflicts should emerge in the Soviet Union clearly confirms this conclusion. What is more disturbing is that some of the Republics of the Soviet Union have begun to organise local armies. From the long term point of view, this will threaten the unity and integrity of the Soviet Union. This is turn may have long term repercussions on all other countries.[1]

The increasing frequency of elections, while strengthtening our democratic roots, is also shaking our social roots. The violence that has come to be associated with elections has successded not only in keeping saner elements from contesting the elections but also from voting. All through the election campaign, local toughs could be seen along with other 'party workers' attempting to influence the voting pattern and 'woo' the poor and helpless. A similar act of madness resulted in the murder of Mr. Rajiv Gandhi. This is not what our founding fathers had in mind when they chartered the country's course on the road of democracy. Violence, whether verbal or otherwise, defeats the purpose of any. All national parties are guilty of violence. No candidate elected through the cult of violence can do the country any service on assuming power. The election commission cannot do much since it does not have the powers to do anything except to order a repoll.[2]

The government should confer more statutory powers on the commission to deal with election related violence.

Does Narasimha Rao see a foreign hand in assassination of Rajiv Gandhi? The matter is being looked into by a commission of inquiry. I hope the terms of reference of the commission would be widened to find answers to questions like this. Meanwhile, I would like to say each one of us has his hunch. Beyond this, I would not like to comment.[3]

As Chief Minister of Andhra Pradesh, Rao could not handle the seperate down. How would you handle the presidentship of the Congress.

You are absolutely wrong in saying I could not handle the separate Andhra agitation. I would perhaps remind you that the Andhra agitation was there for some time, but it was a question of keeping the state together. It was a question of saving the integrity of the state. The agitation could not result in a separate Andhra State. Though there was no question of anyone controlling it or not controlling it, I had to step down to keep the state together. Let there be not mistake about that [4]

Is Rao sticking to the election manifesto presented by the late Rajiv Gandhi.

We will implement it cent per cent. This is our first and fore- most promise. No intention on our part to change the promises made in the manifesto.[5]

Was an amendment made to the Congress constitution to provide that only a Lok Sabha member could be made the leader of the Congress parliamentary Party?

No such amendment was made[6]

There cannot be any doubt that we live in an age of violence, not only does violence play a significant role in our electoral process, but there is an increasing tendency to settle arguments by voilence. It is true that we are still at some distance from the Kalashnikov culture, but it appears to be merely a question of time; if the present trend continues we will accept violence as part of our way of life, as indeed, it is already in some parts of the country. I am not referring to political assassination when I am talking of violence, though it certainly as an aspect of political violence because assassinations can take place even in a society where normal political conventions are observed. The United States, like India, is a violent society, but there violence has tended to be associated with the race problem; the political assassinations that took place in that country could be related to that central problem. In India violence is generalised; in this respect, we resemble some of the Latin American States. I have in mind states with large (red) Indian populations, not only the Central American republics but also the Andean states. These states have one thing in common; they have extremely satrtified societies based on race and colour and any attempt by the disinherited and the dispossessed to improve their conditions leads to savage repression. These are countries which have permanent state of emergency; the only war they wage is against their own people The Central American states were, of course, the original banana republics; not only because their major export was bananas and they were depedent on the United Fruit Company which could change governments and when it pleased, but because the small elite which held power in these countries preferred to bend to external pressures rather than politically enfranchise the Indians. The foreign hand was the result of the refusal of the small elite, who benefited from the system, to end social stratification. I am by no means suggesting that we are on the way to becoming a banana republic, but the ostrich-like policy we have adopted towards social change, the refusal to accept the fact that the political and social outcasts, unless integrated into the social systems by giving them a stake in it, will make it impossible for us to overcome our internal weaknesses; we will be society torn as under by internal striffe, a state in permanent crisis.[7]

Commerce and Law Minister Dr. Subramanian Swamy on June 13, 1991 alleged that there had been "a fair amount of secret contact" between the National Front Government and the LTTE. Some of it through the DMK Government of Tamil Nadu, and urged the NF leaders to "volunteer" information regarding these contacts. All leads of the investigations into the Rajiv Gandhi assassination case pointed to the LTTE's involvement, according to Dr. Swamy, who asked whether a country could allow one of its popular leaders to be killed by a foreign agency. It was "an infringement of our sovereignty", he said. There was no one except the LTTE as per the evidence so far" in Rajiv Gandhi's assassination case. The Sri Lankan organisation, according to him, had been allowed to grow, and even kill its rivals during the National Front Government's rule at the Centre. Dr. Swamy did not think it was "relevant" to seek information about the "secret contacts" that the LTTE had with the Congress-I governments at the centre or with the Tamil Nadu Government headed by the late M.G. Ramachandran.

Dr. Swamy alleged that the LTTE's role during the National Front Government's reign had been such that its worker had helped a NF Union Minister to "capture booths during elections in Bihar". He did not name the Minister, however, but added he would do so in a day or two.

The Liberation Tigers of Tamil Elelam (LTTE), Sri Lanka's dominant Tamil Guerilla group, may or may not have killed Rajiv Gandhi. Even if it did, it would be virtually impossible to prove its involvement. The LTTE is today not only one of the best organised and well-armed guerrilla groups, but it has learnt enough in its 15 years of existence to cover its tracks. To be fair to the LTTE, there are other groups/interests within India and outside which could have wanted to prevent Gandhi from becoming Prime Minister again. The LTTE has itself tried to pin the blame on four forces; militant groups within India, Sri Lanka government, rival Tamil groups and one or more individual Sri Lankan Tamils who might have suffered at the hands of the Indian Peace-Keeping Force (IPKF) and wanted revenge. Some questions raised in the implicit defence of the Tigers since the May 21 assassination are; Why should LTTE kill Gandhi? How would it benefit? Would not the killing destroy the good will the Tigers have in India, particularly in Tamil Nadu? Was not the LTTE trying to end its frosty ties with Gandhi? Is it not true that LTTE does not interfere in Indian politics? To answer these questions, it is necessary to study some of LTTE's past actions and its reactions to those events. We shall begin with the July 1989 assassinations of Appapillai Amirthalingham, MP, and his Tamil United Liberation Front (TULF) colleague V. Yogeswaran in the former's Colombo residence to understand the group's psyche. When Amir once a favourite of Indira Gandhi and the Indian government, was shot dead, the LTTE-which was then holding peace talks with Colombo-initially denied all responsiblity. It maintained it denial even though the three killers were shot dead by policement and one of the assassins, known as Visu, was once known to have been based in the LTTE office in Madras. Indeed, the Tigers, in carefully orchestrated leaks to the then sympathetic Colombo media, made it known that the three had quit the group sometime earlier and were probably working for India's Research and Analysis Wing (RAW) on top of it, many asked such questions (note the resemblance with the queries posed after Gandhi's death). Why would the LTTE kill Amirthalingam? What threat did he pose to them? Wasn't he a political nobody in 1989, unable to win an election (he was nominated to Parliament after his defeat in Batticaloa, Unable to visit Tamil Nadu areas freely? At a time when LTTE was talking peace with the Sri Lankan Government, would they kill such a well-known personality and that too in Colombo. And, on top of all this, weren't the Tigers trying to mend their fences with the TULF top brass? But the LTTE soon put up posters in Sri Lanka's northeast, describing the dead assassins of Amir and Yogeswaran as "martyrs". Next, Gopalasmy Mahendrarajah alias Mahattaya, the LTTE's number two, told an interviewer (even when the peace talks with Colombo were still on) that the Tigers had indeed killed Amir and gave the reasons for his execution. But as important as he belated admission of Amir's killing was the way it was done, which showed the dodgedness and single-mindedness with which the LTTE Pursues its targets.[8]

Rajiv Gandhi, despite losing power in November 1989 continued to take an active interest on Sri Lanka and kept his links with Sri Lankan

Tamils, including those from non-LTTE groups and individuals. After the V.P. Singh Government fell in November 1990, most Sri Lankans were convinced that Gandhi was on his way back. The LTTE must have also realised this. But Gandhi, contrary to what is being made out, was deeply distrustful of the Tigers. This is admitted by nearly all those who were in regular touch with him on the Sri Lankan issue. In a way perhaps Gandhi can be called naive for having let his feelings known to a wide range of people, and even agreeing to meet members of Tamil groups (Kasi Anandan included) who did not match his stature. One Sri Lankan who met him a few months ago recalls that Gandhi, after going through a document on the Tamil question specially prepared for him, remarked: This is fine. But it does not take into account what we (India) should do in case the LTTE does not cooperate. Knowing them (LTTE), we should have a contingency plan where we can proceed without them if necessary. Gandhi, having burnt his fingers in Sri Lanka and in the light of the changing world scenario, had come to take an adament stand on two points. There shall be no compromise on Sri Lanka's territorial integrity and, two while there should be attempts to win over the LTTE, the Tigers should never be given the status of the sole representatives of the Tamil community. Rajiv Gandhi was also genuinely concerned about the safety of A. Varan-daraja Perumal, an EPRLF leader and the former Chief Minister of Sri Lanka's northeast who fled the island just before the IPKF withdrawl and now lives in a safe house in Madhya Pradesh. Gandhi told a Sri Lankan early this year: I am on the hit list of the Panthic Committee so is my family. If they manage to get me, it will not make a big difference to the Indian state vis-a-vis Punjab. But if the Tigers get perumal, it will be a major blow to the Tamil question. Rajiv Gandhi volunteered to give, as a good will gesture, a bullet proof vest to perumal. He also sent a condolence message after the killing of Path-manabha and his group members. There is no love lost between the LTTEE and EPRLF. It is inconceivable that the LTTE did not know Gandhi's mind. If the LTTE did kill Gandhi, then there could be two reasons why the tigers sent Anandan to meet the Indian leader. One, the meeting could be later parotted as "Proof" of their innocence. The world could be told that they were mending their fences with Gandhi, so why should they kill him? The March 5 meeting is indeed being reasoned as the main reason why the LTTE could not have assassinated Gandhi,[9]

It is argued that LTTE would not benefit by Gandhi's exit since the Congress Party is anyway committed to the July 1987 India-Sri Lanka accord. True, But it is equally true that on crucial issues, the stand of a government is influenced by what its leader thinks and how he/she acts. To this extent, Gandhi's death may bring about a change in India's attitude vis-a-vis the Sri Lankan Tamil question. No other Congress leader in the centre took such an active interest on the subject as did Gandhi. The choice of Tamil Nadu as the killing ground may be a coincidence, but it is one place where the Tigers have over the years assiduously established safe houses and sympathisers and where a section of politicians worship Prabhakaran as a hero. The Tigers also continue to ferry men and material between Tamil Nadu and Sri Lanka, and in the recent past have abducted (for brief period though) dozens of Indian fishermen and customs officials without inviting any governmental warth. If rival Tamil groups, who also once enhoyed a presence in Tamil Nadu, are not being suspected as much as the LTTE, it is not without reason. None of them has the kind of commitment and fanatcism which marks out the LTTE. None of these groups would be able to command members to die for a cause. There is another aspect about Rajiv Gandhi's assassination that is interesting Amrithalingam was illed at the height of a New Delhi-Colombo row over the IPKF (TULF sources said later that the LTTE assassins had been itching to meet Amir that very month), Sam Thambimuthu was killed just before he was to fly to London to allegedly report about LTTE activities to Amnesty International, Pathmanabha was killed soon after the LTTE resumed its war against Colombo when there was speculation that Colombo and EPRLF might do a volte face and join hands, and Rajiv Gandhi does just when he was expected to become Prime Minister once again.[10]

Radical measures are afoot to beef up security inside Parliament House to provide a better security cover to top politicians and other VVIPs living under the shadow of terrorism. Official sources said in New Delhi on Jene 7, 1991 tht the watch and ward agency of Parliament, sloley responsible for security arrangements in the complex, was being given more teeth in terms of skilled manpower and spohisticated technical equipment. Gradually the 250 member strong be upgraded to the level of the elite Special Protection Group (SPG), National Security Guards (NSG) and other such agencies involved in VVIP security arrangements in the country. Top most priority was being given to installation of state of the art communication system to replace the age-old present network. Other thrust areas were procuring and pressing into service sophisticated bomb detectors, drug detectors, explosive defusers and gas detectors. The appropriate authorities were also making efforts to set up devices on all 12 entrances to Parliament House to detect plactic explosives as the device was non-existent in the security set-up right now. This is vital as platio explosives are not being increasingly used in terrorist crimes world-wide. In the Rajiv Gandhi assassination too, a plastic explosive is said to be the killer weapon. Till such arrangements are completed the watch and ward staff would be put on a high state of alert to manually check and frisk each entrant to the complex for plastic explosives. While outside Parliament top security agencies provided elaborate security cover to the President, Vice-President, the Prime Minister and other VVIPs. Inside the Parliament it was the responsibility of the watch and ward agency. It was explained that the need to upgrade this agency arose in view of the increased threat perception for these politicians. Right now, the watch and ward agency is dependent on outside agencies like Delhi Police, SPG, NSG and the Intelligence Bureau (IB) for experts, equipment and even vehicles in case of any eventuality. The watch and ward control room, which was set up only few years ago, closes down at night making it impossible to monitor the situation and take prompt steps in case of any incident. They said in the pipeline was a proposal to start an elaborate anti-sabotage drill on a daily basis for Parliament House security this upgradation of security was over. The anti-sabotage drill would help make security arrangements inside Parliament House foolproof in line which the present-day requirements. The personnel of the watch and Ward Staff would also be sent to specialised agencies like the NSG and SPG for a crash training course. A large number of the present watch and ward staff were not conversant with ways and means to tackle terrorist crimes. Declining to divulge the full details of the propose crash training the sources said one of its constituents would be inculcating the instinct to drive offensively in emergency situations.

Attention is now turning to the new government headed by P.V. Narasimha Rao, in New Delhi and its tasks ahead. Hopefully, it will be in full command soon and draw up its priorities. Defence and defence-related issues should be high in the list in the interst of the country's health and economy. Like in most fields of national life, all is not well in the defence front too. Doubtless, the men in the forces are still ready for any sacrifice needed for the country, but discontentment at all levels is increasingly effecting the standards of performance in the armed forces.

That perhaps is one of the reasons why retired military personnel have increasingly chosen to march into political parties-and set things right in the government. What has really frustrated the retired personnel of the armed forces is not the government's repeated failure to honour the promises made to improve their lot, but the bungling on several otherfronts. The word 'BOFORS' has become notorious in the public mind. It caused the fall of a government, rightly or wrongly. But for those who know the forces from inside, the Bofors type of controversies have now become a common feature even though the money involved may not be as large as in case of the 155 mm artillery gun For years we have been invariably rushing abroad for buying military equipment, required or not required, for "national interest" or somebody else's interest; More about it a little later. First about the increasing discontent which has begun to demoralise the forces. One of the major factors in this regard is the in-service conditions. Promotions, transfers and postings are being increasingly politicised, influenced by both bureaucratic and political forces. The appointment of the present Chief of the Naval Staff some months ago really rocked the sea force, which saw for the first time a controversy about the top appointment. No reflection this on the capabilities and suitability of Admiral Ramdas, but the manner in which Tony Jain was done in the eye was questionable and demoralising to the naval force. What has happened in the Indian Air Force just now did not happen in the Navy a few months ago. The Chief of Air staff designate, Air Marshall Suri, was give a few months extension in the Air Marshall rank to enable him to be in uniform until the present chief, Air Chief Marshal S.K. Mehra, retires on July 31. Suri has now been named as Mehra's successor and steps into the next rank on August 1. But unfortunately Vice-Admiral Tony Jain, who was given a few months's extension in Vice-Admiral rank, was not given the Admiral's rank and made Chief of Nava staff even though it was well-known in top defence circles that Jain was to succeed Nadkarni. As a matter of fact, Vice-Admiral Tony Jain's case was stronger than Air Marshal Suri's even though the circumstances in both cases were about the same. Jain's tenure in the rank of Rear Admiral was cut short. He did not complete his term as Director General of Coast Guards and was elevated to the next rank and made Flag Officer commanding-in-Chief, Western Command, considered to be the most prestigious appointment in the Navy. In fact, this charge is considered to be a stepping stone to becoming the Navy Chief. Admiral, Nadkarni too stepped up like that and was given an extension in the Vice-Admiral's rank, But Admiral Jain was deprived of his due. If it is not politics in the defence forces, wht is it? This trend has been increasingly growing after Lt. Gen. Sinha's "premature" exit from the Army and entry into politices. Sinha may not have joined the Janata Dal in Sheer frustration but today several retired military personnel are doing so. There is need to make an in-epth study of this growing trend by the new government. It has to be clearly understood that the nation at this juncture cannot afford the armed forces to face the pollution of the civil services. The Generals, Admirals and Air Marshals who are now becoming quite "vocal" have to be put, in their proper places, in uniform and out of it. But at the same time; please listen to them carefully. They have some genuine complaints-and suggestions too. Air Staff Chief Marshal O.P. Mehra, a former Chief of Air Staff and later a Governor, is a well-meaning person I have known since 1960 when he was the manager of the Indian hockey team to the Rome Olympiad. The former chief made a very frank statement recently at a workshop he addressed on Defence-Industry Cooperation organised jointly by the Economic and Scientific Research Foundation and the Air Force Association, of which he is one of the founders. The former chief who had earlier headed Hindustan Aeronautics Ltd. (HAL), strongly feels the need to review the country's industrial policy vis-a-vis defence production.[11]

Significantly, Air Chief Marshal O.P. Mehra observed that the expansion and modernisation were not carried out on the basis of long-term planning, but mostly driven by expediency. The casualty in the regard, he said, was standardisation of equipment, economics of scale, efficiency etc. He supports the participation of the private-sector in defence production and efficiency in the production units, this move would help strengthen indigenisation". Importantly, he is of the view that indigenisation should be undertaken on a selective basis. Military hardware and avionics are two sectors where stringent quality specificaions are required and the "private sector entering these areas should make an in-depth study to know whether thy could conform to the stringent specifications and standards". Most of the problems of the armed forces stem from production and procurement-from abroad policies of the government. There is a lot of money for defence production and purchases and justifiably people at large do not mind it in the interest of the country's security. Several purchases and procurement of sophisticated military equipment are kept seceret "in the public interest" with the result that large-scale bungling also remains "seccret". This happens at all levels in the defence forces, and the "civil authorities" naturally want to place their own men in the force at crucial positions of authority. Some officers favour certain purchases from abroad to ensure quicker promotions to crucial positions and better post- retirement benefits. Nothing can illustrate this better than the story of a very competent General making one recommendation for the purchase of a gun and then changing his mind within days of becoming the Chief of Army Staff. The same is of the story of a retired Admiral. And who knows how many former Air Marshals too would have succumbed to "civil baits". One could go on and on to prove the deteriorating and demoralising conditions in the armed forces. What is important at this stage is that the new government at the centre needs to apply its mind to this problem as fast as the need to bring the national economy on the rails and to strengthen the democratic institutions in the national.[12]

In the defence sector-perhaps one of the major contributors to the widening deficit-there is need to find out where we are heading and by when. Many of the projects the feasibility of which has been established (missiles) should be taken to their logical conclusion preferably without fanfare. And if the Main Battle Tank (MBT) and the Light Combat Aircraft (LCA) are overdependent on foreign components then in review scientists must be told in no uncertain terms that they must produce results. And that policy must permeate the entire industrial scene because there is a tendency to replace one licence with another very decade or some in many sectors besides defence. Perhaps nothing has been more distorted than Nehru's efforts to promote goodneighbourliness. The ceasefire in Kashmir even as a victorious Indian Army was rolling back the Pakistani invaders in 1948; the return of Hajipur in 1964 was evidence that large and 'Hindu' India was not about to undo the partition-that we were willing to live and let live. Not so the dialogue that has been brought about under US pressure over Siachen. It is a totally different kettle of fish and if the spirit of the Simla Agreement is to prevail then the Narasimha Rao Government would have done the nation valuable service by putting Siachen on the back-burner and confronting the Pakistani leadership (and indeed the US Administration) about their support to the Khalistani and Kashmiri terrorits. A significant portion of our economic woes are security related because we have lost be way of industrial production and greater outlay on the creation and maintenance of a larger and diverse security appratus. The Congress party is fortunate in its secure moorings. The alternative has all the makings of anarchy.[13]

It will be worthwhile to distinguish between the different kinds of violence afflicting India. One cannot deny that the attempts to crush the various insurgencies will rank at the top. As far as I can remember, from the early fifties the military has been active aginst the insurgents in the Northeast and it continues to be active even now, though it is another group that has raised the standard of rebellion. The situation in the Punjab and in Kashmir cannot be said to be normal and there are rumblings of discontent in other parts of the country. It is not my intention to examine the reasons why authority is being systematically challenged, but it is obvious that political institutions and a system of government which fails to accommodate and reconcile difference have failed. Instead of trying to bring about a truly federal polity which will ensure autonomy to the states, the only remedy our leaders are willing to consider is to rein force the powers of the Central Government, failing to realise that it is part of the problem and not a solution to it. It is, perhaps, worth considering whether it is not the continuous intereference of the Central government in the affairs of the States that has created the problem. A second kind of violence is liked to the criminalisation of politics, and I am not referring to booth captureing, poll violence or the number of people connected with crime who seek electoral office, but the increasing use of lumpen elements to terrorise the people. The city mob has always been volatile, it can be used as a battering ram by conservative elements for their own political purpose. If a careful study is made of communal riots or any other kind of riots, it will be seen that interested parties who stood to benefit by the violence had unleashed the lumpen elements. We saw this after the assassination of Mrs. Gandhi and on a smaller scale, after the recent assassination. This is a dangerous tendency and the use of the mob to secure political ends is one of the steps towards fascism. Dangerous as these aspects of political violence are, they pale into insignificance when compared to insititutionalised violence. Institutional violence particularly of the kind I have in mind, is sanctified by custom and usage; it is accepted, or rather accepted till challenged as the natural order of things. Thus in an Indian village, the lower castes and the Scheduled Castes used to know their place; they seldom, if at all owned any land and toiled on the master's land, not for wages but for a certain limited amount of the produce and they were usually indebted to the landlord. Violence was implicit rather than explicit, the low castes never thought of challenging the existing order because they were fully aware of the consequences; the bold ones who did challenge were punished in an exemplary manner to restrain others. Democratic politics did not make any difference in the beginning; the low castes were treated as voting cattle, their votes were delivered by the upper castes. But slowely the village society, inspite of all the efforts of the upper castes, was affected by the outside world. The lower castes, too, become aware that the political process could be used to bring about social changes; the more radical among them were willing to challenge the existing order. The result was that the upper castes who controlled the organs of state power ruthlessly tried to suppress the social revolt; a caste was ravaged the countryside. The lower castes have been made aware of their rights; they want their place in the sun and the possessing classes, benefitting under the existing system, are determined to resist social change at all cost. It is this which has led to unparalleled violence. If the political order fails to incorporate the disadvantaged and the disinherited into the system, it can very well degenerate into a state of permanent internal war. This is what the Central American and canadian States are facing. We can certainly avoid the situation, if we have the political will. But our elite prefer to treat any talk of positive discrimination in favour of the lower castes assubversive. It is not even willing to consider making education compulsory because education might make the lower castes aware of their rights and open windos of opportunity, with such an elite, it will be a miracle if we are able to deal with our social crisis. Are we then condemned to a state of permanent violence? A banana republic in the making?[14]

What is the verdict of my countrymen? That we will watch in mute horror and fear the triumph of evil over good. Are we a nation of impotents that can't even make an attmept to punish the guilty? Will there never be a resurgence and a reawakening? Are we so morally dead? There is the presence of a 'remote control' that is both the cause' and 'the effect'. The assassination of Rajiv Gandhi is not simply the work of the LTTE as so many would like us to believe. In crime and the study of crime 'the obvious' as evidence, clue and theory must be eliminated. In this ghastly murder, the LTTE is too obvious a suspect. Someone, somewhere wants us to believe that it is the LTTE and the LTTE alone which is responsible for the assassination. Yet the LTTE stood to gain little by his death. If the enraged sikh community did not retaliate after the brutal killings in the post-Indira Gandhi assassination riots in 1984, why should the LTTE? The IPKF presence in Sri Lanka was wrong. But for one woman assassin to be so thoroughly motivated and brain-washed as to carry out a suicide mission in Madras, single handedly. No. It was just not the job of a single person. There were accomplices. There were conspirators. There was a certain method to this madness. The plot took shape in the minds of a few. Who were they? Murder was contemplated. Murder was planned. Murder was excuted. Who did it? Who had it done? Not the Sri Lankan Tamils. Not the LTTE. They are the scapegoats, the fall-guys as the expression goes. Do we have only the Sikh militants and the LTTE to pick on? Does the needle of suspicion never point anywhere else? Are we such mindless wonders that we are afraid even to 'think? Exclude the obvious. Besides the LTTE who could have been responsible? Who could have masteminded such a diabolical plot and managed the execution from remote control? And finally the million dollar question-'who stood to gain the most by eliminating Rajiv Gandhi'? The terms of reference of the Verma Commission and the scope of its enquiry and investigators have to performe be enlarged if the consipiracy, the plot and the assassins are to be exposed. Otherwise the very existence of India as a democracy and as a nation is in danger.[15]

The problems of terrorism and militancy in Punjab, Assam and Kashmir are again top priority items which require nerves of steel.

Rao's political base might be wobbly, but he brings with him considerable experience in statecraft in the face of daunting challenges ahead. He has, however, to apply his skills with a wider vision and perspective. A lot will depend on how he builds his team and tackles the affairs of the party, the government and relations with other parties. Clarity of thought and a sense of direction and determination alone can help him to take the country forward. He will do well to remember that slogans alone no longer satisfy the people. He has to redeem the pledge as spelt out in the Congress Party manifesto.

NOTES :

1. Rakesh Gupta. Political violence in Society, *Patriot,* 19 June 1991.
2. P.L. Banwari, Violence in Elections. *The Business and Political Observer*, 19 June 1991.
3. *National Herald,* 3 June 1991.
4. *Ibid.*
5. *Ibid.*
6. *Ibid.*
7. K.M. Panikar. The Violent Society. *Patriot,* 8 June 1991.
8. M.R. Narayanswamay. Tracking the Tigers. *The Hindustan Times,* 16 June 1991.
9. *Ibid.*
10. *Ibid.*
11. B.K. Mathur. Task Ahead on the Forces Front. *The Tribune,* 21 June 1991.
12. *Ibid.*
13. Cecil Victor. Congress and the Nehruvian Model. *Patriot,* 23 June 1991.
14. K.M. Panikkar, *op.cit.*
15. Vijai Singh Monkottia. A summer of Shame. *The Hindustan Times* 16 June 1991.

SEVENTEEN

THE NEHRU-GANDHI LEGACY

It is in times of crises that strong legacies, goodwill and traditions come to the rescue. The congressmen, elderly or the young, senior or junior, realised moments after the great tragedy his them with the severity and suddenness of a vicious torando, that the likes of Rajiv Gandhi can seldom be found. They also realised that their well-being and future lay under the shadow of his public memory, the esteem for the values the party set over several decades, and the goodwill the Nehru-Gandhi's have generated.

Carrying the weight of the Congress on his shoulders cannot be an easy task for Pamulaparti Venkata Narasimha Rao-minus the aura of the Nehru-Gandhi name and even personal charisma. But despite these handicaps, Rao has emerged as the man of the hour. Naturally unpretentious, inclined towards dialogue rather than confrontation, he is endowed with the qualities needed to calm passions in the moment of crisis. The other writes about this self-effacing politician from Andhra Pradesh, who is now India's Prime Minister. Does the man who is 70 on June 28 1991 have the metle needed to lead the Congress. Rao's long inning in the Congress has been marked by steadfast loyalty to Indira Gandhi and her son. That, in turn, helped only to increase his distance from the politics of his home state, Andhra Pradesh, of which he was once Chief Minister. To Rao's credit, he has never even tried to be a regional leader in the way many other Congress leaders are With the protection of the Nehru-Gandhi family removed, it may now be this quality which will help Rao most to keep the Congress party together, casting himself almost in the role of a referee among warring factions. But his ability to perform this vital task has necer beev tested before, and as Jaipal Reddy graphically puts it, "the ability to wield power may be lost through disuse."[1]

Will Narasimha Rao take back old Congressmen, former Congressmen. We have no enemies. Do you want to suggest that if we do not take back anyone they become our enemies.[2]

This is the first time going to the elections without a Nehru- Gandhi family member being either a Congress President or Prime Minister and this is also the first time that he is not suggesting any one as the Prime Minister. The fact that there is no one from the familly which dominated politics of this country for seven decades is not there to guide Rao through elections. Does he think it would affect the electoral fortunes of Congress party? Since he is not saying who is the Prime minister candidate, would that discourage voters.

On the whole I have no such apprehensions. Will Rao project the late Rajiv Gandhi as his main electoral issue in the next phases of the election?

We will not make Rajiv the issue, but to the programmes enunciated by him. That will be our main plank.

The post-Nehru Gandhi Congress is destined to become a democratic and therefore decentralised party. There is no option for it except to slowly gravitate towards a fedaralist platform. It is too early to say what precise from Congress federalism will take and how closely it would approximate the National Front-left front variant of federalism. But the logic of collective leadership and the absence of the "monarchy" dictates the Congress's steady drift away from unitarianism. In time, therefore, there will be broadly two sets of political formations-the centralist and the federalist, The BJP, given its deciplined, cadre-based party structure and its dominance by Brahmins, is now poised to stake its claim to being the principal centralist organisation. It has all along been a unitarian centralist party but its inability to extend its ifluence beyong certain pockets of north India seriously undermined the importance of its assertions on this score. Again, it is too early to say how much the BJP will succeed in convincing the electorate about its being the Congress's real succssor. Further, there is every possibility that a flexible Congress leadership will eventually produce a formula which enables it to retain a centralist appeal while accommodating federalist urges. Also, it is possible that centralism itself will lose much of its appeal if the Congress governs skifully and successfully discards Indira Gandhi's political style while paying lip service to her personality. But whatever happens, the fact is that the BJP has accomplished its aim in this election. Party leaders had been candid from the start that they were not campaigning to come to power in Delhi. In fact, for a few brief weeks before Sriperumbudur, Madras, when it appeared that the BJP might just become the single largest party, there was virtual panic at the headquaters at the thought of being invited to form the government.[3]

Now that it has returned to power at the Centre the Congress party has not just a slender majority protect but a legacy of nationhood at home and equity among the comity of nations in foreign policy that has been under siege. But Nehruvian model by which Prime Minister P.V. Narasimha Rao has shown has enough resilience to withstand the onslaught if the Congress party does not allow itself to devide from tit Central to the Nehru scheme of things was the creation of an industrial and agricultural infrastructure that would make the country self reliant in the first instance in most of the core sectors of the economy which, in turn, would lead to self sufficiency in all those critical sectors that help maintain a nation's freedom of thought and action. Thus it was that the foundations that he laid for the Green Revolution helped the nation to wriggle out of the rigorous of the US PL-480 arrangement and the farsightedness of men like Bhabha and themuch maligned Krishna Menon helped us party unclear blackmail when the Tarapore nuclear plant and the entire Maharashtra industrial belt was threatened with closure. Nothing underscores the fact that national security and industrial growth are interwined than the state of the world today. And Nehru had this to say on the subject.. 'Defence does not consist of people going about marching up and down the road with guns and other weapons. Defence today consists of a country which is industrially prepared for defence and which can produce the goods and equipment.' Read along with his other statement; "We prefer to have-if I may use the word-the second rate weapons that we produce rather than the first rate weapons for which we have to rely on somebody else." The model becomes self-supportive. Over the years, distrotions have crept in and licence-production which Nehru conceived as a stepping stone to self-sufficiency has become a self-perpetuating mantra. Too many of our critical projects are dependent on foreign know-how even while we nurture at tremendous cost to the exchequer a scientific infrasturcture that appears to thrive on creating openings through which foreigners can gain easy passage.[4]

A new phase has begun not only for the Congress party but in the country's political life itself. A country that was nurtured for more than half a century by the Nehru family has suddenly found itself "leaderless". Not that there are no leaders to run the affairs of the country but there is not one in sight who can measure upto the standards set by Jawaharlal Nehru Indira Gandhi and Rajiv Gandhi. Here again the point is not that there is no one who can match any of three leaders intellectually, but that there is one who combines in himself or herself the intellectual excellence political comprehension and wisdom ideological convictions and a nation-wide acceptability. A unique character of the Nehru was that almost all the national policies in practice in every field were the contribution by Jawaharlal Nehru who initiated them during the independence movement itself and had them debated at length for several years. Whether it is the policy of secularism or mixed economy or an independent media the dominating common factor was consensus. The three leaders and Lal Bhadur Shastri strongly believed that unless a national policy was evolved taking into account the sentiments and viewpoints of all sections of society it cannot benefit the country to the extent expected and cannot last long especially in a developing country like India. This was why Jawaharlal Nehru, Indira

Gandhi and Rajiv Gandhi had pursued the policy of consensus as against the politics of confrontation. The effort of all the three leaders was to see that the religious diversity did not produce of climate of confrontation, which would be disastrous for the country. They believed that economic backwardness was the main cause of most if not all religious and cultural conflicts and so devoted their time and energy in devising and pursuing secular policies which precented communal conflict on the one hand and promoted fast and equitable economic development on the other. The underlying philosophy in this approach was to engage all communities in a common endeavour and to help them achieve common goals collectively so that their commitment to protecting the structure thus built would be strong and irrevocable. Nehru found no other way of further cementing the bounds that unite the various religions and communities in the country and he was sure that unless communal harmony was assured this nation would not progress. And lack of progress meant disintegration of India. Throughout their lives the three leaders fought on two major fronts to promote this policy. On the one hand they had to trive to bring together through various ways the diverse communities and on the other face squarely and defeat the communal onslught of fundamentalist sections of the communities. Although there was a consensus among the communities to coexist, work and live together, fricitions created by the fundamentalist forces posed unending problems reducing the effectiveness of the consensual policies pursued. This in turn weakened secular forces and created new threats to the unity and intergrity of the nation in the form of secessionist movements.[5]

Though the communal forces appear to be gaining strength for whatever reasons there is little doubt that the majority of the people are in favour of a secular polity and oppose the secessionist demands too. This was proved beyond doubt in 1977 and in the last one and a half years when the country's political system as well the masses rejected government that had the BJP support. The resounding victory of the Congress in 1980 had shown the preferences of the masses. It was not only the Congress policies that the masses had welcomed back but also the Congress leadership that was closely associated with these policies. Mrs Indira Gandhi was in power when the Congress was defeated in 1977 and he was leading the party when it was given a handsome number of seats in 1980. Similarly Rajiv Gandhi was in power when the Congress was defeated in 1989 and he was on a massive comeback trail when she was assassinated. These two instances show that what the people of this country want not only Nehruvian policies but a leadership that is deeply committed to them. The people are not willing to settle for either of the two. The successive splits in the

Congress proved this. Each split be in the separation of the socialists from the Congress before independence, or the splits in 1969, 1977 and later was engineered by persons who believed that the masses were in favour of either the policies (socialism) or the leaders (syndicate). It was this identification of the policies with the Nehruvian line leadership that ensured continuity and the success of the policies. This was also responsible to a large extent for the problems in succession. The party as well as the masses cannot accept any leader who is not associated in a convicing manner with the Nehruvian policies. The election of Lal Bhadur Shastri as the leader after the death of Jawahar Lal Nehru, instead of Morarji Desai, was prompted by the fact that Shastri was Nehruvian leader, while Desai was not. That Desai was bit the right man to head the government wasp proved by his diastrous short-lived tenure as the Prime Minister of the Janata regime in 1977. But in the Congress party itself he had faced an out right rejection when he challenged Indira Gandhi after the death of Shastri for the leadership of the party. In choosing its leaders the Congress was persuaded by the dominant sentiment in the people. It was this sentiment that prevailed when Rajiv Gandhi was elected the leader unanimously after the death of Indira Gandhi. As was expected he continued with determination the Nehruvian policies and even laid down his life for his convictions. After the dastardly assassination of Rajiv Gandhi the party had applied the same Nehruvian principle in choosing its leader. Though there was some dilly-dallying for a week the choice of Narasimha Rao was a foregone conclusion. His credentials are impecable and his record is spotless. Amongh the Congress leaders of today he is the only one who adhered to the party and its Nehruvian policies whether the party was in power or out of power. True to his reputation he coined a new slogan-secularism with stability for the second phase of election. It is his firlm belief that stability cannot be ensured except through secular policies. Communal harmony is the since quo non for political stability, economic growth and social equilibrium. He echoed Nehruvian sentiments and thought when he told the International Qiraat Competition in New Delhi in 1981 in a inaugural address" Muslims have enriched India's cultural life and civilisation. The influence of Islam manifest itself in every aspect of cultural life." His commitment to secularism is irrevocable. He says "India is a secular country, which implies that any opportunity is available to every Indian, irrespective if the religion he may profess. This entitles each Indian to pursue his own belief." The taks before him are trully awsome in the sense he has to manage the Congress at a time when it is passing throught one of the worst periods in its history. But the main task before him is to steer the party in the post-Nehru era. As the senior most leader of the party he has no one to look up to and he has only collegues to consult with. That is an advantage in the sense that a collective leadership can be developed as the only way to preserve the unity of the party and its ideological quality.[6]

The Congress president, P.V. Narasimha Rao, has said the his party will adhere steadfastly to the Nehru line for there is not other viable line "outside the pale of fascism." In an extended conversation, Narasimha Rao, displaying a combativeness not always associated with his personality, asserted that he did not consider the BJP to be a rival of the Congress "because you have rivals (only) in the same system". What the BJP stands for is totally different from the values, policies and frameworlk of the Congress. "The BJP wants the destruction of the system which the Congress stands for." "The only way to exist in India is to co-exist", Narasimha Rao said.

Rao reitereated his party's opposition to the proposal for a national government suggested by President Venkataraman saying that it would not work and that, in any case, no such government would be necessary in this election since he expects the Congress to form one.

Rao described as "unrealistic for the present moment" various efforts now underway to bring present and former Congressmen together. He also stated that he did not attach any sanctity to either of the two principles: one person, one post or a single person serving both as party president and Prime Minister. Asked whether the Congress could for the first time consider having a Prime Minister who does not belong to the north, the party president argued that the real issue was not whether the Prime Minister belonged to this or that part of the country but whether, as in the past, he or she was acceptable to all regions. He said there are people in his party who do command this kind of pan-Indian loyalty.[7]

"How does it feel, P.V. Narasimha Rao, being made the president of the Congress at this tragic hour when the very existence of the party seems to be at stake?

Well, it's a great challenge; no doubt. All of us are here to face this challenge. The Working Committee, members of the Congress at all levels...the whole organisation is now facing the challenge. We are sure (that) we will succeed in overcoming it. However, I do not think that the very existence of the party is at stake. That is not correct. The Congress has had a long history. It has deep roots everywhere in the country. It has its own ethos; it has its own leadership at all levels. So, I do not agree that the party's existence as such is at stake. Yes, we have had a setback. But we will get over it in the best manner possible to forge ahead."[8]

Has the sudden removal of Rajiv Gandhi from the scene not created a situation where the party has not establish de novo its credentials among the people?

"Again, I would say that this is an over-statement. Yes, the removal of Rajiv Gandhi has been a very, very big blow to us in the Congress. But I'm not really inclined to agree that the party has to establish do novo its credentials among the people. I don't agree with this proposition for the simple reason that I've just stated. The Congress has its own roots, its own existence, its own ethos and its own presence in the consciousness of the people. So, this part, I don't think I can agree with.[9]

Former Congressmen wanting to rejoin the party may have acted in haste in mooting the idea at this juncture. But has the Congress party by publicty rejecting the overtures not sought to discourage trend which requires serious consideration?

They made their move publicly. I am not able to understand how could the Congress Working Committee have done anythign Committee have cone anything privately in response to that? Secondly, the manner and the context in which they did it; the timing they chose. In view of all thism there was hardly anything else the CWC could do. It only did what was necessary at the time it all happened.

So, should Narasimha Rao say that admission of former Congressmen to the Party is not ruled out?

"Congress is a democratic organisation. We have seen people going out of it whenever it suited them. After 10-15 years, they would make a beeline back to the. Congress, Now, all these things have been happening for various reason. You will have to go into the reason in each case. I'll not do that. But what I would say is that this phenomenon is nothing new. And if we treat it as a phenomenon which is already there, the rest will follow only when it is properly done, or properly attempted or propposed. Finally, the decision (to admit former Congressmen) would have to be of the Working Committee.[10]

The 106-year-old political warhorse, the Indian National Congress, limped back to office this week after an 18-month interregnum. Not that its return was in doubt; the question was whether it would get a clear majority. As it turned out, the tally of the Congress and its allies fell 11 seats short, despite a late rally in the wake of a sympathy wave generated by Rajiv Gandhi's assassination. And as it also turned out, the leader's demise caused an upheaval in the party over its choice of the Prime Minister.

When the dust finally settled down, it became apparent that in the absence of the Nehru-Gandhi family the old party was forced to grapple with new realities. The realities have changed for the Congress in more ways than one. First, the churn in the party over the leadership issue signified that the equations within the party were changing. Gone were the days of an all-powerful high command which was the final arbiter of all aprty disputes. It was back to the Syndicate days with regional bosses claiming their share of the cake at the Centre.

Second, the election results threw up another reality. The party's base vote was virtually wiped off in two Hindi-speaking states, Uttar Pradesh and Bihar. Given the importance of these states in Indian politics, the Congress assuming power in Delhi without virtually any representation from UP and Bihar was like the CPSU seeking to rule the Soviet Union without control over the Russain federation. But at the same time, the party demonstrated yet again that the voters of south India are inclined to believe that only the Congress is capable of providing a functional government at the centre.

While the intra-party equations will work themselves out over a period of time with the Congress perhaps moving towards a more federalist style of functioning - an arrangement which will enable accommodation of the aspirations of the regional bosses-the dramatic erosion of the Congress base in the Hindi heart land is perhaps of greater and more immediate concern.[11]

In the south, the Congress swept predictably. In Tamil Nadu, there was a 2.5 per cent swing in favour of the Congress-AIADMK alliance over a sterling performance in the 1989 polls in which if had garnered 57 per cent of the popular vote. In Kerala, it was again a tale of a marginal swing resulting in windfall gains. The Congress led UDF vote increased by a mere 0.4 per cent and the combine bagged 16 of the 20 seats.

Interestingly, in Karnataka the pattern was not the same, though the Congress bagged 21 of the 26 seats. The Congress vote, in fact, slumped by 6.9 per cent. In a sense, the slump was in keeping with the trend in Karantaka. Since 1971, when the Congress got a whopping 70 per cent of the popular vote there has been a decline in each successive election to reach 42 per cent in this poll. If the party won these many seats in the state, it was because the BJP's dramatic entry-and it bagging 29 per cent vote-which hopelessly splintered the non-congress vote.

This has ominous potents for the Congress. The Hindutva forcess can now be expected to make an all-out effort to expand their influence and activities all over the state with a view to oust the Congress. And the BJP may well succeed on this. Clearly, there has been a precedent. Until 1983, the Congress had enjoyed unchallenged supremacy in the state, having ruled it continously since its inception in 1956. But the widespread discontent spawned by the misrule of the Gundu Rao government grace the then Janata Party which until then had no base or organisatin in the state, a golden opportunity to unseat the Congress in 1983.

Despite this, a point needs to be made about the character of the Congress in the South. Unlike the north where the party has studiously maintained a lofty aloofness from other political formations, it has been more flexible in the south and more responsive to new political developments. It created a rainbow coalition, called the UDF (United Dempcratic Front) in Kerala and aligned itself with the dominant regional party in Tamil Nadu, and in the process, turned to the backwrds if necessary-as in Tamil Nadu and Karanataka-or to the minorities where required as in Kerala.

Of the remaining states, the Congress did remarkably well in Maharashra, Orissa, Haryana and Assam, but poorly in the Marxist bastion of West Bengal and Ram-lehar (wave) swept Gujarat. But all in all, the Congress did not maintain an all-India presence, as it did not in 1977 and 1989. The only difference this time is that despite that it has formed a government. Governmancema, therefore, prove difficult. But more importantly it will have to shape a strategy to regain the lost ground in the Hindi Heartland.[12]

The question is loaded as it presupposes that there has been dynastic rule in the Congress in the past. I am afraid this is a popular misconception and something taken for granted without ascertaining what the traits of "dynastic" succession are. In the frist place "dynastic succession" means the invariable and inevitable succession of a child to the parent's office of authority, whatever it be, without anything else intervening or anybody else giving any opinion or view on it.

Secondly, the capability, quality or capacity of the successor in a dynastic succession is never taken into account. There is nothing to prevént a worthless bounder from succeding another worthless bounder and so on. The only requirement is that of blood or linkage and nothing else.

Thirdly, in a dynastic succession nobody elects a successor who becomes perforce an automatic choice merely because he or she is the child of the parent who he or she is succeding. In our new India, to become a Prime Minister a person has first to lead the party, which projects him or her as the future Prime Minister, to victory in a rather tough Parliamentary election held on the basis of adult franchisc. Secondly, after the election he or she has to be elected the leader by the Parliamentary wing of his or her party. Then and then only will the

President send for him or her to become the Prime Minister and to form a government.[13] .

Jawaharlal Nehru was so elected, so was Indira Gandhi and so was Rajiv Gandhi, Moreover, Indira Gandhi was not elected immediately after Jawaharlal Nehru but after the demise of Lal Bhadur Shastri. Who was selected as leader after the passing away of Jawaharlal Nehru. And Indira Gandhi had to face a contested elect on the become the leader of the Parliamentary Party. Rajiv Gandhi also had to face an election although uncontested like Jawaharlal Nehru, before becoming leader.

Dynastic succession on the contary, implies amongst other things succession by even incompetent black ground through an autocratic process of succession and not selection through democratic elections of the best persons available such as Jawaharlal. Indira and Rajiv as also Lal Bhadur Shastri. Perhaps one of these days we shall even hear that Pitt the younger or Winston Churchil or Neville Chamberlian, to mention only a few were also the beneficiaries of the principle of dynastic succession.[14]

How can it be called dynastic rule? The Nehru-Gandhi family is a Congress family. Rajiv was the head of Congress. Dynastic rule has become a cliche. Whom do the countrymen love? The nation is sentimentally attached to the Nehru-Gandhi family and not for nothing. The attachment should not be misconstrued. The Nehru Gandhi family will dominate national politics as long as the ways of assassination by invisible hands and in highly sophisticated manner continue. Only in the case of Congress, Mahatma Gandhi, Indira Gandhi and Rajiv Gandhi were assassinated in an effort to thwart democracy.[15]

What makes us so sure that the dynastic rule has ended? Democracy and dynastic rule can't go together and it doesn't speak well for a big country like India if it cannot find a Prime Minister other than from doesn't make anybody ineligible to lead a country if he or she is otherwise suitable. But the Indian people should get rid of the idea that the king's son is the only suitable successor. We have so far accepted dynastic rule. But from now on there should be a change.[16]

This is an often-asked loaded question which slights the political maturity and wisdom of Indiàn people. Historically, dynastic rule means the role of a particular family royal or otherwise, which captured and enjoyed power over a period of time by virtue of its military might. As did the ancient and medieval dynasties in India or the Bourbons and Hapsburgs in Europe. Was Jawaharlal Nehru as usurper of power? Wasn't Indira Gandhi thrown out of power in 1977 through the ballot box and succeeded in returning to power by the same process in 1980?

Did not it happen to Rajiv Gandhi in 1989? All these only bear testimony to the inherent strength of the Indian democratic process. The Congress (I) as an organisation has undoubtedly been affected by its over- dependence on Nehru-Gandhi family but that is a problem the party itself has to resolve.[17]

The mystique of the Congress (I)'s stability lay in the rule by one or the other Gandhi. Today the party has been left with no leadership. A mentality dating back to the days of yor e persists. It is not very different from those Maharajas, when a lambardar or partwari's son dreamt only of stepping into the shoes of his ancestors. So the dynasty cannot be said to be absolutely over. Anybody can be surprised but not I, Sonia Gandhi can well contest from Amethi. This can just happen. There has already be talk of her keeping the seat warm until Priyanka or Rahul are able to take over. Mrs Gandhi's sister-in-law is already a Minister. Although she fell out with the family after her husband's death. She was not acceptable to the family, particularly Mrs Indira Gandhi, and thus she was not accepted by the Congress (I). Why had I suggested Mrs Maneka Gandhi's name as the likely successor of her husband as the Youth Congress (I) chief when Sanjay Gandhi died in a plane crash? I had only said that the mantle had fallen on her. It was the party that has been seeking the mandate of the people for a successor each time the leader of the party died.[18]

I cannot say much about strengthening Indian democracy in as much as I don't think democracy has found its roots in India as yet. May be it will have a chance to sprout. Unfortunately, the ruling party headed by Nehru and the Gandhis had thrown the basic principles winds. The game of vote-catching was first taught by then without any care whatesoever for the good of the country. That game the ruling parties of all the States have learnt by heart they will cling to power by hook or by crook. This is no democracy. Let us hope that by God's grace and plenty of luck, Indian democracy will thrive gradually. The beginning should begin now.[19]

The Congress has a chance now to build itself as a Centrist organisation; as a political force. Uptil now it had depended on a particular family. Their organisation is an moribund as our's. They have also been mouthing issues but not doing anything about them. So, now they have a chance to build a collective leadership and take up issues. But one has to wait and see whether they are capable of doing that of the ambitions (of various leaders) for getting the topspot and being the undisputed master-which is their tradition-will break the party?[20]

The Congress may be a bit slow in its responses but its members are pretty quick to sense any change in the balance of power at the top. In rallying round P.V. Narasimha Rao the CPP has been true to it character. Its choice of a leader through a consensus was no different from what it would have been in case of a contest since the party made up its mind only after an intensive exercise to gauge the mood of the members and the level of support the two contenders could expect in a secret ballot. Sharad Pawar knew sometime before he withdraw from the contest that the odds were against him and that he could not count on the support of a majority. His decision to press the demand for a secret ballot until the last minute was in the circumstances no more than a futile gesture of defiance. It was perhaps intended to make the point, which he did with needless drama, about his new status in the party. It is not clear whether it was also meant as a warning that, in the party. It is not clear whether it was also meant as a warning that, in the absence of a charsmatic leader, consensus-building in the party could no longer be a one- shot affair but would have to be an on-going process. This warning was addressed not so much to Narasimha Rao, who by temperament is averse to acting on personal caprice, but no those members who have yet to reconcile themselves to the changed situation in the party. Rao is the last man in the Congress to suffer from delusions of grandeur and is more paifully aware than most of his colleagues in the party of the constraints under which the government he heads would have to work. These constraints are built into the very situation in which Narasimha Rao has been sworn in as Prime Minister. The election results have produced another hung Parliament, with no clear mandate for any one party or front, adding to the growing political uncertainties. The new Prime Minister will have to take good care not to alienate any power centre in his own party and not to hurt those outside the party whose support he may need in a division. Narasimha Rao cannot afford to mark time or tinker with big- problems. He would have to fight the secessionists in Punjab and Kashmir with greater determination. Above all, he would have to do something here and now to end the awful economic mess. In the past governments could often save the past by mortgaging the future. This option is no longer available in the face of unmanageable budgetary and balance of payments deficts. It iwll be impossible to get a new IMF loan in the absence of new measures of fiscal disicipline. Such discipline will have to be all the more stringent in case the country perfers to make do without a loan. Whatever the prefered course the task of political management is going to be far more difficult than in the past. In concrete terms a regime of stricter fiscal discipline can only mean cuts in food and other subsidies which will hurt the poor, higher tazes which will alienate the middle classes, curbs on imports which will slow down the growth of industry and higher prices which will make holes in all family budgets.

All these measures will be highly unpopular and can add dangerously to the prevailing political turbulence.[21]

Will the new government be able to mobilise its own party members to support such measures in the face of a rising tide of popular discontent? And will the opposition parties, now busy making polite noises about a positive approach to the new government, be able to resist the temptation to exploit this discontent for partisan ends? The one comforting answer to these question is that no party will be keen to rock the boat since all dread the prospect of another mid-term poll. But this cannot be much of a solace to a hard-pressed government. It is not enough for it to get a particular measure through Parliament. There will be serious difficulties in implementing it if those opposed to it insist on taking the issue to the street. A new awareness of the constraints under which it works on the part of the government will be of no avail unless all the parties exercise a certain measure of restraint on their own cadres and supporters. It is idle to think of a larger political grouping just now unless something is first done to reduce the level of paranoia in public life. Only then it will be possible for like-minded groups to sit together, think coolly of the options available to the country and agree on what kind of concerted measures can be taken to stope the spreading rot in the system. This is precisely where Mr. Narasimha Rao needs to act boldly. The new decision-making process must involve close consultations not only with his senior colleagues but also with leaders of other parties to explore the common ground between the Congress and the rest on every big issue and find ways and means of enlarging it. At the same time there must be a new openness about the difficulties facing the government. It must be frank in explaning the pros and cons of the various options open to it and the reasons which make it prefer a particular course of action. The public is not so deaf as to ignore the difference between a decision taken under duress and one resulting from panic or loss of nerve. This is a question not on public relations intended to put a gloss on government's failures but of public education. The people must know that this is no time for business as usual. Here is the rub. Judging by the reaction of the parties even the interpretation of election results has become part of this business. EM.S. Namboodiripad, for instance, is not perturbed in the least that the elections have produced another hung Parliament. This is the natural state of affairs, he argues. What was unnatural was the long spell of one-party rule, apart perhaps from the special case of West Bengal. This is the sort of logic which makes many people wonder if some parties have a stake in instability at the Centre. V.P. Singh feels that the election results have given his party a mandate to sit on the opposition benches. But why cannot the electorate's decision to cut his party down to size be also interpreted as a verdict against his brand of caste-bassed justice? It has been rather a failure of communication, he says. The people of Bihar alone have been able to grasp the full import of the new politics of caste-based equity. The other will understand in due course.[22]

Hope has survived. The dark clouds which had gathered on our political horizon in the aftermath of Rajiv Gandhi's assassination have given way to sunshine. The postponement of elections and the unconstitutional formualtions had created a rather scary scenario. With the results flowing in the democratic process in this country once again has proved supreme. In the days ahead, when once again a hung Parliament will state us in the face, the leaders of all political parties and those of the Indian National Congress in particular will have a historic role to play. The events of the next few days will have far-reaching implications for out democracy. Faced with the prospect of no party being able to muster a majority on its own in the tenth Lok Sabha also, some analysts may tend to make doomsday forecasts. But this result was not unexpected. All pre-poll surveys had shown that 3 hung Pariliament was round the corner with the Congress emerging as the single largest party. A phase has come when we have to reconcil ourselves to the reality of stability being provided by rational alliances.

The Congress, it seems, has once again failed to get a majority. But more important than this aspect of the election result trend is the fact that myth of the Bharatiya Janata Party's ability to sweep the Hindi heartland has been shattered the Janata Dal has collaspsed and the hopes of the Left parties that a National Front-Left Front combine will be able to stake claim forming a Government have been dashed. In short we may say that while the Congress has retained it s Numero Uno status all others have fared below their own expectations. This indeed is a great achievement for the Congess. Its status as the only national political organisation has remained intact, while the BJP certainly has been able to increase its representation base and has made token inroads into the southern states, it has faced a virtual vote of no confidence in Rajasthan, Madhya Paradesh and Himachal Pradesh, where it has its own state Government. Even in the Lok Sabha seats of Delhi the dingdong battle between the BJP and the Congress candidates, with film star-politician, Mr. Rajesh Khanna, giving Lal Krishna Advani a run for his money, has gone to show that the Ram-lahar (wave in favour of Ram) has not really helped the saffron flag bearers. Secularism has prevailed. BJP has faired well in parts of the country but we can say that Ram-Lahar is not the basis of this performance.[23]

The collapse of the Left-Front in Kerala is an abject lesson for the Leftists. In effect, in five states ruled by non-Congress Parties-kerala, Tamil Nadu, Madhya Pradesh, Himachal Pradesh and Rajasthan-the voteres have gone against the state rulers. In ccontrast, in Karnataka and Maharashtra, two Congress-ruled states the ruling party of these states have retained the voters confidence. In Andhra Pradesh the Telugu Desam has staged a partial comeback, but even then the sway of the ruling Congress party over the state is still evident. In West Bengal, the Left- Front led by Mr. Jyoti Basu has shown that its fortress is envincible, but the Congress seems to have improved its showing here as well. In Uttar Pradesh, Mulayam Singh Yadav may now be regretting his decision to hoodwink his Congress supporters in a pre-dawn Raj Bhavan intrigue, which resulted in the present rout of his party in the State Assembly Poll. The only non-Congress Chief Minister who seems to have delivered fortunes for his party in the form of Lok Sabha seats is Laloo Prasad Yadav of Bihar, but the norms applied for this "performance" have left many question marks. Thus, apart from retaining its Numero Uno status, while the Congress has retained the confidence of the voters in the states ruled by it, the non-Congress benefit from a "sympathy wave"? While certainly in the aftermath of Rajiv Gandhi's assassination a sympathy factor was added, a close scrutiny of the party's performance would show that the Congress did well in all those places where the party put up a united face. In Andhra Pradesh, Bihar and Uttar Pradesh factionalism was a major factor in ensuring an erosion in the party's support base. Also, the Congress performed well in those states where it chose its allies correctly-Kerala and Tamil Nadu bear testimony to this. Contrast to this the blunder of extending support to Mr Mulayam Singh Yadav's regime last November a major reason for the Congress losing many of its traditional voters in Uttar Pradesh becomes clear. In the coming days therefore, when the Congress may have to choose its allies at the Centre, lessons should be drawn from the experience of the permulations worked out in November 1990 and due caution should be ensured by the party's leadership. The Congress certainly is poised to form a Government in New Delhi once again. The choice of the leader of the Congress parliamentary party therefore has generated a lot of interest; and is the subject of intense speculation. It must be remembered that unlike the election of the leader of the National Front Parliamentary Party in 1989, when a factional leader was elected to head a programme-less non-Congress government, the election of the CPP leader now will be viewed by the nation as the election of a leader who will endeavour to provide stability after the fall of the V.P. Singh and Chandra Shekhar regimes. Had destiny not been cruel, then on May 30 itself Rajiv Gandhi would have filled the vacuum after having led his party on a triumphant comeback campaign. The vacuum of Rajiv Gandhi can never be filled. But those who have voted the Congress back to its predominant position in national politics certainly entertain hopes of a stable Government which will symbolise the continuation of the work initiated by Rajiv Gandhi. The nation expects the Congress to chose its leader with due caution. The poor performance in some states where the party was faction- ridden and where manipulation overshadowed party interests has shown that the only force which can defeat the Congress is the Congress itself. The Congress MPs and the party's leadership therefore must ensure that no selfdefeating endavour is undertaken which deprives the nation of the chance of once again enjoying stability under a Congress-led Government. The real test for the Congress now lies ahead.[24]

The shocking death of Rajiv Gandhi had left the people with a sense of profound sorrow and bewildered anger. A panicky Congress party had unseemingly adopted a resolution sponsoring Sonia Gandhi as its successor to the post of party chief. But it goes to the eternal credit of Sonia that while some top leaders of the Congress had lost their bearings, she showed tremendous psychological reserves by not only refusing to get hustled into taking a wrong step in the immediate context, but also by her reported counsel to democratically select the Congress president from among the leaders themselves. The Congress, thus, owes a debt to Sonia Gandhi for her dignified maturity and grace, helping the party to regain its sense of purpose; the people of India are also equally indebted to her for her contribution to the restoration of general sanity. With the unanimous selection of P.V. Narasimha Rao as the Congress president the shaken mood of the party leaders and followers was rapidly overcome. The party even under its psychic shock, would automatically gain in electoral terms from the tragic dimension of the assassination of Rajiv Gandhi. The Indian people are naturally worried over the future of the country in the event of the mother party, Congress, failing to protect Indian democracy. From experience, the people of this country have come to reckon with the fact that till now all the anti-Congress, opportunist combinations have miserably failed India and its masses. This was so in 1967-68, when nine States were under the opportunist conglomerate rule. The later two experiments, that of the Janata Party government at the Centre in 1977 and of the NF dispensation in 1989-90 met the same fate. That is why the people of this country have come back to the Congress after punishing the party whenever they were angry with it. For, the alternatives have disillusioned them much faster with their murky doings all along the line. The same factors have enabled leaders like Pranab Mukherjee, Priyaranjan Das Mushi, Sharad Pawar. A.R. Antulay,

Chenna Reddy or Veerendra Patil, to name only a few to come back to the Congress after a spell of anti-Congress stance outside. Thus, barring the anti- secular and anti-democratic forces, all others ultimately have sought the democratic umbrella of the Congress to ensure their own growth, instead of getting swamped by Indian facism lurking in the form of organised communalism. Neither the people nor the secular parties outside it, will seriously nurse any intention of destroying the century-old Congress roots, sustaining them till now. That is why paying glorious tribute to Rajiv Gandhi on behalf of his party and himself in the Rajya Sabha, Samar Mukherjee, the CPI-M politburo member, said "We think it was an attack (the assassination) not only on Rajiv Gandhi as a person, but on the very unity and integrity of the country". He made it abundantly clear that his tribute was not merely a personal one, but by his entire party. Dwelling on the national significance of the dastardly killing, he added "It is an attack on secularism, it is an attack on democracy". True, this avowal underlines the glaring contradiction of the electoral formulation of the CPI-M and the entire Left to the effect that they were confronting "Congress authoritarianism and BJP communalism" simulataneously in the ongoing elections. But the realistic approach to the dangerous implications of Rajiv's assassination had evidently induced fundamental clarity of vision among the top CPI-M leadership. This turned-around the CPI-M from its blind anti- Congressism can certainly be branded, at the facile level, as rank opportunism. But such denigration does not explain the CPI- M, and in general the Left's, dilemma, which always presumed the existence of the Congress as the main safeguard for the survivial of Indian democracy; while at the same time, advancing the Left sway and retaining its strong holds from being swamped by the Congress.[25]

The best tribute the Congress can pay to Rajiv Gandhi is to resume where he stopped what could have been the greatest enterprise of his public career. The reference is of course to the one initiative with which he electrified the country more than by anything he did before or after that. His initiative, that is, at the AICC session in Bombay, in December 1985, when he declared he would rebuild the Congress from the grassroots up, democratising the base and clearing out the "power-brokers" who had occupied the top. The two aims are in fact a part of the same. If he had aimed his fire only at the power-brokers, it might have been thought that he only wanted to replace an inherited coterie with one of his own choice, and that would have only amounted to a change of power-brokers, not the scattering of their system. But he also promised democracy, and because there is a nexus between the end of democracy in the Congress and the rise of the power-brokers, it was rightly assumed that he meant to root out the system if brokerage for good. The nexus becomes clear if one traces the ancestory of the coterie system back to the "Sanjay brigade" of the late 1970s, then to the "kitchen cabinet" of the late 1960s, the "syndicate", and still farther back to the "old guard". The earliest ancestors, the "old guard", were a more or less honourable group of old fashioned but nevertheless authentic leaders of the Congress, drawn from different parts of the country, if there was any odour about them it was only because they had managed to stay on too long. They had managed to do so, of course only because with the decay of inner-party democracy in the party, there was no way that fresh blood could rise to the top. Those among them who had more than their share of colout and durability became the "syndicate". As the name implies, they became the first generation of power- brokers. They sought to control Indira Gandhi from behind the throne but they were not by any means a tainted lot, and like the old guard they too were the popular leaders of their own respective regions and in their own right. They were not creatures of Indira Gandhi's patronage. The creatures began to creep in with the "kitchen cabinet", which Indira Gandhi created for her own purposes and by her own methods of secretive politics. She carefully chose only those who had little support in their own right, in their own regions, and therefore were wholly dependent upon her favours. In the meantime the old guard and the syndicate were withering on the vine because inner party democracy had wholly dried up in the party by now, and no nourishment was travelling up to anyone at the top except only Mrs Gandhi, who had perfected her own direct access to the people, by-passing the party.[26]

This begs the question that if Rajiv Gandhi could not do it despite his unprecedented mandate in 1984-85, can anyone else do it now? I believe so, because the mandate and its beneficiaries were a part of the problem, not a part of the solution. The mandate convinced everyone who was already predisposed to believing it, that this was the way to perpetual glory: an organisation addicted to the charisma of "the leader" and free of such an inconvenient thing as a mind of its own or multiple voices, and run by a faceless coterie which knows how to use power without the constraints of responsibility. Or, to change the metaphor, an enfeebled body will always reach for the crunch if it sees one, and a charismatic leader to whom all burdens of responsibility can be transferred is a very seductive crunch. Therefore the party and the coterie were equally happy to perpetuate what had paid off. Now all that has changed. The impact of the change may be diluted but cannot be eliminated even, if, in his death, Rajiv Gandhi proves to be a better vote puller (which itself is not certain) than he appeared likely to be when he was alive. Besides, his was the first effort, and had the problems of first efforts. Now a second one is called for and would be more timely. There is no central dominating figure now two whom homage must be paid, and from whom candid advice must be withheld for fear of inviting lethal displeasure.[27]

I must now come to the Congress. It has won a reprieve. But it is only a reprieve. The loss of popularity of the Congress in the two most populous States of Bihar and Uttar Pradesh-and also Gujarat-should be the greatest cause of worry for the Congress party. it has alienated important segments of the population. The Harijans who blindly supported the party have deserted it. The communal riots under the Congress Rraj in the Congress raj in the eighties hurt the Muslims. The hobnobbing with the Muslims obscurantists over the Shah Bano case irritated the Hindus. Its flirting with the VHP and Shilanyas in 1989 further angered the Muslims without pleasing the Hindus. Its long standing failure to implement the reservation policy in the Northern states and at the Centre, with suitable modifications, lost the support of the non-Dwija castes which are the mainstary of the Congress south of the Narmada. Its support of Mulayam Singh in Uttar Pradesh scandalised the upper caste Hindus; its opportunist alliance with Chimanbhai Patel lost the sympathy of Gujarat voters. Its game of musical chairs in the States demoralised the Congress organisation and eroded the ordered state. Its dependence on one man or woman stopped the process of creating new leaders with a national perspective and deep understanding of the country and its problems. It produced parochial power-crazy politicians. The Congress must correct these mistakes. It must become again a vibrant mainstream party. It must introduce new blood. It must cultivate the art of power sharing within the party. It must develop team work and learn to govern firmly and imaginatively. And finally, without cutting off its link with the Indian tradition, it must develop a modern outlook and a growth oriented economic programme.[28]

The election of Narasimha Rao as party chief will not only come as a big relief to Congressmen, but hopefully, restore the regime of consensus in the party. That the party should have done this days after Sonia Gandhi had determinedly said no to the apparatchiks does it little credit. But it can all be blamed on the conduct of some of its leaders who habitually affirm their loyalty to the party's leader and its ideals. The Congress may still attempt to persuade the late leaders family to help it work up a sympathy wave, but that is unnecessary. The people of this country have always stood by their martyrs and Rajiv Gandhi has undoubtedly fallen a martyr to the cause of national unity and integrity and the dream of a modern, secular India. All those who stood by him can reasonable hope to benefit from the people's sympathy. It is still, however, a fortnight to the polls and it would be naive to assume that other parties will give the Congress a sympathy wolkover.

The Janata Dal, the Bharatiya Janata Party and the Left Front are already changing their poll strategies. While the JD and the Left have all but given up the anti-Congressist platform and identified the BJP as their main adversary, the latter is projecting itself as the sole inheritor of Rajiv Gandhi's stability card. While the former are claiming the Nehru-Gandhi legacy of secular egalitarianism and populism, the latter is lying claim to its uncompormising nationalism. The time the Congress has already lost in resolving its leadership question could turn out to be crucial in the ultimate reckoning. The retrive the lost ground will be mean task for the Congress particularly because it will be starting with a double disadvantage. For one, in projecting the late Rajiv Gandhi as the sole leader, it had reduced all its other leaders to the state or regional level. It will not be easy to project them collectively at the national stage within such a short time. Secondly, the party of late had relied for perspective and stra tegies on the late leader and his advisers. It shall now not only have to do its own thinking but, more importantly, appear to be doing so. [29] For, it will be a Himalayan blunder for the new leadership to hope that a sympathy wave alone will do the trick. For all one knows, it may turn out to be merely a ripple and what may ultimately determine the voters' choice may be the quality of the leadership the Congress can provide at this juncture.

NOTES :

1. Jaydeep Gupta. P.V. Narasimha Rao. *The Sunday Observer,* 2 June 1991.
2. *National Hearld,* 3 June 1991.
3. Chandan Mitra. For the BJP It was a Famous Victory. *The Sunday Observer,* 23 June 1997.
4. Cecil victor. Congress and the Nehruvian Model. *Patriot*, 23 June 1991.
5. K.V.S. Rama Sarma. In keeping with Nehru spirit. *National Herald,* 3 June 1991.
6. *Ibid.*
7. *New Wave,* 9 June 1991.
8. P.V. Narasimha Rao Talks to Vinod Sharma. *The Hindustan Times*, 9 June 1991.
9. *Ibid.*

11. Arindam Sen Gupta. Congress: Grappling with New Realities. *The Sunday Observer*, 23 June 1991.
12. *Ibid.*
13. Siddha rtha Shankar Ray in *The Statesman,* 23 June 1991.
14. *Ibid.*
15. Sitaram Kesari in *The Statesman,* 23 June 1991.
16. B.R. Chowdhury. *Ibid.*
17. Nemani Sadhan Bose. *Ibid.*
18. Khushwant Singh in the Statesman, 23 June 1991.
19. Budhadev Guha. *Ibid.*
20. Ajit Singh Teles Vinod Sharma. *The Hindustan Times,* 23 June 1991.
21. Sham Lal. Time For Hard Decisions. *The Time of India,* 22 June 1991.
22. *Ibid.*
23. Shubhabrata Bhattacharya. The Real Test for Congress. *National Heraled*, 17 June 1991.
24. *Ibid.*
25. Ashis Barman. Compulsive Post Rajiv Pointers. *Patriot,* 14 June 1991.
26. Pran Chopra. Rebuilding Congress. *The Hindustan Times,* 13 June 1991.
27. *Ibid.*
28. Madhu Limaye. Verdict '91: What it means? *The Hindustan Times*, 20 June 1991.
29. *The Business and Political Observer,* 30 May 1991.

EIGHTEEN

TWO CONG-I BROTHERS - NARASIMHA RAO AND SHARAD PAWAR

"Narasimha Rao's contribution to the Congress Party as well as the nation is much longer than my own life", the Congress leader Sharad Pawar has said. Happily, two Cong-I brothers are on the fornt line of national politics to serve the great Indian nation and people. Pawar has taken over as a Union Cabinet member with defence portfolio on June 26, 1991.

Perhaps the most striking thing about Sharad Pawar is his self-image. He holds the second most important office in the country, next only to that of Prime Minister's. He rightly thinks, "I have just saved the nation."

The campaign for Sharad Pawar as Prime Minister has got a boost with the reported split in the so-called Congress "coterie". His supporters, who continued their hectic lobbying claim that they have been successful in enlisting the support of a section of the close confidents of Rajiv Gandhi. According to a Rajya Sabha member from Maharashtra, who has become very active during the last two days despite his failing health, two close associates of Mr. Rajiv Gandhi-R.K. Dhawan and Makhanal Fotedar-are willing to support the candidature of Sharad Pawar for the pirme ministership. During the last two days, a number of prominent Congress leaders, including Madhya Pradesh Congress Chief Arjun Singh, called on Sharad Pawar at Kaharashtra Sadan, which has become the headquarters of "Sharad Pawar as Prime Minister Campaign". It is believed that in his talks with various Congress leaders, the Maharashtra Chief Minister is emphsising the need to revive the democratic process in the party. He reportedly refers to the context between Indira Gandhi and Morarji Desai after the 1967 general elections. It is argued on behalf of the Sharad Pawar group that any attempt to impose a leader from above will not only be undemocratic but also embarrass the parties which are willing to support the Congress in the formation of a miniority government. They point out that any consensus among the members of either the Congress Parliamentary Board or the Congress Working Committee will be treated as an imposition of their choice on the Congress Parliamentary Party. They insist on a secret ballot in the CPP. With Dr. Jagannath Mishra and Narayan Dutt Tiwari losing their Parliamentary seats, the supporters of Sharad Pawar has become more confident. They find that they have to battle only aginst Congress president P.V. Narasimha Rao, who rates his chances high only by a consensus. The

Sharad Pawar group insists that if the party president has to work for a consensus, the he has to make it clear that he is not one of the contenders for the top post. They remind that in 1965, after the death of Lal Bhadur Shastri, the then Congress president K. Kamraj, who brought about a consesus in favour of Indira Gandhi, was not a contender for the Prime ministership. But those who are opposed to Sharad Pawar argue that open lobbying and a context for the prime ministership will lead to dissension in the party ranks. Apart from the supporters of Narasimha Rao, the group of Rajya Sabha MPs campaigning in the name of Sonia Gandhi insist on a consensus. The group working for bringing back Sonia Gandhi in the fray has made it clear that even if a secret ballot is accepted, it will appeal to the newly elected MP's to make another gesture to Sonia Gandhi by offering her the leadership of the Congress Parliamentary Party and the prime ministership. It argues that a secret ballot should be taken only of Gandhi again declines the offer. This group is confident that Gandhi will not reject the offer, as the threat of a secret ballot also envisages dissession in the party. But sources close to Sonia Gandhi point out that she is not willing to revise her decision not to join politics at this juncture. The supporters of Narasimha Rao have floated a new idea to uphold the principle of "one person one post". They point out that if Rao is accepted as the consensus choice for the prime ministership, then a leader from the Hindi heartland can be elected party president. In this connection, the name of Arjun Singh has been proposed. As far as Sharad Pawar is concerned, the supporters of Rao propose that he can join the Government as Deputy Prime Minister with charge of an important portfolio like Home. They argue that Pawar does not have any experience of working at the Centre and is not well versed with the gigantic problems which the nation faces at this juncture. The problems faced by the country and the demands of consensus politics to make the Government stable require an experienced leader like Narasimha Rao to head the minority Government, they insist.[1]

Maharashtra Chief Minister, Sharad Pawar, said on June 22, 1991 his state got a raw deal in the Constitution of the Union Council of Ministers but maintained that he would join the Cabinet. Addressing a press conference in Bombay Pawar expressed the confidence that the party high command would take due not of it (raw deal) and mete out justice. He said his joining the Union Cabinet will be delayed till a successor to him is decided by the Congress Legislature Party in the presence of AICC observers. He said the Legislature Party is likely to meet on June 24 or June 25 according the observers convenience. Reporters asked Pawar as to what he would do if the state legislators demanded that he should stay in Maharashtra. He replied that it was the decision of the head of the party to invite him to join the central Cabniet and "I will obey the decision", he added. When asked about the press reports that he was tipped for the Home or Industry portfolio, Pawar said he did not know about it. It was the prerogative of the Prime Minister to allocate the portfolios, he said. Pawar was busy throughout the day consulting his party legislators and prominent leaders to pave a smooth way in choosing his successor. When asked whether his successor would be elected hy a secret ballot, Pawar said the procedure laid down by the Centreal Parliamentary Board in electing the new Prime Minister would be followed in the state. He said that every legislator would be given an opportunity to express his or her choice in the presence of the observers. Replying to a question on inadequate representation to Maharashtra in the Central Government, the Chief Minister said that it was a fact that the state got a raw deal. At the same time, he expressed confidence that the party high command would take due note of it and mete out justice.

Pawar said he did not visualise a mid-poll in the state as the Government was stable and voters were not immediately prepared for another election. He was answering a question whether there would be any possibility of a mid-term poll in the state in view of the minority government after he moved to Delhi.

The National Front will adopt a "wait and watch" policy for the first six months, and possibly review its stand after that, based largely on how the Congress tackles the economic and other pressing problems of the day. "We won't support the government but we will not create difficulties for them," said Fernandes. In Parliament, the party will see to it that government does not fall during voting on budget or money bills. The party could also abstain from voting, if so required, said Fernandes. At the same time, the Congress is expected to "behave in a responsible way and give up its arrogance". Ram Vilas Paswan is more emphatic about it "not being the NF's sole responsibility" to ensure that the government does not come down. It is as much the BJP's responsibility to see that another mid-term poll is aovided, he maintains. He cautions that the Congress should not take this "support" for granted. If the JD does not agree with the Congress stand on major national issues, social issued (read Mandal), it won't hesitate in withdrawing support, according to Paswan. The Left Front was quick to fall in line with the National Front decision on extendign issue-based support to the Congress government. Neither the CPI nor the CPM sees any similarity between the present crisis and the 1969 situation when they supported the "progressive" minority government led by Indira Gandhi against the Syndicate. As CPI's M. Farooqi puts it. "Today the Congress does not have a progressive image as Mrs. Gandhi did when he introduced bank nationalisation and abolished privy purses. Saifuddin Chaudhary, the CPM-MP from West Bengal, believes that in the interests of its own self-preservation, the Congress will be compelled to adopt a consensus approach towards the National Front-Left Front. According to the CPM Central Secretariat member Prakash Karat, a broad framework of issues on which the party could support the government was discussed over the last two days at the Politburo and Central Committee meetings of the party. "We will certainly support the govenment if it initiates positive steps on issues like Punjab, but are bound to oppose it if it takes an anti-people stand". Asked how the Congress could prove its majority in the House at the end of 30 days without a tangible show of support by the NF-LF, he retorted: "That is a problem that the Congress and the President must resolve. Why should we take upon ourselves the sole responsibility of offering any assurances of support?" CPI leader Inderjit Gupta is even more emphatic: "Let them (Congress leaders) first come to us with a concrete programme. Why should we jump forward and offer any guarantees of support? Let us see how they behave over the next four weeks. Whether they consult us on important issues. Whether they adopt a progressive stand on matters of national interest. Why should we rush and make a statement? After all 30 days is not 30 minutes."[2]

Although the CPM and the CPI publicly disclaimed any interest in the leadership struggle within the Congress, privately members indicated their predilections. According to sources, the CPM preferred Narasimha Rao. As a party member said, "who is Sharad Pawar? He may have a following in Maharashtra but he is not a leader of national stature like Narasimha Rao. All he has to back him is money power, because he is ruling over the industrial capital of the country." Despite the antipathy towards Pawar, however, the CPM appreciated attempts to democratise the election of the Congress leader. In the CPI, it was felt that while Narasimha Rao was a respected figure, he was not in the prime of health, which would make it difficult for him to shoulder the responsibilities of the high-pressure prime ministerial post. Pawar, on the other hand, while lacking the stature of Narasimha Rao, had established himself as a Chief minster with considerable clout, with the backing of a strong lobby of industrialists. This would certainly help the party strengthen itself. His secular credentials too were impressive, since had successfully contained the BJP and the Shiv Sena within his state.[3]

The "Counter Pawar" campaign was multi-pronged. The foremost pitch used was the now-familiar. "Now is the time for all good men to come to the aid of the party" line. A contest at this juncture would show the Congress party in poor light, especially when it looked certain to be short of a majority, and then, so soon after the death of the leader. Then there was the question of "Loyalists" vs "Newcomers", Pranab Mukherjee (of all people) rustled up a vigorous campaign questioning Pawar's defection from the Congress in 1978 conveniently forgetting his own contretemps after Mrs. Gandhi's death. And finally this was perhaps the most valid argument of all-came the question of who was most qualified to lead the party and country in terms of vision, experience and ability to keep the party together. Whether or not Narasimha Rao was a candidate of the coterie, the indisputable fact was that he was administratively the most experienced Congressman arround; he was trusted by Rajiv Gandhi and was his most senior coleague; and his intellectual and linguistic acumen meant he was better placed to lead the party at this juncture. The Pawar campaign's response to this aggressive counter was feeble. Madhavrao Scindia argued that if the Conservative Party of England could elect its leader by a secret ballot, why could not the Congress party? Shiv Shankar's refrain was defeating Narasimha Rao would signal an important blow to the Bhrahminical domination of the Congress Party. Besides, the party could do with the dynamic leadership of a younger man. And more than everything, what better chance was there to break the stranglehold of the coterie? At another level, the Pawar group also argued that they would not have opposed the consensus idea, had the "referee"-the AICC president-not been a candidate himself. Behind the Pawar group's insistence on a secret ballot was the firm belief that in that scenario, at least 80 per cent of the MPs would vote in that scenario, in favour of the Maharashtra strongman. These, however, included several who were not expected to come out openly in favour of Pawar, for fear of offending the coterie, which had been alatantly using Sonia's name through the week, to put the "fear of Good" into the newly elected MPs. Besides, Pawar, with the financial clout of the Bombay moneybags behind him could outpurchase the coterie (a number of Bombay industrialis parked themselves in the Capital throughout the duration of the crisis; all except one tycoon who has traditionally backed Congress, were behind Pawar this time.) These arguments were quickly sidelined by Tuesday when the arithmetic changed dramatically. It began perhaps with the arrival of K. Karunakaran, the former chief minister of Kerla and current chief minister-designate. A mild-mannered Congressman in his 70's with a perpetually toothy grinm Karunakaran, along with his lieutenant P.C. Chacko (a former president of the Kerala PCC- S, Pawar's defunct outfit) was counted in by the Pawar group. A vastly experienced

Congressman and a member of the parliamentary board and the Working Committee for many years, Karunakaran, along with Narasimha Rao, had saved Pawar's neck when the coterie was out to topple him as chief minister. The Pawar group also made some gross tactical errors: they assumed that PV was an exclusively coterie candidate which turned out to be incorrect. On his own PV did command respect of several southern MPs. The chalengers also erred in assuming that Pawar could graduate to prime ministership from chief ministership. This has never happened in Congress history. Recognised now as a challender, Pawar's every move in Delhi now will be watched carefully and attempts will be made by other Congress heavy weights to stymie him. Whether this chieftain will salvage a good treaty from this humiliating defeat will determine his political future.[4]

While the Congress's improved performance in the 10th Elections has been welcomed by Opposition parties, including the BJP promising it constructive support and cooperation to run the Government as no party wants another mid-term poll soon. One hopes that the Prime Minister will soon tide over the teething troubles that are inherent in a situation like the present when the Congress Party is finding its feet after the end of the Nehru-Gandhi's era.[5] The difficulties arose when a new Congress president had to be found after the assassination of Rajiv Gandhi. The party's working committee post-haste gave the post to Sonia Gandhi, obviously at the behest of the "coterie". After she declined to involve herself in the succession struggle it was Narasimha Rao, who was named president, with the understanding that he would be the Prime Minister if the party came to power. But when the time came for making the chose, the coterie which has guided the affairs of the country and the party from behind the scenes and suggested that the issue be decided by consensus. Sharad Pawar, the Maharashtra Chief Minister, who was also a contender, demanded that the next Prime Minister be chosen by secret ballot by the Congress Parliamentary Party. It was fairly obvious that the consensus choice was Narasimha Rao, but Pawar persisted and withdrew his secret ballot proposal only when he found that the large Maharashtra contingent of MPs apart, all the southern MPs were backing Narasimha Rao. Elsewhere the Congress did not matter very much. At that stage Narasimha Rao suggested that Pawar come over to Delhi to assist him. Pawar declined in the first instance, saying "Bombay is my home and I belong there", to presumably lay his claim at a later stage. But before returning to Bombay he called on Narasimha Rao and had a look at the list of names of the new Minsters, of state and Deputy Ministers. He was aghast at seeing it bristling with members of the coterie, who had succeeded in rejecting his claim to the Delhi crown on the ground that he had deserted the party on two occasions earlier, the time of Indira Gandhi and was therefore untrustworthy. Pawar then decided on the spur of the moment that he would be spoilling all chances of his ever coming to Delhi if he kept himself ensconced in Bombay. He told the Prime Minister that he was thinking of coming to Delhi and would like to have the Home portfolio. He also wanted to have some of his adherents, notably N.K.P. Salve, P. Shiv Shankar and Suresh Kalmadi-those who had led the secret, ballot move on his behalf-to be included in the Government. Meanwhile, he wanted to go to Bombay and install a trusted follower, presumably A.R. Antulay, to succeed him as Maharashtra Chief Minister. But in Bombay Pawar found himself hoist by his own petard for there too the coterie had engineered to make the succession difficult by challenging his undisputed sway in Maharashtra Congress politics. The coterie has launched moves to get the Pradesh Congress president Shivajirao Patil Nilangekar, elected as the new Chief Minister in Pawar's place, and to frustrate his move to have his own nominee in the post. To add to his frustration, Pawar finds that Salve, Shiv Shankar or even Shiviraj Patel have not been included in the Union Cabinet. It appears that the Prime Minister, going by the advice of the coterie, has appointed an inordinately large number of members in his Minsterial Council, leaving little scope for making adjustments, for he cannot enlarge the Cabinet to include very many more Ministers. Apparently the coterie had its way and pushed. Narasimha Rao to filling almost all the slots, leaving little room for either. Salve, Shiv Shankar or Shivraj Patil. The latter can at best be brought in as the Speaker of the Lok Sabha, but the Opposition is pressing its own candidate and the Congress does not have a majority in the House, thus there is little scope for accommodating more of Pawar's nominees. How the Prime Minsiter could produce a list of as many as 58 Union Ministers, Ministers of state and Deputy Ministers in a matter of a few hours on the morning of June 21, 1991 is a mystery-unless it had all been decided for him by the coterie and some other advisers. The Prime Minister's well-wishers think that he ought to have begun with a small council of Ministers and then added to it, or even substracted from it on the basis of performance, as all previous Prime Ministers had done in the past. The wholesale manner in which the Ministerial council was filled in great haste is now giving rise to problems. The new MPs are now openly expressing themselves on the formation of the Ministerial council as Congress MPs have never done in the past. The followers of Mr. Arjun Singh are grumbling that V.C. Shukla and H.R. Bhardwaj have been taken in the Government from Madhya Pradesh, even though at least Shukla joined the party only recently. The anti-Arjun Singh group is making no bones of their hostility to Dalbir Singh and Kamal Nath, entrants in the Ministerial council who are said to be associated with Mr. Arjun Singh. They are opposed to the high profile Minister that is proposed to be given to Arjun Singh, whose record is not altogether unblemished. P. Chidambaram, it is stated, has a grudge that although a Minister of State for Home Affairs in the Rajiv Government and a member of the Political Affairs Committee, he continues to have the same status, whereas Mr. Ghulam Nabi Azad has been promoted to full-ranking Ministership. Mr. Giridhar Gomango, who has been sworn in as a Minister of State, is understood to have written to the Prime Minister saying that earlier he held the post of Minister of state for Communication with independent charge.

The Maharashtra group feels it has been marginalized and party MPs from Tamil Nadu are upset that no one from the State has been made a Cabinet Minister. Indeed, there are not many Congress (I) MPs who are not grumbling that their case has gone by default. They would have lived in hope if the Ministerial council had not been filled all at one go. Party analysis agree that discountent is acute. But they think that there may be another aspect to it. In the post-Rajiv era, the lid of censorship that remained foisted on Congressmen has now been lifted, and they are speaking openly, indicating that with the end of the "dynasty", there is now more inner-party democracy. As far as the coterie is concerned, they think they are upholding the Indira-Rajiv legacy as "loyalists". They feel that it is a time of transition and that the Prime Minister by his amicbloe and accommodating nature and outstanding stature in the party would be able to eventually harmonize and sort out the contradictory elements. The process of adjustment may be slow but the optimists think that Narasimha Rao, more than anyone else, can cope with the situation and will succeed eventually in pacifying the discordant elements, thus restoring a measure of inner-party democracy.[6]

To anyone who has watched the rapid developments of last week-the emergence of the Congress as the single largest political party, winning as many as 242 seats along with its allies, the unanimous election of Narasimha Rao as the leader of the Congress Parliamentary Party, the formation of the new government, and above all, the induction of Sharad Pawar in the Cabinet-it is abundantly clear that Congressmen at every level have begun to draw appropriate lessons from the current situation in the country. It is not merely the survival instinct which has asserted itself. The popular response to the Congress election campaign has induced a new self confidence in the party. To say this does not mean that the Congressman have grasped the gravity of the political and economic situation in the country. The Congressmen out of power are a different commodity. Since their party has remained in power for nearly four decades except for five years, between 1977-80 and 1989-91, they have yet to realise that their party is at the crossroads and Indian people have given them yet another opportunity to live up to their expectations, both in political and economic terms. The harsh Indian political reality today is that an ancient nation is bleeding with wounds-a serious economic situation, rise of terrorism, phenomenal increase in the mass influerice of communal and casteist forces, growth of cynicism among the people, and above all, erosion of the credibility of all secular forces. The growing discontent among the people is being exploited by certain forces. The obvious lesson from this is that the Congress will have to rouse the patriotic and secular instincts of the people on the basis of the national consensus.[7]

The man, the team and the job-all the three will be under close scrutiny in the coming days by discerning people. They will expect exacting standards in judging the performance of the new Government and keep constant watch on whether and, if so, to what extent, it succeeds in grappling with the many intractable problems. First, the man-Prime Minister P.V. Narasimha Rao, there are no two opinions about his competence, experience and other qualities, his assets for the new job. Because of that he begins his term with tremendous goodwill. Forgotten, for the time being, is the fact that the ruling party does not have a majority and that, technically, it could be outnumbered at a crucial moment. Mr. Rao's experience in managing political affairs under difficult conditions in the past should help him get over the constraints imposed on him by the verdict of the electorate. He moved to New Delhi in 1974 and soon after came the Emergency with its excesses and the choking political environment. Not a very happy period to be in Delhi for a State Congress leader to start at the national level. Rao made the best of the inhospitable situation, rendered more so because of his disturbed equation with the Congress president of the day, D.K. Borooah. From 1980 to 1989, when his party lost power at the Centre, he handled the affairs of important ministries with skill. After Rajiv Gandhi's assassination, he emerged as the top- first as the Congress (I) president and then as leader of the Parliamentary Party and, in that capacity, as Prime Minister. He played his cards well-while others were seen working hard, and using various means, fair and not so fair, to grab the positions rendered vacant by Rajiv Gandhi's demise, Rao conducted himself coolly, managing not to betray even the slightest sign of anxiety. Think of the material distributed at the Maharashtra Sadan by the over-enthusiastic supporters of Sharad Pawar, the contender for the Prime Minister's post-a note referring to

Rao's alleged connections with Chandraswami or the statements by individuals or groups of party members opposing the move for a consensus to choose the leader of the Parliamentary Party-and Rao's action in stopping the release of a joint statement by over 100 members of Parliament pledging support to him and the contrast will be clear.

Sharad Pawar said in Bombay, on June 24, 1991 that he does not regret his stand on choosing the Congres Parliamentary party leader through secret ballot. He observed that the campaign his supporters orchestrated in Delhi had helped establish certain democratic norms. Pawar also said that his observation about the state not being given inadequate representation in the union cabinet was taken seriously by the Prime Minister. SB Chavan becoming the home minister was proof that the message had reached, said the Congress leader. He said that he was ready to take any responsibility and it was the Prime Minister's prerogative to allocate prtfolios. The major decision taken in the last cabinet meeting under his leadership, concerned naxalite activity in Gadchiroli district. The cabinet viewed.

NOTES :

1. Shameem Faizee. Sharad Pawar. *Patriot,* 19 June 1991.
2. Vandana Mandlekar and Prema Vishwanathan. All Ill-Defined Support. *The Times of India,* 23 June 1991.
3. *Ibid.*
4. Chidanand Rajghatta. The Pawar Game. *The Times of India*, 23 June 1991.
5. *The Statesman,* 24 June 1991.
6. *Ibid.*
7. V.D. Chopra. After P.V. Government, What Next? *Patriot,* 24 June 1991.

NINETEEN

NEW CHALLENGES

After the death of Rajiv Gandhi, what challenges does Narasimha Rao think the Congress will face in this election? I do not see any fresh challenge in the election. The challenges are the same as they existed in the late Rajiv Gandhi's time, What I feel and understand is that the people have made up their mind. They are firm that the Congress has to be brought back to power in this election. They have become sick of the misrule of other parties during these past 18 months. I am sure they are going to usher in the Center's rule once again. I am sure this would be confirmed during my election tour starting from tomorrow. It would confirm the polarisation in this regard.[1]

What challenges does Narasimha Rao forsee for the nation and for himself in the post-Nehru-Gandhi dynasty?

Where is the talk of this dynasty? And, where is dynasty? What do you think? Who took over after Pt-Nehru's death? Your theory of dynastic rule broke down at the very first step. Who brought Indira Gandhi. Were they not the people of India? Again, were they not the people of India who brought Rajiv Gandhi as the leader of the nation and as Prime Minister? What right has anyone to talk of dynastic rule? Were there not non-dynastic Prime Ministers also in between? But, they were short-lived. The Congress could not make them survive longer in office. Who prevented them from making themselves perpetual, at least for five years? What is answer to this? I am not suggesting anything. It is for every one to see. You are free to draw your own conclusion from your past experience. I have nothing to add to that.[2]

Professor Milton Friedman, the Nobel Prize winner for economics, concludes in the Tyranny of the status Quo that no elected head of state has more than six to nine months to initiate major policy changes. Thereafter, the force of status quo take over. This borne out by the Indian experience. Nani Palkiwala has gone on record to say more than once that the best budget India ever had was in 1985. It wa less than six months after Rajiv Gandhi took over. Subsequent efforts of the administration were to undo whatever good was done. And whatever results were delivered had their origin in the irreversible policy initiatives of the first six months. The phenomenon would flummox anyone not conversant with the dynamics of power. By all accounts, Rajiv Gandhi has a charismatic personality and was supported by a brute majority in Parliament. He did his best to be a good leader and motivate people but fell prey, by his own admission, to the machinations of the power-brokers surrounding him. There is a lesson. Good managers must know the leadership and motivation theories. But their success would depend on their ability to understand and practice "power" the prime mover of organisation. Unfortunately, prominent management experts appear to be allergic to the word though they do mention the subject in a round about way by using terms like authority, motivation, incentives and so on. However, these terms do not do justice to reality, as power is the synergic output of these individual elements. The resultant force is far greater than the sum of individual inputs. Some of these inputs are nebulous, others incomplete. Let us consider authority. Authority is defined as the ability of job holder to give orders and exact obedience to use organisational resources for achieving goals and to take decisions and have them implemented. Authority flows from the top to the bottom through a chain of command. Our experience demonstrates that even heads of states, with all the authority at their disposal, are rendered ineffective by a handful of people who can scuttle any move.

Management specialists call them informal leaders to be accommodated in the system. But they are not the only fly in the ointment. Even a petty official can inordinately delay an important project by misfiling a report of misplacing a file. Managerial authority remains only on a paper. Satellite leaders known as a coterie, caucus or cabal, are always able to execute their plans. They do not need any authority. They have the 'power'. They study of motivation has attracted a large number of scholars. One is baffled by the number of theories and their implications. Maslow, the father of the work-motivation theory states that people have a hierarchy of needs, each with a predetermined degree of intensity. People work for their satisfaction in the given order.[3]

Herzberg and his colleagues restated this theory by saying that lower level need satisfaction (physiological, security and social) can bring forth only the minimum necessary effort from employees, People are fired to give their best only by higher level needs like ego and self actualisation. Douglas McGregor, in the mean time, came up with his own Theory X and Theory Y. One fails to understand why his contribution is labeled as the theory of motivation. The focus of his work relate to the assumption made by leaders regarding their subordinates' behavior and its resultant effect on their performance. It is more a management philosophy that a theory of motivation. Room adds a new dimension to the subject. He mentions with sufficient justification, that earlier theories assumed that a donkey will a always go for the carrot oblivious of his needs and capabilities. In real life, before embarking on a venture a person will consider not only the attraction of the rewards but also hi chances of success. The implications for managers are that he must know not only what is desired by each subordinate but also how he rates his changes of success.[4]

What is know from the unpublicised findings of serious exit polls suggests that in the first round of polling on May 20, 1991 Rajiv's Congress fared rather poorly, some what worse that predicated by the public opinion polls (and drastically worse than predicated by Surjit Bhalla). But then this is a strangely split election, something that has not taken place anywhere else in the world to my knowledge. The Congress's obvious game plan is to turn mass sympathy for Rajiv and is family into a clear voting edge in the next two rounds to make up for a below-par performance in the first round. It would require a great deal of political denseness not to maintain an appearance and minimum unity submerging the factional conflicts and competitions and the unseemly ambitions of regional satraps-in the name of carrying forward Rajiv's vision and policies.

But assessing the political scenario of the intermediate, if not the immediate, future must to beyond questions relatiing to the number of Lok Sabha and State Assembly seats the party will win. Analytical attention must focus on two question: What causes division and splits in India's oldest political party and what is the outcome of the working these internal contraditions over time? Secondly, what explains the Congress party's internally volatile, sometimes unstable, condition as well as its resilience and strength? Political scientists as well as lay journalists are perfectly aware that the Congress in the wake of the 1969 split, and decided after the 1971 triumph for Indira Gandhi, has been a very different party from the one that was founded in 1985 and played a leading part in the freedom struggle. It used to be, at least at a formal level, a mass party with a dues-paying membership divided into a primary and active category, with a defined organisational structure, involving some kind of internal elections covering the local, district, state and national levels, with a hierarchy of leadershipging up to the All India Congress Committee and with an elected president at its head. Other structures which mattered included the State and Central Parliamentary Boards. Now only the shell of this historically developed organisational structue is intact. Even in the old days factionalism was on of the key laws of motion of this organisation; much of the 'dues-paying' membership rneolled by the faction leaders was only on paper, and there were frequent allegations of 'bogus enrolments' and manipulation, Nevertheless, the party of government in Independent

India remained, in the words, of the political scientist Paul Brass, "a highly factionalised, internally competitive party".[5]

But with Indira Gandhi's truimph in 1971, which overcame the crisis which had seized the party and had endangered its hegemony in the polity, and with the disintegration of the 'syndicate' which challenged her leadership style and policies, the organisation became "in effect, her personal party, dependent upon her populist, sometimes demagogic leadership rather than on local party organisation, win elections". The internal elective principle was blotted out. A national political party became, in other words, a patrimony or political estate understood by everyone to belong to the Nehru-Indira Gandhi family. But interestingly, although the succession seemed dynastically determined in a republic it seemed to work-because the supreme leader conducted mass politics on a gigantic scale and mobilised tremendous resources and organisational energy and enthusiasm to keep the party going, taking advantage of opposition 'disunity'. Essentially this ensured that the popular support for the Congress-a most revealing name-remained much broader than its leadership'. This chapter in India's political history has now come to an end. Narasimha Rao, it is clear, will be Chairman of the Board, primus inter pares (first among equals), rather than supreme leader of the party. Aside from being required to guide the party to a victory, it is claear that he must reverse course, do away with arbitrary, non-elective modes and styles of functining within the organisation and restore a credible collective leadership-if his pre-eminence is to survived. If this cannot be achieved in a short time after the elections, further splits and self-damaging feuds within the party are guranteed in 1991. The crisis of the Congress, which is not apparent at this juncture but lurks beneath the surface, can be described in the following terms: the leadership cannot rule the organisation interacting with its mass constituencies in the old way and the organisation, as India's largest and most powerful party, cannot be ruled in the old way. How will Narasimha Rao, and the rest of the Congress leadership, respond to this challenge?[6]

Chandra Shekhar on June 20, 1991 urged the new Government assuming office on June 21 to immediately set its mind to the grave challenges, particularly the economic crisis facing the country, by ensuring the willing cooperation of the people. In a farewell broadcast to the nation, the Prime Minister said the recent elections had proved that democracy was firmly entrenched in the country. But some elements had been trying to divide the country of the basis of caste and religion, and the new Government must immediately find ways to tackle this threat. Chandra Shekhar said the democratic experiment initiated by the founding fathers had proved successful, but some elements had sought to disrupt the unity of the country. He was, however, confident that the spirit of reconciliation would take the country forward. He said the new Government would take over from Friday and called upon the people to weolcome this democratic change. The Prime Minister expressed his gratitude to the people for their cooperation to his Government, and extended his best wishes to them in a very brief telecast.

A vital point that has been left unattended relates to the Congress's electoral base which too is upset by teh sudden disappearance of Rajiv Gandhi. This section spreadover the entire country continues to be nonplussed. It has to be convinced without loss of time that Congress can survive on its own and that the assassination of Rajiv Gandhi has not ineapaciated the organisation to the point of liquidation. There are reports that while congress was suffering a trauma for a week or son its adver-saries and active political workers went round the country side in Uttar Pradesh, Bihar and else where spreading the impression that there was nothing leeft in Congress now. It had a demoralising effect on certain sections of Congress supporters where next phase of polling was due. It is necessary, therefore, for the party leaders to conduct themselves in a manner that may convince the people that the party is relevant and that it can survive this tragedy. Charisman may have gone, but there are even now scores of leaders who are suprior to their counterparts in the opposition. There could be no denying the fact that in the killing of Mr. Rajiv Gandhi, the most powerful contender of Prime Ministership has been eleminated. This has put Congress (I) to a disadvantagious position. It has demoralised the party at all ranks as the question as to who would be the Prime Minister if the party returned to power is of crucial importance as the slogan of stability was linked with Rajiv. On earlier occassions the party and almost readymade answers to this question eversince the death of Nehru in 1964. Successor to Indira Gandhi who succeeded with the initiative of the then President Zail Singh, kept the party together. The present situation is entirely different and complex. The party's links with Nehruvian nomenclature stands snaped. Question of instant acceptability is doubtful so far as Mrs. Sonia Gandhi is concerned and Priyanka is too young to be considered. She will, however, continue to haunt the Congress mind and all eyes will be fixed on her as a future choice at a suitable time. It may look too early to think of it, but is too pertinent to make a note of it. The survival instinct of Congress is too strong to leave any avenue of sustenance untapped and unexplored.[7]

There has never been any dearth of suitable remedial prescriptions for the Congress to act upon. As the party stands at the most dangerous crossroads in its hundred year old career, rush of suggestions has been intensified. As a matter of fact, there is harldy anything new or extraordinary in the suggestions. Most of these are stereotyped and pedastrian in nature. Basically, Congress has to think whether it has outlived it s utility or its has still to play a role assigned to it by history. In case it fails to stand on its feet and does not come up to the task ahead, it may be devoured of its right to exist. Challenges confronting it have multiplied many fold and the encounter is going to be really stiff. A taste of it is evident in the current mid-term poll to Lok Sabha.

In the present political scenario overcast with ideological conflicts, Congress was expected to play role in safeguarding the basic, ideological edifice of secular, democratic India. On ideological plane, it is faced with the new challenges of communalism, casteism and separatist forces which have succeeded in changing the national agenda and put the secular forces in defensive. Admittedly Congress finding it difficult to paly its assigned role under the present dispensensions. It is in this specific context that the new role or Mr. Rajiv Gandhi has to be seen. Rajiv had taken up the challenge and was in a state of interaction with the people with all the courage of conviction at his command. He was not only fighting an election, but was engaged in fighting for a cause and identify his party with the basic perceptions which sustend the country so long. He was convinced that only rededication to the basic ideological formulations will make the party find its rightful place in the country. His voice has been stilled. Congress has to find a leadership which lead it on the path of ideological reconstruction. The party has to do some heart cherishing and think of its task ahead. Unity and discipline by resorting inner party democracy will be the first requirement to be fulfilled. Organisational elections had been hanging fire for long. This has to be gone through. it will necessitate rigorous handling of party affairs. This makes the task of Narasimha Rao rather difficult. Only a collective leadership can generate hope for the future if the party is not totally beaten and is alive of its historic role. Altogether new challenges have been added to the lists already perforating problems relating to the task of countering ideological aberrations and conflicting views. The danger of threat to democracy, institutionalisation of the cult of violence in political dealings, combating terrorism, lack of responsiveness to the voice of sanity, pressures on the national unity and integrity etc will need concerted action on political plane which cannot be the exclusive concern of the Congress. Only a joint endeavour on the basis of maximum possible consensus can produce results. Punjab, Kashmir and Assam should be the concern of all and must not be assigned to Congress or any party alone. In any case, Congress, being the largest political force, may have to take a lead and initiate a move in these directions.[8]

Like hen scurrying into the coop at the first sign of perceived danger, the Congress Working Committee, composed as it is of people distinguished more for their chamchagiri (sychophancy) than for anything they have done on their own for the public did what came normal to it: it decided to co-opt yet another member of the Gandhi clan as its president. That Sonia Gandhi, politely declined the honour speaks well for the Working Committee which behaved with singular unmanliness. Through sheer force of hanit Congressmen had come to regard the Nehru-Gandhi family as the sheeranchor of their party. When Jawaharlal Nehru died, many of the old Guard were still alive-men like Nijalingappa and Kamaraj- who had the courage to back Lal Bhadur Shastri as Nehru's successor. But following Shastri's untimely death and the induction of Indira Gandhi to the party leadership it was all over the old Guard which was subsequently bested by Indira Gandhi in her bid for total power: After that it was downhill all the way. Indira Gandhi schemed against the old Gurard to form her own Congress-R. Jagjivan Ram who was named president of the breakaway section at the Bombay session (1969) allowed himself to be manipulated by her. The affable Shankar Dayal Sharma who became party president at the Calcutta session in 1971 was no great improvement on his predecessor. The worst was Dev Kant Barooah who became president of the party in 1975 and held on to the post through the Emergency. He was to earn notoriety for coining the dubious phrase: 'Indira is India and India is Indira'. Thereafter Indira Gandhi gave up the pretense of ruling by proxy and assumed direct charge of the party from 1978 onwards.

It was not that the Congress fell effortlessly into the grasping hands of the Nehru clan right away. In 1946, with independence round the corner Gandhiji wanted Jawaharlal to succeed Maulana Abul Kalam Azad as Congress president. The party rank and file wanted Vallabhbhai Patel to succeed Azad. Indeed, his nomination papers had been put in. But the Mahatma wanted Jawaharlal to be president as that put him automatically in line to be India's first Prime Minister after independence. The Mahatma felt that Nehru 'cannot be replaced', especially since 'he is a Harrow boy, a cambridge graduate and a barrister and is wanted to carry on negotiations with the Englishmen'. Another consideration with the Mahatma was that Vallabhbhai did not have a good repport with Muslims. In the circumstances, Vallabhbhai was persuaded to withdraw his nomination as he had done earlier in 1929, 1937 and 1939 all at Gandhiji's request. Another candidate,

Acharya JB Kripalani, also withdrew his candidature. The way was clear for Nehru to assume power with the consent of the party and the blessing of the Mahatma.[9]

But Nehru to give up his chair when he became prime minister and the man who succeeded him was the Acharya who was to insist on retaining the supremacy of the organisational wing of the Congress over its parliamentary wing, on which issue he fell out bothe with Nehru and the Sardar. Thereafter, he tendered his resignation and went into political wilderness. Next came Dr. Pattabi sitaramayya who became president at the jaipur session of the Congress in 1948. Pattabhi Sitaramayya was never a real threat to Nehru, pattabhi had won the election-yes, there were elections in those days-against purshottam Dall Tandon by a narrow margin of 1199 votes to Tandon's 1085. Sardar has upported Tandon while Nehru gave his nod to Pattabhi, but in the elections that followed 18 months later at the Nasik session, it was Tandon who finally got in.

After Sardar's death it was to be Nehru-raj all the way. he took over the reins of the party at the 1951 party session in Delhi and stayed in the post till 1955 when he handed over charge to Uchcharangray Navalshankar Dhebar at the famous Avadi session when the parrty voted for a 'Socialistic patten' of society. Dhebar was not one to rock the Nehru boat and he continued as president for five long years, till 1959 when he faded away. For a fairly unknown man outside of Saurashtra, Dhebar stayed as Congress President (Amritsar 1956, Indore 1957, Guwahati 1958 and Nagpur 1959 with Nehru's support, knowing fully well his place in the scheme of things. He was to be followed by two other men, Neelam Sanjeeva Reddy (Bangalore 1960, Bhavanagar 1961 and Patna 1962) and Kamaraj (Bhubhaneswar 1964, Durgapur 1955 and Jaipur 1966) who could be relied upon to play to Nehru's tune. It will be remembered that it was at Nehru's instigation that Kamaraj proposed his famous plan that saw the elimination of many of Nehru's challenges.[10]

There is the problem of the future snape of the Congress which has yet to figure in the discussion on the current political scene. It is self-evident that under Rajiv Gandhi it ceased to be the hegemonic party which it was firmly under Nehru and not so firmly under Indira Gandhi. But despite its near total eclipse in the curcial states of UP and Bihar now, it has not become a regional party either. Anyone who knows anything about Indian history will know that it must either seek to regain its earlier position of shrink further and shrink not to become a regional party but to become a regional party but to be reduced to insignificance on the pattern of former socialist parties of various names. A regional identity is clearly dependent on language. Those who talk of the end of anti-Congressism and of country entering the era of coalition politics on a long-term basis are ignorant of Indian history and the compulsions of Indian social reality which emphasises unity as much as it accommodates diversity. But that reckoning, the struggle for the place the Congress has occupied has to continue.

The problems the country faced in the fields of economy, security and law and order are heart-breaking. But if they demand a political truce under a Congress dispensation, they also rule out an anti-BJP alignment except as an alibi for keeping a government in existence.

We need a grand vision and determination for orderly and humane societal transformation. It is a difficult proposition to today's situation with politicians pulling the polity in different directions for their vote banks and sectarian gain. All the same, we need but to respond positively to new changes and accordingly manage necessary structural transformation.

We do need new concepts in politico-economic and social management so as to enable us to select, synthesise and conceptualise the full implications and the significance of the challenges we face, of the changes we are going through, and of the means we will choose to meet these problems. The V.P. Singh of the polity divide it. They lack a modern vision of faster growth with a human touch. They do not seem appreciate the fact that the demands of different segments of society have to be blended harmoniously and intelligently not only for our survival but for competing effectively with other advanced world communities. We need to pause and ponder over the deeper malaise afflicting the polity and see if new areas of national consensus could be explored. The choice is clear: either we act fast or perish. For, even for a tolerable future for all of us, rich or poor, weak or strong, we will have to liberate it from the antiquated concepts and isms and past prejudices and pranks. The challenges can be successfully faced if we help to develop the capacity of old and new socio-economic forces of human understanding and help each interest group to look beyond and relate and trust other groups as a part of adjustment exercise. We will have to learn to live with the increasing vulnerability of extremely complex sectarian interests and an extremely fragile and complex multi-ethnic polity. We will have to learn even how to manage our fears if we are not to be overawed by trigger happy terrorist groups and opportunists and exploiters of different shades and hues.[11]

Freedom is not divisible but bread is, and since bread is, and since bread is the main problem of life, there are as many divisions on this as there are men in the world. The task before the polity is to find an aggregation which is viable. As long as the Congress fought for freedom, it held together, but the moment it came to possess the key to the store house, the divisions multiplied. The task before it and other national parties at this critical juncture is to find an adhesive which can accommodate varied interests and help the process of a harmonious change in the system. Political theory has little to say on this. Democracies take it for granted that conflicting interests can be reconciled. It is easier said than done. No democracy in the world has come near perfection in this matter, As for communist societies, theoretically there is not place of new forces in a classless society although even this myth has has exploded in the Soviet Union. Thus, we have little to go by on how to accommodate the ever increasing number of forces thrown up by our society. The tragedy is that while every potential splitter of society promises to deliver the goods, he is actually taking his group away from its realisation. Form the more you split, the weaker you become. Unfortunately, this has become the bane of our national life. It is said that we have copied the western model. This is not wholly true. Actually what we have created is a travesty of the western model. Societies of the west are more or less homogenous. They have split along conservative and radical lines, or on the basis of economic and social issues. Ours being a country of extreme diversity, we tend to break at the seems at the slightest provocation. Western Political thinking can be of not much help to us here. Unfortunately, we have not done much deep thinking on how to hold our society together while advancing the interests of its various sections.[12]

Till the eighties, three distinct ideologies were contending for power-the left-of centre Nehruism (a sort of democratic socialism), the nationalist ideology of the Jana Sangh and the communism. The Congress enjoyed unbroken rule because it was an amorphous organisation supposed to represent the interests of one and all. In reality, it was nothing of the sort. But the illusion stayed for long, so long the Congress was able to accomodate its various constituents. Now those who are disillusioned with the present order are up in revolt or have already came a cropper so long its constituency consisted of only Brahmins and traders. Only the communists had a coherent ideology and distinct constituency. Thus, while the Congress had all elements of breaking up, the Jana Sangh has to expand its base to make its ideology credible. In any case, it was not likely to make progress unless the Congress was found to fail on nationalism. But having won freedom for the country, the charge that it was not nationalistic enough could not stick. Times have changed. The decline of the Congress set in when different regions began to assert their rights. The power configurations within the party did not permit an equitable distribution of resources which led to centre-state conflicts. With the growth of economy, while industrial interests demanded a free hand, the growing kulak lobby was able to influence the power structure. Similarly, the growth of the trade unions and the small-scale sector led to new forces which had to be accommodated.[13]

Never before since Independence did India face such frightening convergence of a grim economic crisis, acute social tensions and widespread violence and disturbing political uncertainties. If the memories of the 1977 emergency were not fresh in our minds, the situation today would fully justify the declaration of financial emergency. The need to avoid that extreme step should not come in the way of pursuing the same objective by consent, consultation and consensus. Only a prime minister who can act in national interests without worrying, at all, about the impact of the steps taken by his government on his future political career can take the tough decisions that the present challenges demand. The Congress parliamentary party's choice of the leader has given to the country exactly such a leader at this critical juncture. P.V. Narasimha Rao can afford to take unpopular, but necessary steps. In doing so, he will require to draw upon his vast experience and astuteness to steer the country out of an extremely difficult corner.

Even if the Congress party had secured an absolute majority, the new prime minister could not do without the support of other parties and groups; for, the challenges are so grave that they can be met only if there is a national consensus on remedial measures. In a way therefore, the fact that the Congress party will require the support and understanding of other parties and groups in the Lok Sabha for smooth governance should be welcomed. It will force the ruling party to shun arrogant indifference towards the views of other political groups and to genuinely rely on building a national consensus. To begin with, the following deserve immediate attention.[14]

Imperiled as we are let us not deviate from the immediate task of consolidating ourselves as a cohesive, homogenous and integrated people. The state of the nation is such that it cries for radical reforms. From being a leader of the Third World, we have slumped to being just a "Third Rate' Third World country. Our economy lies shattered. The rupee, if devalued further as per the pre- conditions being imposed by the IMF for the release of the second installment of the loan, will simply crash. Our worst fears of India becoming a banana republic would have come true. Chandra Shekhar's caretaker government has sold 20 M.T. of Gold from our Reserves to tide over the financial crisis. A questionable decision. Is a caretaker government competent to take such a major step? On the other hand we are witnessing another strange drama be being enacted on the election front. A greater muddle was never seen as this current election. A parallel centre of power has been created and the entire poll schedule has been turned into some kind of a farce. Perhaps all this blood-shed, the senseless killings and the hatred could have been avoided if we had planned and had a one day poll in the entire county. This particular election will go down in our history as a never-ending agony, in which issues have been lost and in the ultimate analysis the nation's prestige has been lost.

Not even the richest and the most stable democracies anywhere in the world can afford a two month election extravaganza. If this is not mid-summer-madness, what is such an election should be for all times the last of a bitter, bloody and disgraceful election. This has indeed been a summer of shame.[15]

The fact that the Congress strength in the new Lok Sabha falls short of a majority indicates that in the country as a whole the party has made no headway by way of its organisation and influence in the last two years. On the contrary, the Congress score in this election would have shown a decline but for the impact of Rajiv's assassination on the public which helped it to improve its position, though in its classic home in UP, it has suffered a humiliating defeat, handing over the State to the BJP. It appears that the leaders of the Congress are by and large aware of this shortcoming, and one noticed an urgency of staying together when the question of choosing a new leader for its parliamentary party. Despite the fact that powerful vested interests were found to be backing important leaders in the race for leadership, ultimately the overriding consideration that weighed with all the factions was not to let the party be divided but stand united through the choice of a leader who is acceptable to all by consensus. Hence came the election of Narasimha Rao as Prime Minister-a person who is the very embodiment of consensus both within his own party and outside in its relations with other parties. Consciously low key in his demeanour, Narasimha Rao possesses the humility of a true Intellectual-a characteristic rarely to be seen in politics now a days. The Council of Ministers he had chosen is by all counts a very mixed bag where persons of seniority, experience and eminence find themselves in the company of proven mediocrity of bordering on the bully. The ministerial team reflects by and large the state of the Congress today while one noticed special attention paid to the northeast along with fairly even representation of all regions and interests.

Placed as he is, Narasimha Rao will have to run the Government with broad consensus from other parties belonging to the Naitonal

Front and the Left. The decision of this Opposition bloc slightly larger in number than the one led by the BJP-to extend responsive cooperation from issue-to-issue instead of blanket support, is a reflect of the present realities. This would impose upon both the Congress and the Left-of Centre Opposition certain constraints, rather responsibilities. Apart from the unwritten embargo on the toppling of the Minister for fear of inviting another mid-term which is unacceptable to all parties, one has to take into account the fact that on all major issues confronting the Rao Government there could be no solution by forcing decisions by majority votes. Irrespective of whether a government commands parliamentary majority or not, it can hardly expect to make any headway towards solving any of the important problems today without striving to secure the consent of the major parties in Parliament. In most cases, this has to include the BJP group as well. Because, the issues facing the public in general will affect the BJP as it concerns the others in this field. Consensus thus has become the order of the day for Indian politics. The challenge to the present government really lies in its acumen and sagacity in hammering out such consensus on all the major issues- not by flamboyant, hi-fi political gimmicks. A new chapter in Indian politics has just arrived.[16]

Rao as Prime Minister is not expected to remain at the head of the Congress party. Aside from the strain entailed by the twin burden, this would not be a precedent he would want to continue. There are several Congress leaders of outstanding ability and any of these can be entrusted with the responsibility of reviving the Congress and its inner-party democracy. Illustratively, Arjun Singh, once vice-president of the Congress, is one of those possessed of the right credentials who can be asked to fill the Congress presidency for completing the party election, including the election of all elective officals of the party. Maharashtra's Sharad Pawar, having given the much-needed jolt to the Delhi- based 'coterie', has wisely withdrawn from the contest. Age favours him and he can wait as he takes a more direct interest in all-India affairs. Hopefully, he would not make the mistake of his poitical mentor and guru, the late Y.B. Chavan, who never really took much interest in the affairs of states other than Maharashtra. This failure limited him, and he was timed and again passed over.[17]

And now it is a challenge ahead. The ability to communiciate a linguist who knows 15 languages-is his strong point. Charisma is missing. But Narasimha Rao has the ability to get on with the younger elements and it is a surprise that a number of young MPs, not all of them members of the maligned coterie, were pitching for him. His views on foreign policy and economics are not clearly defined but he is generally inclined to take collective decision. In a way Rao may well be a stop-gap and make way for younger people to take over the reins. The timing is just right not only for Rao but also the Congress (I) which is hoping to steer the country ahead at a time when all seems gloomy.[18]

It is above all the Congress which must not be influenced by the thesis of the Parliament of 1991 being "hung". If it even concedes something to this thesis the people will hang it. It has been given a mandate to govern and govern it must certainly it must do its best to secure the cooperation of all patriotic and progressive parties. It has to strike for a national consensus. But it has above all to be itself proud of being itself and refuse to be patronised or intimidated by any other party. It is the Congress which has been given the responsibility of governance by the people. It cannot forget that the people gave it their mandate on the basis of the manifesto it presented and the claim that it made that Congress and its allies along can give to the nation and the people the stability that the natin so urgently needs. It is the duty of other parties, if they have the nation's interests upphermost in their hearts and minds to be at least as responsive to the Congress as the latter would be to it. Cooperation cannot be a oneway street in either case. The Congress must boldly and promptly start the implementation of the time-bound schedules of its manifesto. It has been given a historic chance and task. It must prepare to advance.[19]

NOTES :

1. *National Herald,* 3 June 1991.
2. *Ibid.*
3. Inderjit Sharma. The Authority of power. *The Business and political observer,* 19, June 1991.
4. *Ibid.*
5. N.Ram. A Whole New Ball Game. *Current,* 8 June 1991.
6. *Ibid.*
7. B.N. Thakur. Charisma to Consensus. *New Wave,* 1 June 1991.
8. *Ibid.*
9. M.V. Kamath. Congress Then and Now. *Current,* 8 June 1991.
10. *Ibid.*
11. Hari Jaisingh. The search for Harmony. *The Business and Political Observer,* 15 June 1991.
12. Hari Jaisingh the search for Harmony. *The Business and Political Observer* 15 June 1991.
13. *Ibid.*
14. R.K. Mishra. PV: The Tasks Ahead. *The Business and Political Observer,* 21 June 1991.

15. Vijai Singh Mankottia. A Summer of Shame. *The Hindustan Times* 16 June 1991.
16. Nikenil Chakravartty. Indian Politics. *Patriot,* 23 June 1991.
17. *Patriot*, 21 June 1991.
18. *The Statesman,* 21 June 1991.
19. Mohit Sen. Prepare for Advance. *National Herald,* 21 June 1991.

Appendix I

CONGRESS LEADERSHIP

Prime Minister, Chandra Shekhar, said in New Delhi, on June 6, 1991 there was no paucity of leaders in the Congress and expressed the belief that the party would "find its own leader".

The assassination of Rajiv Gandhi would not cause a "vacuum... for all times to come" and therefore would not "have any lasting impact on the stability of the country," he said in an interview to Bulgarian television.

Reminded that he had been a former Congressman and asked about a possible political realignment, he said he did not subscribe to the theory of paucity of leaders in the Congress as it was a party with an old history and it would be "unfair to the party... to harp on that theory."

"There is no dearth of leaders because leaders are made overnight. If you elect a person to be the prime minister of the country, he will carry the country one way or the other," he said.

Acknowledging that the assassination of Rajiv Gandhi had created apprehensions about the future of the country, Chandra Shekhar said he was confident that the country would come out of the crisis.

"I see no reason why the Indian people will not rally around to make cohesive efforts to come out of the present crisis," he said.

"I do not see any reason to be pessimistic about future because in the last four decades India has faced many a problem of serious nature but the Indian people have behaved in a very mature manner and risen to the occasion at all times...they will come out of the crisis. I am quite confident about it," Chandra Shekhar added.

Referring to the security arrangement for Rajiv Gandhi, he said the government had taken all necessary precautions "but no one expected that a human bomb would be used to eliminate Rajiv Gandh."

Stressing that this was the first time in world history "when a human bomb was used to eliminate one individual," Chandra Shekhar, however, would not comment on the investigations into the assassination "until there is some conclusive evidence about the whole incident".

Speaking about the political situation in the country, Chandra Shekhar said that the BJP would not be able to provide a stable government and opined that the current upsurge in support of the BJP was a short-term phenomenon.

"Ultimately the people will be guided by their economic and social considerations for which I do not think the BJP has much of an answer,

because retrograde ideas are not going to create a new sense of confidence," he said.

"This party (BJP) has played upon the religious feelings of our people. So it may be a short-term aberration that they get support of the people but these religious questions are not going to solve the problems of bread, butter, illiteracy and inequality in society," he said.

"I cannot say that they will not get some support but that support is in no way, in the wildest imagination, any answer to India's problems," he declared while saying that BJP's coming to power was "a remote possibility."

The Prime Minister admitted that events in the rest of the world and in the region had impact on some developments in India.

"The BJP gets encouragement if Islamic fundamentalism gets encouragement in the Arab world or Pakistan or Bangaladesh. It is always fanatic forces opposing each other which held each other because fanaticism breeds fanaticism," he said.

Referring to the recent developments in the world, particularly in eastern Europe, Soviet Union and the Gulf, Chandra Shekhar said, "in the world of today you cannot just ignore the changes that are taking place...they will have their impact."

He, however, added "I do not think we should be overconcerned about this because Indian people will determine their own future in their own way. They have not been influenced by outside in the past, they are not going to be influenced now."

The Prime Minister said every nation faced its own problems and these could be solved only if "you tutor your ideological consideration according to the circumstances...and until this indigenous thinking is there no nation will be able to match with the problems it has to face."

Stressing that India would play a positive role in world affairs because a country of its size and potential could not be ignored, he said, "India cannot be lost because of media projections in some quarters. India has to survive and India has to play a major role."

Replying to a question on the refuelling controversy during the Gulf war, Chandra Shekhar said the problem was "unnecessarily exaggerated beyond a point."

He said that refuelling of planes was a bilateral matter and India availed of the same facility in several countries.

Criticising the attempt to politicise the problem, Chandra Shekhar said, "we were ready to give this facility to Iraq if they wanted landing facility for providing medical help. I told everybody that for humanitarian considerations we will not stop anyone."

Speaking about developments in the Gulf, Chandra Shekhar said he was opposed to the presence of foreign troops in any part of the world.

"Any power having presence outside its territory is not good for world peace," he said and added while referring to the U.S. presence in the Gulf "It is not in the interest of the U.S. itself. "No country should take police duty in another part of the world,"

Appendix II

NEHRU LINE OF CO-EXISTENCE NECESSARY –P.V. NARASIMHA RAO

Following are the excerpts from the conversation he has with Mr. Dileep Padgaonkar, Editor of The Times of India. New Delhi (see also New wave, 9 June 1991).

DP: The Congress is going into the second round of elections without projecting anyone as Prime Minister. Will this be a disadvantage to the party" ? If it is, how do you propose to overcome it?

PV: The Congress and its leadership have always been treated as one whole. Sometimes the leader has been able to give the organisation the necessary impetus and the charisma. This has made up certain deficiencies in the organisation. There have been occasions when the reverse has been the case.

Today, whatever people might say, the Congress is a united force. When Rajivji left us, the Congress felt bewildered and shatered. But after the Congressmen realised the full import of what had happened they decided to sink their differences and give the Congress a unity which to a considerable extent can make up for the loss of the charismatic leader.

There are many Congressmen who have been running the party at different levels quite successfully for decades and decades. You just cannot write them off as non-entities. It is true that we were seen following the leader and I don't regret it at all. The image projected by the Congress was that of a command and also of a good following.

At*the same time once that command suddenly leaves, we do take some time to build another one. Today we are not without command. What needs to be understood is that there are people who have worked all their lives for the Congress. They are known, they have been tested, they have been tried. So it is not as if we are facing a blank wall after the leader left us. When you compare this to what has been happening in other parties you will find that the Congress has the upper hand.*

Q: *The instant reaction of the Congress after Mr Rajiv Gandhi's assassination was to turn to Mrs Sonia Gandhi. Did this have an adverse impact on the country?*

A: *No, it did not. Quite the contrary. If you had accompanied the urn to Allahabad on the train and watched the faces of people who swarmed the stations in their thousands without being specifically asked to come then you would cetainly have revised your opinion.*

Q: *In the past few days there have been calls from various quarters that Congressmen and former Congressmen should come together. I refer in particular to Mr Mohan Dharia's letter. How do you react to movement of this kind?*

A: *Mr Mohan Dharia is a very good friend and so are the leaders who were once upon a time in the Congress but who are now in other parties. I have read Mohan's letter. I find that when he talks about all Congressmen coming together, he concentrates only on one party and its leader. He suggests that they should immediately be taken into the Congress or that they should come together with the Congress. He, then, actually proposes a plan of action. All this is very unrealistic at the present moment. We are facing each other. We are all in the election fray. We are facing each other. How can this be the moment for anyone to follow Mohan's idea? I think it is illtimed.*

Q: *It is your feeling that the opposition parties will try and score propaganda points because your own election is of a provisional nature?*

A: *That is the Constitutional provision. The working committee has no power to elect a regular permanent president. It has the power to elect the president, but that election needs to be ratified by the AICC. In all other respects the person elected president by the working committee is the president.*

Q: *The Congress is entering an unprecedented phase in its long history. The Nehru-Gandhi family has for better or worse dominated the party and the country. How do you see the Congress evolving in the future? Will it have a more federal approach in its functioning than has been the case in the past?*

A: *I have very clear views of my own on this question of the fanily. Take my own case. When I entered politics, I was not personally acquainted with Mr Jawaharlal Nehru or Mrs Indira Gandhi. But the Congress and Nehru's writings and teachings and what he stood for created a new family. My cohesion was with that ideological family. It has been as strong as in any other social kind of family. From that point of view thousands like me in those days thoug Nehrufamily. Coming to the socalled dynastic theory, let me say that it broke down even at the very first demise. Mr Lal Bahadur Shastri was not from the restricted Nehru family. This ideologi-*

cal cohesion has endured over the decades. So long as Congressmen subscribe to this vision the feeling of the family is bound to remain. The father, then Mr Lal Bahadur Shastri, then the daughter, then the grandson came to the helm of affairs. This was because the Congress wanted them to come. The people endorsed it in a big way. If there is one thing that is going to continue, it is this feeling of an ideological identity. I call it the Nehru line. The restricted family is part and parcel of the large family and is identified with the sentiments and aspirations of the people. don't call it dynasty. I have not heritation in saying that the Nehru line will abide. The alternative to the Nehru line in India is fascism.

Q: *At no time since independence has the Nehru line come under such systematic and relentless assault as it has in the past few months. The Congress response so far, at an ideological level, at least, has not been firm enough. How are you going to ensure that the line regains vigour and its ability to riposte these forces?*

A: *There has never been any reservation about the Nehru line in the Congress. Those who had the reservation about the Nehru line in the Congress. Those who had the reservation about the Nehru line in the Congress. Those who had the reservation separated at the time of the successive splits. I don't say they left just because of the ideological factor. There were other factors too. But then those who wanted to stick to the line stuck to it inspite of difficulties and inducements from the other side. Inspite of all that has happened, the Nehru line has survived. I do not see any other viable line, outside the pale of fascism. The ground of the Nehru line might have got splintered now and then for various reasons. Still it is there for anyone to see. It has the vitality to lead the country, to give the necessary lead from time to time from vicissitude to vicissitude. And we were convinced that was the correct line. The main plank of the line is that we have a plural society and all segments of the society should exist in freedom and equality. The only way to exist in India is to co-exist. This is the long and short of it.*

Q: *In this context can one deduce that you regard the BJP as the main rival of the Congress in this election?*

A: *I do not consider the BJP a rival because you have rivals in the same system. The BJP system is totally different from that of the Congress. Indeed, it wants the destruction of the system which the Congress stands for.*

Q: *Do you agree that in purely electoral terms the BJP does constitute a threat to the Congress in the remaining elections.?*

A: Yes, in some parts of the country they are posing as if they are going to sweep the polls, which they are not going to happen.

Q: *Should the Congress be voted to power, it will be called upon to urgently tackle the Ayodhya dispute. Do you think that it is possible to reach an amicable solution to it?*

A: *I have no doubt that it can be done. Once you get out of the electoral politics the solution can be found. In fact, as soon as a solution was being found, it was politicised. As it happened in 1989, there was an agreement which has the virtue of taking further steps in the matter beyond the election. But some forces didn't like this. They wanted it through and through to be an election issue. That is why the agreement was scuttled at the last moment.*

Q: *What would be your party's attitude to Punjab if it comes to power?*

A: *It will be the same attitude the we have always had. The solution to be within the context of India's unity and integrity. The Rajiv-Longowal accord was the solution which was considered to be viable. But for Sant Longowal's assassination it could have worked. That accord is already on the table. One could work on it, adding consideration of my new details that may have arisen meanwhile.*

Q: *Your party had expressed certain reservations about elections in Punjab.*

A: *Our position on elections in Punjab was categorical. We do not want to participate in an election which has been interpreted by one of the participating parties as a referendum for Khalistan. I know no way of participating in an election which is not completely within the four corners of the Indian Constitution. You cannot have secession as an issue.*

Q: *How would you now rate the prospects of the Congress?*

A: *I rate it high. I think we are going to have a comfortable majority. The stability platform cannot be appropriated by other parties for the simple reason that they cannot give it.*

Q: *In case the Congress falls short of a majority in Parliament, what system would you favour. A national government, a coalition, a government, which enjoys support from the outside? People who are going to vote in the coming elections would like to be assured that some kind of thought is being given to either of these eventualities.*

A: *This is something which no one can refuse to think about. But if you ask any party today about the election I am afraid there will be only one answer. I am confident of forming the government. Why should I comment on any other scenario? Coming to the proposal for coalition all I will say is that this can be discussed only if there is similarity in their thinking. A national government is by definition a kind of hold-all government in which parties which agree or disagree all come together. However, as I said, this is not going to be necessary in this election.*

Q: *Can the Congress, for the very first time, to have a Prime Minister who does not come from the northern states?*

A: *I don't think there was any conscious decision at any time that the Prime Minister should come from state A or state B. You know that our Prime Ministers from the north have invariably got strong, unstinting support from the south. So they have not really been considered in terms of north and south. I don't see why we should do so now.*

Q: *This was certainly true of all the Congress Prime Ministers so far. But the feeling is that in the second rung of leadership, which has now surged to the fore, may not command this kind of loyalty, a pan-India loyalty.*

A: *I am sure there are people who do. The leadership in the Congress has always been to some extent patent and, to a comparatively smaller extent, latent. The patent leadership has been of the leader and the latent one has been of those who worked with the leader. Perhaps this is how we consciously worked it out.*

Q: *Do you propose to organise inner party elections? These have been postponed again and again.*

A: *Yes. Rajivji, in the press conference he held at the time of releasing the manifesto, very clearly stated that party elections will be taken up from the point where they were interrupted by the Lok Sabha elections. I am convinced there can be no future for the Congress or the future which the Congress envisages unless we have people manning the Congress through the democratic process.*

Q: *Do you favour the principle of one person, one post?*

A: *We can take that decision only after the elections. I don't attach any sanctity to one pattern or the other.*

Q: *The Congress manifesto has gone some way the direction of ensuring speedy economic growth even while emphasising programmes for the direct alleviation of poverty. Wher do you stand on the issue?*

A: *I am not an economist though I am one of the members of a team which is studying the conduct of economic policies. I am quite conviced that direct benefits have to be given to the poor. But that is not all. To give a poor man something to alleviate his suffering is one thing that is necessary. But what really counts is how to make him economically viable. You give him a piece of land, you give him a buffalo-these are real programmes which make him viable. If you don't make him viable he continues to be a dead\weight on society. Both are necessary because right now even when he is not in a position to till the land that you give him he needs some aid. If you do give him land you need to give it along with some loans and concessions which makes him viable; otherwise he* *will sell the land to the nearest landlord. Therefore, it is not only a question of civic relief. It is more important to make every poor family viable, to enable it to stand on its own feet.*

Q: *The world has changed radiaclly in the past three years. How do you think India should respond to it?*

A: *I am convinced that India should resume the very important role it has played in the Non-Aligned Movement (NAM). It is more relevant today than ever before. Remember that NAM has always changed according to the needs of the time. See where it started and where it stands now. The Belgrade summit has given many leads. It is a different matter that those leads seem to remain where they were. Any government of India worth its salt should start on those lines. India cannot have an interest which is totally outside that of the whole world. If something is wrong somewhere it is bound to have repercussions on our internal matters. This is something which India must always bear in mind.*

Appendix III

THE FOLLOWING IS THE TEXT OF THE STATEMENT ISSUED BY FORMER UNION MINISTER VASANT SATHE IN NEW DELHI ON JUNE 19, 1991.

We are at a crucial period in the history not only for the Congress but for the entiry nation. This calls for a great deal of sagacity and maturity in creating the right image and impression of unity after the vacuum created by the removal of the undisputed leadership of Rajivji.

Taking into account the various factors and the loss of Congress majority in the North, it would be in the fitness of things to elect a leader of the Congress Parliamentary Party from the regions from where majority of Congress MPs have been elected.

(i) The leader should be one who should be able to stand the stress and strain of running the central government in this crucial period. He should have the capacity of commanding full support and confidence of the majority of MPs, in his own as well as other Congress states.

(ii) He should be able to communicate in languages that can be understood both in North and South.

(iii) He should have the capacity and temperament of carry with him not only his party colleagues but also leaders of the Opposition.

(iv) He should be fully dedicated to the Congress policies and programmes and should have a broad growth-oriented vision.

The Congress has many stalwarts who can fulfil the above criteria. It would be better at this juncture to avoid an election because whatever be the result and although as a last resort the only democratic alternative is an election, it would not be desirable at this juncture when the party has not got a clear majority to expose a division among our ranks of MPs.

I sincerely hope that our experienced and intelligent Members of CPP will rise to the occasion and live up to the expectations of the nation.

Sd/-
(Vasant Sathe)

Appendix IV

The following is the text of the statement issued by Mr Sharad Pawar in New Delhi on June 20, 1991.

I welcome the Congress President's acceptance of my demand for ascertaining the views of the members of the CPP in the decision of the leadership of the party.

I want to clarify that my whole endeavour was for no other purpose except the affirmation of democratic principle in the functioning of the party.

It is my firm conviction that only a united and democratic Indian National Congress can respond to the aspirations of the people for a strong and stable government.

It is only the INC which can pull the country out of the deep economic quagmire and restore the fonfidence and credibility of the nation.

It is only a strong and united INC which can confront the forces of communalism and terrorism which threaten the unity of the country.

The achievement of these goals would be the most befitting tribute to the martydom of our young and dynamic national leader the late Mr Rajiv Gandhi.

In view of this I appeal to all the members of the CPP to support Mr P.V. Narsimha Rao and thus arrive at a unanimous decision.

Sd/-
(Sharad Pawar)

Appendix V

TENTH LOK SABHA SEATS

The results of 503 of the 511 Lok Sabha seats which went to the polls are:

Congress	*224*
AIADMK	*11*
IUML	*2*
Janata Dal(G)	*1*
Total	*238*

This alliance is expected to be supported by the MIM (Hyderabad)- 1, the Sikkim Sangram Parishad-1, and the Kerala Congress-1 taking the total to 241 seats.

The National Front-left alliance:

Janata Dal	*53*
Telgu Desam Party	*13*
Jharkand Mukti Morcha	*6*
Congress(S)	*1*
CPI(M)	*34*
CPI	*13*
Revolutionary Socialist Party	*4*
Forward Bloc	*3*
Total	*127*

The BJP, Siva Sena combine:

BJP	*119*
Shiv Sena	*4*
Total	*123*

The 12 other are:

Samajwadi Janata Party	*5*
Haryana Vikas Party	*1*
Bahujan Samaj Party	*1*
Asom Gana Parishad	*1*
ASDC (Assam)	*1*
Manipur People's Party	*1*
Nagaland People's Conf.	*1*
Independent (Assam)	*1*

The result from eight Lok Sabha constituences which went to the polls between May 20 and June 15 have not yet come in for various reasons.

In two constituencies the Election Commission had announced that the results declared by the returning officers are "null and void" as these were declared in defiance of the its specific orders. These are Davangers (Karnataka) and Aurangabad (Bihar).

The commission has ordered an inquiry into certain irregualrities in the case of Monghyr and Begusarai, both in Bihar. Results have been delayed from four constituencies-Guwahati and Salempur (U.P.), Sasaram and Bikarmaganj in Bihar. In the case of the last two, the results were witheld as the commission was earlier under the impression that the returning officer had announced the resluts despite written instructions to the contrary. That embargo was lifted as it was established that the commission's instructions reached the returning officer after the declaration of results. T.N. Seshan, Chief Election Commissioner, clarifed this today. The result from Banka (Bihar) had also been similarly held up, but has come in now.

The Lok Sabha has a strength of 545 members. Two are nominatea from the Anglo-Indian community by the President. In Jammu and Kashmir the elections have not been held thereby reducing the number to six more and in Punjab (13 seats) the elections have not yet taken place. Besides, in eight constituencies the elections were countermanded because of deaths of candidates- Barh, Gaya and Madhepura in Bihar-Kutch (Gujarat), Nanded (Maharashtra), Cuddapah (Andhra Pradesh), Dharwas South (Karnataka) and Dhenkanal (Orissa). In five other constituencies the elections were countermanded after polling on May 20. These are Patna and Purnea in Bihar and Meerut, Bulandshahr and Etawah in Uttar Pradesh.

The results which will not be available in time for being included in the notification of the Commission constituting the Tenth Lok Sabha, will be notified separately as they come in.

Appendix VI

NEW COUNCIL OF MINISTERS

The follwing are the members of the Union Council of Ministers who took oath of office, on June 21, 1991.

Mr P.V. Narasimha Rao (Prime Minister)

CABINET MINISTERS

Dr. Manmohan Singh

Mr Balram Jakhar
Mr Arjun Singh
Mrs Shiela Kaul
Mr C.K. jaffer Shanef
Mr B. Shankaranand
Mr K. Vijaya Bhaskara Reddy
Mr Sitaram Kesri
Mr M.L. Fotedar
Mr Madhavsinh Solanki
Mr S.B. Chavan
Mr V.C. Shukla
Mr Madhav Rao Scindia and
Mr Ghulam Nabi Azad
Mr Sharad Pawar

MINISTERS OF STATE IN DEPENDENT CHARCE

Mr P. Chidambaram
Mr Ajit Kumar Panja
Mr Ashok Gehlot
Mr Rajesh Pilot
Mr Kamal Nath
Mr Jagdish Tytler
Mr Kalpnth Rai
Mr Margaret Alva
Mr Tarun Gogoi
Mr K. Ramamurthy
Mr Bal Ram Singh Yadav
Mr Santosh Mohan Dev
Mr P.A. Sangma and
Mr H.R. Bhardwaj

MINISTERS OF STATE

Mr P.J. Kurien
Mr Mullapally Ramachandran
Mr S. Krishna Kumar
Mr M.M. Jacob
Mr Rangarajan Kumaramangalam

Mr M. Arunachalam
Mr Shantaram Potdukhe
Mr P.K. Thungon
Mr Mamata Banerjee
Mr Chinta Mohan
Mr Kamaluddin Ahmed
Mr Dalbir Singh
Mr M.O.H. Farook
Mr G. Venkatswamy
Mr Giridhar Gomango
Mr K.C. Lenka
Mr Eduardo Faleiro
Uttambhai H. Patel and
Mr M. Mallikarjun
Mr. Rameshwar Thakur
Ms Tara Devi

DEPUTY MINISTERS

Miss Girijia Vyas
Mr Salman Khursheed
Mrs K. Kamala Kumari
Mr Paban Singh Ghatowar
Mr Ram Lal Rahi and
Mr P.V. Rangayya Naidu
Mr S.D. Nayama Gowda

Appendix VII

Revise Congress strategy

Reproduced below is a translated extract of E.M.S. Namboodiripad's open letter to P.V. Narasimha Rao, which appeared in the CPI(M)'s Malayalam organ, Deshabhimani.

Thiruvanthapuram, May 30, 1991.

Dear Shri Narasimha Rao,

The Congress under Indira Gandhi became all powerful. With that, innerparty democracy disappeared from the Congress. From the national to the village level, nominated persons became Congress leaders. It is the result of this style for 20 years that crisis gripped the Congress after the assassination of Rajiv Gandhi. One section wanted to install Sonia Gandhi in the place of Indira Gandhi and Rajiv. Within that section the president with a prime minister subservient to her. The coterie that was around Indira and Rajiv thought it could run things as it wanted. It wanted Sonia Gandhi as a tool in its hands. What observers see in your election is the collapse of this plot. Not only that, several leaders have issued statements stressing the need for restoring innerparty democracy. I see it as the beginning of a new chapter in the history of India as well as the Congress. I wish that you make a positive contribution to the completion of this process. I take this opportunity to call upon you and other Congressmen to do an introspection on the role of the Congress in post-Independence India.

Though Congress, as the party which led the freedom struggle, was quite strong, the Communist party was growing as an independent political force, while the Socialists in the Congress had moved over to the opposition. At the same time, because of the peculiarities of the situation, Hindu communalism also had begun to take a political form. Regional parties such as Dravid Prasthanam were also mushrooming.

While these developments were happening outside the Congress, within that party itself their impact was felt. Even before the death of Mahatma Gandhi there were two groups in the Congress-the left and the right under the leaderships of Prime Minister Nehru and Deputy Prime Minister Patel, respectively. Had that process been allowed to go on, probably there would have been a polarisation between the leftists and rightists within the Congress. Probably other developments such as a party based on Hindutva or similar manifestations of Islamic, Christian and Sikh religions also might have surfaced. Thus a healthy ideological struggle would have developed. But that was prevented and an artificial unity established in the Congress to dominate other parties. It is this line which enabled the emergence of the individualistic leadership of Indira Gandhi and Rajiv Gandhi, with the result that when both of them were assassinated the Congress was devoid of a leader.

Permit me to remind you that it is your duty to launch a discussion on what should be done to rescue the Congress and the nation from this situation....

....Following the murder of Rajiv Gandhi, Indian politics is at a crossroads. In this context should not your party's attitude towards the Left be re-examined? Will it do good either to the Congress or the country if your party's current electoral strategy, based on hostility towards the CPM-led alliances in Kerala, West Bengal and Tripura and the National Front, is not changed? Should it not be revised even before the June 12 elections?

Sd/-
E.M.S. Namboodiripad

Appendix-VIII

WHY DID MOHAN DHARIA WRITE TO THE CONGRESS WORKING COMMITTEE

Sitting in my chamber at the Planning Commission, I am often anugished with the way the country is moving. The many serious economic problems along with our failure to contain the growing population and underemployment are all cause for serious concern. Compiling material during the drafting of the Eighth Five-Year Plan has driven home the point more cruelly than even before. When you are confronted by the fact that over 40 crores of our people (more than the total population at Independence and about 50 per cent of the population today) are illiterate, unemployed and underemployed, that about 50 per cent fo our area is wasteland, that 2 lakh villages today are without potable water, and that 85 per cent of our population has not seen a laterine- then you are forced to sit up and think about where we have gone wrong. Equally disconcertation in which the basic tenets of secularism and social justice are being threatened. Besides, we face the danger of extremist elements taking over-be it in Kashmir, Punjab, Assam or Tamil Nadu. The question is, how do we tackle these dangerous trends?

It is this concern alone that prompted me to appeal to the Congress Working Committee to bring together all Congressmen, both within and outside the party. I wanted them to consider the possibility of all like-minded persons, like Chandra Shekhar who is essentially a congressmman, coming together in the Congress to counter the dangers that confront us.

I have been in touch with several leaders within the Congress in this regard for quite some time. But it was the brutal assassination of Rajiv Gandhi and the need for a large popular mandate to a single party, that prompted me to write the lettle to the CWC, particularly since there was very little etime between its meeting on May 29 and the second and third phase of elections on June 12 and 15. My decision was largely impromptu and taken only on the morning of May 29.

I had hoped the CWC would consider the proposal seriously in the larger interest of the country since it is my feeling that no single party will get a majority. I do not believe there will be a sympathy wave, and even if a single party gets a majority, it will only be marginal. This is not enough for the vibrancy of the democratic process which only a stable government, supported by the masses, can provide. I am aware that many countries like France and Italy are increasingly moving towards a coalition arrangement but they do not have to face the conditions that we do in this country. I believe that in this point of our history, the country needs nothing more than a large popular mandate which will ensure a concerted attempt at develoment.

I would like to stress that I have no personal motivation in this at all. I am not personally interested a public office or any position in the party. I might mention that I had no desire to be appointed the deputy chairman of the Planning Commission either. It was only at the insistence of Chandra Shekhar that I agreed to do so. Nor have I acted at the behest of anyone, including Chandra Shekhar. I do not need to do that. After all, I am an individual in my own right, and as a freedom fighter and a person who has had a long association with the Congress, I have my own dreams for the country. I had hoped that this arrangement between all Congressmen and like-minded people today would surcharge the whole wave of confidence among the people. Unfortunately, this has not happened.

Several people are sceptical about my initiative because I am a close friend, associate and confidant of Chandra Shekhar. To an extent I understand this. But my proximity to Chandra Shekhar should not be misunderstood. I truly believe, and in this I know I represent several people, that Chandra Shekhar has excelled himself as Prime Minister, even though he did not have the people's mandate. Indeed, he has proved only too well that he is a people's Prime Minister. I do not say this because he is my dear friend but because of his vision and the way he has handled several very sensitive situations. This has been commented upon by several heads of state as well. What is wrong in suggesting that the president of the Congress and Chandra Shekhar tour the country together and reach some sort of seat adjustment?

And what is wrong in suggesting that Chandra Shekhar should head the Congress even in Parliament? It is the individual personality around which people always rally. Was this not the case with Pandit Nehru, Mrs Gandhi or for that matter, Rajiv Gandhi? It is being alleged that my concern that the Samajvadi Janata Party may be completely wiped out in this election has prompted my action. This is completely untrue. My sole concern is the larger national interest and the imperative need for a stable government. It was this that had prompted a group of us to try in 1975 to get Mrs Gandhi and Jayaprakash Narayan into dialogue. We had thought then, and I maintain this view, that a spirit of conciliation is far more important that one of confrontation. However, it was not appreciated then and we were promptly sent from the Central Hall to the central Jail! The situation has not changed much in all these years and the opposition to my proposal proves this.

I am not disappointed that my initiative has failed. I am only disappointed over the fact that it did not receive as much importance by the CWC that it deserved. It only reflects the inability of the Congress leadership today to view the situation in the right spirit and perspective. For it requires magnanimity of mind and heart and courage to digest such unpalatable suggestions which are directed at the general interest of the country. It is yet possible that there will be a realignment of forces after the elections. However, it may not be possible to secure the solid backing of the country even if by chance a party comes to power with a slender majority.

Nevertheless, I truly believe in the resilience of our people and their ability to overcome the most trying circumstances. I am an optimist and I have good reason to be so.

(Mohan Dharia, formerly one of the 'Young Turks' of the Congress, is currently deputy chairman of the Planning Commission) (Courtesy. The Times of India, 2 June 1991)

Appendix IX

CONGRESS ON NATIONAL CRISIS

The following is the text of the statement issued by 43 Congress MPs, including Mr Shiv Shankar, Mr N.K.P. Salve and Ms Najma Heptullah, in New Delhi on June 18, 1991.

In this hour of grave national crisis following the tragic and brutal assassination of our beloved leader Mr Rajiv Gandhi, the nation looks up to the Congress to provide a strong and state government only a united and strong congress can meet the serious challenges and provide the right kind of governance.

To strengthen the democratic traditions of our great 106-year-old party, it is vital that the Congress Parliamentary Party is left free to elect its own leader as the scope of the consensual process is not clear. This will be in keeping with the precedence already established and would not only be in the interest of the party but also in the national interest. Democratic processes are indispensable for ensuring the party's stability and unity as well as that of nation's political stability and integrity.

Therefore, the newly constituted CPP, consequent upon elections to the 10th Lok Sabha, must be left free to exercise its democratic right in electing a leader. As loyal and disciplined soldiers of the Congress, we feel that the best homage to our leader, Mr Rajiv Gandhi, would be for the CPP to opt for the democratic process of election.

The Indian National Congress today needs courage, commitment, dynamism and an undiluted adherence to the ideology of the party and the principles of democracy. That is the only way it can meet the challenge of free India's history.

Appendix X

NARASIMHA RAO'S ADDRESS TO THE NATION

The following is the text of Prime Minister P.V. Narsimha Rao's address to the nation. On June 22, 1991.

I address you at a difficult time. Rajiv Gandhi's assassination brought home to us in a brutal manner the grave dange to the stability and integrity of the nation. A barbaric act snatched away from us a great leader in his prime. But his vision of India will live on and will continue to inspire and guide future generations.

In their hour of crisis the people of India have stood as one. They have given a befitting reply to the forces which seek to destabilise the country and subvert democracy. The electoral process just completed has yet again demonstrated the strength and vitality of Indian democracy. It has once again demonstrated that the unity of the Indian people is beyond challenge.

The dangers posed to the country by problems in Punjab, Kashmir and Assam are very real. The general law and order situation is a matter for alarm, as is the communal situation.

Government will address itself to these problems with determination and singleminderdness. We will ensure that the unity and integrity of the country are safeguraded. While genuine grievances of the people will be redressed, terrorism and other fissiparous tendencies will be dealt with firmly.

I am cetain in my mind that we shall succeed in this endeavour for we draw our strength from our people who have behind them a long tradition of amity, coooperation and togetherness and deep love for their motherland.

The economy is in a crisis, is exceedingly difficult The balance of payments situation. Inflationary pressures on the price level are considerable. There is no time to lose. The Government and the country cannot keep living beyond their means year after year. There are no soft options left. We must tighten our belt and be prepared to make the necessary sacrifices to preserve our economic independence which is an integral part of our vision for a strong nation.

In the pursuit of this objective, my Government attaches the highest priority to restoration of the health of the economy. In the past, we have faced such crises and overcome them the economy has the strength and the resilence. The people have to resolve together, we shall overcome. This is a national endeavour, in the pursuit of which we should rise above sectional interests and partisan cooperation of all.

We are determined to address the problems of the economy in a decisive manner. The postponed Union Budget will be presented in month. India shall maintain its unblemished and perfect record in meeting its international obligations the dialogue with the multilateral financial institutions, in particular the IMF, would be continued.

Fiscal discipline must be observed hard decisions would have to be implemented to manage the balance of payments situation and to curb inflation at the same time, we will ensure that the process of adjustment is managed in such a manner that it protects the poor and sustains the momentum of growth.

This Government is committed to removing the cobwebs that come in the way of rapid industrialisation. We will work towards making India internationally competitive, taking full advantage of modern science and technology and the opportunities offered by the evolving global economy utmost efficiency will be postered.

We cannot tolarate waste, inefficiency and indifference to quality, in the public or any other sector. We also welcome foreign direct investment, so as to accelerate the tempo of development, upgrade our technologies and to promote our exports.

Obstacles that come in the way of allocating foreign investment on a sizeable scale will be removed. A time-bound programme will be worked out to streamline our industrial policies and programmes to achieve the goal of a vibrant economy that rewards creativity, enterprise and innovativeness. I see a very special role for non-resident Indians to play in this process. We shall make investment in India a rewarding experience.

Agriculture will receive the Government's close attention. The progress made so far should be consolidated and conditions created for greater and diversified progress. Close attention will be paid to expanding irrigation and the development of dry land agriculture. Extension services will be strengthened and modern technology brought to the doorsteps of our farmers. Fair and remunerative price for farm produce will be ensured.

It will be our endeavour to improve the quality of life of milions of our people who are living in want and deprivation. Their betterment of the rural poor will receive the Government's closest attention.

It will be our endeavour to develop appropriate linkages so that the pressure of land on rural areas is eased and more employment opportunities are generated with a view to tackling the problems of unemployment undermployment and low incomes. Administration will be made more responsive and it will be ensured that every rupee spent on development reaches the intended beneficiaries.

Existing policies on financail assistance will be paid to the improvement of the primary health care infrastructure, particularly in rural areas.

The strengthening of the public distribution system will receive the Government's immediate attnetion. The PD's would be expanded not only to cover the rural areas but would also sharply target the poor.

The public distribution system would be made an important instrument in our fight against rural poverty and in improving the quality of life of our people. We have to evolve a strategy that at once combines policy initiatives with the full endorcement of the corecive laws of the land.

We are committed to protect the constitutional and legal right and the legitimate interests of the religious, linguistic and ethnic minorities. We shall set up special courts to try communal coffences.

A composite paid action force will be constituted to quell communal riots. The Minorities Commission will be provided statutory statys with a view to enhancing its effectiveness.

It will be the endeavour of my Government to restore India to its place of honour in the comity of nations and ensure that India's voice is once again heard with respect and attention in the world fora. Our relations with neighbours will enjoy the priority they deserve so that our region becomes an area of peace, prosperity and stability.

I have formed a broad-based weaker section-oriented Council of Ministers. This is only the beginning in the beginning of a programme to reach out to the men and women of India in every nook and corner. My term understands the beartbeat of the people.

Our vision is to create employment, eradicate poverty and reduce inequality. We want social harmony and communal amity. We want a more humance society. As the twentieth century draws to a close, we cannot live with poverty and destitution among large sections of our population. Gandhiji said that it was his ambitious to wipe every tear from every eye. This is the vision which will inspire the wore of my Government.

Appendix XI

COUCIL OF MINISTERS

Following is the list of Council of Ministers recommended by Prime Minister P.V. Narasimha Rao to President R. Venkataraman on June 23, 1991.

P.V. Narasimha Rao-Prime Minister

-Personnel, Public Grievances, Science and Technology, Space, Ocean, Development, Electronics, Atomic Energy, Chemical and Fertilisers, Rural Development, Civil Supplies and Public Distribution. Additional Charge of Industry.

CABINET MINISTERS

1. *Dr Manmohan Singh* - *Finance*
2. *Mr Balram Jakhar* - *Agriculture*
3. *Mr Arjun Singh* - *Human Resources Development*
4. *Mrs Sheilla Kaul* - *Urban Development*

5. *Mr C.K. jaffer Sharief* - *Railways*
6. *Mr B. Shankaranand* - *Petroleum and Natural Gas*
7. *Mr K. Vijaya Bhaskara Reddy* - *Law Justice and Company Affairs*
8. *Mr Sitaram Kesri* - *Welfare*
9. *Mr M.L. Fotedar* - *Health and Family Welfare*
10. *Mr Madhavsinh Solanki* - *External Affairs*
11. *Mr S.B. Chavan* - *Home*
12. *Mr V.C. shukla* - *Water Resources*
13. *Mr Madhav Rao Scindia* - *Civil Aviation and Tourism*
14. *Mr Ghulam Nabi Azad* - *Parliamentary Affairs*
15. *Mr Sharad Pawar* *Defence*

MINISTERS OF STATE (INDEPENDENT CHARGE)

1. *Mr H.R. Bhardwaj* - *Planning Programme Implementation*
2. *Mr P. Chidambaram* - *Commerce*
3. *Mr Santosh Mohan Deb* - *Steel*
4. *Mr Ajit Kumar Panja* - *Information and Broadcasting*
5. *Mr Ashok Gehlot* - *Textiles*
6. *Mr Rajesh Pilot* - *Communications*
7. *Mr Kamal Nath* - *Environment and Forests*
8. *Mr Jagdish Tytler* - *Surface Transport*
9. *Mr Kalpanth Rai* - *Power and Non-conventional Energy Sources*
10. *Mr K Ramamurthy* - *Labour*
11. *Mr Balram Singh Yadav* - *Mines*
12. *P.A. Sangma* -*Coal*
13. *Tarun Gogoi* - *Food*
14. *Mr girdhar Gamango* - *Food Processing Industries*

MINISTERS OF STATE

1. *Mr Kamaluddin Ahmed* -*Civil Supplies and Public Distribution*
2. *Mrs Margaret Alva* - *Personal, Public Grievances and Pensions*
4. *Kum Mamta Banerjee* - *Human Resources Development (Dept of youth Affairs and Sports)*

5. *Mr Eduardo Faleiro* - *Extermal Affairs*
6. *Mr M.O.H. Farook* - *Civil Aviation and Tourism*
7. *Mr M.M. Jacob* - *Paliamentary Affairs and Home*
8. *Rangarajan Kumaramangalam* -*Parliamentary Affairs. Law, justice and Company Affairs*
9. *Mr. S. Krishna Kumar* - *Petroleum and Natural Gas*
10. *Mr P.J. Kurien* - *Industry*
11. *Mr K.C. Lenka* - *Agriculture*
12. *Mr M. Mallikarjun* · *Railways*
13. *Mr Chinta Mohan* - *Chemicals and Fertilisers*
14. *Mr Uttambhai Patel* - *Rural Development*
15. *Mr Shantaram Potdukhe* - *Finance*
16. *Mr Mullappally Ramachandran-Agriculture*
17. *Mr Dalbir Singh* - *Finance*
18. *Mr G. Venkat Swamy* - *Rural Development*
19. *Mr P.K. Thungon* - *Industry*
20. *Mr Rameshwar Thakur* *Finance*
21. *Ms D.K. Tara Devi* *Health*

DEPUTY MINISTERS

1. *Kum Girija Vyas* - *Information and Broadcasting*
2. *Mr Salman Khursheed* - *Commerce*
3. *Smt K. Kamala Kumari* - *Welfare*
4. *Mr Paban Sing Ghatowar* - *Labour*
5. *Mr Ram Lal Rahi* - *Home Affairs*
6. *Mr P.V. Rangayya Naidu* - *Communication*
7. *Mr S.D. Nayana Gowda* *Coal*